Wild Law – In Practice

Wild Law – In Practice aims to facilitate the transition of Earth Jurisprudence from theory into practice. Earth Jurisprudence is an emerging philosophy of law, coined by cultural historian and geologian, Thomas Berry. It seeks to provide the foundation for a radical shift in law and governance from an exclusive focus on human beings to recognition of human interconnectedness with the comprehensive Earth community.

This volume addresses a range of topics including the effectiveness of environmental law, developments in domestic law recognising the rights of nature, the role of civil society in legal change, the regulation of sustainability and limits to growth. *Wild Law – In Practice* is the first book to focus specifically on the practical legal implications of Earth Jurisprudence.

Michelle Maloney is based at Griffith Law School; **Peter Burdon** teaches at the University of Adelaide.

Law, Justice and Ecology
Series editor: Anna Grear, Cardiff Law School,
Cardiff University, UK

In an age of climate change, scarcity of resources, and the deployment of new technologies that put into question the very idea of the 'natural', this book series offers a cross-disciplinary, novel engagement with the connections between law and ecology. The fundamental challenge taken up by the series concerns the pressing need to interrogate and to re-imagine prevailing conceptions of legal responsibility, legal community and legal subjectivity, by embracing the wider recognition that human existence is materially embedded in living systems and shared with multiple networks of non-humans.

Encouraging cross-disciplinary engagement and reflection upon relevant empirical, policy and theoretical issues, the series pursues a thoroughgoing, radical and timely exploration of the multiple relationships between law, justice and ecology.

Titles in the series:

Law and Ecology
New environmental foundations
Andreas Philippopoulos-Mihalopoulos

Law and the Question of the Animal
Edited by Yoriko Otomo and Edward Mussawir

Wild Law – In Practice
Edited by Michelle Maloney and Peter Burdon

Forthcoming:

Earth Jurisprudence
Private property and the environment
Peter Burdon

Wild Law – In Practice

Edited by
Michelle Maloney and
Peter Burdon

LONDON AND NEW YORK

First published 2014
by Routledge
2 Park Square, Milton Park, Abingdon, Oxfordshire OX14 4RN

and by Routledge
711 Third Avenue, New York, NY 10017

First issued in paperback 2015

Routledge is an imprint of the Taylor & Francis Group, an informa business

© 2014 Michelle Maloney and Peter Burdon

The right of Michelle Maloney and Peter Burdon to be identified as editors of this work, and the individual chapter authors for their individual material has been asserted in accordance with sections 77 and 78 of the Copyright, Designs and Patents Act 1988.

All rights reserved. No part of this book may be reprinted or reproduced or utilised in any form or by any electronic, mechanical, or other means, now known or hereafter invented, including photocopying and recording, or in any information storage or retrieval system, without permission in writing from the publishers.

Trademark notice: Product or corporate names may be trademarks or registered trademarks, and are used only for identification and explanation without intent to infringe.

British Library Cataloguing in Publication Data
A catalogue record for this book is available from the British Library

Library of Congress Cataloging-in-Publication Data
Wild law : in practice / edited by Michelle Maloney, Peter Burdon.
pages cm. – (Law, justice and ecology)

1. Environmental law–Congresses. 2. Environmental law, International–Congresses. 3. Environmental law–Philosophy–Congresses. I. Maloney, Michelle M., editor of compilation. II. Burdon, Peter, editor of compilation.
K3584.8.W55 2014
344.04'6–dc23
2013036613

ISBN 13: 978-1-138-94493-0 (pbk)
ISBN 13: 978-0-415-66334-2 (hbk)

Typeset in Baskerville
by Cenveo Publisher Services

Contents

Notes on contributors		vii
Series editor's preface		xii
Editors' introduction		xiii

INTRODUCTION   1

1 **Wild Law embodies values for a sustainable future**   3
    IAN LOWE

PART I
Agency and implementation   17

2 **Earth Jurisprudence and the project of Earth democracy**   19
    PETER D BURDON

3 **Wild Law from below: examining the anarchist challenge to Earth Jurisprudence**   31
    SAMUEL ALEXANDER

4 **Peoples' Sustainability Treaties at Rio+20: giving voice to the other**   45
    KAREN MORROW

5 **The challenges of putting Wild Law into practice: reflections on the Australian Environmental Defender's Office movement**   58
    BRENDAN SYDES

PART II
Jurisprudential challenges   73

6 **Internalizing ecocentrism in environmental law**   75
    THE HON. JUSTICE BRIAN J PRESTON

7	**Jurisprudential challenges to the protection of the natural environment** D E FISHER	95
8	**Who's afraid of the founding fathers? Retelling constitutional law wildly** NICOLE ROGERS	113

PART III
The rights of nature — 131

9	**Decolonizing personhood** ERIN FITZ-HENRY	133
10	**Building an international movement for Rights of Nature** MARI MARGIL	149
11	**'Water as the way': achieving wellbeing through 'right relationship' with water** LINDA SHEEHAN	161
12	**Earth laws, rights of nature and legal pluralism** ALESSANDRO PELIZZON	176

PART IV
A Wild Law perspective on environmental stewardship — 191

13	**Ecological limits, planetary boundaries and Earth Jurisprudence** M MALONEY	193
14	**Biodiversity offsets: a dangerous trade in wildlife?** BRENDAN GRIGG	213
15	**Emissions trading and Earth Jurisprudence: will liabilities protect the atmospheric commons?** FELICITY DEANE	230
16	**Wild Law and animal law: some commonalities and differences** STEVEN WHITE	247
	Index	263

Notes on contributors

Samuel Alexander

Dr Samuel Alexander is a Lecturer with the Office for Environmental Programs, University of Melbourne, where he teaches an interdisciplinary course called 'Consumerism and the Growth Paradigm'. He is also co-director of the Simplicity Institute (www.simplicityinstitute.org) and founder of the Simplicity Collective (www.simplicitycollective.com). His research focuses on voluntary simplicity, degrowth economics, and the implications of peak oil and energy descent. He is active in his local 'transition initiative', Transition Coburg, and is currently writing a book on the economics of sufficiency.

Peter D Burdon

Peter Burdon is a Senior Lecturer at the Adelaide Law School. His PhD was in the field of ecological law. It won the Bonython Prize and a University of Adelaide Research Medal for best original thesis. Since 2005 he has worked with Friends of the Earth Adelaide in the Clean Futures Collective. He also sits on the Ethics Specialist Group of the International Union for the Conservation of Nature, the executive committee of the Australian Earth Laws Alliance and on the management committee of the Environmental Defender's Office (SA). He lives in the Adelaide plains with his beautiful wife, dancing daughter and baby boy.

Felicity Deane

Felicity Deane recently completed her PhD in Law at the Queensland University of Technology, on the topic of Australia's Clean Energy Package and the World Trade Organisation. She holds a Bachelor of Law and a Bachelor of Commerce from the University of Queensland (1999) and a Post Graduate Diploma in Legal Practice from Monash University (2004). She has held positions as a financial accountant and legal consultant in Australia and as a managerial accountant in the USA. Prior to this she worked as a Senior Policy Officer for the Queensland Police Service and assisted in the establishment of the state-based Domestic and Family Violence Unit in the Office of the Commissioner.

D E Fisher

Douglas Fisher joined the Queensland University of Technology as Professor of Law in 1991. Prior to this he held appointments at the University of Edinburgh, the University of Queensland, the Australian National University and the University of Dundee, before being appointed as Professor of Law at Victoria University (Wellington, New Zealand) in 1982, where he was Dean during 1988, 1989 and 1990. He also practised law in the public sector with the United Kingdom government and was for some 10 years a consultant with Phillips Fox in Brisbane. His principal teaching and research interests are currently in the areas of environmental law and natural resources law.

Brendan Grigg

Brendan Grigg is a Lecturer at Flinders University Law School, Australia. Before joining the Flinders Law School in 2010 he worked in the South Australian Crown Solicitor's Office where he practised in native title law and in environmental law. This included a role as in-house solicitor to the South Australian Environment Protection Authority. He has also practised at a specialist planning and development law firm in Adelaide.

Erin Fitz-Henry

Dr Erin Fitz-Henry joined the School of Social and Political Sciences at the University of Melbourne in 2011. She completed an MDiv at Harvard University and a PhD in anthropology at Princeton University, where she previously served as a lecturer. She has long-standing interests in social movement organising, and is currently finalising a book manuscript based on her dissertation research on and around a US military base in Manta, Ecuador. Her second major project looks at the Rights of Nature movement in Ecuador and Bolivia, the first two countries in the world to grant ecosystems the same legal rights accorded citizens. She is particularly interested in the ways in which these environmental rights are being differently implemented and challenged by states, local citizen groups, and industry personnel in the oil and mineral sectors.

Ian Lowe

Professor Ian Lowe (BSc, NSW; DPhil, York (UK)) is an Emeritus Professor in the School of Science at Griffith University, an Adjunct Professor at two Australian universities and is the President of the Australian Conservation Foundation. His principal research interests are in policy decisions influencing the use of energy, science and technology; energy use in industrialised countries; large-scale environmental issues and sustainable development. Professor Lowe has been appointed to the Australian National Commission for UNESCO and is a consultant to the CSIRO Division of Sustainable Ecosystems. In 1988 he was Director of the Commission for the Future, and was named Australian Humanist of the Year.

M Maloney

Michelle Maloney is an environmental lawyer and activist. She is co-founder and National Convenor of the Australian Earth Laws Alliance (www.earthlaws.org.au), Executive Committee Member of the Global Alliance for the Rights of Nature and Chairperson of the Environmental Defender's Office Queensland. Michelle is currently completing her PhD at Griffith University and her thesis uses an Earth jurisprudence framework to examine the role of law and regulation in reducing unsustainable consumption.

Mari Margil

Mari Margil is the Associate Director of the Community Environmental Legal Defense Fund where she leads the organisation's international Rights of Nature work. In 2008, she assisted Ecuador's Constitutional Assembly to draft Rights of Nature constitutional provisions. Mari received her Master's degree in Public Policy and Urban Planning from Harvard University's John F. Kennedy School of Government. She is a co-author of *The Public Health or the Bottom Line* published by Oxford University Press in 2010, and *Exploring Wild Law: The Philosophy of Earth Jurisprudence* published by Wakefield Press in 2011.

Karen Morrow

Karen Morrow graduated from the Law Faculty of the Queen's University of Belfast in 1991 and obtained a Master's degree at King's College London in 1992. She has held posts in law at the University of Buckingham, the Queen's University of Belfast, the University of Durham and Leeds University and has, since January 2007 been a Chair at Swansea University where she is co-director of the Centre for Environmental and Energy Law (CEELP). Her research specialism is in UK, EU and international environmental law, focusing primarily on rights-based questions and public participation in these areas.

Alessandro Pelizzon

Alessandro Pelizzon completed his LLB/LLM in Law in Italy, specialising in comparative law and legal anthropology. He has been involved in indigenous rights for over 15 years, firstly by supporting the drafting of the UN Declaration on the Rights of Indigenous Peoples in Geneva and then completing his PhD thesis at the University of Wollongong on native title and legal pluralism in the Illawarra. He is one of the founding members of the Global Alliance for the Rights of Nature, the Australian Earth Laws Alliance and the Earth Laws Network at Southern Cross University. His main areas of research are legal anthropology, comparative law, legal theory, indigenous rights and ecological jurisprudence.

Justice Preston

Justice Brian Preston is the Chief Judge of the Land and Environment Court in New South Wales. Prior to being appointed in 2005, he was a senior counsel practising primarily in New South Wales in environmental, planning, administrative and property law. He is an Adjunct Professor at Sydney Law School and has lectured in postgraduate environmental law for over 20 years, both in Australia and overseas. He is the author of Australia's first book on environmental litigation (in 1989) and 76 articles, book chapters and reviews on environmental, administrative and criminal law.

Nicole Rogers

Dr Nicole Rogers is a Senior Lecturer in the School of Law and Justice, Southern Cross University, Lismore. She has published in the areas of climate change litigation, Wild Law, environmental activism, and the interdisciplinary area of performance studies theory and the law. Her doctorate was on the playfulness of law. She has a background in environmental activism.

Linda Sheehan

As Executive Director of Earth Law Center, Linda Sheehan develops new laws and governance models that acknowledge the natural world's rights to exist, thrive and evolve. For her prior NGO work 'fight[ing] pollution of the Pacific and the streams and rivers that flow into it', she was recognised as a 'California Coastal Hero'. She is also Summer Session Faculty at Vermont Law School, where she teaches 'Earth Law', and was a Visiting Research Fellow at the University of Victoria, BC. She is a contributing author to *Exploring Wild Law: The Philosophy of Earth Jurisprudence*, and a member of the IUCN's Commission on Environmental Law. She holds a BS in chemical engineering from the Massachusetts Institute of Technology; an MPP from the University of California, Berkeley's Goldman School of Public Policy; and a JD from the University of California, Berkeley's Boalt Hall School of Law.

Brendan Sydes

Brendan Sydes is Principal Solicitor with the Environment Defender's Office Victoria, a community legal centre specialising in environmental law. His work at the EDO involves providing legal advice and representation to community groups and environmental NGOs working to protect and enhance the environment, policy and law reform work and overseeing the EDO's community legal education activities. Brendan has volunteered as a legal adviser and committee member at community legal centres in Victoria and NSW and is presently Chair of the Committee of Management of the Federation of Community Legal Centres, Victoria.

Steven White

Steven White is a Lecturer at Griffith University Law School, specialising in animal law. He is also a member of Griffith University's Key Centre for Ethics, Law, Justice and Governance and the Socio-Legal Research Centre. Steven has written extensively on animal law issues and he created and continues to teach one of the first undergraduate courses on animal law ever offered in Australia. His doctorate examined the regulation of companion and farmed animals in Australia.

Wild Law
Series editor's preface

The series *Law, Justice and Ecology* seeks to publish diverse engagements with the complex and challenging factors involved in the profound human and ecological crises characterizing the early twenty-first century.

Wild Law presents a fresh attempt to address important challenges presented to mainstream environmental law and governance structures by Earth Jurisprudence and Wild Law. The book is organized as a response to one central question: how can the theory and practice of Wild Law be developed in meaningful, practical and transformative ways? Drawing from papers initially presented at a multidisciplinary conference in Brisbane, Australia in September 2011, *Wild Law* centrally engages with Thomas Berry's challenge to humankind to embrace the 'Great Work' of finding a way to make 'the transition from a period of human devastation of the Earth to a period when humans would be present to the planet in a mutually beneficial manner'.

This edited collection aims to bring important ground-level perspectives to bear on key contemporary challenges and issues concerning the application of Wild Law, while also offering some invigorating theoretical engagements with its central theme. The contributions are refreshingly varied. Some are written on the basis of long experience in the courts or in litigation-facing legal-environmental initiatives; others reflect engagement with indigenous peoples' groups and initiatives; others are based on scholarly engagements with a range of themes and concerns. The result is a collection drawing together scholarship, policy considerations, practice and activism that, in various ways and from various angles, challenges – in practical ways – the ecocidal status quo in which neoliberal structures (including law and legal systems) are complicit.

For anyone concerned to reflect upon the practical implementation of Wild Law in the company of a committed, passionate group of commentators and experts, this book provides a valuable introduction to some potential responses and strategies aimed at unfolding the 'great work' that Thomas Berry urged humanity to embrace.

Anna Grear

Editors' introduction

For those of us who care deeply about the state of the world and find the apparently endless downward spiral of environmental indicators a cause for great despair, the writings of Thomas Berry are a greatly needed source of guidance, inspiration and optimism. His intellectual legacy is immense and includes: a new narrative or Universe Story to provide the context for a viable human presence on the Earth; a soulful critique of modern industrial society and of the complicity of social institutions such as law, religion, the university and the economy in perpetuating environmental harm; and his challenge to develop more intimate relationships with the non-human world and with local bioregions.

But it is Thomas Berry's gifts to us as lawyers and as people interested in the meta-structures and minutiae of modern governance – the rules, systems, institutions and decision making processes that underpin our societies – that provide the starting point for this book. The chapters that follow were selected from presentations given at a multidisciplinary conference held in Brisbane, Australia, in September 2011. The conference brought together more than 150 people, including legal academics, lawyers, scientists, politicians, activists, philosophers, priests and interested members of the public. Each participant was committed to the single question that informs this book – how can we work collaboratively to build the theory and practice of Wild Law?

Why a book about Wild Law in practice?

Wild Law is an emerging theory of earth-centred law and governance that is stimulating a burgeoning field of academic literature and grassroots activism. While it draws broadly on the insights of environmental philosophy, Wild Law also has something new to offer. Its proponents have inspired a growing international movement of activists, researchers and advocates who are implementing ecological law in domestic legal systems. Individual organisations involved in this work include the Center for Earth Jurisprudence, USA;

the Community Environment Legal Defence Fund, USA; the Center for Earth Law, USA; Wild Law United Kingdom; the Pachamama Alliance, Ecuador; Navdanya, India; the Australian Earth Laws Alliance; and the Earth Law Alliance New Zealand. The international umbrella network that brings many of these groups together is the Global Alliance for the Rights of Nature which represents more than 60 organisations around the world.

The aim of this book is to capture some of the stories about the progress, success and challenges faced by the practical implementation of Wild Law. Unlike most books of this kind, many of the chapters offer insights into the daily practice of activists engaged with articulating and advocating for Earth centred law and governance. Other chapters offer new frameworks and theoretical insights for thinking about the practical implementation of Wild Law.

Introduction

Ian Lowe sets the tone for the volume, arguing that environmental laws and regulations have not fundamentally changed the rate of environmental destruction. He reminds us that despite 50 years of awareness of environmental issues and 35 years of environmental law, all of the important indicators are worsening. At best, he argues, environmental laws are merely slowing down the rate of degradation of natural systems. Following this critique, Lowe maps out a range of reforms that would be required to move legal systems towards an improved capacity to protect the natural world. He also highlights the importance of Wild Law and other strands of utopian thinking for progressing humankind toward a sustainable future.

Part I Agency and implementation

We then move to four chapters that focus on the methods through which Wild Law can be introduced into our existing, anthropocentric and pro-growth legal systems. Peter Burdon and Samuel Alexander both consider how Wild Law can be introduced into the present legal and political systems of western industrialised nations. Burdon argues that the power structures that presently prevent our transformation to a healthy Earth Community can be countered by projects such as 'The Project for Earth Democracy'. He argues that attempts to fuse ecocentric ethics with deeper forms of democracy and public participation can help 'shift the power structure that dominates contemporary decision making from private interests, to the collective'. Alexander suggests a radical rethink of how we create the transition to an Earth-centred governance system and suggests the building of a grassroots movement that can force change throughout society, and eventually also lead to 'top down' change. Karen Morrow examines the growing role of civil society in challenging existing nation-state structures and in offering up increasingly sophisticated, well-organised agendas for action and change.

Brendan Sydes reflects on how Wild Law can be implemented within the only network of public environmental law organisations in Australia, called the Environmental Defender's Offices. He suggests that while there are significant barriers to introducing Wild Law into the 'administrative rationalist' framework that has shaped Australian environmental law and the work of the EDOs, Wild Law may offer a new paradigm for supporting the intrinsic values of the natural world.

Part II Jurisprudential challenges

Two chapters from leading Australian jurists then explore how Earth-centred principles and practice can be implemented in our judicial and legislative systems. Justice Preston, Chief Judge of the New South Wales Land and Environment Court, raises a number of critical issues relating to access to justice and statutory approaches to regulating human impact on the environment, that need to be addressed if principles of Wild Law are to be integrated into western legal systems. Douglas Fisher examines the jurisprudential foundations of environmental law, including the structure of selected international and national instruments, and suggests that an ecocentric basis for environmental law is emerging. Following these chapters, Nicole Rogers examines the challenges of integrating Wild Law into western constitutions in general, and the Australian Constitution in particular, and highlights the potential for radically retelling important High Court cases from a Wild Law perspective. In so doing, she highlights the potential for alternative narratives to inform the process of adjudication.

Part III The rights of nature

Four chapters then explore different aspects of how one of the most prominent elements of Wild Law, Rights of Nature legislation, is being interpreted and implemented in various jurisdictions. Erin Fitz-Henry examines the barriers currently being addressed by Rights of Nature advocates in Ecuador and reminds us that the struggle for environmental protection continues even after progressive legislation has been enacted. Mari Margil provides an overview of the Rights of Nature movement around the world and sets it within the broader context of how social movements form and prevail in the face of initial attitudinal and structural barriers. Linda Sheehan examines current governance structures for managing water and criticises the dualistic approach which treats water as human property. She argues for new water governance methodologies grounded in the collective, shared rights of people and the natural world. Alessandro Pelizzon's chapter examines Rights of Nature and legal pluralism, and offers insights into how the Wild Law movement can both learn from and create spaces to engage with indigenous knowledge.

Part IV A Wild Law perspective on environmental stewardship

The final section provides an Earth jurisprudence perspective of current practice in areas as diverse as biodiversity offset schemes and carbon pricing. Michelle Maloney applies a Wild Law framework to examine the debate about, and offer a practical framework for progressing, the idea of living within our ecological limits. Brendan Grigg uses a Wild Law lens to examine biodiversity offset schemes and the property rights they create and argues that such schemes must be severely limited in scope and operation if our legal and economic systems are to respect the natural world. Felicity Deane creates an Earth jurisprudence framework to examine the emissions-trading schemes of the European Union, New Zealand and Australia and argues that the current schemes, though a positive step forward in curbing humanity's atmospheric pollution, merely perpetuate the status quo and do not protect the atmospheric commons. Finally, Steven White writes a valuable piece that examines the commonalities and differences between Wild Law and animal law and lays the groundwork for a dialogue between these two fields of work.

Individually, each of these chapters offers an important contribution to the development of specific aspects of Wild Law and environmental governance. Collectively the chapters provide fascinating insights into the current state of Wild Law in practice. It is our hope that this volume inspires others to focus on the nexus between theoretical development and practical implementation.

Michelle Maloney and Peter Burdon
July 2013

Introduction

Chapter 1

Wild Law embodies values for a sustainable future

Ian Lowe

The current legal framework (in Australia and around the world) is clearly failing to prevent environmental damage. Environmental law in Australia began formally with the passing of the *Environmental Assessment (Impact of Proposals) Act* by the Whitlam government in 1974. State and Territory legislation followed in those jurisdictions. The capacity of the Australian government to over-rule States to protect the environment was confirmed by the Franklin Dams case (*Commonwealth v Tasmania* (1983) 158 CLR 1), when the High Court agreed that the foreign affairs power of the Constitution allowed the Commonwealth to act in accord with its treaty obligations. The Howard government subsequently passed the *Environmental Protection and Biodiversity Conservation Act* (1999), which explicitly empowers the government to intervene if a proposed development threatens an endangered species or an ecosystem which is at risk.

State environment courts have not generally been proactive in protecting the environment. One elected official in a large city told me he was seriously questioning whether it was fiscally responsible to prohibit irresponsible development proposals, because the developer inevitably appealed to the court which invariably upheld the appeal (L. Ardill 1983, pers. comm.). Generally the presumption has been that any development which is commercially viable should be allowed to go ahead unless there is overwhelming evidence that it would be environmentally disastrous. Since it is usually individuals or community groups who are trying to stop a project and developers with very deep pockets who are supporting the proposal, the legal battle is rarely an equal one. In some cases in which I have appeared as an expert witness, the lawyers acting *pro bono* for the objectors have faced a legal team led by a top silk, with barrow-loads of supporting documents and well-paid consultants flown in to promote their cause (for example, *Xstrata Coal Queensland Pty Ltd & Ors v Friends of the Earth – Brisbane Co-Op Ltd & Ors* 2012).

While there are clear shortcomings in the process, discussed in the following section, the real test of environmental law is whether it is working to protect the environment. The only legitimate conclusion is that the law is failing. While objectors win occasional battles, natural systems are clearly losing the war. At the national level, the first independent report on the state of the Australian environment in 1996 identified serious problems that needed to be addressed: loss of biodiversity, the state of inland rivers, degradation of large areas of productive land, growing pressures on the coastal zone and spiralling levels of greenhouse gas emissions (SoEAC 1996: 7–9). Three subsequent reports at five-year intervals have documented the steady worsening of all of those problems (SoEC 2011: 9). At the global level, the emergence of serious environmental problems has demanded political attention (Paavola and Lowe 2005). Successive reports in the UNEP series on Global Environmental Outlook have described the decline of natural systems. The most recent, GEO5, noted that the changes in Earth systems in recent decades are unprecedented in human history (UNEP 2012: 6). It warned that many local, regional and global systems have critical thresholds, beyond which they will change rapidly and irreversibly, with very serious impacts on the future of human civilization (UNEP 2012: 6).

Failings of the Australian legal system

There are some clear limits on Australian environmental law which have reduced its capacity to slow the decline of natural values. Restrictions on standing in some jurisdictions have prevented legal action on behalf of natural systems. Environmental regulations usually assume that development will go ahead unless it can be proven beyond reasonable doubt that the consequences would be unacceptable (McGrath 2011: 36). This presumption raises two issues: the burden of proof and the standard of proof. The burden of proof lies with the objectors, often individuals or community groups with limited resources engaged in a legal battle with well-resourced corporations whose activities would be regarded as tax-deductible costs of doing business and so are supported from the public purse. The standard of proof is the same test used in criminal law – the applicant's case must be established beyond reasonable doubt. This stands in contrast to the standard of civil law where the case must be proven on the balance of probabilities.

The interaction between these dual factors raises the issue of scientific evidence, on which environmental cases often hinge. The legal system of sworn evidence and cross-examination is designed to allow observers to make a judgement about who is giving a truthful account of events and which witnesses are less credible. But science rarely gives a black-and-white answer to complex questions. A competent and honest scientist will usually give a qualified and nuanced response. So there is a real risk in the court that 'junk science' – bald and confident assertions from 'experts' who are either less competent or less honest – will appear more convincing than a qualified opinion. In any case, the qualified opinion is less likely to meet the implicit standard of proof beyond all reasonable doubt. The New South Wales Land and Environment Court has trialled a process to use science more effectively, as discussed below (Preston 2011).

The legal system is designed to consider each case on its individual merits. It is not equipped to consider cumulative impacts. Thus each proposal for a coastal development might be acceptable if it were the only change to be allowed, but the cumulative impact of allowing them all could be seriously damaging to the coastal zone. At the level of global problems, denial of responsibility for cumulative impacts had been a common defence against legal attempts to restrain new projects that accelerate climate change (McGrath 2008). The approach taken by proponents of large export coal mines, in several cases where I have appeared as an expert witness, is to argue that no specific environmental harm can be attributed to that particular project. The proponents have accepted that climate change is happening, even accepted that its consequences could be catastrophic, but deny any responsibility for their specific contribution to the cumulative impacts. In one specific example, proponents of a large coal mine accepted their responsibility for emissions directly associated with mining and processing the coal, but argued successfully that they would not be responsible for the impacts of the subsequent burning of the coal as well as claiming that no specific environmental problem could be attributed to their emissions (*Xstrata Coal Queensland Pty Ltd & Ors v Friends of the Earth – Brisbane Co-Op Ltd & Ors* 2012). With this approach common, there has effectively been no legal means to restrict the damage being done to the global climate system.

The report of the World Commission on Environment and Development (1987) brought into common use both the concept of sustainable development and the idea of the precautionary principle. The report recognized that there will be situations in which the science is not conclusive and proposed that the response should be proportionate to the risks of getting it wrong. Where the consequences could be serious or irreversible, the report stated, lack of full scientific certainty should not be a reason for failing to intervene. Courts have been generally reluctant to use the precautionary principle, faced with arguments from proponents of developments that it is too restrictive. So proposals that could have serious or irreversible consequences are routinely approved (Cleary 2013: 83–90). The New South Wales Land and Environment Court has set out a notable exception to the general rule. Since the relevant legislation requires the use of the precautionary principle, the Court has decided that the burden lies with objectors to make a scientifically credible case that there is indeed a risk of serious or irreversible consequences. If that case is made to the satisfaction of the Court, the proponent of the development then bears the burden of proof to show that the risk is acceptable (Preston 2006).

Courts rarely revisit earlier decisions and most governments have both limited capacity and little political will to ensure conditions imposed on developments are actually enforced. The Australian government does not even fund its environmental department to oversee enforcement. The department has a section for 'assessment and approvals', which is at least an honest descriptor. To make an obvious point, if a law is not enforced its existence is ineffective. The failure to enforce conditions imposed at the approval stage is a fundamental failing of environmental law (Cleary 2013: 75).

As a final point, the whole legal process effectively privileges this generation over all future generations, who cannot take legal action or present their views in court. It also privileges human interests over the needs of all other species, who are equally unable to present their interests. Australia's environmental protection framework is overtly anthropocentric and is focused on the short-term commercial interests of this generation over the health and flourishing of the rest of the ecosystem. Scholarship in the broad field of futures studies has developed the notion of our responsibility to future generations (Kim and Dator, 1999) and Dator (2005) cite one legal precedent, when the Supreme Court of the Philippines granted standing to people professing to represent the interests of future generations (*Oposa vs Factoran Jr* 1993). More recently, negotiations between the New Zealand government and the Whanganui Iwi led to recognition of the river, Te Awa Tupua, as a legal entity with standing before the courts (NZ Government 2012). These are the only instances I have been able to identify in the 40 years since it was argued that trees should have legal standing (Stone 1972).

Reforming environmental protection law

It is entirely possible, at least in principle, to reform Australian law to remedy some of the most egregious deficiencies in the current legislative framework. Fowler (2009) has argued that environmental law has evolved in a piecemeal way but is under-theorised and lacks a clear philosophical foundation consistent with its purported goals of environmental protection. Recent attempts to incorporate the principle of ecologically sustainable development (ESD) are aimed at shoring up the environmental law with an ESD philosophical basis. But the pressures to find a 'balance' between social, environmental and economic considerations almost inevitably steer decision-makers back to the old emphasis on the economy.

In the absence of fundamental reform, which would incorporate the basic principle of Wild Law and give it constitutional recognition, I suggest a series of steps that would correct some of the worst aspects of current practice, using the acronym STOP CRIME. The changes would be to have Scientific panels informing process, Transfer the burden of proof to proponents of developments, Overhaul the standard of proof, have Past advice evaluated, have Cumulative impacts explicitly considered, Real consideration of future generations, Independent assessment, Monitoring in the light of claims and Enforcement of conditions.

Scientific panels

As mentioned above, the New South Wales environment court has trialled a system to ensure that its adjudicative function is informed by science (Preston 2011). Where the experts provided by the proponents and opponents of a development disagree, those experts are required to attend a conciliation process that leads to a consolidated statement for the court. The statement sets out the agreed science, the areas of disagreement and the scientific basis for the arguments of the two sides concerning those areas of contention. This allows the court at least to understand what is agreed and what scientific credibility the respective contending views have. Similar processes, aimed at ensuring that judges understand scientific arguments, have also been trialled outside of Australia. In India, for example, the High Court has required the judiciary to do in-service training in environmental science (Balakrishnan 2006).

Transfer the burden of proof to proponents of developments and overhaul the standard of proof

Given the damage that has been done to natural systems in recent decades, and our lucky escapes from even more serious harm, I think it would be reasonable for those proposing major new developments to bear the burden of proof. They should have to show that the proposal is benign. I would also overhaul the standard of proof, so the proponent would have to show beyond any reasonable doubt that the impacts are acceptable. There would still be occasions when the science of the day did not reveal a problem that turned out to be serious. As an obvious example, chlorofluorocarbons (CFCs) were widely used for decades before the science showing that they would deplete the ozone layer was carried out. Even after this finding, it took another decade to persuade legislators to respond (Lowe 1989). Despite this, it would be much more difficult to justify large new hydro-electric projects or export coal mines if the proponents were required to prove beyond any reasonable doubt that the impacts were benign.

Past advice evaluated

Evaluating past advice would hold experts to account for the consequences of dishonest or inadequate evidence. I suspect that some of the less credible 'expert' support for projects would not be provided if there were provisions for holding to account those who gave evidence in court.

Cumulative impacts explicitly considered

Considering cumulative impacts would be a major step forward, not just in such obvious areas as coastal development but also in allowing the courts to take into account contributions to global problems such as climate change and loss of biodiversity. Climate change is the extreme example of the failure of current environmental law. The proponents of massive new coal mines, explicitly designed to ensure that huge amounts of fossil carbon are added to the atmosphere, have consistently argued that no particular increment of climate change can be attributed to their actions (*Xstrata Coal Queensland Pty Ltd & Ors v Friends of the Earth – Brisbane Co-Op Ltd & Ors* 2012; McGrath 2007). A reasonable approach would be to say that adding further carbon dioxide into the atmosphere is unacceptable and that any proposal for a coal-fired power plant could only be approved if its carbon emissions were captured and safely stored for geological time.

Real consideration of future generations

Real consideration of future generations requires that we factor into our decision-marking the impact that our resource use will have on society in the future. One approach would be to appoint a specific representative for future generations who could advocate on their behalf in a court of law. An alternative would be to explicitly require both government ministers and the courts to take into account the needs of future generations when approving or evaluating new projects. This would provide a mechanism for ethically assessing the rate of resource depletion and its likely impact on future generations.

Independent assessment

Independent assessment of environmental impacts would be a major change for the better. Under Australian law, proponents of a development commission an assessment. It would be entirely understandable for proponents to seek out consultants who are likely to give a favourable report. Either this is already happening or new developments proposed are remarkably well considered, since the assessments almost invariably find that the proposal is acceptable (Cleary 2013: 97, 186). In the real world, consultants know that their chances of getting regular business depends on their giving their clients the desired advice, so it is reasonable to conclude that successful consultants are skilled in putting the best possible emphasis on the proposals they assess. It seems clear that the public interest would be better served if the process required genuinely independent assessment by a public agency. As Cleary (2013: 186) argues: 'Independent EISs managed by an independent regulator are the only way to ensure that the public gets a full and frank account of the risks'.

Enforcement of conditions

If we were serious about our environmental responsibility, monitoring would be resourced and seriously undertaken to ensure that assurances given at the assessment stage were well founded. Under the current system in Australia, there is no routine monitoring of developments and action is only taken if there is clear evidence of a problem. Given that a former judge of the NSW Land And Environment Court has said that developers are so influential that proposals are approved 'however irrational or environmentally damaging' they are (Cleary 2013: 62), it should not be surprising that there are cases of approved developments leading to unacceptable environmental impacts. Those who opposed coal mines because they feared negative impacts have in some cases been proven correct when the developments went ahead, but no effective remedial action has been taken (Ibid: 62–9).

Finally, Australian environment courts can impose conditions on proposals, such as requiring mines to prevent pollution of waterways or to rehabilitate land. However, unless there is enforcement of these conditions, they may well be overlooked by managers anxious to improve the profitability of the project. Most jurisdictions in Australia have little capacity or political will to enforce conditions imposed on developments. Cleary (2013) gives several examples of approved mines leading to serious impacts on local landholders, with no effective response to their complaints.

In summary, it is clearly possible to envisage a better system of environmental law to avoid the most glaring shortcomings of the present system. Since that case is clear, the obvious question to ask is why such obvious measures have not been introduced. Cormac Cullinan (2011a) has written of an epiphany when he found himself 'encountering conceptual difficulties that could not be resolved by simply amending legislation because they had their roots in the underlying legal philosophies (jurisprudence)' (Cullinan 2011a: 14). That is a fundamental point. The legal system inevitably embodies and reifies the values of those who make the laws, as Hall (1989) argued in his elaboration of Oliver Wendell Holmes' view that the law is a 'magic mirror' reflecting the culture and history of the particular society. In a democratic system, that means that the laws reflect the values of the political class, who in turn are strongly influenced by the interests of the economy in general and large corporations in particular. Since those values are incompatible with the concept of living sustainably, in balance with natural systems without degrading those systems, the framework of environmental law which embodies those values inevitably fails to protect the environment. Unless the law is based on the values needed for a sustainable future, applying cosmetic changes to the legal system will be futile. As an extreme demonstration of this underlying problem, on two rare occasions when objectors to a proposed development were successful in court, the relevant State government immediately passed a new law to overturn the ruling and allow the proposal to go ahead (Cleary 2013: 54–63; McGrath 2007).

Those who are concerned about the failings of environmental law, as any observer concerned about the degradation of natural systems should be, need to engage with the underlying system of values on which the law is based. That reflection needs to incorporate analysis of the values that would be consistent with the aim of living sustainably and in balance with natural systems for the foreseeable future.

Values for a sustainable future

The first independent national report on the state of the Australian environment identified a range of serious environmental problems that needed to be addressed if the declared goal of living sustainably was to be achieved: loss of biodiversity, the condition of inland rivers, degradation of large areas of productive land through over-grazing, salinity and erosion, pressures on the coastal zone and rapidly increasing greenhouse gas emissions (SoEAC 1996: 4). Just to emphasize the importance of those issues, three later reports have all noted that every one of those trends is still worsening (SoEC 2011: 9–12). The first report attributed the environmental problems to 'the cumulative consequences of population growth and distribution, lifestyles, technologies and demands on natural resources'. It went on to point out that 'progress towards ecological sustainability requires recognition that human society is part of the ecological system', calling for 'integration of ecological thinking into all social and economic planning' (SoEAC 1996: 4). More explicitly, it can be seen that the drivers of environmental degradation are growing human numbers, increasing consumption per head and the societal values which see these trends as acceptable or even desirable, rather than a threat to the survival of human civilization.

Raskin (2006) argues that the values which have underpinned human development for the last century have been domination of nature, individualism and materialist consumerism. These values, he proposes, are now a fundamental obstacle to the goal of a sustainable future. He argues further that we need a new triad, with domination of nature being replaced by ecological sensitivity, individualism by a sense of solidarity with the entire human community, and materialist consumerism by an emphasis on the quality of life. Bosselmann (2011) developed an acronym for the dominant approach, giving it the appropriate name of DAMAGE: 'Dualism (of humans and nature), Anthropocentrism, Materialism, Atomism, Greed (individualism gone mad) and Economism (the myth of no boundaries and limitless opportunities)' (Bosselman 2011: 205).

By way of contrast, I have sketched out what I see as the basis of a sustainable future, imagining myself looking back from a future time when we have achieved that goal (Lowe 2005a). We would have stabilized both our population and its footprint, its level of resource demands. Our cities would be much more energy efficient, with better building standards and urban design to create liveable communities with services within easy reach. Rain water would be collected and waste water cleaned for reuse, allowing us to meet our needs with less pressure on natural systems. We would have dramatically reduced our greenhouse pollution by embracing renewable energy and world's best practice efficiency levels. More of our food would be produced locally; we would have healthier diets and greater levels of physical activity. We would have invested in education, skills and innovation to secure our future, based on the goal of producing 'globo sapiens': wise global citizens, aware of their responsibilities and having the courage to courage to take considered action (Kelly 2008). Social cohesion would have been improved by measures aimed at reducing inequality. Proposals for new development would be given a serious triple-bottom-line assessment and then considered by a participative process, allowing us to take difficult decisions as a community and ensuring that the winners from these changes compensate the losers. To ensure that new developments are biodiversity-positive, any clearing of natural vegetation would be balanced by investing in the restoration or enhancement of other natural areas.

An acronym that summarises this future sustainable society is HEALTHIER (Lowe 2005b: 82–98). It will be Humane in the sense of developing technologies and approaches that can, at least in principle, be extended to the whole human family. It will take an Eco-centric Approach, recognizing that we have no future if we fail to maintain the capacity of natural systems to provide breathable air, drinkable water and the capacity to produce our food. It will have a Long Time Horizon, recognizing that the decisions we are taking now have implications decades or centuries into the future. It will be Informed, having invested in a dramatically improved understanding of complex natural systems and our effects on them. It will be Efficient, turning resources much more effectively into the services we need. It will be Resourced, having managed the transition from depleting geological resources to living on renewable energy flows.

Values and Wild Law

Apart from some attempts to include procedural rights, the legal profession has paid little attention to the alternative approach of a rights-based environmental law. Fowler (2009) has suggested three layers of rights: procedural rights such as standing, access to information, access to legal support and immunity from punitive costs; human rights, such as the right to a clean and healthy environment, the right to equitable development and the right to water; and substantive rights for nature. The Ecuadorian Constitution was changed by referendum in 2008 to incorporate a provision that Nature (or Pachamama, the Andean Earth goddess) 'where life is reproduced and exists, has the right to exist, persist, maintain and regenerate its vital cycles, structure, functions and its processes in evolution'. It goes on to say that '[e]very person, people, community or nationality, will be able to demand the recognition of rights for nature before the public bodies'.

In similar terms, Higgins (2010) has argued for international legal action to prevent environmental harm. Her suggestion is to amend the Rome Statute, the basis for the International Court of Justice, which was established in recognition of the problem that some of the most egregious crimes against humanity were justified by the law in a particular nation state. Higgins (2010: 2) argued that ecocide, defined as 'extensive destruction of or damage to ecosystems' should be a crime for which offenders could be prosecuted at the global level, even if their actions were sanctioned by a local legal system.

The underlying principle of Wild Law or Earth Jurisprudence is that the human law should be based on and respect the laws of nature. Graham (2011: 259) argues 'it is important, indeed necessary, to situate the system of laws within the physical context of the Earth's systems'. We are as dependent on the health of those natural systems as any other species is, but 'the law currently situates itself above or separate to the physical realm' (Graham 2011: 259).

In support, Burdon (2011: 86) notes, science has gradually changed our understanding of our place in the universe. First the Copernican revolution, then Darwin's insights, followed by modern cosmology, have totally transformed our view of humans. Where once we regarded ourselves as the summit of creation in the centre of the universe, we now recognize that we are the temporarily dominant predator species on a small planet orbiting an undistinguished star in a remote corner of an ordinary galaxy, one of perhaps 100 billion such systems of stars. Despite this radical transformation of our understanding, our legal systems have arguably evolved backwards. Where hunter-gatherer societies recognized the need for a system of customs, practice and law that allowed them to live in balance with their natural resources like food and water, our legal system is based on the delusion that natural systems only have value when transformed for human use.

Recalling Bosselmann's approach, we need to halt what he called DAMAGE (Bosselmann 2011: 205). So the legal framework needs to recognize that humans are not separate from nature, but inextricably entwined within it. We are as dependent on natural systems as elm trees or elephants, sparrows or sharks. Every molecule in my body was formerly part of the plant or animal kingdoms, and every molecule in my body will in time return to the Earth's systems. We need to move away from the anthropocentric delusion that we are the centre and masters of the Earth's natural systems. Our dependence on the health of natural systems should impel development of a legal system that is founded on the need to maintain the health of those systems.

Our materialism, the delusion that we will be more fulfilled if we are surrounded by more material possessions, needs to be replaced by what Raskin (2006: 1) called an appreciation of the quality of life, the quality of our human experience, rather than the quantity of material we possess.

By Atomism, Bosselmann (2011: 205) means the reductionist mindset that assumes soil, water, plants, animals and air can be separately regulated, when their health is intrinsically intertwined. Greed, or 'individualism gone mad', is the psychological flaw of not being content with enough, always wanting more and failing to recognize that more of a good thing may not even benefit us as individuals, even if it were possible to continue expanding production to meet the apparently insatiable demands for more. Finally, and most fundamentally, we need to recognize that the economy is a sub-set of our society. It is an important sub-set, but economic development should be seen as a means to the end of human happiness, rather than an end in itself. It is clearly a delusion to believe that contentment will inevitably increase if the gross domestic product becomes more gross, given that GDP is simply the aggregate of all spending and so increased by crime, violence, illness and war.

Reversing those presumptions leads us, as Bosselmann (ibid) argues, to a recognition that we should base our legal system on a set of principles which assume that our primary goal is a sustainable future. The Earth Charter is, he proposes, such a foundation. My copy of the Earth Charter is always before me on my desk as I write, constantly informing my thinking. Launched in 2000, it has a set of overarching core principles: respect and care for the community of life, ecological integrity, social and economic justice, democracy, non-violence and peace. These are equally important headings. Under the principle of ecological integrity, the Earth Charter sets out four goals:

- *Protect and restore the integrity of Earth's ecological systems, with special concern for biological diversity and the natural processes that sustain life.*
- *Prevent harm as the best method of environmental protection and, when knowledge is limited, apply a precautionary approach.*
- *Adopt patterns of production, consumption, and reproduction that safeguard Earth's regenerative capacities, human rights and community well-being.*
- *Advance the study of ecological sustainability and promote the open exchange and wide application of the knowledge acquired.*
  (Earth Charter International Secretariat 2005)

These are obviously similar to the basis for Wild Law and are the principles on which our legal system should be based if we are serious about the goal of sustainability. As Bosselmann argues, 'the modern secular myth that humans are in control and above nature' has outlived its usefulness and is now a barrier to our development. We need a new myth 'that celebrates life in all its bounty and variety' to 'inspire the cultural change that we need' (2011: 211). That is the promise of Earth Jurisprudence, or Wild Law: the new underpinning that would provide a durable basis for human civilization.

Conclusion

Some people think the vision of a sustainable future is utopian, but that has been said about all the important reform movements. Those who opposed slavery 200 years ago were told that no economy could function without slave labour, while the suffragettes were persecuted when they demanded the vote for women 100 years ago. Only 40 years ago, Indigenous people did not count as Australian citizens. Twenty-five years ago it was still utopian to dream of Berlin without the wall, or South Africa without apartheid, or an African-American as President of the USA – or even such modest goals as good coffee and civilized licensing laws in the part of Australia where I live! Many social reforms we now take for granted were initially denounced as utopian. They happened because determined people worked for a better world.

The US economist Lester Thurow has been attributed with saying that it is hard to tell people the party is over, especially if they haven't got to the bar yet! Describing the legal basis of a sustainable future society is, in those terms, telling you that one type of party is coming to an end; the party based on delusions of unlimited resources and a natural world that is immune to the insults we throw at it. But it is also describing a better party that is starting up, to which we are all invited. It is a better party because it won't run out of food and drink. It is a better party because it won't leave us with a very nasty hangover of radioactive waste or disrupted global climate or despoiled natural systems. It is a better party because it is based on the quality of human experience rather than gluttonous consumption. It is a better party because the neighbours won't be enviously peering through the windows or throwing rocks on the roof, because they will all be invited. And it's a better party because our children will be able to keep enjoying it after we are gone.

Rowan Williams, then Archbishop of Canterbury, reminded British voters before their 2005 election that there are always excuses for avoiding these important issues (Williams 2005). Without a strong mandate for change, he said, we can't be surprised when courage fails and progress is limited. As Rowan Williams said, we all have a responsibility to help change popular views and give courage to our leaders – literally encourage them – to take responsibility for our future.

It would be much easier for those of us in the developed world to ignore these difficult issues, to enjoy our material comforts and our wonderful lifestyle – but a sustainable future is clearly a better future. Working for it is our moral duty to the countless millions of other species that we share this planet with, and the future generations for whom we hold it in trust. Earth Jurisprudence is the only foundation on which such a future can be built.

References

Balakrishnan, K.G. (2006) 'Judicial activism and the role of green benches in India', paper presented at Asian Justices Forum, online. Available at: <http://highcourtchd.gov.in/sub_pages/left_menu/publish/articles/articles_pdf/judicial.htm> (accessed 27 September 2013).

Berry, T. (1999) *The Great Work: Our Way into the Future*, New York: Three Rivers Press.

Bosselmann, K. (2011) 'From reductionist environmental law to sustainability law', in P. Burdon (ed.) *Exploring Wild Law: The Philosophy of Earth Jurisprudence*, Kent Town, SA: Wakefield Press, 204–213.

Burdon, P. (2011) 'The great jurisprudence', in P. Burdon (ed.) *Exploring Wild Law: The Philosophy of Earth Jurisprudence*, Kent Town, SA: Wakefield Press, 59–78.

Cleary, P. (2013) *Too Much Luck: The Mining Boom and Australia's Future*, Melbourne: Black Ink.

Cullinan, C. (2011a) 'A history of wild law', in P. Burdon (ed.) *Exploring Wild Law: The Philosophy of Earth Jurisprudence*, Kent Town, SA: Wakefield Press, 12–23.

Cullinan, C. (2011b) *Wild Law*, Green Books: Totnes.

Dator, J. (2005) 'Assuming "responsibility for our rose"', in J. Paavola and I. Lowe (eds) (2005) *Environmental Values in a Globalising World*, Abingdon: Routledge, 215–235.

Earth Charter International Secretariat (2005) *The Earth Charter*, online. Available at: <www.earthcharter.org> (accessed 14 April 2013).

Fowler, R. (2009) 'Environmental regulation, the state perspective', paper presented at the First Australian Conference on Wild Law and Earth Jurisprudence, Adelaide, September 2009.

Graham, N. (2011) 'Owning the Earth', in P. Burdon (ed.) *Exploring Wild Law: The Philosophy of Earth Jurisprudence*, Kent Town, SA: Wakefield Press, 259–269.

Hall, K.L. (1989), *The Magic Mirror: Law in American Society*, New York: Oxford University Press.

Harding, S. (2011) 'Gaia and Earth Jurisprudence', in P. Burdon (ed.) *Exploring Wild Law: The Philosophy of Earth Jurisprudence*, Kent Town, SA: Wakefield Press, 79–84.

Higgins, P. (2010) *Eradicating Ecocide*, London: Shepheard-Walwyn.

Kelly, P. (2008) *Towards Globo Sapiens: Transforming Learners in Higher Education*, Sense Publishers: Rotterdam.

Kim, T-C. and Dator, J. (eds) (1999) *Co-creating a Public Philosophy for Future Generations*, London: Adamantine Press.

Lowe, I. (1989) *Living in the Greenhouse*, Brunswick, Victoria: Scribe Books.

Lowe, I. (2005a) 'Achieving a sustainable future', in J. Goldie, B. Douglas and B. Furnass (eds) *In Search of Sustainability*, Collingwood, Victoria: CSIRO Publishing.

Lowe, I. (2005b; 2nd edn 2009) *A Big Fix*, Melbourne: Black Inc.

McGrath, C. (2007) 'The Xstrata Case: Pyrrhic victory or harbinger?', in T. Bonyhady and P. Christoff (eds), *Climate Law in Australia*, Sydney: Federation Press.

McGrath, C. (2008) 'Regulating greenhouse gas emissions from Australian coal mines', in W. Gumley and T. Daya-Winterbottom (eds) *Climate Change Law: Comparative, Contractual and Regulatory Considerations*, Sydney: Lawbook Co.

McGrath, C. (2011) *Synopsis of the Queensland Environmental Legal System*, East Brisbane: Environmental Law Publishing. Available at www.envlaw.com.au/sqels5.pdf (accessed 20 August 2013).

New Zealand Government (2012) Whanganui River agreement signed, media release. Available at http://www.beehive.govt.nz/release/whanganui-river-agreement-signed (accessed 20 July 2013).

Oposa vs Factoran Jr, 224 Philippines Supreme Court Reports Annotated 792–818 (1993).

Paavola, J. and Lowe, I. (eds) (2005) *Environmental Values in a Globalising World*, Abingdon: Routledge.

Preston, B.J. (2006) 'Principles of ecologically sustainable development', online. Available at: <http://www.lec.lawlink.nsw.gov.au/agdbasev7wr/_assets/lec/m4203011721754/preston_principles%20of%20ecologically%20sustainable%20development.pdf> (accessed 14 April 2013).

Preston, B.J. (2011) 'Internalising ecocentrism in environmental law', paper presented at the Third Wild Law Conference: Earth Jurisprudence – Building Theory and Practice, September 2011, Griffith University, Queensland, online. Available at: <http://www.lec.lawlink.nsw.gov.au/lec/speeches_papers.html#Justice_Preston,_Chi> (accessed 14 April 2013).

Raskin, P. (2006) *The Great Transition Today: A Report from the Future*, Boston, MA: Great Transition Initiative, GTI Paper no. 2.

State of the Environment Advisory Council (1996) *State of the Environment Australia*, Collingwood, Victoria: CSIRO Publishing.

State of the Environment Committee (2011) *Australia State of the Environment 2011 In Brief*, Canberra: Blue Star.

Stone, C. (1972) 'Should trees have standing? Towards legal rights for natural objects', *Southern California Law Review* 45: 3–53, available at http://isites.harvard.edu/fs/docs/icb.topic498371.files/Stone.Trees_Standing.pdf, (accessed 16 July 2013).

UNEP (2012) *Global Environmental Outlook 5 Summary for Policy-Makers*, online. Available at: <http://www.unep.org/geo/pdfs/GEO5_SPM_English.pdf> (accessed 14 April 2013).

Williams R. (2005) 'A planet on the brink', *The Independent*, Sunday 17 April, available at http://www.independent.co.uk/voices/commentators/rowan-williams-a-planet-on-the-brink-489537.html (accessed 20 August 2013).

World Commission on Environment and Development (1987) *Our Common Future*, Oxford: Oxford University Press.

Xstrata Coal Queensland Pty Ltd & Ors v Friends of the Earth – Brisbane Co-Op Ltd & Ors (2012) QLC 013 at [490]–[499], available at http://www.landcourt.qld.gov.au/documents/decisions/MRA092-11%20Xstrata.pdf (accessed 17 July 2013).

Part I

Agency and implementation

Chapter 2

Earth Jurisprudence and the project of Earth democracy

Peter D Burdon

Human civilization is currently in the grip of social and ecological decline. We no longer have to discuss this crisis in future tense – it is part of the daily reality for many of the world's people. Arguably the most frustrating aspect of collapse is that many of its current manifestations could have been avoided. In 1992, the Union of Concerned Scientists issued a warning to humanity which read: 'Human beings and the natural world are on a collision course… No more than a few decades remain before the chance to avert the threats we now confront will be lost and the prospects for humanity diminished.' Yet, despite a growing public acceptance of the need for radical change, our laws, economics and powerful vested interests have maintained a program of business as usual. Thus, in 2005, the United Nations Millennium Ecosystem Assessment (MEA) (2005) reported that *every living system* in the biosphere was in a state of decline, the rate of which was increasing. The MEA further estimates that humans are responsible for the extinction of between 50–55 thousand species per year, a rate unequalled since the last great extinction some 65 million years ago. More recent studies of future energy consumption (International Energy Agency 2013) and ecological sustainability (Randers 2012) continue to project human society into a dangerous and ultimately fatal future.

Earth Jurisprudence is a vision for radically re-configuring our legal system and governance structures so that they support rather than undermine the health and integrity of the Earth community. To introduce this vision, I will proceed in four parts. In part one, I argue that the root causes of the present environmental crisis are an anthropocentric worldview coupled with neoliberal growth economics. In part two, I illustrate how these root causes have shaped the development of environmental protection law since the industrial revolution. In particular, I argue that environmental law is currently developed by a plutocracy which has vested interests in limiting its application. In part three, I unpack two important elements of Earth Jurisprudence. First, I describe Earth Jurisprudence as an ecocentric concept of law. This concept holds that human laws are subordinate to the ecological integrity of nature. Purported laws that contravene this standard are judged as defective and provide a justification for civil disobedience. Following this, I examine ecocentric governance and the project of Earth democracy. I argue that democratic frameworks should be deepened to allow for greater public participation and to achieve dilution of moneyed interests. I contend that decisions made by the collective will reflect social and ecological interests better than those made by private interests operating within a plutocracy.

The search for root causes

There is a long history in environmental studies of locating and developing methods to combat the 'root causes' of the environmental crisis. Canadian philosopher John Livingston (1981: 24) explains this approach, noting: 'Oil spills, endangered species, ozone depletion and so forth are presented as separate incidents and the overwhelming nature of these events means that we seldom look deeper.' 'However', Livingston argues (1981: 24), 'these issues are analogous to the tip of an iceberg, they are simply the visible portion of a much larger entity, most of which lies beneath the surface, beyond our daily inspection.'

In my view, the most sophisticated attempt to locate a root cause was developed by social ecologist, Murray Bookchin. According to Bookchin, the domination of nature by human beings stems from and takes the same form as the myriad of ways human beings exploit each other. The key to this analysis is 'hierarchy' – a term that encompasses 'cultural, traditional and psychological systems of obedience and command' (Bookchin 2005: 3). This includes the domination of the young by the old, of women by men, of one ethnic group by another, of the wealthy over the poor and of human beings over nature. Thus, according to Bookchin (2007: 13), to separate ecological problems from social problems or even to play down or to give token recognition to their relationship 'would be to grossly misconstrue the source of the growing environmental crisis'.

What attracts me to Bookchin's analysis is that it allows us to acknowledge and go beyond the common explanation for environmental exploitation advocated by many environmental philosophers – namely anthropocentrism.[1] According to this view, human beings exploit the environment because they conceive it as *existing* for their own personal use and benefit. Anthropocentric logic assigns value to human beings alone and assigns a significantly greater amount of value to human beings than to non-human entities. Anthropocentrism regards humans as the central fact or final aim and end of the universe and views and interprets everything in terms of human experience and values. Finally, anthropocentrism promotes a separation of people from nature and positions us at the imagined centre of the universe. From this perspective, the environment is rendered peripheral and understood as a resource to satisfy human needs, desires and wants.[2] Human beings are not understood as members of the mammalian class. We are 'culturally determined and distinguished' and 'set apart from all other uncultured parts of nature' (Graham 2011: 28).

While certainly instructive, the exclusive focus on mental ideas like anthropocentrism to explain the environmental crisis suffers from mental determinism. Adopting such a narrow perspective is a common shortcoming in social theory. Karl Marx, for example, is often accused of technological determinism (Cohen 1978), or of class struggle determinism (Marx and Engels 1879). Other theorists place the nature dictates argument (Diamond 2005), the process of production (Holloway 2002), changes in lifestyle or consumption (Hawken 2007) or mental conceptions of the world (Klein 2008) as being sufficient to cause social change. Certainly, mental determinism is as insufficient as any other narrow project.[3] In practice, major social transformations occur through a dialectic of transformations across a range of moments and develop unevenly in space and time to produce all manner of local contingencies. This is evidenced in the contrast between the Occupy movement and the second Arab revolt. A deterministic stance fails to capture this complex interplay and produces a contingency in social development (Harvey 2010: 196).

Another reason for moving away from a strict mental explanation for the environmental crisis is that it ignores structural forms that perpetuate exploitation independent of a particular philosophical worldview. The most important of these is industrial capitalism. Capitalism's inherent thirst for short-term growth and self-expansion[4] is fundamentally inconsistent with environmental protection (Magdoff and Foster 2011). Since the industrial revolution (1750), capitalism has grown at a compound rate of 2.5 per cent. In good years, growth is measured at an average of 3 per cent (at this percentage, the rate of growth doubles every 24 years). This growth is subject to uneven geographical development, particularly since the onset of neoliberal economics in the 1970s (Harvey 2006: 87–119). When capitalism was first constituted and material resources were abundant, 3 per cent compound growth was not considered a problem. However, this is no longer the case in the age of scarcity and resource wars (Klare 2002; 2012). Indeed, the total economy in 1750 was approximately US$135 billion. It had grown to US$4 trillion by 1950 and US$40 trillion at the beginning of the new millennium. If the global economy doubles over the next decade, it will have grown to US$100 trillion and by 2030 will need to find US$3 trillion profitable opportunities for growth. There are limits to growth and we have hit those limits, both environmentally and socially (Heinberg 2011).

Further, the systemic attributes of capitalism mean that the personality and worldview of individual capitalists is largely irrelevant. It simply does not matter if the director of Exxon Mobile or BHP Billiton is a good person or holds an ecological worldview. No amount of eco-literature, bush walking or Buddhist retreats will release a corporate director from the structural economic and legal pressures that pertain to a capitalist mode of production. Karl Marx makes this point forcefully in volume one of *Das Kapital*. The capitalists, according to Marx, have no real freedom – they are mere cogs in a mechanism who have to reinvest a portion of their profits and grow their enterprise because the 'coercive laws of competition force them to' (Marx 1992: 652). Put otherwise, the coercive laws of competition force capitalists to take a portion of their surplus and put it into expanding production (more labour, or new technology). The alternative is to go out of business and lose social status. As capital personified, their psychology is focused on the augmentation of exchange-value and the accumulation of social power in limitless money-form. If capitalists show any sign of drifting away from their central mission, the laws of competition bring them back into line. Therefore 'accumulation for the sake of accumulation, production for the sake of production' (Marx 1992: 652) becomes the central mantra of a capitalist mode of production.

Environmental protection in a plutocracy

The specific development and orientation of environmental law must be understood with reference to the growth of industrial capitalism from 1750. Harvard historian Morton Horowitz (1977: 32) notes that prior to this period, property rights were underpinned by an 'explicitly anti-development theory' that limited landowners to what courts regarded as natural use. The 'natural use' idea of private property equated to strong trespass law, which barred all uncontested physical entries, and nuisance law that prohibited neighbours from indirectly impairing a neighbour's enjoyment of land. For example, in the context of river systems a landowner could not disturb the natural drainage of land or take water from a river to the extent that it 'diminished its quality or quantity' for landowners downstream (Freyfogle 2001: 4).

It was quickly recognized that the 'natural use' conception of property stood in the way of economic progress. To promote development, lawmakers were pressured by economic interests to 'materially change the meaning of landownership to facilitate... intensive land uses' (Freyfogle 2001: 4). Horwitz comments:

> Law once conceived of as protective, regulative, paternalistic and above all, a paramount expression of the moral sense of the community, had come to be thought of as facilitative of individual desires and as simply reflective of the existing organization of economic and political power.
> (Horowitz 1977: 253)

This shift toward development was guided by the understanding that economic growth required more intensive land use than had been practised by previous generations. For example, communities that once enjoyed water laws that protected natural flow had these removed so that industries could draw more water and even introduce pollutants into the water system. Industrial parties required the right to emit smoke that degraded air quality; to make noise that scared livestock and on occasion to emit sparks which had the potential to set wheat fields on fire. Waterwheels disrupted the migration of fish, tall buildings blocked sunlight (Freyfogle 2001: 4). To promote these economic activities the environmental protections were deliberately eroded to promote market growth 'at the expense of farmers, workers, consumers' (Horwitz 1977: 254).

Many of the environmental problems that we face today can be traced back to the weakening of environmental protections that occurred during the industrial revolution. Further, the influence that industrial parties have over governments and the legislative process has further strengthened. Indeed, today it is most accurate to describe the governance framework in Western democracies as state-capitalist. State capitalism is a regressive and highly inadequate social theory. It is also fundamentally inconsistent with sustainability and basic principles of democracy.

These inconsistencies can be explained by distinguishing two systems of power – the political system and the economic system. The political system consists of elected representatives who set public policy. In contrast, the economic system consists of private power that is relatively free from public input and control. There are several immediate consequences of this organization of society. First, the range of decisions that are subject to democratic control is quite narrow. For example, it excludes decisions made within the commercial, industrial and financial system. Second, even within the narrow range of issues that are subject to public participation, the centres of private power exert an inordinately heavy influence through financial contributions, lobbying, media control/propaganda and by supplying the personal for the political system itself. Further, corporate leaders not only collaborate intimately with government representatives but acquire a 'strong role in writing legislation, determining public policies, and setting regulatory frameworks' (Chomsky 2005: 48). Perhaps the most striking recent example of this was documented by Paul Krugman and concerned the role of the American Legislative Exchange Council in providing the language for Florida's controversial Stand Your Ground laws.[5]

In short, contemporary democratic institutions function within a narrow range in a capitalist democracy and even within this narrow range, their function is inordinately weighted toward private power. Indeed, state-capitalism is a plutocracy – rule by moneyed interests where people simply vote periodically for 'political entrepreneurs, who seek out their vote much like commercial interests seek out dollars in the marketplace' (Magdoff and Foster 2011: 13). While I do not want to suggest that environmental laws and regulations have had no effect, their impact has always been limited to the extent that they challenge the facilitation of economic growth. Under a plutocracy, progressive lawmakers may tinker at the edges of the growth paradigm, but they will never give environmental law the teeth to fundamentally challenge the power structure of state capitalism. Indeed, so long as a certain elite group is in power, it will make decisions that promote the interests that it serves. And so long as governance is tied to the imperative of economic growth, social and environmental justice will remain a distant concern. To expect otherwise is folly.

Earth Jurisprudence and the project of earth democracy

> The universe is communion of subjects and not a collection of objects.
> (Swimme and Berry 1992: 243)

Earth Jurisprudence is an emerging theory of law that emphasizes human interconnectedness with the environment. It maintains that legal recognition of interconnectedness is a prerequisite for ecological sustainability and should be recognized as a foundation of our legal system. To this end, Earth Jurisprudence seeks to catalyse a paradigm shift in law from an anthropocentric/growth paradigm and toward the ecocentric concept of 'Earth community'. As described by Thomas Berry, the term Earth community provides several fundamental insights. Among them is the notion that ecosystems involve the individual behaviours of organisms. These organisms are understood as members (not isolated parts) of ecosystems (Berry 1999: 4). Also, he argues that ecosystems have various degrees of interiority or subjectivity (Berry 1999: 162–3). In Earth Jurisprudence, the concept of Earth community has several critical implications for law. The first pertains to our concept of law and the second to the way laws are made. I will briefly outline each of these insights in turn.[6]

Re-conceptualising our concept of law

The contemporary concept of law in analytic jurisprudence is fundamentally human centred. The two dominant schools of thought – natural law and legal positivism – are concerned ultimately with relations between individuals, between communities, between states and between elementary groupings of these categories. Only in rare circumstances does legal theory consider the environment as relevant to our concept of law. Indeed, the 'separation and hierarchical ordering of the human and non-human worlds constitutes the primary assumption from which most Western legal theory begins' (Graham 2011: 15). Legal positivism promotes the view that only human beings or corporate 'persons' are subjects and that nature is an object. Nature is not considered to possess inherent value and receives instrumental value and protection from human property rights.

In contrast, the fundamental starting point for Earth Jurisprudence is the 'ecological integrity' of the Earth community (Burdon 2013). This reference point acts as a bedrock standard or measure for the legal quality of a purported law. Thus, laws that contravene the standard of ecological integrity are considered defective and do not bind a population in conscience. Put otherwise, purported laws that undermine the health and future flourishing of the Earth community are not binding and citizens are justified in engaging in non-violent acts of civil disobedience to amend or repeal the law. By advocating a necessary connection between law and ecological integrity, Earth Jurisprudence seeks to ensure that environmental ideas are not imposed from the outside in an ad hoc or limited way. Instead, they are inherent to our very concept of law and provide an immediate measure of legal quality.

The concept of 'ecological integrity' originated as an ethical concept as part of Aldo Leopold's classic 'land ethic' (1966) and has been recognized in legislative instruments such as the *Clean Water Act U.S.* (1972).[7] As described by Laura Westra (2005: 574), the generic concept of integrity 'connotes a valuable whole, the state of being whole or undiminished, unimpaired, or in perfect condition'. Because of the extent of human exploitation of the environment, wild nature provides the paradigmatic example of ecological integrity.

Among the most important aspects of ecological integrity are first the autopoietic capacities of life to regenerate and evolve over time at a specific location (Swimme and Berry 1992: 75–7). Thus, integrity provides a place-based analysis of the evolutionary and biogeographical process of an ecosystem (Angermeier and Karr 1994). A second aspect concerns the requirements that are needed to maintain native ecosystems (Karr and Chu 1999). Climatic conditions and other biophysical phenomena can also be analysed as interconnected ecological systems. A third aspect is that ecological integrity is both 'valued and valuable as it bridges the concerns of science and public policy' (Westra 2000: 20). To bridge this chasm, models such as the multimetric Index of Biological Integrity allow scientists to approximate the extent to which systems deviate from verifiable integrity levels calibrated from a baseline condition of wild nature (Karr 1996: 96). Degradation or loss of integrity is thus comprised of any human-induced positive or negative divergence from this baseline standard (Westra 2000: 21). Finally, if given appropriate legal status, 'ecological integrity' recognizes the intrinsic value of ecosystems and can help curb the excess of human development and exploitation of nature.

Eco-centric governance: deepening democracy

The Project of Earth Democracy is another fundamental aspect of Earth Jurisprudence. Distilled to a sentence, Earth Democracy is an attempt to fuse ecocentric ethics with deeper forms of democracy and public participation.

The scope of ideas circulating in this space is stunning and includes bioregional governance (Plant et al. 2008; Snyder 2008); and libertarian-socialist concepts of participatory democracy (Bookchin 2007). Arguably the most visible attempt to fuse concepts such as Earth community with democracy is the Earth Charter. The preamble to the Charter reads:

> To move forward we must recognise that in the midst of a magnificent diversity of cultures and life forms we are one human family and one Earth community with a common destiny. We must join together to bring forth a sustainable global society founded on respect for nature, universal human rights, economic justice and a culture of peace.[8]

As described in the Charter, democracy is not an end in itself – it is a means for achieving social and environmental goals. Thus, the Charter's positive affirmation of democratic ideals should not be confused with a general endorsement for existing states. As Klaus Bosselmann (2010: 92) notes: '[a]ny attempt to find an example of successful governance for sustainability among existing states must fail. It simply does not exist.'

In thinking about how existing democratic structures can be deepened to facilitate ecological and social goals, I believe that energy should be directed toward developing new social relationships and re-skilling citizens to occupy decision-making roles in their communities. The importance of pre-figurative politics has been well documented in contemporary literature (Epstein 1993; Hopkins 2008; Bosselmann et al. 2008). Just what the pre-figurative forms are is an open question and must be considered with reference to local conditions, politics and levels of expertise. Four pathways for deepening democracy deserve specific mention:[9]

(i) Participatory budgeting originated in Porto Alegre, Brazil and is a process of democratic deliberation and decision-making in which citizens decide on how to allocate funds of a municipal or council budget (Wampler 2009).
(ii) Communal councils have been established in Venezuela and seek to empower citizens to form neighbourhood-based elected councils that initiate and oversee local policies and projects for community development (Martinez et al. 2010).
(iii) Workers cooperatives represent one part of what Michael Albert (2003) calls 'participatory economics'. A worker cooperative is a cooperative owned and democratically managed by its worker-owners. While this model exists in all industrial countries, a particularly interesting case study is the Mondragon Corporation,[10] whose federation extends over the Basque region of Spain. In the 2012 European financial crisis, unemployment in the Basque region only rose to 6 per cent. This can

be contrasted with the rest of Spain which simultaneously experienced unemployment levels at 25 per cent with youth unemployment at 50 per cent.[11]

(iv) The reclaiming of public space for community decision making, which has been integral to the decentralised and open decision-making processes employed by the Occupy movement (Blumenkranz 2011).

These and other examples intend to shift the power structure that dominates contemporary decision making from private interests, to the collective. It is surely conceivable, perhaps even likely, that decisions made by the collective will reflect both community and ecological interests better than those made by corporate executives or members of parliament operating within the structure of state capitalism. Properly conceived, democracy is about securing the conditions that make it possible for ordinary people to better their lives by becoming political beings or what Bosselmann (2010: 105) calls Ecological Citizens. What is at stake is whether citizens can become empowered to recognize that their concerns are best addressed and protected under a governance structure governed by principles of commonality, ecological integrity, equality and fairness; a governance model in which taking part in politics becomes a way of staking out and sharing in a common life and cultivating a deep respect and relationship with the broader Earth community.

Conclusion

In his final book, Thomas Berry identified a 'Great Work' that lies before humankind. 'The Great Work now', he writes, 'is to carry out the transition from a period of human devastation of the Earth to a period when humans would be present to the planet in a mutually beneficial manner' (Berry 1999: 3). Berry was under no illusion concerning the immensity of this task, nor its urgency. Indeed, reflecting on the present environmental crisis, he argues that perhaps the most 'valuable heritage' we can provide for future generations, is some indication of how this work can be fulfilled in an effective manner (Berry 1999: 7). This is not a task we have chosen for ourselves. However, Berry maintains that '[t]he nobility of our lives... depends upon the manner in which we come to understand and fulfil our assigned role' (Berry 1999: 7).

The analysis of Earth Jurisprudence and governance presented in this chapter represents a modest contribution to this task. The next important question is – *so who is going to do it?* If we have any possibility of avoiding the worst ravages of ecological collapse then I contend that Berry's Great Work must also become our own. We must stop waiting for our governments and private interests to act with respect for the environment and work collaboratively toward change. We can begin today to re-define our relationship to the natural world and as a community reconceptualize our concept of law to reflect ecocentric goals. We can also build (or join existing) alternative decision-making structures and re-skill ourselves in the practice of democracy. In the final analysis, a plutocracy is not something that we can bring down with force – instead, as Gustav Landauer (2010: 214) recognized: 'we destroy it by contracting other relationships, by behaving differently toward one another.'

Notes

1 See for example (Berry 1999: 4): 'The deepest cause of the present devastation is found in a mode of consciousness that has established a radical discontinuity between the human and other modes of being.'
2 Contemporary examples of this thinking can be witnessed in the debate concerning the preservation of the spotted owl in America's Northwest. Rush Limbaugh argued: 'If the owl can't adapt to the superiority of humans, screw it... if a spotted owl can't adapt, does the Earth really need that particular species so much that hardship to human beings is worth enduring in the process of saving it?' cited in (Jamieson 2008: 181–82).
3 Despite his representation as a deterministic social theorist, Karl Marx offers an interesting analysis of social change in Marx 1992: 494–495, fn 4. Here he argues that social change is predicated by a complex interplay of six identifiable conceptual elements. These include, technology, relation to nature, the process of production, the production and reproduction of daily life, social relations and mental conceptions.
4 Immanuel Wallerstein (1993: 14). Wallerstein characterizes the capitalist mode of production in the following terms: 'it was this relentless and curiously self-regarding goal of the holder of capital, the accumulation of still more capital, and the relations of this holder of capital had therefore to establish with other persons in order to achieve this goal, which we denominate as capitalist.'
5 This article can be viewed at <http://www.nytimes.com/2012/03/26/opinion/krugman-lobbyists-guns-and-money.html>. See also the investigative website ALEC Exposed <http://www.alecexposed.org/wiki/ALEC_Exposed>.
6 For a more advanced introduction refer to Burdon (2013).
7 Section 101(a) has its objective 'to restore and maintain the chemical, physical, and biological integrity of the Nation's waters.'
8 Read the Earth Charter online at <http://www.earthcharterinaction.org/>.
9 See the movie 'Beyond Elections' at <http://www.beyondelections.com/>.
10 For further information on the Mondragon Corporation see <http://www.mondragon-corporation.com/language/en-US/ENG.aspx>.
11 BBC, News, Basque co-operative Mondragon Defies Spain's Slump, 14 August 2012 <http://www.bbc.co.uk/news/world-europe-19213425>.

References

Albert, M. (2003) *Parecon: Life After Capitalism*, New York: Verso.
Angermeier, P. and Karr, J. (1994) 'Protecting biotic resources: Biological integrity versus biological diversity as policy directives', *BioScience*, 44(10): 690.
Berry, T. (1999) *The Great Work: Our Way Into the Future*, New York: Bell Tower.
Blumenkranz, C. (2011) *Occupy!: Scenes from Occupied America*, New York: Verso.

Bookchin, M. (2005) *The Ecology of Freedom: The Emergence and Dissolution of Hierarchy*, Oakland, CA: AK Press.
Bookchin, M. (2007) *Social Ecology and Communalism*, Oakland, CA: AK Press.
Bosselmann, K., Engel, R. and Taylor, P. (2008) *Governance for Sustainability – Issues, Challenges and Successes*, Bonn: World Conservation Union.
Bosselmann, K. (2010) *Earth Democracy: Institutionalizing Sustainability and Ecological Integrity*, in J.R. Engel, L. Westra and K. Bosselmann (eds) *Democracy, Ecological Integrity and International Law*, London: Cambridge Scholars Publishing.
Burdon, P. (2013) *Earth Jurisprudence: Private Property and the Environment*. London: Routledge.
Chomsky, N. (2005) *Government in the Future*, New York: Seven Stories Press.
Cohen, G. (1978) *Karl Marx's Theory of History: A Defence*, Princeton, NJ: Princeton University Press.
Diamond, J. (2005) *Guns, Germs, and Steel: The Fates of Human Societies*, New York: WW Norton & Company.
Engel, J.R. Westra, L. and Bosselmann, K. (2010) *Democracy, Ecological Integrity and International Law*, London: Cambridge Scholars Publishing.
Epstein, B. (1993) *Political Protest and Cultural Revolution: Nonviolent Direct Action in the 1970s and 1980s*, Berkeley, CA: University of California Press.
Freyfogle, E. (2001) 'Property rights, the markets and environmental change in twentieth-century America', *Illinois Public Law and Legal Theory Research Papers Series*, 01.
Graham, N. (2011) *Lawscape: Property, Environment, Law*, London: Routledge.
Harvey, D. (2006) *A Brief History of Neoliberalism*, Oxford: Oxford University Press.
Harvey, D. (2010) *A Companion to Marx's Capital*, New York: Verso.
Hawken, P. (2007) *Blessed Unrest: How the Largest Social Movement in History Is Restoring Grace, Justice, and Beauty to the World*, London: Penguin Books.
Heinberg, R. (2011) *The End of Growth: Adapting to Our New Economic Reality*, Gabriola Island, Canada: New Society Publishers.
Hopkins, R. (2008) *The Transition Handbook: From Oil Dependency to Local Resilience*, Totnes: Green Books.
Holloway, J. (2002) *Change the World Without Taking Power*, Melbourne: Pluto Press.
Horowitz, M. (1977) *The Transformation of American Law, 1870–1960: The Crisis of Legal Orthodoxy*. Oxford: Oxford University Press.
International Energy Agency (2013) *World Energy Outlook 2013*, Paris: Organization for Economic Cooperation and Development.
Jamieson, D. (2008) *Ethics and the Environment: An Introduction*, Cambridge, MA: Cambridge University Press.
Karr, J. (1996) 'Ecological integrity and ecological health are not the same', in Peter C. Schulze (ed.) *Engineering Within Ecological Constraints*, Washington, DC: National Academy Press.
Karr, J. and Chu, E. (1999) *Restoring Life in Running Waters*, Washington, DC: Island Press.
Klare, M. (2002) *Resource Wars: The New Landscape of Global Conflict*, New York: Holt Paperbacks.
Klare, M. (2012) *The Race for What's Left: The Global Scramble for the World's Last Resources*, New York: Metropolitan Books.
Klein, N. (2008) *The Shock Doctrine: The Rise of Disaster Capitalism*, Sydney: Picador.

Kraughammer, C. (1991) 'The Spotted Owl', *Time Magazine*, 82.
Landauer, G. (2010) *Revolution and Other Writings: A Political Reader*, Oakland, CA: PM Press.
Leopold, A. (1966) *A Sand County Almanac: Essays on Conservation from Round River*, New York: Ballantine Books.
Livingston, J. (1981) *Arctic Oil*, Toronto: CBC Merchandising for the Canadian Broadcasting Corporation.
Magdoff, F. and Foster, J.B. (2011) *What Every Environmentalist Needs to Know About Capitalism*, New York: Monthly Review Press.
Martinez, C., Fox, M. and Farrell, J. (2010) *Venezuela Speaks!: Voices from the Grassroots*, Oakland, CA: PM Press..
Marx, K. and Engels, F. (1879) 'Strategy and tactics of the class struggle', online. Available at: <http://www.marxists.org/archive/marx/works/1879/09/17.htm> (accessed 02 November 2011).
Marx, K. (1992) *Capital Volume One*, Sydney: Penguin Books.
Millennium Ecosystem Assessment (2005) *Ecosystems and Human Well-Being*, online. Available at: <http://www.unep.org/Maweb/en/index.aspx> (accessed 2 October 2013).
Plant, J., Andruss, V. and Wright, E. (2008) *Home! A Bioregional Reader*, Gabriola Island, Canada: New Catalyst Books.
Randers, J. (2012) *2052: A Global Forecast for the Next Forty Years*, White River Junction, VT: Chelsea Green Publishing.
Snyder, G. (2008) *The Practice of the Wild*, Berkeley, CA: Counterpoint.
Swimme, B. and Berry, T. (1992) *The Universe Story*, San Francisco, CA: Harper.
Wallerstein, I. (1993) *Historical Capitalism*, New York: Verso.
Wallerstein, I. (2011) 'Wallerstein on the Arab Revolts', *Against the Grain*, online. Available at: <http://www.againstthegrain.org/program/437/id/222240/tues-5-31-11-wallerstein-arab-revolts> (accessed 12 December 2012).
Wampler, B. (2009) *Participatory Budgeting in Brazil: Contestation, Cooperation, and Accountability*, University Park, PA: Pennsylvania State University Press.
Westra, L. (2000) 'Ecological integrity and the aims of the Global Ecological Integrity Project', in D. Pimentel, L. Westra, and R. Noss (eds) *Ecological Integrity: Integrating Environment, Conservation and Health*. Washington, DC: Island Press.
Westra, L. (2005) 'Ecological integrity', *Encyclopaedia of Science, Technology, and Ethics*, 2: 574.

Chapter 3

Wild Law from below
Examining the anarchist challenge to Earth Jurisprudence

Samuel Alexander

> You never change things by fighting the existing reality. To change something, build a new model that makes the existing model obsolete.
> Buckminster Fuller

At least since Marx there has been a line of critical theory that conceptualizes the capitalist state as merely a tool for advancing and entrenching the narrow economic interests of the rich and powerful, to the detriment of wider society (Marx 1983). A broader critique has arisen more recently that holds that governments across the political spectrum have developed a 'growth fetish' (Hamilton 2003), through which all societal goals, including or especially environmental ones, are subordinated to the overarching aim of maximizing economic growth. These critical perspectives raise challenging issues for progressive legal theorists and activists who seek to advance their social or environmental causes by way of 'top down' legal change. Given that Earth Jurisprudence can be understood, first and foremost, as a movement that treats ecological sustainability as a fundamental legal principle (Berry 1999; Bosselmann 2008) – more fundamental even than the growth imperative (Alexander 2011a, 2011b) – the question of whether law will ever accept such a principle in a growth-orientated world is a confronting question that ought not to be avoided. After all, what if the institutions of law are so compromised by growth fetishism and corporate interests that the changes needed to create a sustainable and just society will never be generated from the 'top down'? Put otherwise, what if asking law to produce a sustainable and just society is like asking a zebra to change its stripes? We may desire the zebra to do so, and it may tell us it will change, but all history suggests that by nature it will not.

Furthermore, if the changes needed to produce a sustainable and just society will never be driven from the 'top down', but could only arise through social movements 'from below' (Trainer 2010), what are the implications of this for Earth Jurisprudence, which to date has been characterized almost exclusively by the attempt to formulate and justify 'top down' legal approaches to environmental law? Is Wild Law a coherent category if the society it vaguely implies is something that could only be created among the grassroots of social movements, as opposed to something that could be produced by the legislature or the judiciary? These are some of the issues I wish to examine in this chapter, although my purpose is to raise questions rather than to lay down answers or provide solutions. I confess that the sands of my own thinking are shifting with uncertainty beneath my feet as I write, owing in part to the complexity of the issues involved (see Bollier and Weston 2013; Healy et al. 2012). Nevertheless, what I am convinced of is that the importance of the questions posed justifies the attempt to grapple with them, so I ask that this exploratory essay be treated merely as an 'invitation to discuss'.

The central issue I would like to raise for Earth jurists, and for oppositional lawyers more generally, is the question of 'strategy'. That is to say, I would like to raise the question of how best to direct our limited energies and resources, for if change is truly what we desire, our energies and resources must be used to their fullest practical effect. Earth Jurisprudence, after all, is not an intellectual game we play to amuse ourselves. It is a framework for deep societal transition, and if we truly believe in the 'ends' for which we ostensibly struggle, then surely we must take care that the 'means' we employ are the best we have available.

To be clear, I do not seek to question the 'ends' or 'principles' of Earth Jurisprudence, with which I am deeply sympathetic (Burdon 2011a). Rather, this chapter seeks to evaluate the 'means' which Earth jurists (including myself) have generally taken up to try to achieve or realise those 'ends.' More directly, I want to ask the question of whether 'top down' change is really where we should be directing our energies, and to suggest that perhaps we should be directing more of our energies toward building the new society at a grassroots level; building it beneath the legal structures of the existing society with the aim that one day new societal structures will emerge 'from below' to replace the outdated forms we know today. In this sense, it could be said, I am presenting an 'anarchist' challenge to Earth Jurisprudence, in the limited sense, at least, that I am proposing that we consider ignoring the state rather than trying to use the state to advance 'deep green' causes which it seems wholly uninterested in supporting.

I feel this perspective could be easily misunderstood, so before developing my line of reasoning a word of clarification is immediately in order. I do not wish to suggest that strong 'top down' environmental laws, such as those proposed by Earth jurists, are not desirable. On the contrary, it is perfectly clear to me that the judiciary and especially parliament could do many things to protect and conserve Earth's ecosystems (see Bollier and Weston 2013), and over the last decade or so Earth Jurisprudence has been, and continues to be, a rich source of inspiration for what an ecocentric legal system might look like (Burdon 2011a). My tentative thesis, however, is that growth fetishism has such a strong hold on the branches of government that efforts directed toward producing strong 'top down' environmental law will essentially be ignored by lawmakers, and thus those efforts for progressive 'top down' change could well be wasted. We do not, of course, have a surplus of oppositional energy or resources to waste or misdirect, so if it is the case that the zebra of law will not change its stripes, it arguably follows that we should not dedicate our efforts toward convincing it to do so, no matter how desirable that 'top down' change may be. Rather, we should dedicate our efforts toward areas with the greatest leverage – with the greatest potential to effect positive change – and I have come to suspect that the areas that have the greatest leverage lie among the grassroots of social movements, not parliament or the courts.

I do not pretend to be able to do this line of thinking justice in the space available; nor could I expect to convince the reader of its veracity, since I have already implied that in my eyes its veracity remains an open question. All I hope to do is raise the question of 'strategy' – the question of how best to direct our limited energies and resources – and if I can do that successfully I feel the chapter should serve a worthwhile purpose. I begin unpacking these ideas in the next section by describing briefly how the growth model of progress has come to shape law. I proceed to outline ways that law has attempted (without success) to deal with the ecological impacts of growth and how Earth Jurisprudence opens up space for an alternative, post-growth approach to legal governance. Insofar as it confronts growth, however, Earth Jurisprudence arguably renders itself politically unpalatable, and so I conclude by delving deeper into the question of 'strategy' in order to explore the prospects or even the possibility of a Wild Law 'from below.'

Law and the growth model of progress

With the development of the steam engine in the early decades of the eighteenth century, for the first time humankind was able to harness the vast stores of energy embodied in fossil fuels – coal, at first, and later oil and gas. This led to the industrialization of economies around the world, a process that is still continuing to this day. Not since the Agricultural Revolution around 10,000 years earlier had there been such a radical change in the way human beings lived on Earth. The productive capacity of industrializing nations grew at exponential rates, driven onward by the seemingly endless supply of cheap and abundant energy, and this growth of production and trade provided industrializing nations and their inhabitants with what seemed like an endless supply of resources with which to meet their every desire. As a result, economic growth became the overriding objective of governments – the solution to all problems – especially in the Western world but increasingly elsewhere (Purdey 2010). Indeed, growth of the global economy seems to have become synonymous with 'progress' itself, and today this remains the dominant paradigm or lens through which social, economic, and political success is judged.

Unsurprisingly, perhaps, this growth paradigm also came to shape legal systems around the world, such that law, in many jurisdictions, can be seen to have developed a pro-growth structure (Alexander 2011a). The dynamics at play here are relatively straightforward: when economic growth, as measured by increases in GDP, is considered synonymous with national progress, laws that foster economic growth are presumptively justified, while laws that inhibit, slow, or reduce economic growth are presumptively unjustified. Over time this 'normative filter' has given legal systems their pro-growth structures, and while one could point to exceptions to this general statement (e.g. Filgueira and Mason 2011), they are just that, exceptions within a growth paradigm that marginalizes them.

Economic growth has brought with it many social benefits, of course, lifting millions of people out of poverty and providing many with a high material standard of living that would have been unimaginable only a few generations earlier. When focusing only on these types of material provision, the growth paradigm has some initial plausibility, especially since there are billions of people on the planet who clearly still need to develop their economic capacities in some form, just to provide for their most basic material needs. At first consideration, then, it is quite understandable why economic growth is widely considered to be an appropriate, even necessary, social goal. It is arguably a goal that not only *does* but also *should* shape our social, economic, and political structures, including our legal systems.

Economic growth, however, is a two-edged sword, one that produces both benefits and costs, especially ecological costs. Vast bodies of rigorous scientific evidence now indicate that today the size of the global economy exceeds, by some way, the sustainable carrying capacity of the planet (see, e.g., Vale and Vale 2013). Furthermore, despite extraordinary technological advances in recent decades – advances that were supposed to solve the ecological crises – the overall impacts of economic activity continue to grow and intensify, not decline (Jackson 2009). These facts radically call into question the legitimacy of the growth paradigm, at least in the most developed parts of the world, for if there is to be any 'ecological room' for an expanding human population to live at a dignified material standard of living, the richest societies must not continue increasing their material demands on a finite planet (Meadows et al. 2004). Rather than rethink the growth paradigm, however, the international community has fudged the issue by talking of 'sustainable development,' which sounds lovely but has been rendered meaningless by decades of greenwash. Today, sustainable development has come to signify the attempt to produce and consume more sustainably, *provided this does not interfere with continued economic growth.* This description might sound cynical, but even a glance at reality will testify to its accuracy (Worldwatch Institute 2013). As the global economy struggles to emerge from the global financial crisis, it is clear that 'growth fetishism' is alive and well – growth appears more important now than ever, the environment be damned – and this paradigm continues to provide a normative filter that determines which environmental laws are allowed to pass through the institutions of capitalism. It is at least arguable, then, that any approach to environmental law that seriously challenges the growth paradigm will never make it through this normative filter, and it is now worth taking a closer look at the various approaches to environmental law in order to better understand the forces that are at play here.

Three broad approaches to environmental law

In the legal sphere it could be said that there are three broad approaches to dealing with the environmental impacts of economic activity – 'market-based' approaches; 'command-and-control' approaches; and the 'deep green' approach of Earth Jurisprudence. I will now briefly outline these three approaches and emphasise the relationship of each approach to the growth paradigm.

'Free market' environmentalism

Within advanced capitalist societies today, the dominant approach to environmental law is based on neoclassical economics, exemplified most clearly by law-and-economics scholarship but which also has a much broader influence (Posner 1986). This approach (which comes in many varieties) assumes that the best way to maximize utility in a society, over the long term, is to create a well-functioning 'free market' economy. To oversimplify, this broadly involves the state protecting private property rights and enforcing contracts, but otherwise generally 'staying out' of the economy. In such an economy it is assumed that there will be price incentives in place to ensure that natural resources are exploited to an 'optimal' degree, but not further. If natural resources are overexploited in such a way as to engender sustainability concerns, this can only be because the costs of production are not fully internalized, often because the degradation of common resources is not being built into the price of the commodities produced, leading to overconsumption (i.e. a 'market failure'). Accordingly, within this model, environmental law aims to internalize any externalities, and privatize common resources, but otherwise let prices and market mechanisms determine how the economy functions in relation to the natural environment.

Without going further into the details of this complex theory of law, the point to emphasise presently is how easily this approach to environmental law sits within the growth model. Far from challenging growth, the neoclassical approach to environmental law assumes that the common good will be advanced most efficiently if individuals, businesses, and governments seek to maximize profits and grow the economy. Growth provides money, after all, and money provides individuals and governments with power to satisfy their desires, including environmental desires. The role of law is simply to create structures to ensure that markets function in an 'optimal' way. From this view, environmental problems are not due to economic growth, as such, but due to imperfect structures within which economic activity occurs. Accordingly, growth itself is not questioned.[1]

'Command-and-control' environmentalism

The 'free market' approach to environmental law might work nicely in theory, but its relationship with reality has proven to be tenuous indeed. An alternative approach can broadly be called 'command-and-control' environmentalism, which arose due to the failures of 'free market' environmentalism to protect nature. The command-and-control approach (which also comes in many varieties) does not accept that market mechanisms will ever be sufficient, on their own, to adequately protect planetary ecosystems. Rather, this broad school holds that more direct regulation of the economy is needed. While the command-and-control approach might accept that internalising externalities is an important step in the right direction, it nevertheless insists that 'market failures' are so pervasive, and ultimately unavoidable to some degree, that direct governmental involvement is required, at least to address the most egregious environmental harms. Advocates of the 'free market' respond with the argument that such paternalism is an inefficient mode of governance, and that the same ends can be achieved more efficiently via market mechanisms. However, advocates of the command-and-control approach typically consider certain inefficiencies an acceptable price to pay for the more direct environmental regulation.

Again, the many nuances of this approach, and the intricate debate between approaches, cannot be unpacked further here (see Godden and Peel 2010). For present purposes, the point to note is that, like the 'free market' approach, the 'command-and-control' approach does not question the growth paradigm, but rather tries to better regulate economic activity in order to diminish the ecological costs of growth. The more direct regulation may, at times, slow growth to some extent, but this is considered an unfortunate side effect of environmental protection, not one of its aims. The underlying aim remains growth, although it is usually softened by such as terms as 'green growth', 'smart growth', or that now dangerous euphemism, 'sustainable development' (Worldwatch Institute 2013).

Earth Jurisprudence

When one asks advocates of 'free market' or 'command-and-control' environmentalism why the overall ecological impacts of economic activity are still increasing, both parties will claim that it is because their own systems of governance have not yet been fully or properly implemented. Advocates of the 'free market' will insist that with a bit more deregulation and some tweaking of prices here and there, the 'invisible hand' will ensure that both growth and sustainability are achieved as a natural result of market forces. Advocates of 'command-and-control' will argue that with some stricter regulation of the growth economy, the ecological costs of growth can be reduced within safe boundaries. But there is another reason for why both approaches have failed to produce sustainability, and I would argue that that it is because neither approach questions the growth paradigm (Alexander 2012a, 2012b). By assuming the legitimacy and desirability of growth, the mainstream approaches to environmental law outlined above formulate strategies for environmental protection within a macro-economic framework that is inherently unsustainable. It should come as no surprise, therefore, that those strategies fail. In order for environmental law to have any chance of being effective, what is needed, first and foremost, is a jurisprudence 'beyond growth', and I have argued elsewhere that Earth Jurisprudence is the most promising place for such a jurisprudence to take hold (Alexander 2011b).

Earth Jurisprudence is far from being a homogenous body of literature (Burdon 2011a), but there do seem to be threads of commonality that unite the various forms. First among them is the idea that nature – the life-support system upon which the entire community of life depends – is more than a 'resource' to be exploited for human gratification. Nature is something that should not be, and indeed, cannot be understood merely in economic terms. An old growth forest or a marsh, for example, should be valued not merely (or at all) in terms of dollars, or treated as resources to be developed in ways that maximize profits, but primarily in terms of the role they play in maintaining the health and integrity of planetary ecosystems. In this sense Earth Jurisprudence treats ecological sustainability as fundamental, and accordingly seeks ways to construct legal systems in order to achieve that defining goal. If this approach interferes with economic development, then it is 'development' that must be reconsidered, not the 'principle of sustainability' (Bosselmann 2008). From this view, then, law should seek to facilitate the creation of 'post-growth economies' that sit safely within ecological limits, rather than trying make 'growth economies' sustainable, as mainstream environmentalism tries to do, without success. Earth Jurisprudence must hack at the roots of unsustainability, not merely the branches, and I believe that this means operating beyond the growth paradigm.

As noted earlier, it is not the purpose of this chapter to unpack the details of what an Earth-centred jurisprudence would look it or how it might function. Those issues have been taken up with rigour in other chapters of this book, and elsewhere (Burdon 2011a). Nor have I attempted to present the case against growth in any detail, a critique that has been made many times before (e.g. Meadows et al. 2004; Jackson 2009). Instead, the present analysis seeks to evaluate the prospects of a post-growth Earth Jurisprudence in a growth-orientated world, and, in particular, to consider whether 'top down' change is a strategy that Earth jurists should be focusing on. I am now in a position to consider these issues in a little more detail and bring my argument to a head.

Three strategies for change: democratic, socialist, anarchist

My analysis so far has been based on the following two premises: (1) that the growth paradigm acts as a normative filter which over time has given law a pro-growth structure; and (2) that the growth paradigm is inherently unsustainable. Upon those premises I argued that environmental laws that do not question the growth paradigm have failed and will always fail to achieve sustainability, and that Earth Jurisprudence must therefore be a post-growth jurisprudence if it is to succeed where 'free market' and 'command-and-control' environmentalism have failed. The issue I will now address is the question of what strategies could or should be taken if the aim is to create an Earth Jurisprudence beyond growth.

The strategy that Earth jurists (including myself) have generally taken up to advance their causes is what can be called the 'democratic' strategy. This essentially involves formulating and defending 'top down' legal proposals that embody the principles and values of Earth Jurisprudence. This strategy trusts that when the majority see the desirability of developing an ecocentric legal system, that sentiment will filter upward and eventually manifest in law. With particular reference to the legislature, the democratic strategy expects that when there is a culture that wants Earth Jurisprudence, those cultural values will be embraced by representative politicians and used to shape public policy in order to win or maintain office (Alexander 2013).

This strategy is perfectly coherent in theory, but it assumes that representative democracies are functioning well, and a strong case can be made that many so-called democracies are under the undue influence of corporate interests (e.g. Tham 2010). If that is so, even a culture shift in favour of Earth Jurisprudence would not necessarily bring about the required 'top down' structural change, because we can be sure that the corporate interests influencing public policies are not interested Earth Jurisprudence, certainly not an Earth Jurisprudence beyond growth. In the Australian context, a disheartening example of corporate influence in politics occurred in 2010 when the then Prime Minister, Kevin Rudd, sought to impose a relatively small tax on the mining industry, only to be subjected to a multi-million dollar, corporate-funded, scare campaign that ultimately resulted in Rudd being booted out of office and replaced with a more 'moderate', more corporate-friendly, Prime Minister. The most worrying aspect to this political event was the fact that the tax being proposed was hardly radical, and yet corporate interests shut down even this moderate legal reform. On a global scale, the same point could be made with respect to how the state responded to the Occupy Movement. As soon as the movement looked like it could potentially develop some real momentum, the state bore down with the full force of executive power and ensured that this fundamentally anti-capitalist political demonstration was nipped in the bud.

These are but particularly explicit examples of what is generally a more insidious process of control. Arguably the deeper forms of undemocratic influence come from political parties' dependence on corporations for political campaign funding, or from privately-owned media conglomerates feeding the public only or mainly what is in the corporate interest, thereby 'manufacturing consent' and keeping politicians in line (Chomsky and Herman 1994). Of course, culture often puts pressure on politicians to act this way or that, and sometimes, in accordance with democratic theory, the politicians are forced to abide or lose office. Fragments of an Earth Jurisprudence might even slip through law's normative filter (e.g. Filgueira and Mason 2011), as might some advances in social justice. But as soon as politicians, or the culture which those politicians are supposed to represent, seriously threaten to confront corporate power, it seems that a sophisticated political and ideological process is set in motion that functions to maintain, more or less, the existing order of things. In such circumstances, what hope is there for a 'top down' Earth Jurisprudence beyond growth? Empire, we can be sure, will not contemplate self-annihilation (Hardt and Negri, 2000); it will struggle for existence all the way down.

Marxists essentially accept this critical view of representative democracy, arguing that, indeed, the capitalist state is merely a tool for maintaining the status quo and furthering the narrow interests of economic elites. From this perspective, the deep changes that are arguably needed for Earth Jurisprudence depend not on the citizenry putting upward pressure on representative politicians, but on the citizenry taking control of the state more directly in order to advance the common good by way of state socialism. Since the economic elites will never voluntarily give up their hold on power, it follows that the Marxist or socialist revolution must be a violent revolution. In theory, at least, state socialism presents Earth Jurisprudence with a second strategy for achieving its environmental goals.

The problem with this strategy for societal change, however – aside from the acceptance of violence which seems fundamentally contrary to the ethics of Earth Jurisprudence – is that Marxism, and socialism more generally, have almost without exception remained embedded within the growth paradigm that I have argued Earth Jurisprudence must reject. In other words, state socialists have tended to seek state power, not to use that power to move away from the growth economy, but to facilitate continued growth only in more socially just ways and with a broader distribution of wealth. The same could be said of social democrats. While it is possible to imagine an eco-socialist Earth Jurisprudence – certainly it is easier than imagining a state capitalist Earth Jurisprudence! – there arguably remains the concern that states of *any type* – whether capitalist, socialist, or some other variety – are in and of themselves structurally inclined to be pro-growth. The basic critique here, which I cannot detail presently, is that all states are dependent for their existence on a taxable economy, and the larger the tax-base, the more funds the state can draw from to carry out its policies. This is the basic incentive structure that makes governments of any variety inclined toward growth.

This line of reasoning leads to a third, broad vision of social change, arising out of the anarchist tradition – the environmental anarchists, in particular, such as Murray Bookchin (1990) and Ted Trainer (2010). Although these theorists have their important differences, they essentially agree with Marxists that state capitalism is unjustifiable on the grounds that it is being used unjustly as a tool to maintain the existing order. But unlike Marxists, they do not think the solution is taking control of the state. They think the solution is building the new society at the local, grassroots level, where communities create self-governing, localized, participatory democracies. Part of the disagreement with Marxists here is because these 'deep green' anarchists think that the state is inextricably intertwined with economic violence against nature, and so from this perspective, no state, not even state eco-socialism, is going to lead to sustainability. But even if there were hope of a green state, these theorists would not advocate that people direct their energies toward top-down change, because they think that state governance is an unjustifiable form of hierarchy and rule, no matter how 'green' it might be. Accordingly, they believe that if a just and sustainable society is to emerge, it has to be built without help from the state (and probably with a lot of resistance). Far from giving up on democracy, however, these theorists are demanding it – in the most direct form possible.

While this brief review does a disservice to the richness of the ideas and thinkers discussed, it does serve the purpose of raising questions about how any transition to a sustainable way of life could unfold. Would it (or could it) be somehow voted in through the mechanisms of parliamentary democracy? Would it require a political revolution and the introduction of some form of eco-socialism? Or would it require grassroots movements to essentially do it mostly themselves, building the new economy underneath the existing economy, without state assistance? I have tentatively argued that efforts to convince or pressure the state to adopt a post-growth Earth Jurisprudence might be an exercise in futility, on the basis that governments seem to be fundamentally committed to growth economics. Not only can the argument be made that governments are effectively tools used for securing and advancing the narrow interests of economic elites, as Marxists have long asserted, but a broader critique suggests that governments across the political spectrum, whether capitalist or socialist, are in the grip of a 'growth fetish' (Hamilton 2003). If either or both of these diagnoses are correct, then this raises challenging questions about how and where Earth jurists should be directing their efforts. I have come to think that a post-growth Earth Jurisprudence is, and for the foreseeable future will be, politically unpalatable, and this suggests to me that, as a matter of strategy, Earth jurists should be dedicating more of their efforts toward building the Earth-centred society at the grassroots level, where – if you will excuse the metaphor – we are likely to get a better 'return on investment'. Strategy will always be a context-dependent issue, of course, and there may be times when attempting to push on governments might be the best strategic use of our efforts. That is for each of us to assess as individual agents embedded in unique contexts. But given the limits of oppositional energy at our disposal, it is important that not one joule of it is wasted, and saying that 'top down' change is *desirable* is not a sufficient excuse for misdirecting that energy. Of course 'top down' change is desirable! But the question I have posed in this chapter is the question of how to achieve the 'ends' of Earth Jurisprudence *most effectively*, and the tentative thesis I have presented is that this might involve working toward a Wild Law 'from below'.

Wild law from below: A coherent legal category?

Before closing I would like to offer a word about whether it is appropriate to speak of Wild Law if the changes aimed for are brought about 'from below' rather than from the 'top down'. After all, conventional use of the word 'law' implies a rule or body of rules emanating from parliament or the courts, and indeed Earth jurists accept that '[i]n Earth Jurisprudence, "human law" is the essence of what is meant by the term law. Its meaning is largely consistent with orthodox theory' (Burdon 2011b: 67). This raises the question of whether Wild Law is even a coherent category if it were something that could only emerge in the social sphere, beneath parliament and the courts. Perhaps 'law' is not the right word for the mode of governance to which I refer?

If 'law' were interpreted narrowly as meaning the rules emanating from parliament and the courts, then it would follow that Wild Law 'from below' is not a coherent category on the grounds that it is not law, proper. However, this conventional understanding of law is arguably unduly narrow, evidenced by the fact that jurists have long accepted 'customary law' to be a legitimate form of law, despite in such cases there being an absence of conventional lawmaking institutions, such as parliament or courts as we know them today (Bollier and Weston 2013). The customary laws of many indigenous communities are a case in point, where cultures were governed, and to some extent still are, by sets of knowable and enforceable rules that arose from elders, myth, and tradition – from customs – rather than from parliament or courts. As Ng'ang'a Thiong'o writes of Earth Jurisprudence in an African context:

> In Africa, wilderness, or what you call 'wild law,' is the great source of law, not written common law. In fact, our traditional law is oral and is passed from one generation to another orally, through music, art, dance, drumming, and through the 'do's and don'ts' of the community.
> (Ng'ang'a Thiong'o 2011: 183)

While I am not arguing that systems of common law or civil law should adopt African customary law, I am suggesting that there could be space, even in the West, for a customary Wild Law to develop beneath conventional lawmaking institutions (see also Bollier and Weston 2013: Chapters 4 and 8 especially). This would depend, however, on a cultural revolution of sorts, through which the values and principles of Earth Jurisprudence become broadly accepted and acted upon at the community level, irrespective of, and perhaps in defiance of, state-based law. 'The force behind customary law', Thiong'o (2011: 175) writes, 'is that legitimisation comes from the community', and that '[i]t is important to see [customary law] as a way of life, rather than hard, cold, legal norms imposed from elsewhere' (Thiong'o 2011: 174). Could it not be, then, that over time a Wild Law 'from below' could develop at the community level, changing the structures of society, not as a result of new statutes or case law, but as a result of new social and economic customs based on principles of ecological sustainability? That is indeed the possibility I have tried to raise in this chapter. Having only sketched out a skeletal framework, however, it follows these bones must await another occasion to be fleshed out.

Conclusion

An objection that is likely to be levelled at the thesis presented in this chapter is that I have unwisely or inappropriately privileged one mode of transition (grassroots social movements) above another ('top down' legal change), when both modes are equally necessary to create a sustainable society and thus both modes should be pursued. It is important that this objection and my response to it are understood, otherwise it could be very easy for my argument to be misunderstood. My argument has not been that 'top down' legal change could not help facilitate the transition to a sustainable society. Obviously there is much that parliament and the courts could and should do to help in such a transition (see, e.g., Bollier and Weston, 2013), and for many years Earth jurists, among others, have been explicating some of the laws and legal principles upon which such a transition could be based. Rather, my argument has been that the formal institutions of law may be so compromised by the growth paradigm that expecting those institutions to produce a fundamentally Earth-centred legal system, at the expense of growth, is akin to expecting a zebra to change its stripes. I do not claim to have established this thesis to any level of certainty. My aim has simply been to bring this issue to the surface, because if my tentative thesis that 'law is a growth-orientated zebra' were more or less correct, this has significant implications on how and where oppositional lawyers should direct their energies and resources. More specifically, it suggests that trying to convince a growth-orientated state to use the vehicle of law to create a post-growth society might be futile, a waste of our efforts. If that were so, it would seem to be more fruitful for oppositional lawyers to dedicate their energies and resources toward advancing their causes at the grassroots level and attempting to build the new society 'from below', rather than trying to bring it about from the 'top down'. Put otherwise, I am suggesting, as an Earth jurist, that we consider ignoring the state that is almost certainly going to ignore us, and instead attempt to create ecocentric customs of Wild Law among the grassroots of our local communities. How we might do that, and what it might look like, are subjects for another occasion.

Note

1 It is worth noting, however, that if all environmental externalities were actually internalized this might so radically change the nature of economic activity that something very different from a growth economy might arise. In fact, neoclassicism could well be its own worst enemy, in the sense that the only reason neoclassicists promote growth is because they do not understand the radical implications of their own theory (see Alexander, 2011a: 245–6).

References

Alexander, S. (2011a) 'Property beyond growth: Toward a politics of voluntary simplicity', doctoral thesis, Melbourne University.
Alexander, S. (2011b) 'Earth jurisprudence and the ecological case for degrowth,' in P. Burdon (ed.) *Exploring Wild Law: The Philosophy of Earth Jurisprudence*, Kent Town, SA: Wakefield Press.
Alexander, S. (2012a) 'Planned economic contraction: The emerging case for degrowth', *Environmental Politics*, 21(3): 349–68.
Alexander, S. (2012b) 'Peak oil and the twilight of growth', *Alternative Law Journal*, 37(2): 86–90.
Alexander, S. (2013) 'Voluntary simplicity and the social reconstruction of law: Degrowth from the grassroots up', *Environmental Values*, 22(2): 287–308.
Berry, T. (1999) *The Great Work: Our Way into the Future*, New York: Bell Tower.
Bollier, D. and Weston, B.H. (2013) *Green Governance: Ecological Survival, Human Rights, and the Law of the Commons*, Cambridge: Cambridge University Press.
Bookchin, M. (1990) *Remaking Society: Pathways to a Green Future*, Cambridge, MA: South End Press.

Bosselmann, K. (2008) *The Principle of Sustainability*, Burlington, VT: Ashgate Publishing.

Burdon, P. (ed.) (2011a) *Exploring Wild Law: The Philosophy of Earth Jurisprudence*, Kent Town, SA: Wakefield Press.

Burdon. P. (2011b) 'The great jurisprudence', in P. Burdon (ed.) *Exploring Wild Law: The Philosophy of Earth Jurisprudence*, Kent Town, SA: Wakefield Press.

Chomsky, N. and Herman, E. (1994) *Manufacturing Consent: The Political Economy of Mass Media*, London: Vintage.

Filgueira, B. and Mason, I. (2011) 'Is there any evidence of earth jurisprudence in existing law', in P. Burdon (ed.) *Exploring Wild Law: The Philosophy of Earth Jurisprudence*, Kent Town, SA: Wakefield Press.

Godden, L. and Peel, J. (2010) *Environmental Law: Scientific, Policy, and Regulatory Dimensions*. London: Oxford University Press.

Hamilton, C. (2003) *Growth Fetish*, Crows Nest, NSW: Allen & Unwin.

Hardt, M. and Negri, A. (2000) *Empire*, London: Harvard University Press.

Healy, H., Martinez-Alier, J., Temper, L., Walter, M., Gerber, J.F. (2012) *Ecological Economics from the Ground Up*, London: Routledge.

Jackson, T. (2009) *Prosperity without Growth: Economics for a Finite Planet*, London: Earthscan.

Marx, K. (1983) *The Portable Marx* (edited by Kamenka, E.), London: Penguin.

Meadows, D., Randers, J. and Meadows, D. (2004) *Limits to Growth: The 30-year Update*, White River Junction, VT: Chelsea Green Publishers.

Posner, R. (1986) *Economic Analysis of Law*, Boston: Little, Brown.

Purdey, S. (2010) *Economic Growth, the Environment, and International Relations: The Growth Paradigm*, New York: Routledge.

Tham, J.C. (2010) *Money and Politics: The Democracy We Can't Afford*, Sydney: University of New South Wales Press.

Trainer, T. (2010) *The Transition to a Sustainable and Just World*, Sydney: Envirobook.

Thiong'o, N. (2011) 'Earth jurisprudence in the African context', in P. Burdon (ed.) *Exploring Wild Law: The Philosophy of Earth Jurisprudence*, Kent Town, SA: Wakefield Press.

Vale, R., and Vale, B. (2013) *Living within a Fair Share Ecological Footprint*, London: Earthscan.

Worldwatch Institute, (2013) *Is Sustainability Still Possible?* (State of the World 2013) London: Island Press.

Chapter 4

Peoples' Sustainability Treaties at Rio+20

Giving voice to the other

Karen Morrow

The emergence of the Peoples' Sustainability Treaties (PSTs) initiative in the run-up to the UN's 2012 Conference on Sustainable Development (Rio+20) was a significant development for sustainability praxis. At the same time it offered a strikingly concrete manifestation of civil society's increasing discontent with the (ironically) glacial progress of the international governance community in addressing the pressing interconnected environmental, social and economic sustainability challenges that have come to characterize the early twenty-first century. The paucity of progress in the flailing climate change negotiations and the dispiriting level of state interest in the pre-Rio+20 negotiations themselves provide but two examples of the wider problem. In response to the near moribund state of international environmental law, civil society was moved to attempt to offer the direction and leadership that it felt signally lacking. In marked contrast to most state actors, civil society attacked the Rio+20 process vigorously on a number of fronts. In the first instance it engaged in what it suspected would be a largely bootless attempt to influence state and international non-governmental organization stances on progressing the sustainability agenda. Civil society also actively engaged with the Rio+20 process in its own right and as an opportunity to facilitate the development of a more coherent approach towards its own global activities (De Zoysa 2012; DPTSP 2012). PSTs were envisaged as performing a crucial role in each of these contexts.

While the PSTs that emerged in the run-up to Rio+20 covered a broad range of sustainability topics, discussion here will focus specifically on those with primarily 'environmental' credentials, in particular where they espouse Wild Law influenced thinking. A purposely broad and inclusive line is taken towards the identification of Wild Law approaches here as sharing at base a common understanding that the Earth/human relationship paradigm requires urgent and fundamental reshaping in order to secure the survival and flourishing of the planetary biosphere and humanity within it. As comprehensive coverage of the wealth of Earth Jurisprudence/Wild Law thought is not possible here, discussion will be confined to identifying commonalities between wider thinking in this area and developments in the PSTs.

Shared drivers for the developing Wild Law agenda and its manifestation in the PSTs

There are a whole range of drivers behind the development of Earth Jurisprudence and Wild Law that are also present in the 'environmental' PSTs which provide a recent example of its incarnation. Each, in its own distinctive way, contributes to an emerging understanding of the holistic nature of what may be termed the Earth Community. This ecocentric conception of the Earth/human relationship is rooted in the seminal works of Thomas Berry (Berry 1999). It envisages extending first moral considerability and consequently legal protection beyond the human and even living nature, to encompass the whole biosphere. Berry's initial philosophical approach and the far-reaching ideas that it encapsulates have been the subject of considerable debate and development (Burdon 2012). Key among incidences of this new ecocentrism in the PST context are creative re-imaginings of the Earth/human paradigm deriving from a range of sources, including radical science; resurgent indigenous cosmologies and their increasingly prominent expression in politics and law; and last, but not least, theoretical (and particularly jurisprudential) explorations of this relationship.

The scientific drivers of Wild Law are rooted in radical thinking on the Earth/human relationship expressed in multiple sources, for example, the divisive work by the Club of Rome on the limits to growth (Meadows et al. 1972). They are also present in Lovelock's (2009: 121) initially controversial but increasingly accepted Gaia theory, viewing the earth as a self-regulating system and his comment that:

> [i]f it is real it demotes us from ownership of the Earth to being one of many animal species. It still allows us to be important and powerful, but the Earth can proceed without us.

This type of systemic thinking oriented standpoint is also moving into the mainstream as one of the underpinnings of the emerging but already influential work on planetary boundaries (Rockström et al. 2009). This adopts a more holistic and biosphere-based Earth System perspective on the impacts of human activities on the environment than previous work in this area. In this context the Earth System is defined as:

> the integrated biophysical and socioeconomic processes and interactions (cycles) among the atmosphere, hydrosphere, cryosphere, biosphere, geosphere, and anthroposphere (human enterprise) in both spatial – from local to global – and temporal scales, which determine the environmental state of the planet within its current position in the universe. Thus, humans and their activities are fully part of the Earth System, interacting with other components. (Rockström et al. 2009: footnote i)

While not explicitly 'Wild Law' oriented, this approach, with its view of humanity and the biosphere as intimately interdependent, is inclining thinking about and rethinking of the Earth/human paradigm in the same direction, at least in terms of challenging anthropocentrism.

The influence of resurgent indigenous cosmologies in an explicit campaign to invoke rights-based protection for the environment had, until recently, been most evident in its legal impacts in domestic law in South America, notably in Ecuador's inclusion of provision for the rights of nature in its 2008 constitution and Bolivia's passing in 2010 of a Law of the Rights of Mother Earth (Adelman 2013). The ongoing activities of the social movement that prompted these developments, ensured that the PSTs, rather than existing in a sort of activist isolation, were paralleled in the official Rio+20 process by a number of radical, Wild Law inspired initiatives by South American states. These included Bolivian proposals for 'the rights of nature'; Paraguayan proposals for 'harmony with nature'; and the Ecuadorian proposal for a 'Universal Declaration of the Rights of Nature' (*Proposals of Bolivia Ecuador and Paraguay for Rio+20 2012*). The wider UN system too has, once again prompted by Bolivia, accommodated at least to some degree, innovative international discussion in this area, initiating a 'Harmony with Nature' intergovernmental negotiating process and inaugurating International Mother Earth Day. This has been done in recognition of the 'interdependence that exists among human beings, other living species and the planet we all inhabit' (United Nations 2009: para 1).

Modern jurisprudential debate on ascribing rights to nature is itself the product of a history that harks backs to the very origins of law and an equally distinguished broader philosophical background. More specifically it was seeded by the ground-breaking work of writers such as Leopold (1968) and Stone (1972) and latterly owes its cultivation to the work of a diverse group of scholars inspired by Cullinan's influential work on what is now termed Wild Law (Cullinan, 2011). The various strands of Earth Jurisprudence that underpin Wild Law thinking encapsulate a whole range of views as to how to achieve the crucial task of reframing the Earth/human relationship; they are variously expressed and include: Earth-centred; Ecological Governance; and Community of Nature approaches (Filgueira and Mason 2009). Each of these would provide a theoretical basis that could facilitate the development of Wild Law approaches to the practicalities of legislating to secure an ecologically sustainable and viable future. They may all be understood as being founded on the understanding that the current exploitative instrumental and property-based approach that dominates the Earth/human relationship is both morally repugnant and practically dangerous, facilitating a model of development that serves to place the biosphere under a veritable phalanx of unsustainable pressures. The alternative, Earth Jurisprudence approaches, albeit for a variety of reasons, press towards according intrinsic value to nature in a variety of ways in order to develop a new and sustainable paradigm for human interaction with(in) the biosphere.

As a minimum, Wild Law oriented approaches are contextualized in a view of humanity as both dependent upon and integral to the biosphere, though they range widely to include much more ambitious elements such as the development of ecology-based governance models and espousing rights-based legal protection for the natural world. It is therefore worth pointing out that, in expressing a range of views of what may loosely be termed 'Wild Law' based thought, the PSTs are in many ways typical of the fluidity of the broader debate in this emerging area (GARON 2009–12).

Why 'civil society', 'rights' and 'treaties'? The antecedents of PSTs

Civil society, law and rights

The PST initiative is not a random development, rather it is firmly grounded in the milieu of established civil society interactions within and beyond the framework of the international community more generally. The last couple of decades in particular have seen the role of civil society in the international polis slowly shift from the periphery of United Nations law and policy-making processes to a location of significantly greater and more direct influence in a number of areas. A well-worn route to exerting this influence has been in the quest to shape policy developments and both hard and soft legal provision. Broadly speaking, the former category encapsulates legally binding instruments agreed among states (such as treaties, conventions and protocols) and here civil society exerts only indirect influence. The latter category covers a whole range of different types of agreement that are not legally binding as such and which can be developed among states but also by a whole range of international actors (or indeed a combination of the two) and this allows civil society to manifest both direct and indirect influence. Civil society activity in this sphere has often necessitated head-on engagement with the socially, politically and jurisprudentially dominant (though by no means unquestioned) concept of universal rights based legal provision (Otto 1997). In this context, civil society has been instrumental in calling for more or less radical expansions in existing regimes to accommodate both extended notions of rights and (albeit to a lesser extent) rights holders. One clear example of this can be found in the transformative initiative concerned with human rights provision for indigenous peoples culminating (after over two decades of wrangling) in the adoption of the soft law United Nations Declaration on the Rights of Indigenous Peoples (DRIP) (United Nations 2007). While what was involved in the DRIP was, in political and jurisprudential terms, a great deal less radical than a Wild Law-based attempt to invoke the expansion of rights-based coverage to the natural world, it does arguably provide a number of parallels to the latter situation.

First, on a theoretical level, indigenous peoples have long shared (what ecofeminists and others would view as) nature's status as 'other' in the globally dominant Western legal paradigm and suffered as a result of the ripeness for exploitation that this entails (Morrow 2013). In each case, this type of legally sanctioned manipulation, treating other entities as simply means to our own ends, arguably morally diminishes the exploiter at the same time as generating manifold adverse impacts for the exploited. In addition, where the abuse of nature is concerned, there is also a practical argument to be made concerning exploitation of the 'other', as untrammelled unsustainable human activity has now reached the point where it threatens the biosphere of which we are both part and dependent upon for our survival (Rockström et al. 2009). In the current context, these arguments make it incumbent upon us to act to ensure the 'survival dignity and well-being' (United Nations 2007: article 43) of the exploited other both on the basis of principle and for reasons of enlightened self-interest. Given the primacy of the role ascribed to rights-based regimes in modern law, giving serious consideration to the adoption of an expansive rights-based approach to the protection of the other is arguably difficult to avoid.

Second, on a more practical level, the DRIP's substantive coverage is of some relevance to environmental protection, for example in referring to the right of indigenous peoples to '... the conservation and protection of the environment and the productive capacity of their lands or territories and resources' and consequently invoking state obligations in this regard (United Nations 2007: article 29).

Third, in addition to matters of principle and substance, the soft law legal status of the DRIP and its implications are worth examining more closely here. While a lawyer's instinct may be to favour hard law over soft law, the vagaries of the international legal system actually mean that the soft law status of the DRIP can be viewed as acting to its advantage rather than limiting its impact. For present purposes this is most significant in opening up the negotiating process to civil society actors rather than limiting participation to states and intergovernmental organizations as would have been the case in a hard law treaty negotiation process. This resulted in its significant enrichment (Barelli 2009).

The fourth and final way in which looking to the DRIP may be instructive in the current context lies in the process by which it was made and to the influence that this had on its content. The DRIP in part showed what can be achieved by the forces of a globally networked and participatory civil society initiative, operating in an area where its activities are encouraged by UN institutions and some nation states. The active engagement of civil society in the DRIP decisively shaped the coverage in the final document, ultimately pushing at the established boundaries of human rights law by achieving at degree mainstreaming for the collective human rights that indigenous people hold necessary. This represented a radical departure from the prevailing individualistic rights norm (Barelli 2009).

Civil society in the environment/sustainability context

The 2012 PST initiative itself was rooted in like developments to those pertaining to the DRIP made evident in the environment/sustainability sphere. This can be traced to the emergence of parallel civil society conferences and outputs alongside the UN Conference on Environment and Development in Rio in 1992 and in the flourishing global movement that they helped to root in this sector. Notable among the developments prompted by the first Rio summit was the Women's Environment and Development Organisation's World Women's Congress for a Healthy Planet (WWCHP), which was held in Miami in 1991. Working on the UN's draft of Agenda 21, this event produced a comprehensive 'gender aware' revision of the original supposedly 'gender neutral' (but actually 'gender blind') text resulting in significant changes to the content of that document as finally adopted. The adoption of a summit-style format and the production of a revised treaty document at the WWCHP proved significant in a number of ways, not least in resonating with the official Rio process into which it would ultimately feed. Arguably just as significant was the fact that the WWCHP process was carried out in such a way as to allow civil society to stake claims to both competence and legitimacy through its foundation on expert grassroots opinion and the inclusive global representation and participation praxis that was adopted throughout. These factors served to both augment the status of the process and establish civil society's credentials in this area. The success of the WWCHP was also symptomatic of the very nature of the conception of sustainability that would ultimately be enshrined within the Rio process and outcomes. This strongly emphasized the cultivation of 'bottom-up' societal engagement as a necessary corollary to 'top down' state action (Morrow 2012). This necessarily endorsed the activism of civil society on a global scale and continues to serve to make this area of global governance one that is particularly conducive to civil society activity. The Rio summit and its working legacy were instrumental in spawning stakeholder and later partnership approaches to sustainability. This was particularly the case in the ongoing collaborative endeavour between the United Nation's Commission on Sustainable Development and 'major groups' under Agenda 21. While this arguably led to some aspects of civil society activity being effectively 'captured' or co-opted by UN institutions, at the same time (facilitated by the growth in global communications and information technology) it seeded and then nurtured considerable growth in global civil society networks.

Improved civil society networking and a growing confidence in engaging with the global polis in turn spawned innovative thinking, one manifestation of which was the emergence of concentrated efforts to influence the international legal agenda. These included the UN initiated (but civil society fostered and adopted) Earth Charter Initiative (TECI 2000). This was particularly notable in expressing an explicit aspiration to soft-law status for the Earth Charter which sought to advance the ethical basis of sustainability. The development of the Earth Charter was furthered by an innovative, global, participative, civil-society-led drafting process which produced both a concrete outcome in the form of the Charter and also established an ongoing and diverse worldwide network to support it. The Earth Charter is also of interest for present purposes in that it exhibited some Wild Law credentials, notably recognising in its preamble that '... we are one human family and one Earth community with a common destiny' and in article 1a. that '... all beings are interdependent and every form of life has value regardless of its worth to human beings' (TECI 2000).

Wild Law approaches have come even more strongly to the fore in more recent developments, notably the 2010 World Peoples Conference on Climate Change and the Rights of Mother Earth which adopted the much discussed Universal Declaration of the Rights of Mother Earth. This document, in its quasi-legal form, language and substance (Cullinan 2010), is specifically geared to show just how Wild Law thinking could be viably embodied in international environmental law. The resonance and credibility to be gained by adopting processes and generating outcome documents modelled on those of the international legal community is thus once again at issue here.

The cultivation of an active role for civil society on a global scale is also increasingly viewed on a strategic level, as one necessary response to the understanding that, in light of pressing environmental, social and economic constraints we need to undertake a paradigm shifting 'great transition' in order to function on all levels as a planetary society. The imaginative and influential *Great Transition Report* that posits this also adopts aspects of Wild Law thinking. It makes specific reference to the need to nurture our '... awareness of the connectedness of human beings to one another, [and] to the wider community of life and to the future ...' (Raskin et al. 2002: 62–3) as providing the conceptual foundation of finding a sustainable path to continued survival and flourishing (Raskin et al. 2002). The *Great Transitions* report is most explicitly in favour of a Wild Law approach in its consideration of what it terms the 'rights revolution'. The authors argue that rights-based approaches can be harnessed and should be 'accelerated' in order to safeguard the planet's life-support functions and provide better coverage to the 'inviolable rights of people and nature' (Raskin et al. 2002: 59). In the latter area, the report suggests the need to go well beyond existing nature protection regimes to take a progressive 'natural communities and ecosystems' based approach towards rights for nature.

Significantly, in seeking to promote the flourishing of the whole Earth community, the *Great Transitions Report* very clearly marks civil society alongside more usually identified intergovernmental organizations and transnational corporations as the key global actors taking centre stage in the transition to a sustainable society (Raskin et al. 2002: 49–54). The rapid and pervasive growth in non-governmental organization activities at local, national, regional and latterly global levels and increasingly in networking across them provides the most concrete (albeit still fragmented) manifestation of civil society. It has also, as we have seen, enthusiastically forged a role in making an informed and participative alternative case on environmental and sustainability issues, exploiting in full the opportunities which international environmental and sustainability law and policy provide and indeed often pushing their boundaries in ways which have already irrevocably changed the shape of the global polis (Raskin et al. 2002: 52).

The PST project then built on established activist foundations bent on mainstreaming radical and outsider perspectives, including Wild Law, though it was arguably even grander in its conception than its predecessors, forming a strategic element in the wider ongoing project (TWC 2010) seeking to secure the development of a Global Citizen's Movement. This is geared towards fostering greater coherence and cohesiveness in global civil society in order to tackle the problems inherent in its fragmented nature and improve its impact on intergovernmental processes. The PST process at Rio culminated in the adoption of a Manifesto of the Peoples' Sustainability Treaties, which called, in line with another tenet of Wild Law, for subsidiarity in an equity-based global environmental governance regime, fuelled by a participatory global citizen's movement (*Peoples Sustainability Manifesto* 2012).

The Wild Law credentials of the PSTs

In addition to providing one demonstration of the wider evolving role of global civil society, the PSTs set out, in the first instance, to fashion a number of 'independent collective agreements' reflecting 'the public interest and aspirations of a sustainable world' that sought to have an impact on the intergovernmental negotiations at Rio+20 (De Zoysa 2012). To this end, a number of potential PSTs were set up in the run-up to the summit, several of which were endorsed by a variety of (civil society) actors there. The PSTs, which were each jointly facilitated (ideally by a combination of organizations from the North and South) were subject to a common template-based drafting process and predicated on an open and inclusive 'engagement methodology'. Each was envisaged as being widely publicized, in particular on the internet, thus facilitating potentially global participation of partner organizations, states and the public (PST 2012).

Most of the proposed treaties were influenced by ecological perspectives to some degree, according specific coverage to the imperative need to promote and secure viable environmental protection (see for example, the Rights for Sustainability Treaty, and the Environmental Education for Sustainable Societies and Global Responsibility Treaty). Time and space will not, however, allow us to discuss all of them here. Instead coverage will focus on the two PSTs that exhibited particularly strong Wild Law credentials, specifically foregrounding rights for nature in various guises, namely the Rights of Mother Earth Treaty (RMET), and the Radical Ecological Democracy Treaty (REDT). A third PST, the Charter of Universal Responsibilities (CUR) is also briefly considered as it raised a particularly interesting synthesis of anthropocentrism and Wild Law by explicitly grafting notions of responsibility on to an expanded view of established human rights-based approaches (PST 2012). While full content analysis of these PSTs is not viable here, it is still possible to give a flavour of the coverage offered by them and to indicate their various Wild Law credentials.

The RMET from the outset situates humanity as an integral part of Mother Earth which is expressed as being 'an indivisible, living community of interrelated and interdependent beings with a common destiny'. It thus eschews the dominant models of governance that view humanity as separate from and 'above' nature in favour of one that recognizes the 'ecological partnership' that exists between people and the planet. As its title suggests, the RMET's first principle recognises the 'inherent rights of Mother Earth and all ecosystems and species of which she is composed' (PST 2012).

The REDT in its preamble points to the causes of our ongoing multi-dimensional environmental crises as being rooted in a top-down, ecologically unsustainable model of development and proposes in the alternative '... a radically different vision of human well-being, one that is tune with nature and respects other people'. The PST's first underlying principle is therefore ecological integrity and its seventh specifically invokes the rights of nature (PST 2012).

Finally, while the CUR's focus is rather different from the other PSTs that have been considered here, and its coverage is necessarily (given the fact that only humans have the moral agency required in order to exercise responsibility) more anthropocentric, it still retains a pronounced Wild Law influenced component. Thus its first principle is not only concerned with 'interdependences' within the human community but also between 'humankind and the biosphere' and its fifth refers to the 'awareness of our shared responsibilities to the planet' as a 'condition for the survival and progress on humankind' (PST 2012).

These 'environmental' PSTs seem to be chiefly rooted in the three broadly mutually reinforcing developments outlined above: first in Earth Jurisprudence thinking; second in an emerging scientific understanding of the need to view humans as integrated into ecosystems and ultimately the biosphere; and third in the reclamation and resurgence of indigenous cosmologies across the world, but particularly in the global South, that also see humans and the earth as locked in inseparable symbiosis. All of these approaches are in the process of shifting from being regarded as extreme outsider perspectives into at least being ideas with which mainstream thought is now willing to countenance even if it is not fully conversant with them.

The Rio+20 outcome document: 'the future we want'

While the Rio+20 summit was widely regarded as achieving little, the emergence of a fledgling role for Wild Law in the otherwise decidedly unimpressive outcome document, 'The Future We Want' (FWW) (United Nations 2012) was one of the few bright spots to emerge in an otherwise bleak landscape. The tone of the outcome document as a whole is very much one of 'business as usual', dominated as its content is by the oft-repeated entrenched positions of the variously vested interests of the international community. It is therefore somewhat unexpected that Earth-centred thinking also found a small but significant place in the FWW. While this clearly rose to prominence in the outcome document through both the ongoing domestic and summit-specific activities of the ecologically radical South American states referred to above, in common with these, it was strongly flavoured by the activities and views of civil society, in this case as notably and prominently expressed in the PST initiative. In this vein the FWW states:

> We recognize that the planet Earth and its ecosystems are our home and that Mother Earth is a common expression in a number of countries and regions and we note that some countries recognize the rights of nature in the context of the promotion of sustainable development. We are convinced that in order to achieve a just balance among the economic, social and environment needs of present and future generations, it is necessary to promote harmony with nature.
>
> We call for holistic and integrated approaches to sustainable development which will guide humanity to live in harmony with nature and lead to efforts to restore the health and integrity of the Earth's ecosystem.
>
> (United Nations 2012: paras 39–40)

While hardly amounting to a ringing endorsement of Wild Law thinking, the FWW does at least pay lip-service to a number of its core elements, notably to the need for humanity to live in 'harmony with nature' and the need to secure patterns of Earth/human interaction that secure ongoing ecosystem health. More surprisingly, the FWW even goes so far as to refer to the endorsement of the 'rights of Mother Earth' approach by some states. In any event, the fact that what is still very much an emerging and minority view, and a radical one to boot, managed to gain sufficient traction to achieve inclusion in any form in a UN official document is significant. Furthermore, this development gives some much needed ground for hope that our failure of imagination in grappling with the existential challenge of sustainability is neither inevitable nor perpetual. At the very least its inclusion, albeit in a rather rudimentary fashion, in the FWW places Earth Jurisprudence and the possibility of Wild Law on the international community's mainstream agenda – no longer is it to be readily relegated to the periphery as a matter of course.

Concluding (or perhaps more accurately belated new beginning) thoughts

The PSTs, in addition to operating on their own merits in prompting debate on core issues, and in particular in articulating the values that need to inform our dealings with and as an integral part of the biosphere, expressed an approach which ultimately made its presence felt to a degree in the Rio+20 outcome document. They also played a significant strategic role in the broader attempt to construct a more cohesive and coherent identity for civil society in the run up to Rio+20 (DPTSF 2012). Moreover, by pressing PSTs into service in the drive to construct a Global Citizens Movement, the initiative was, from the outset, envisaged as a component of a 'living document' that would extend its reach beyond the Rio+20 process and its outcome (De Zoysa 2012). This was a clever, far-sighted and indeed necessary move as the summit itself was, given the global economic climate, arguably doomed to disappoint those seeking the impetus for a more sustainable future (Morrow 2012). The fact that the PSTs were created to play a role extending beyond their specific content thus ensured that they were not in danger of becoming dead letters simply because the summit and its outcome were underwhelming. Rather they stand, as they were intended to do, as a spur to further action, prompting us to the paradigm shift that is required to shape a future that is truly sustainable for the whole Earth community.

References

Adelman, S. (2013) 'Rio+20: sustainable injustice in a time of crises', *Journal of Human Rights and the Environment*, 4(1): 6–31.
Barelli, M. (2009) 'The role of soft law in the international legal system: the case of the United Nations Declaration on the Rights of Indigenous Peoples', *International and Comparative Law Quarterly*, 58(4): 957–83.
Berry, T. (2000) *The Great Work: Our Way Into the Future*, New York: Harmony Books.

Burdon, P. (2012) 'Self, community and ecological jurisprudence', online. Available at: <http://opo.iisj.net/index.php/osis/author/submission/251> (accessed 4 February 2013).

Cullinan, C. (2010) 'The legal case for the Universal Declaration of the Rights of Mother Earth', online. Available at: <http://www.therightsofnature.org/wp-content/uploads/pdfs/Legal-Case-for-Universal-Declaration-Cormac-Cullinan.pdf> (accessed 27 November 2011).

Cullinan, C. (2011) *Wild Law: A Manifesto for Earth Jurisprudence*, 2nd edn, Totnes: Green Books.

De Zoysa, U. (2012) 'People's sustainability treaties for Rio+20' *Perspectives No. 3 UNEP*, online. Available at: <http://www.unep.org/> (accessed 21 November 2012).

Dialogue Platform of the Thematic Social Forum (DPTSP) (2012) 'Another future is possible', online. Available at: <http://rio20.net/en/iniciativas/another-future-is-possible> (accessed 27 November 2012).

Filgueira, B. and Mason, I. (2009) *Is there any Evidence of Earth Jurisprudence in Existing Law and Practice?* An International Research Project, online, United Kingdom Environmental Law Association (UKELA) and the Gaia Foundation. Available at: <http://www.ukela.org/content/page/1090/Wild%20Law%20Research%20Report%20published%20March%202009.pdf> (accessed 4 December 2012).

Global Alliance for the Rights of Nature (GARON) (2009–2012), in particular 'What is (*sic*) rights of nature', online. Available at: <http://therightsofnature.org/what-is-rights-of-nature/> (accessed 27 November 2012).

Leopold, A. (1968) *A Sand County Almanac*, London: Oxford University Press.

Lovelock, J. (2009) *The Vanishing Face of Gaia: A Final Warning*, London: Allen Lane.

Meadows, D.H., Meadows, D.L., Randers, J. and Behrens, W.W. (1972) *The Limits to Growth: A Report for the Club of Rome's Project on the Predicament of Mankind*, London: Earth Island.

Morrow, K. (2012) 'Rio+20, the green economy and re-orienting sustainable development', *Environmental Law Review*, 14(4): 166–297.

Morrow, K. (forthcoming) 'Ecofeminism and the environment', in M. Davies and V. Munro (eds) *Ashgate Research Companion to Feminist Legal Theory*, Farnham: Ashgate.

Otto, D. (1997) 'Rethinking the universality of Human Rights law', *Columbia Human Rights Law Review*, 29: 1–46.

Peoples Sustainability Manifesto (2012) online. Available at: <http://www.oree.org/_script/ntsp-document-file_download.php?document_id=2274> (accessed 29 October 2013).

Proposals of Bolivia, Ecuador and Paraguay for Rio+20 (2012) online. Available at: <http://rio20.net/en/propuestas/proposals-of-bolivia-ecuador-and-paraguay-for-rio20> (accessed 23 November 2012).

PST (2012) 'Peoples sustainability treaties', online. Available at: <http://sustainabilitytreaties.org/> (accessed 14 November 2012).

Raskin, P., Banuri, T., Gallopin, G., Gutman, P., Hammond, A., Kates, R. and Swart, R. (2002) *Great Transition: The Promise and Lure of the Times Ahead*, Global Scenario Group, Boston: Stockholm Environment Institute.

Rockström, J., Steffen, W., Noone, K., Persson, Å., Chapin III, F.S., Lambin, E., Lenton, T.M., Scheffer, M., Folke, C., Schellnhuber, H., Nykvist, B., De Wit, C.A., Hughes, T., van der Leeuw, S., Rodhe, H., Sörlin, S., Snyder, P.K., Costanza, R.,

Svedin, U., Falkenmark, M., Karlberg, L., Corell, R.W., Fabry, V.J., Hansen, J., Walker, B., Liverman, D., Richardson, K., Crutzen, P. and Foley, J. (2009) 'Planetary boundaries: exploring the safe operating space for humanity', *Ecology and Society*, 14(2): 32. Available at: http://www.ecologyandsociety.org/vol14/iss2/art32/ (accessed 16 April 2013).

Stone, C. (1972) 'Should trees have standing', *California Law Review*, 45: 450.

The Earth Charter Initiative (TECI) (2000) 'The Earth Charter', online. Available at: <http://www.earthcharterinaction.org/content/pages/Read-the-Charter.html> (accessed 27 November 2012).

The Widening Circle (TWC) (2010) 'Imagine all the people', online. Available at: <http://www.wideningcircle.org/documents/TWC%20Readings/GTI-Perspectives-Imagine_All_the_People.pdf> (accessed 4 December 2012).

United Nations (2007) 'Declaration on the Rights of Indigenous Peoples', Resolution 61/295, online. Available at: <http://www.un.org/esa/socdev/unpfii/documents/DRIPS_en.pdf> (accessed 23 November 2012).

United Nations (2009) 'International Mother Earth Day', Resolution 63/278, online. Available at: <http://harmonywithnatureun.org/index.html> (accessed 23 November 2012).

United Nations (2012) 'The future we want: outcome document adopted at the Rio+20', online. Available at: <http://www.uncsd2012.org/content/documents/727The%20Future%20We%20Want%2019%20June%201230pm.pdf> (accessed 8 October 2012).

Chapter 5

The challenges of putting Wild Law into practice
Reflections on the Australian Environmental Defender's Office movement

Brendan Sydes

This chapter explores some of the practical implications of Wild Law and the possibility of 'Wild Lawyering' from the perspective of the Environmental Defender's Office (EDO) movement, a collection of public interest environmental law practices in Australia.

The Australian legal system, including Australian environmental law, is a long way from anything that might be described as ecocentric or 'Wild Law' in character. As the discussion that follows will demonstrate, attempts to pursue Wild Law in practice in Australia face some significant challenges. I will argue, however, that it is possible to identify elements of an agenda for EDOs and others to take Wild Law in Australia beyond a critique of the deficiencies of the existing system to something that can be described as Wild Law in practice.

I commence with an outline of the challenges that Wild Law presents to current conceptions of public interest environmental law. I then describe the EDO movement, followed by an analysis of the current Australian legal system before providing some suggestions as to how the EDO movement might work within this system to develop an agenda for Wild Law in practice. In particular, I will focus on approaches to legal practice, engagement with substantive legal issues, and policy and reform work. It is my hope that this analysis and the practical ideas that I discuss are of relevance, not only to the community legal sector in Australia, but also around the world.

Wild Law and the challenge to public interest legal practice

EDOs are legal practices which aim to advance the public interest rather than to make a profit. In the absence of a profit motive, the nature of the work that should be done, the clients that ought to be assisted and the methods that ought to be employed become prominent questions that need to be answered by reference to some other set of principles or objectives. As we will see, in the case of the EDO movement these principles or objectives are often not particularly explicit or articulated in any great detail and are in many cases simply assumed.

These principles and objectives can be characterized as 'administrative rationalism', an approach that is based on the contention that environmental issues, once identified, can be dealt with within the existing legal system by using legislation to bring these issues under administrative control (Godden and Peel 2009). The role of public interest environmental lawyers under this model is to ensure that the task of bringing environmental issues under administrative control occurs firstly by the development of new legislation or the extension of existing legislation, and secondly by holding governments accountable in their administration of these legislative schemes. A particularly important role for public interest environmental lawyers under this model is to facilitate the exercise of third party standing rights and to act as enablers of citizen participation in decision making under these administrative regimes.

The Wild Law critique raises some significant questions about this approach that in turn present some interesting challenges to the EDO movement. For example, in common with other areas of critical legal theory such as feminist legal theory, Wild Law suggests that problems and their solutions are to be found not just at the level of the development and implementation of particular laws, but deep within the structure of our legal system and the often unarticulated assumptions upon which the system is based. In particular, the Wild Law argument contends, our whole legal system is built upon anthropocentric foundations that are not simply suboptimal (and therefore amenable to reform) when it comes to tackling environmental issues, but actually contravene fundamental principles of Earth Jurisprudence.

Less obviously perhaps but no less importantly Wild Law raises some interesting issues with respect to the practice of law and methods of lawyering. Redefining the issue leads to a need to redefine the approach to the practice of law and once again throws up ideas that might not only seem foreign but also distinctly uncomfortable to lawyers accustomed to legal practice in the traditional manner, including current methods of public interest lawyering (Rivers 2006: 28).

Exploring these questions and the challenges presented by Wild Law has the potential to be thought provoking and invigorating for public interest environmental lawyers such as those involved in the EDO movement. This provocation and invigoration is timely, firstly because it is becoming increasingly clear that the 'business as usual approach' to environmental regulation is insufficient to meet challenges such as climate change, the unsustainable consumption of resources and environmental sinks, and biodiversity loss.

Secondly, provocation and invigoration is necessary and welcome because it is becoming increasingly clear that a vision of EDOs as publicly funded enablers of citizen participation in administrative decision making under our current system of governance has run its course. I think it is becoming increasingly necessary for EDOs to be able to present a new positive vision for a legal system that sees humans as an inextricable part of nature, with laws and legal systems that respect and enable this interdependency rather than undermine it. In the UK and Europe for example, public interest environmental law organization ClientEarth has the mission to 'use law as a tool to mend the relationship between human societies and the Earth'(ClientEarth 2013).

The EDO movement – historical development and current practice

The first Environmental Defender's Office to open its doors was EDO NSW, which commenced operation in 1985. The need for a dedicated organization of environmental lawyers to provide support to conservation organizations, community groups and individuals had been discussed for some time prior to this in New South Wales and Victoria especially, but lack of funding support and in some cases hostility from the private legal profession meant that it was some time before organizations could be established. Separately constituted organizations were established in other states (Queensland, South Australia and Victoria) in the late 1980s and early 1990s. Additional offices were established in other states and territories (Western Australia, Tasmania, Northern Territory, Australian Capital Territory and a second Queensland office in north Queensland) in 1995 and 1996.

The establishment of these remaining offices in 1995 and 1996 followed the commencement of (limited) Commonwealth government funding of the Environmental Defender's Office Program, a significant step in the evolution of the EDO movement which had until that time subsisted on some state government funding as well as donations and philanthropic support.

All of the EDOs are independent incorporated organizations. Although the precise constitutional purposes and governance arrangements differ from organization to organization, all employ at least one or more professional staff and are managed by a voluntary Board or Committee of Management. Historically these boards have been largely comprised of legal practitioners, a situation that reflects the historic and continuing interest of individual members of the legal profession.

As independently constituted and managed organizations with significantly different levels of resources, the nature of the activities undertaken across different offices varies. However, in common with the broader community legal centre movement of which the EDOs are a part the work is commonly categorized into three broad areas:

1. Providing legal information, advice and legal representation. All EDO offices provide services (typically for free or at greatly reduced rates) to

individual citizens, community groups and conservation organizations. Advice and assistance is provided on the implementation and operation of environmental regulation such as land use planning and development controls, pollution regulation and biodiversity protection laws. Less frequently, advice and assistance is provided with respect to other legal matters in an environmental context including in such areas as protester rights, defamation law and consumer protection. Significant test case or impact litigation is beyond the capacity of all but the larger well-funded offices and is also significantly limited in states other than New South Wales by the lack of broad standing provisions in environmental regulation.

2. Community legal information activities including training, workshops and publication of factsheets, handbooks and kits. In common with other 'community lawyering' work of the community legal centre movement, all EDOs deliver a range of information and training designed to facilitate public participation in environmental decision making and to ensure that environmental law is accessible to non-legally trained citizens involved in a range of environmental issues. Such work strongly emphasizes the value of empowering individuals and community groups to participate in processes under environmental legislation, both from the point of view of democratic participation and also from the perspective of environmental protection.

3. Policy and law reform work. All offices engage to some degree in policy and law reform work around the development of new legislation and the reform of existing legislation, although in recent years at least the better-resourced offices of EDO NSW and EDO Victoria have been more prominent in this area, particularly with respect to national issues. This policy and law reform work has historically mostly comprised engagement with policy and law reform processes undertaken by government through activities such as submission writing and appearances before reviews and inquiries. However, there are also some significant examples of more proactive law reform and policy work that have been undertaken in recent times where EDOs have worked independently or with collaborators in conservation NGOs to develop proposals for law reform.

As noted above, discerning with precision the objectives which underpin the work of EDOs is not straightforward. Objectives are often not particularly explicit or articulated in any great detail and are in many cases simply assumed. There is nothing as simple and direct as a 'charter' or statement of common purposes and principles that provides a ready catalogue of the aims and the aspirations of the movement. Aims and objectives contained in the organizations' formal constitutions tend to be broad and enabling rather than specific.

Notwithstanding the challenges these limitations present, the following objectives seem to be evidenced both in routine discussions and descriptions from the various offices as well as being implicit in the work that is performed:

1. Protection of the environment through the law and especially environmental legislation. The development of the EDO movement followed the development of environmental regulation and the consequent emergence of environmental legal practice as a specialist expertise. A core objective of the EDOs is to act as a source of this expertise for individual citizens and organizations that are not serviced by the private profession and by government lawyers.
2. Securing accountability of government and the administrators of environmental law for its implementation, both in terms of consistency of decision making with regulatory frameworks as well as enforcement of environmental regulation.
3. Improving environmental regulation. Policy and law reform work is perhaps the area of EDO activity that comes close to systemic advocacy, although typically EDO work has focused on advocating for the adoption, or more thoroughgoing adoption, of accepted and established norms, objectives and principles such as ecologically sustainable development and the precautionary principle.
4. The value of 'community participation' in environmental decision making and processes. A common thread through all EDO work is the objective of facilitating the effective participation of individual environmentalists and groups in environmental decision making. Various grounds are advanced in support of this including rights of individuals to participate in decisions that affect them, the accountability of decision makers and the value in terms of the quality of decisions made as a result of the extra scrutiny and the provision of information that participation encourages.

Notably in the context of a discussion about the implications of the critique presented by Wild Law, the work of EDOs often specifically disavows any political grounding or ethical choice. This is not to say that individual lawyers might not hold strong personal views, but the actual content of laws and the methods of lawyering are often styled more as matters of technical expertise rather than any particular policy choice or ethical stance other than the social value of 'access to justice' and 'public participation'. This is an approach to law and legal practice that aligns closely with a view of the role of lawyers as one of applying technical expertise and expert legal judgement to instructions and directions provided by clients whose interests it is the lawyers' duty to serve, subject only to the paramount duty to the court.

The Australian legal system

An understanding of the current legal system is critical to a realistic analysis of the possibilities of developing Wild Law in practice. If, as appears to be the case, Wild Law is to be developed incrementally from the foundations of existing systems of governance, then an understanding of how this system of governance is constructed and its foundational principles is essential.

The Australian legal system is part of the common law tradition inherited from England so it shares a common heritage with English and other common law systems. One significant feature that differentiates the Australian legal system from the English is that Australia is a federation with the Australian Constitution governing the division of responsibilities between state and federal levels of government. Under this system it is the states that have plenary powers with respect to natural resources and the environment. Commonwealth government lawmaking with respect to the environment rests on other indirect heads of power, in particular the power available to the Commonwealth under the constitution to implement international agreements.

As would be expected under this system, historically the development of environmental law has occurred at the level of state governments. To varying degrees, state and territory governments have developed laws to govern natural resource management (mining, forestry, water resources), the reservation and management of public land, the use and development of private land, and, particularly since the 1970s, matters such as pollution control and biodiversity protection. This is a familiar narrative common in textbook accounts of Australian environmental law – firstly, the evolution of environmental regulation over the past 30 to 40 years from earlier natural resource management regimes, spurred by a growing environmental awareness and recognition of the limitations of the common law in dealing with issues such as pollution; and secondly, the importance of international environmental legal instruments in providing a constitutional foundation for an increasing Commonwealth role.

In their text on environmental law, Godden and Peel characterize the model of environmental governance that has emerged as 'administrative rationalism':

> Given the history of administrative control over land and resources within Australia, when environmental concerns surfaced as a focus for public policy in the 1970s, it was unsurprising that such problems were seen as amenable to administrative and governmental control and responsibility…These developments facilitated the development of a classic administrative rationalist mode of governance as the dominant model found in Australian environmental law. In accordance with this model, environmental problem solving largely is to be effected through

legislation administered by state departments, rather than through the development of common law principles and doctrines.

(Godden and Peel 2009: 85)

Basic elements of a legal system implementing Wild Law seem to include rights-based approaches that extend rights to non-human subjects, legal recognition of intrinsic values of nature, and non-instrumentalist approaches to the recognition of nature in law and policy. Three points can be made about the Australian legal system, roughly corresponding to these possibilities.

The first point is that the notion of legal recognition of fundamental rights, whether founded in the common law, statute or the constitution is not a feature of the Australian legal system. 'The Constitution of Australia is a vehicle for delivering the infrastructure of federal government, not a document that guarantees fundamental rights and expectations' (Bates 2010: 91). Apart from some limited implied rights that the High Court has found in the Constitution, equal opportunity legislation and the like, and some state-based human rights charters, there are few express rights and attempts to introduce human rights in Australia have met with little or limited success (Saunders 2010). There is not the strong rights-based culture that seems to be a feature of other jurisdictions and in fact recent exploration of the introduction of a national human rights charter was met with significant hostility from some quarters, one reason being the view that such rights represent an undesirable transfer of power to the judiciary at the expense of the executive and parliamentary arms of government.

For example, former Prime Minister John Howard argued against the introduction of a bill of rights (Howard 2009): 'The essence of my objection to a Bill of Rights is that, contrary to its very description, it reduces the rights of citizens to determine matters over which they should continue to exercise control. It does this by transferring decision making authority to unelected judges, accountable to no one except in the barest theoretical sense'. The prospects of successfully advocating for the introduction of legally entrenched 'rights for nature' in Australia (as has been done in Ecuador for instance (Margil 2011)) seem remote if not impossible when an attempt to legislate for basic human rights has proved so difficult.

The second point is that global norms derived from international environmental legal instruments have been prominent in the development of Australian environmental law. This is especially the case with respect to Commonwealth environmental law making where it is the domestic implementation of international treaties and agreements that has formed the constitutional foundation for legislative intervention in an area that historically was solely the province of the states.

The significance of the prominence of international legal instruments in the Australian legal context is that it is in the adoption of international norms such as ecologically sustainable development that Australian environmental law comes closest to giving effect to notions of nature having intrinsic values. It does so by recognizing biodiversity conservation and ecological integrity as a component of ecologically sustainable development, albeit as something that is to be balanced or integrated with other objectives. The *Environment Protection and Biodiversity Conservation Act 1999 (Cth)*, for example, implements a range of international environmental treaties and agreements, including the Convention on Biodiversity. Its objectives, contained in section 3A, provide that one of the objectives of the Act is that 'the conservation of biological diversity and ecological integrity should be a fundamental consideration in decision-making'.

This reliance on global norms is consistent with Australia acting as a global citizen and joining in shared responses to issues of global concern such as biodiversity loss. An advantage is that the domestic implementation of principles such as ecologically sustainable development and the precautionary principle are arguably given extra force by virtue of their international pedigree. On the flip side, however, there is a tendency to view these international norms and principles in a crude instrumental fashion, as something that the Commonwealth has to draw on to secure a constitutional mandate rather than as an expression of a genuine commitment to the principles they contain (Williams 2012). Similarly, rather than an expression of global citizenship, entry into international agreements and subjection to even the weak accountability mechanisms contained in these agreements is often characterized as an undesirable ceding of Australian sovereignty. A consequence is that to the extent that these global norms introduce some notions of intrinsic values in nature into Australian environmental laws, these notions end up seeming remote and imposed from on high rather than the legal expression of strongly held local values.

A third and final point about the general nature of environmental law in Australia is that the 'administrative rationalist' underpinning of environmental law discussed above is increasingly associated with an 'economic rationalist' or neoliberal approach to environmental regulation (and regulation of business activity generally) that defines nature in an increasingly instrumentalist manner. This manifests itself as a hostility to regulation generally, evidenced by an enthusiasm for deregulation and cutting 'red tape' (all corporate regulation) and especially 'green tape' (environmental regulation), particularly where such regulation impedes mining, property development and other economic activity. This neoliberal philosophy also manifests itself in preference for 'market-based' approaches to policy implementation instead of so-called 'command and control' regulatory approaches. So, in the context of Australian environmental regulation, the creation of new markets has been the preferred approach to carbon pollution and water resource management, and is also prominent in other mechanisms such as biodiversity offsets. These market-based approaches and the idea of ecosystem services (as well as offsets and other market phenomena) can be seen as reconstituting citizens as consumers of 'ecosystem services', and nature as the provider of these services, and thus are strongly anthropocentric in character. Intrinsic values or rights for nature only register to the extent that they represent human preferences in the markets created.

Wild Law in practice – some possibilities

If public interest lawyers like those who work in EDOs and their clients and collaborators were inspired to pursue a Wild Law agenda in Australia, where might they start and what might it look like? The challenges here should not be underestimated. I have outlined a legal system founded on 'administrative rationalism' that has never really left behind its natural resource management roots, an absence of a rights culture if not an outright hostility to the idea that even human rights ought to be legally entrenched, international norms that approach valuing nature in and of itself but are undermined by being seen as instrumental and remote from domestic concerns, an emerging hostility toward environmental regulation and an associated trend to see markets as the solution to environmental problems.

One could be forgiven for thinking that the prospects of Wild Law in practice are rather remote. However, I think it is possible to identify elements of an agenda for EDOs and others to take Wild Law in Australia beyond a critique of the deficiencies of the existing system to Wild Law in practice. Some things might be quite novel, but the foundations of others are already there in work currently undertaken by EDOs.

Wild Law and legal practice

Before discussing some suggestions focused on substantive law and how Wild Law might begin to take shape it is worth reflecting on the practice of law and what Wild Lawyering might involve. Cormac Cullinan, in *Wild Law*, argues that governance needs 'soul'. He then goes further: 'Simply recognising the need for "soul" is not enough. Earth jurisprudence is not merely a theory, it must be a living practice, a way of life. We must learn to observe the earth jurisprudence personally' (Cullinan 2002: 228). This sort of thinking is very unfamiliar and uncomfortable to lawyers accustomed to working within the 'administrative rationalist' framework, even if, like EDO lawyers, we are working at public interest fringe of legal practice.

The practice of law is frequently 'soul destroying' and it is notorious that depression and mental health problems are all too common in the legal profession relative to other professions. Addressing these issues has become the subject of professional concern (Brett Young 2008) and a growing body of literature (Keeva 2009). It is not too long a bow to draw to suggest that this is not just a symptom of long hours and a lack of 'work-life balance' but also, at least in the area of environmental law, the manifest disconnect between the 'administrative rationalist' system and ecological reality.

In the UK, Elizabeth Rivers has explored some of these ideas further and provides some useful suggestions in her article, 'How to become a Wild Lawyer' (Rivers 2006). She suggests that being a Wild Lawyer might involve actions like cultivating holistic rather than linear thinking, multidisciplinary approaches to problem solving, nurturing creativity and the like. I think it would be well worth EDO lawyers actively exploring some of these ideas and experimenting and innovating in how we go about legal practice. In reality this should not be too difficult a task – as part of the broader community legal centre movement we are already a part of a long tradition of unconventional lawyering and we also distinguish ourselves from a very large part of the broader legal community by deliberately eschewing billable hours, bonuses and high salaries as the goal of legal practice.

A distinguishing feature of EDO legal practice is its collaborative nature. Very few clients are individuals and even those are typically part of a broader movement or campaign. Most clients are collectives of some sort organized around a common cause or issue of concern, a feature of EDO work that has been noted by others discussing the role of the community legal centre movement in Australia (Rich 2009: 77). Particularly in the case of small grassroots community organizations, EDO lawyers have developed a particular expertise in not only working with and but also enabling the collaborative and collective modes of governance that by necessity characterize these small community-based organizations. The prominence of community legal education workshops and the like as part of the EDO mode of practice is part of this phenomenon, reflecting as it does an objective to empower people to be active participants in environmental issues that concern them.

There is much that could be characterized as Wild Lawyering in this style of practice already even if it is not labelled as such. However, there are some of examples or insights from the Wild Law literature that could be used to refine and extend the model further. EDOs not only work within the 'administrative rationalist' model but also in the main are dependent on public funding from that system for day-to-day operations. The need to maintain that funding can result in a tendency to emphasize and adopt a gatekeeper role that can stifle or constrain dissent. Public funders want to hear reassuring reports about 'constructive engagement' and lawyers acting as gatekeepers or filters who thereby assist in the efficient administration of courts and other decision-making processes. (This phenomenon of capture by funders is not limited to the EDO movement – see Rice 2012.) I have no doubt about the broad societal value of the work of EDOs in assisting with the efficient administration of justice, but I also think that there is a risk that it is overemphasized. Based on the insights from Wild Law we do, I think, need to be more open to the idea that more overt social activism may be called for in circumstances where existing laws are so manifestly contrary to Earth Jurisprudence.

Peter Burdon has noted a similar phenomenon in terms of the manner in which environmental regulation channels the resources and energies of environmentalists. He argues that 'the only things regulated by environmental law are environmentalists. The laws regulate the way environmentalists respond, and make them predictable' (Burdon 2009). While this is not always an accurate description of how environmentalists engage with and use legal strategies it is nonetheless a situation that would be recognizable to EDO lawyers and clients. It is very dispiriting for lawyer and client involved in processes like environmental impact assessment to find that the rules and unwritten expectations of the process were stacked against them from the beginning, that in effect citizen aspirations for the law far exceed what our current system of laws can deliver. Enormous amounts of time, money and emotional energy can be devoted to addressing 'relevant considerations' that bear little relationship to actual concerns. This is not to say that these processes and tactical battles ought not be engaged in (often they are all there is in terms of legal rights to participate in decision making) or that there is not the possibility to avoid being regulated in the manner Burdon describes, but it is perhaps necessary to explore ways to practise law and meet the associated ethical obligations while at the same time avoiding unwittingly becoming 'part of the problem'.

In terms of working with communities there is a much more developed model of 'law and organizing' described in the US literature that has also attracted considerable interest among those in the community legal centre movement here in Australia (Rich 2009). An organization that adopts this grassroots, community empowerment-oriented approach that is often cited in discussions about Wild Law is the Community Environmental Legal Defense Fund. Originally formed with an objective not dissimilar to that of the EDO movement, CELDF worked for many years to help communities navigate their way through processes established under environmental regulation. Then, as Mari Margil explains, 'after several years we stopped doing that work. We realised that we weren't helping anyone to protect anything' (Margil 2011: 249). CELDF now works very differently, running 'Democracy Schools' that provide communities with the encouragement and assistance to develop their own laws that actually protect the environment. According to Margil, 'the people we work with recognise that the structure of the law was never intended to protect the environment, but instead to regulate its exploitation, and that they must write new structures of laws – maybe writing their own constitutions – to replace it' (Margil 2011: 255).

Some of the projects pursued by CELDF, such as passing local laws banning corporations, would not be possible in Australia as our local government is very much subordinate to state legislatures. However, the broad model of engaging with communities through training and workshops is a familiar one to EDOs and it would not perhaps be too much of a stretch to extend existing workshop programs focused on assisting communities to engage in environmental legal processes to something similar to the CELDF Democracy Schools with the intention of deepening community understanding as to how laws work and how they might be transformed to something more aligned with community aspirations for environmental protection.

Substantive law

The discussion so far has focused on the practice of law and the inspiration Wild Law might present in terms of pursuing existing priorities in a different manner. I will now turn to substantive law. A prominent area of EDO activity is pursuing litigation, that is acting as legal representatives in cases that in some way meet our public interest criteria. This can be by protecting a particular area or something that the community values (such as a threatened species) or by seeking to clarify or extend a particular area of the law through a 'test case'. EDOs have a remarkable track record of pursuing significant environmental law cases and in certain areas such as the application and interpretation of the EPBC Act a significant proportion and probably the majority of cases that can be said to have developed and extended the jurisprudence around key concepts in the legislation have been pursued by EDOs, especially the Queensland and New South Wales organizations.

Almost the entirety of this work, however, has been pursued within the parameters of environmental legislation. The development of common law jurisprudence, in areas such as the public trust for instance, has not been a focus of EDO test case litigation which is perhaps one of the reasons why the public trust doctrine barely rates a mention in Australian jurisprudence. (See Bates 2010, 41–43 for an outline of the history of the reception of the public trust doctrine in Australia.) The public trust doctrine has been identified as one way in which Wild Law principles might be put into practice (Kimbrell 2008), so attempting to remedy this gap could be a useful priority for EDOs, albeit one that that is likely to be met with significant obstacles in terms of the receptivity of the Australian legal system (Finn 2012).

Even within the parameters of existing environmental regulation the potential of concepts like ecologically sustainable development to form a foundation for a more widespread transformation of jurisprudence remains underexplored, I think. In Victoria, the jurisdiction in which I practice, for instance, it is striking that basic concepts like the precautionary principle have only been considered by appellate courts in the last few years despite apparently being part of a legislative and policy framework since the mid 1990s. Some may have some qualms about the degree to which 'ecologically sustainable development' is consistent with a Wild Law approach, but commentators such as Klaus Bosselman are convincing that a strong approach to ESD would be one way of giving concepts such as ecological integrity much greater prominence than is presently the case (Bosselmann 2011). Also, as noted above, ESD and other global norms are perhaps the most significant example of intrinsic values for nature being recognized in our legal system at the moment and it is incumbent on us to try and breathe some life into the otherwise empty rhetoric.

Finally, another significant part of the work of some EDO lawyers is what we call 'policy and law reform'. This has been described above, as has the fact that to a large degree this work mostly involves advocating for the adoption, or more thoroughgoing adoption, of accepted and established norms, objectives and principles such as ecologically sustainable development and the precautionary principle. It is very much in the reformist mode and does not, intentionally anyway, attempt to delve into broader jurisprudential questions or involve advocacy for something like a non-anthropocentric legal system, for instance. EDOs to varying degrees have sought to position themselves as something other than campaigning organizations (an attempt that has not really succeeded in explaining with great clarity what it is that we actually do in my view), a position informed in part by the idea that others in the conservation movement develop campaign goals and pursue the political activities necessary to see them implemented. The role of the public interest EDO lawyer in this model is to supply the technical and legal expertise to those in the conservation movement who are actively initiating and pursuing change.

This situation aligns with Elizabeth Rivers' observation that 'traditional' lawyering involves the implementation of policy developed by others rather than the development of policy. Her thoughts are, I think, a useful challenge to the EDO movement to extend its current narrow thinking to something more ambitious:

> Lawyers are generally cautious, risk-averse and concerned with maintaining the status quo. Wild Law challenges lawyers to take on a different identity as agents of change, which will feel unfamiliar and possibly uncomfortable to many lawyers.
>
> Wild Law has identified that governance is a crucial aspect of creating a healthy relationship with the planet, so lawyers have a vital role to play in redesigning our governance system so that it can operate effectively. If lawyers do not seize this opportunity, it is likely to be taken by others and lawyers will be sidelined.
>
> (Rivers 2006: 28)

Embracing this idea seems attractive, not least because it would be considerably more challenging and interesting than some of the drudgery of making submissions to government inquiries. Rivers discusses how the potential for lawyers to play a 'vital role' and the need to 'seize the opportunity' demonstrate that Wild Law or something like it could be used by the EDO movement and fellow public interest environmental lawyers to develop ideas that could be used to inspire a broader public about the positive possibilities of the legal system and regulation in developing a more harmonious relationship with nature. There is a real need to be able to present this positive vision I think, something that is especially important to counter the prevalent view put by vested interests and so eagerly adopted by governments that environmental regulation is only to be viewed in negative terms, as so much 'green tape' that only gets in the way of the real task of economic development. Although this is the view of certain business and government elites I do not think it represents the view of most people; but we are at the moment lacking a clear vision to counter it and to inspire those who view the world in different terms to a new system of regulation and governance.

Conclusion – Wild Law in practice?

The ideas outlined above for putting Wild Law into practice in Australia are very preliminary. The fact that there is very little in the way of concrete ideas for putting Wild Law into practice demonstrates a real need for some further and more rigorous work by EDOs and others on how Wild Law might develop in a not particularly receptive Australian legal context. The Wild Law idea has clearly struck a chord with many, and the critique of the anthropocentric nature of our legal system undoubtedly resonates with those who struggle to see nature valued in legal and political processes. However, the real test for Wild Law must surely now be translating the insights arising from the critique into practice.

References

Bates, G.M. (2010) *Environmental Law in Australia*, 7th edn, Chatswood, NSW: LexisNexis Butterworths.
Bosselmann, K. (2011) 'From reductionist environmental law to sustainability law', in P. Burdon (ed.) *Exploring Wild Law: The Philosophy of Earth Jurisprudence*, Kent Town, SA: Wakefield Press, 204.
Brett Young, M. (2008) 'Law Institute of Victoria – depression warning', online. Available at: <http://www.liv.asn.au/Practice-Resources/News-Centre/CEO-s-Page/Depression-warning> (accessed 27 March 2013).
Burdon, P. (2009) 'Towards an earth-friendly legal system', *Eureka Street*, online. Available at: <http://www.eurekastreet.com.au/article.aspx?aeid=13932> (accessed 27 March 2013).
ClientEarth (2013) 'Vision', online. Available at: <http://www.clientearth.org/about/vision/> (accessed 27 March 2013).
Cullinan, C. (2002) *Wild Law: Governing People for Earth*. Claremont, South Africa: Johannesburg: Siber Ink in association with the Gaia Foundation & EnACT Intl.; [Distributed by] Thorold's Africana Books.

Finn, P. (2012) 'Public trusts and fiduciary relations', in K. Coghill, C.J.G. Sampford and T. Smith (eds) *Fiduciary Duty and the Atmospheric Trust*, Law, Ethics and Governance Series, Burlington, VT: Ashgate Publishing Company.

Godden, L. and Peel, J (2009) *Environmental Law: Scientific, Policy and Regulatory Dimensions*, South Melbourne, Vic: Oxford University Press Australia & New Zealand.

Howard, J. (2009) '2009 Menzies Lecture by John Howard (full text)', *The Australian*, online. Available at: <http://www.theaustralian.com.au/politics/menzies-lecture-by-john-howard-full-text/story-e6frgczf-1225766613925> (accessed 27 March 2013).

Keeva, S. (2009) *Transforming Practices: Finding Joy and Satisfaction in the Legal Life*, 10th anniversary edn, Chicago, IL: American Bar Association.

Kimbrell, A. (2008) 'Halting the global meltdown: can environmental law play a role?', *Environmental Law and Management*, 20(2): 64.

Margil, M. (2011) 'Stories from the environmental frontier', in P. Burdon (ed.) *Exploring Wild Law: The Philosophy of Earth Jurisprudence*, Kent Town, SA: Wakefield Press, 204.

Rice, S. (2012) 'Are CLCs finished?' *Alternative Law Journal*, 37(1): 16–21.

Rich, N. (2009) 'Reclaiming community legal centres. Maximising our potential so we can help clients realise theirs', Victoria Law Foundation Community Legal Centre Fellowship Final Report, online. Available at: <http://consumeraction.org.au/wp-content/uploads/2012/04/Reclaiming-community-legal-centres.pdf> (accessed 27 March 2013).

Rivers, E. (2006) 'How to become a Wild Lawyer', *Environmental Law and Management* 18: 28–31. online. Available at: <http://earthjuris.org/pdfs/How-to-Wild-Lawyer.pdf> (accessed 27 March 2013).

Saunders, C. (2010) 'The Australian Constitution and our rights', in H. Sykes (ed.) *Future Justice*, Albert Park, Vic: Future Leaders, 117–35.

Williams, G. (2012) 'Murray Darling Basin Plan', *Sydney Morning Herald*, online. Available at: <http://www.smh.com.au/opinion/politics/when-water-pours-into-legal-minefields-20101025-170uf.html> (accessed 27 March 2013).

Part II

Jurisprudential challenges

Chapter 6

Internalizing ecocentrism in environmental law

The Hon. Justice Brian J Preston

This chapter posits some ways in which a nature-centred approach, ecocentrism, may be incorporated into environmental law. I do not propose to articulate the case for adopting an ecocentric approach. It will suffice if I simply describe ecocentrism as taking a nature-centred approach rather than a human-centred approach, where the Earth is valued not merely instrumentally as a commodity belonging to us but also intrinsically as a community to which we belong.

My survey of ways in which the law might embrace ecocentrism cannot be comprehensive; this chapter does not permit such an exhaustive approach. So I will be selective, focusing on what appear to me to be two key topics. The first topic I will look at is the statutory approaches that are characteristic in Australia to regulating the use and exploitation or the conservation of the environment. I will identify five aspects of regulation: statutory objects; relevant considerations; burden of proof; substantive rights, duties and obligations; and implementation and enforcement. I will suggest ways in which these aspects of regulation could embrace an ecocentric approach. The second general topic I wish to address is access to justice, including access to environmental justice. Under this topic I will note some of the features needed to facilitate access to justice. These include institutions, funding, procedures and remedies.

The theme of my chapter could also have warranted an examination of particular branches of the law, such as criminal law, property law, tort law and contract law, to identify ways in which substantive law can adopt an ecocentric approach and align with the laws of ecology. Elsewhere, I have started to sketch the influence of the environment on the law (Preston 2008b: 180). However, there is insufficient space to develop these ideas here.

Statutory approaches to environmental regulation

The objects clause

I turn now to my first topic, statutory approaches to environmental regulation. Virtually all modern statutes contain an objects clause stating the objects of the statute. This statement can be merely an historical explanation of the background leading up to the passing of the statute, a form of recital, or it can be a statement of the purpose of the statute. The former type of statement will not be particularly helpful, other than perhaps assisting in understanding the motive of the legislature or the mischief which the statute was intended to address.

The latter type of statement is more helpful but it is still limited to being an interpretative tool to resolve uncertainty and ambiguity in the meaning of other provisions of the statute. An objects clause does not control clear statutory language or command a particular outcome of exercise of discretionary power under a provision of the statute. This was highlighted, to the dismay of the challengers, in the judicial review challenges to the Bengalla coalmine in the Hunter Valley and to the residential subdivision and development on the flood-constrained coastal plain at Sandon Point on the New South Wales south coast (*Minister for Urban Affairs and Planning v Rosemount Estates Pty Limited* (1996) 91 LGERA 31 at 78; *Minister for Planning v Walker* (2008) 161 LGERA 423 at 453–4). Both cases held that consideration of a particular object, increased opportunity for public involvement and participation in environmental planning in the first case, and encouragement of ecologically sustainable development ('ESD') in the second case, did not command a particular outcome of exercise of the discretionary power in question.

Objects clauses in environmental statutes are often drafted at a high level of generality and are hortatory and aspirational. They are objects for all seasons. An object of conservation, for example, is so wide as to embrace sustained development as much as ESD. It embraces utilitarianism as much as, or more likely more than, ecocentrism.

The objects enumerated in an objects clause might also be potentially conflicting, such as by encouraging economic development but also environmental protection. Indeed, even a single object, such as encouragement of ESD, in fact involves multiple objects, because the concept of ESD involves multiple principles, which might pull in different directions.

What can be done to improve the efficacy of objects clauses in environmental statutes? The first step would be to identify with greater precision what is the intended purpose of including an objects clause in the environmental statute and then draft the objects clause to articulate that purpose.

Secondly, the language used to describe each object in the objects clause must be sufficiently specific to identify with precision what falls within and without the ambit of each object. If ecocentric considerations, such as the intrinsic value of the environment and its components, are to be included, these need to be specified.

Thirdly, if there is potential for conflict, either within an object or between objects, the clause should state how such conflict is to be resolved. This could be done by assigning weight or priority to matters within an object or between objects. If it is intended that any one of the principles of ESD should take precedence over others in any particular situation, this should be stated. Similarly, if one or more objects should take priority over other objects, this should be stated. For example, section 9(1) of the *Water Management Act 2000* (NSW) states that as between the principles for water sharing set out in section 5(3), priority is to be given to those principles in the order in which they are set out in that subsection. A second example is section 3(2) of the *Fisheries Management Act 1994* (NSW) which provides that the objects of the Act include pursuing three specified objects relating to environmental protection but then specifies four other objects relating to economic and other uses of resources which are to be pursued 'consistently with those objects'.

A third example is the recast clause recommended by the *Australian Environment Act: Report of the Independent Review of the Environment Protection and Biodiversity Conservation Act 1999* (October 2009). The report recommended that the objects clause in the *Environment Protection and Biodiversity Conservation Act 1999* ('EPBC Act') clearly articulate and prioritize the objects of the EPBC Act in part as follows:

(1) The primary object of this Act is to protect the environment, through the conservation of ecological integrity and nationally important biological diversity and heritage.
(2) In particular, this Act protects matters of national environmental significance and, consistent with this, seeks to promote beneficial economic and social outcomes.

(Commonwealth of Australia 2009: 17)

Fourthly, the objects clause should influence the exercise of discretionary powers under the statute. There is a gradient of influence. Least influentially, the objects clause can be used in statutory interpretation to resolve uncertainty and ambiguity if they arise. More influentially, the statute could provide for repositories of power to consider or have regard to the objects in the exercise of powers and functions under the statute. The statute may provide that a decision-maker must consider the principles of ESD in determining whether or not to grant or refuse an approval. The Report of the Independent Review of the EPBC Act recommended, after articulating the primary object of the Act of protecting the environment, that:

(3) The primary object is to be achieved by applying the principles of ecologically sustainable development as enunciated in the Act.
(4) The Minister and all agencies and persons involved in the administration of the Act must have regard to, and seek to further, the primary object of this Act.

(Commonwealth of Australia 2009: 17)

Most influentially, the statute could provide for repositories of power to exercise powers and functions under the statute so as to achieve the object. One example is section 2A(2) and (3) of the *National Parks and Wildlife Act 1974* (NSW) which provides:

(2) The objects of this Act are to be achieved by applying the principles of ecologically sustainable development.
(3) In carrying out functions under this Act, the Minister, the Director-General and the Service are to give effect to the following:

   (a) the objects of this Act;
   (b) the public interest in the protection of the values for which land is reserved under this Act and the appropriate management of those lands.

However, such a provision could go further. For example, the statute could provide that a decision-maker must not grant an approval unless to do so is consistent with achieving ESD.

Another example is section 5 of the *Environmental Protection Act 1994* (Qld) which provides:

> If, under this Act, a function or power is conferred on a person, the person must perform the function or exercise the power in the way that best achieves the object of the Act.

The object of the Act is stated in section 3 to be 'to protect Queensland's environment while allowing for development that improves the total quality of life, both now and in the future, in a way that maintains the ecological processes on which life depends (ecologically sustainable development)'.

Relevant matters to consider

The second aspect under the topic of statutory approaches I wish to consider is the statement of relevant matters that a repository of power is bound to consider in the exercise of powers and functions under the statute. The relevant matters a decision-maker is bound to consider in the exercise of powers and functions are determined by statutory construction of the statute conferring the discretion. Statutes might expressly state the matters that need to be taken into account or they can be determined by implication from the subject matter, scope and purpose of the statute (*Minister for Aboriginal Affairs v Peko-Wallsend Ltd* (1986) 162 CLR 24 at 39–40, 55).

There has been a trend for legislatures to reduce both the number of matters expressly stated in the statute to be considered as well as the specificity of the matters stated; the expressly stated, relevant matters have become fewer and more general. An illustration of this trend was when the lengthy and detailed list of relevant matters to be considered by a consent authority in determining a development application under the *Environmental Planning and Assessment Act 1979* (NSW) ('EPA Act') was omitted (from the former section 90) and a smaller and more general list was inserted instead (in section 79C).

The reasons for this trend have not been clearly articulated. One reason may be to increase flexibility and agility in decision-making. Another reason, however, may be to prevent, or at least make more difficult, judicial review by the courts of the exercise of powers under the statute by the executive. A decision-maker commits no reviewable error warranting intervention by the courts by not considering a matter that the decision-maker is not bound to consider.

This is what occurred in *Anvil Hill Project Watch Association Inc v Minister for the Environment and Water Resources* (2007) 159 LGERA 8 at 20–1, where the particular matter alleged by the challenger (that greenhouse gas emissions resulting from the coalmine would contribute to the loss of climatic habitat) was held not to be a relevant consideration that the Commonwealth Minister was bound to take into account in making a determination under section 75 of the EPBC Act of whether the action was a controlled action.

Hence, the fewer matters expressly stated in a statute to be relevant matters, the less scope for judicial review.

Expressing the relevant matter at a level of generality, rather than at a level of particularity, also reduces the risk of judicial review being successful. A decision-maker is more likely to be found to have had regard to some facts and issues under the rubric of a generally stated relevant matter than a particular one. Again, this was discovered to the applicants' dismay in various challenges to decisions on the ground of failure to consider the relevant matter of the principles of ESD. The principles of ESD are so broad that proving that a decision-maker has failed to consider them is difficult in practice. (See, for example, *Drake-Brockman v Minister for Planning* [2007] NSWLEC 490; (2007) 158 LGERA 349 at 387–8; *Blue Wedges Inc v Minister for Environment, Heritage and the Arts* [2008] FCA 399; (2008) 157 LGERA 428 at 447–8.)

The reduction in the number of expressly stated matters does not necessarily exclude other matters, not expressly stated, from being relevant matters. As I have said, a matter might be impliedly relevant by reference to the subject matter, scope and purpose of the statute. However, this involves statutory interpretation and there is an increased risk that a matter will not be held to be relevant. An example is the difficulty encountered in *Minister for Planning v Walker* [2008] NSWCA 224; (2008) 161 LGERA 423 at 454, in implying the principles of ESD to be relevant matters to be considered by the Minister in approving a concept plan under the former Part 3A of the EPA Act.

The solutions to these problems I have identified are similar to those which I have suggested in relation to objects clauses. First, desired ecocentric considerations need to be expressly and specifically identified as relevant matters which must be taken into account in the exercise of powers and functions under the statute.

Secondly, if there is potential for conflict within or between relevant matters, the priority or relevant weight to be accorded to each matter needs to be stated.

Thirdly, if the relevant matter involves an outcome or standard to be achieved, then the statute needs to be drafted so as to require the decision-maker to exercise the relevant power or function so as to achieve that result and not merely to consider the matter in the exercise of the power or function. I return to the example that I gave earlier: a statutory provision should state that powers and functions are to be exercised to achieve ESD and not merely to consider the principles of ESD in the exercise of a power or function.

Another weakness often found in Australian environmental statutes is the omission of a requirement for a repository of power to consider the cumulative effects of an exercise of a power or function. There is a tendency for proposed activities to be assessed in a self-contained manner, independently of other past, present and future activities. This failure to deal with cumulative environmental effects is particularly encountered in the fields of biodiversity, water and climate change regulation (Peel 2011: 15, 17–18).

The absence of an expressly stated requirement to undertake cumulative impact assessment has led to challengers arguing that such assessment is impliedly required. In *Gray v Minister for Planning* [2006] NSWLEC 720; (2006) 152 LGERA 258 at 293–4, 296, a requirement for cumulative impact assessment was found to be inherent in the EPA Act's reference to principles of ESD, including the principle of intergenerational equity and the precautionary principle. However, this resort to implication carries risks. In a challenge in the Federal Court to the same project as in *Gray*, the Federal Court rejected the challenger's contention that the likelihood of the coalmine having a significant impact on matters of national environmental significance under the EPBC Act should be assessed, among other things, by comparison to other actions that might reasonably be assessed under the EPBC Act (*Anvil Hill Project Watch Association v Minister for the Environment and Water Resources* [2007] FCA 1480; (2007) 159 LGERA 8 at 19).

A solution is for the statute to require expressly cumulative impact assessment. An example is the US *National Environmental Policy Act 1969* ('NEPA') 42 USC §§ 4321–4370 which requires preparation of a detailed environmental impact statement for proposals for legislation and other major federal actions significantly affecting the quality of the human environment (*National Environmental Policy Act 1969* § 102(C), 42 USC § 4332(C)). The statement's assessment of the environmental impacts of the proposed action is assisted by the regulations made by the Council on Environmental

Quality implementing the procedural provisions of NEPA. These regulations define cumulative effects as 'the impact on the environment which results from the incremental impact of the action when added to other past, present, and reasonably foreseeable future actions regardless of what agency (federal or non-federal) or person undertakes such other actions. Cumulative impacts can result from individually minor but collectively significant actions taking place over a period of time' (40 CFR § 1508.7 (2011); Council on Environmental Quality January 1997).

Burden of proof

The third aspect under this topic of statutory approaches I wish to consider concerns the burden of proof. A common regulatory approach under environmental statutes is to prohibit some activity which uses, exploits or harms the environment but then permit persons to apply for some form of statutory approval enabling them to undertake such activity. The statute may also provide for a dissatisfied applicant for approval to appeal to a court or tribunal which undertakes a merits review of the decision and re-exercises the power to determine whether to grant or refuse approval to the activity.

Typically, the statute is silent as to the burden of proof, both in the original application for approval and on any merits review appeal. Judicial decisions have held that there is no legal burden of proof on an applicant for approval. There is, no doubt, a persuasive burden – the applicant needs to persuade the approval authority to exercise the power to grant the approval – but this falls short of a legal burden. The statutes also do not typically impose a burden on the applicant for approval to establish an absence of a particular type of environmental harm (such as a significant impact on threatened species, populations or ecological communities) or that the proposed activity will achieve some acceptable environmental outcome or standard (such as ESD), or that the economic or social benefits of the proposed activity will outweigh the environmental costs.

In practice, especially for larger and more significant activities, there seems to be a presumption that approvals ought to be granted unless good reason is demonstrated to the contrary. This effects a transfer of the burden to those opposing an activity to prove that the approval should not be granted in the particular circumstances of the case.

The economic cost and inconvenience of taking measures to prevent environmental harm have also been used as reasons for not undertaking or postponing such measures where there is a lack of full scientific certainty as to the efficacy of such measures. This approach has led to the promotion of the precautionary principle. This principle provides that 'if there are threats of serious or irreversible environmental damage, lack of full scientific certainty should not be used as a reason for postponing measures to prevent environmental degradation' (see, for example *Protection of the Environment*

Administration Act 1991 (NSW) section 6(2)). The precautionary principle, once invoked, effects a transfer of the evidentiary burden to a proponent of an activity to prove that a threat of environmental damage does not in fact exist or is negligible (*Telstra Corporation Ltd v Hornsby Shire Council* (2006) 67 NSWLR 256 at 273; 146 LGERA 10 at 43).

The issue of the burden of proof arises in another way. Persons who consume or exploit the environment will prevail over persons who do not consume or exploit the environment. This is simply because consuming users by exercising their demands foreclose non-consuming users from exercising theirs, but the contrary does not hold true. This results in a loaded system. Even in a system with laws regulating the use and exploitation of the environment, the leverage inherently exerted by consuming users of the environment means that they can continue until they are sued and restrained by court order. Consuming users will, therefore, be defendants and non-consuming users or persons wishing to preserve the environment will be plaintiffs. In our legal system, plaintiffs bear the burden of proving that the defendants' conduct is in breach of the law. In cases of doubt, the plaintiff will not succeed and use or exploitation of the environment will prevail (Krier 1970; Preston 1986: 221).

The solution to these problems concerning burden of proof is to allocate the burden to those who propose to use, exploit or harm the environment. This involves applicants for approval for an activity to use, exploit or harm the environment having to bear the burden of proving that the activity will not cause particular types of environmental harm which have been specified as material; the activity will achieve some environmental outcome or standard specified to be acceptable; the economic or social benefits of the proposed activity outweigh the environmental costs; and the approval ought to be granted for the proposed activity.

The precautionary principle should be specified to be applicable in the exercise of powers and functions under environmental statutes, including in the assessment and approval of applications to carry out proposed activities.

In court proceedings, the burden of proof should be allocated to an applicant in merits reviews appeals to establish the same matters I have suggested that an applicant should be required to establish before the original decision-maker, including that approval ought to be granted to undertake the activity. In civil enforcement proceedings to remedy and restrain a breach of environmental statutes, statutory provisions can raise certain evidentiary presumptions, such as the absence of lawful authority, unless rebutted by evidence to the contrary. This allocates the burden of proof to the defendant to rebut the presumptions raised. One example is under section 1703(1) of the Michigan *Natural Resources and Environmental Protection Act* of 1994. When a plaintiff in an action has made a prima facie showing that the conduct of the defendant has polluted, impaired or destroyed, or is likely to pollute, impair or destroy, the air, water, or other natural resources or the public trust in these resources, the defendant may rebut the prima facie showing by submission of evidence to the contrary. The defendant may also show, by way of an affirmative defence, that there is no feasible and prudent alternative to the defendant's conduct and that the conduct is consistent with the promotion of the public health, safety and welfare in light of the State of Michigan's paramount concern for the protection of its natural resources from pollution, impairment or destruction.

Substantive rights, duties and obligations

The fourth aspect under this topic of statutory approaches I wish to address concerns substantive rights, duties and obligations under environmental statutes. I will start with statutory duties on regulatory authorities. A striking feature of environmental statutes in Australia is that they prescribe conditional, but not absolute, rules of what can and cannot be used or exploited in the environment. Consider statutes concerning threatened species, populations and ecological communities. These statutes adopt the typical regulatory approach of first prohibiting the harming of listed threatened species, populations and ecological communities but then giving power to the regulatory authority to grant approval to persons who wish to harm a particular threatened species, population or ecological community. The statutes prescribe the process for making, considering and approving the application to harm the threatened species, population or ecological community. At no point do the statutes state that approval cannot be granted. There is, therefore, no absolute rule protecting all or some particularly significant threatened species, populations and ecological communities against all or some particularly significant harm in all or particular circumstances. The prohibition on harming threatened species, populations and ecological communities is entirely conditional and provisional.

The solution to this problem is for the legislature to enunciate in the statute some absolute rule. This could be identifying those areas or components of the environment that are unconditionally to be protected from all harm. It could involve identifying environmental outcomes or standards that are not to be compromised or are to be achieved, as the case may be. An ecocentric approach could inform the enunciation of these unconditional outcomes and standards. One example might be to enunciate the outcome of the maintenance of biodiversity and ecological integrity, including ecosystem processing and functioning.

A related feature of environmental statutes is that they are replete with discretionary powers but barely burdened by duties and obligations. As I have noted, the typical regulatory approach is to start with a prohibition on an activity causing some environmental harm but then give power to the regulatory authority to relax that prohibition by applications being made, considered and approved. There is rarely a duty on the regulatory authority either of a positive nature, to achieve some environmental outcome or standard, or of a negative nature, to ensure that some environmental outcome or standard is not compromised. One rare instance of a public duty on a regulatory authority was judicially enforced in the Manila Bay case (*Metropolitan Manila Development Authority v Concerned Residents of Manila Bay* GR No 171947-48, 18 December 2008). The Supreme Court of the Philippines issued a continuing mandamus compelling the Manila Development Authority to perform its statutory duties in cleaning up and preserving the polluted Manila Bay and obliged the authority to submit quarterly progress reports to the court for monitoring.

Reform could, therefore, be usefully focused on statutes imposing more duties on regulatory authorities to achieve or to prevent the compromising of specified environmental outcomes or standards.

Next, I will deal with statutory obligations on persons regulated by the statute. Under the typical environmental statute, the obligations imposed on persons are usually of a negative nature, that is to say, obligations that a person not do certain acts. These might be obligations not to carry out an activity at all, not to carry out an activity in a certain way, or not to carry out an activity with a certain consequence such as causing environmental harm of some kind. If persons wish to be relieved of this obligation, they need to apply for some form of approval authorizing the activity. However, positive obligations do exist in some statutes and, if an ecocentric approach is to be adopted, could be more frequently employed. Landowners might be under positive obligations to conserve land and things on or attached to it.

A landowner might be required, in relation to a listed heritage item on the land, to undertake a minimum standard of maintenance and repair to avoid demolition of the heritage item by neglect (*Heritage Act 1977* (NSW) section 118; *Heritage Regulations 2005* (NSW) Pt 3). A landowner might enter into a private property agreement, whereby the landowner undertakes to conserve the land and things attached to it. Examples are heritage agreements in relation to heritage items on land (*Heritage Act 1977* (NSW) Pt 3B), conservation agreements in relation to flora and fauna (*National Parks and Wildlife Act 1974* (NSW) Pt 4 Div 12; *Threatened Species Conservation Act 1995* (NSW) section 126A), and property vegetation plans (*Native Vegetation Act 2003* (NSW) Pt 4; see also heritage agreements under *Native Vegetation Act 1991* (SA) ss 23, 23A). An owner of land might also be under a positive obligation to control noxious weeds or prescribed alien species of fauna (*Noxious Weeds Act 1993* (NSW) section 12; *Natural Resources Management Act 2004* (SA) section 182).

Positive obligations will also arise where the land is the subject of a carbon offsets project or a biobanking agreement. The owner of the land sells a credit for the native vegetation growing on the land either to an emitter of greenhouse gases (such as a coal-fired, electric power station) for the benefit the vegetation affords as a sink for the sequestration of carbon or to a person who causes the loss of biological diversity in the course of development of other land. The owner, having sold the credit, will be obliged to maintain the vegetation on the land. For example, Pt 7A of the *Threatened Species Conservation Act 1995* (NSW) allows the Minister to enter into an agreement with an owner of land for the purpose of establishing a biobank site. This agreement may require the owner of the land to carry out specified actions on the land, remedial measures in the event that any contingency has a negative impact on the biodiversity values protected by the agreement or that prevents or interrupts the continuation of the management action, as well as restrict use of the biobank site. The *Carbon Credits (Carbon Farming Initiative) Act 2011 (Cth)* allows for carbon credits to be issued for certain projects, including sequestration of carbon through replanting native trees on non-forested land. To be an eligible offsets project of this kind, the project must establish and then maintain through direct planting or seeding, trees with the potential to attain crown cover of at least 20 per cent of the area across the land and a height of at least two metres (*Carbon Farming (Quantifying Carbon Sequestration by Permanent Environmental Plantings of Native Tree Species using the CFI Reforestation Modelling Tool) Methodology Determination 2012* cl 2.1). In addition to the positive requirement to establish and maintain the trees, several negative obligations apply following the commencement of such a project, including that plants must not be removed from the site for fencing, and livestock grazing must not occur in the area if it would prevent the regeneration of trees (cl 2.1).

Positive obligations may arise by consent authorities, in granting development consent, imposing conditions requiring the preservation or improvement of the environment on the land the subject of the development or requiring the carrying out of works on adjoining land (*Environmental Planning and Assessment Act 1979* (NSW) sections 80, 80A(1)(f)).

An increasing recognition of the first law of ecology – that everything is connected to everything else and that the Earth's ecosystem is, in a sense, a spaceship, may necessitate more sweeping positive obligations on landowners (Boulding 1970: 96; Commoner 1972: 33). Sax argues that 'property owners must bear affirmative obligations to use their property in the service of a habitable planet' (Sax 1989: 11). Sax recommends that:

> We increasingly will have to employ land and other natural resources to maintain and restore the natural functioning of natural systems.
> More forest land will have to be left as forest, both to play a role in climate and as habitat. More water will have to be left instream to maintain marine ecosystems. More coastal wetland will have to be left as zones of biological productivity. We already recognise that there is no right to use air and water as waste sinks, and no right to contaminate the underground with toxic residue. In short there will be – there is being – imposed a servitude on our resources, a first call on them to play a role in maintaining a habitable and congenial planet ...

We shall have to move that way, for only when the demands of the abovementioned public servitude of habitability has been met will resources be available for private benefits. To fulfil the demands of that servitude, each owner will have to bear an affirmative responsibility, to act as a trustee insofar as the fate of the earth is entrusted to him. Each inhabitant will effectively have a right in all such property sufficient to ensure servitude is enforced. Every opportunity for private gain will have to yield to the exigencies of a life-sustaining planet.

(Sax 1989: 13–14)

Sax's call for private gain to yield to the existences of a life-sustaining planet is encapsulated in the concept of ESD. The Australian National Strategy of Ecologically Sustainable Development defines the concept as 'development that improves the total quality of life, both now and in the future, in a way that maintains the ecological processes on which life depends'. Statutes could enhance implementation of ESD by imposing positive obligations on landowners to achieve ESD, including by the conservation of biological diversity and ecological integrity.

Finally, I will deal with statutory rights afforded under environmental statutes. Overwhelmingly, environmental statutes, insofar as they afford rights, afford rights to humans. The environment, and components of it such as flora and fauna, has no rights under the statute. Historically, this is entirely understandable. The environment has instrumental, utilitarian value – value for the benefits its use and exploitation yields to humans. But the environment also can be seen, and an ecocentric approach demands it to be seen, as having intrinsic value – value for its own sake quite apart from any instrumental or utilitarian value to humans. A statute can recognize this intrinsic value of the environment and afford it rights. The constitution of Ecuador does just this. Article 71 provides that nature has 'the right to integral respect for its existence and for the maintenance and regeneration of its life cycles, structure, functions and evolutionary processes' and article 72 provides that nature has a right to be restored, a right stated to be apart from the obligation of the state and natural persons and legal entities to compensate individuals and communities that depend on affected natural systems.

Implementation and enforcement

The fifth and final aspect of this topic of statutory approaches that I want to address is implementation and enforcement of environmental statutes. Implementation involves the relevant regulatory authority exercising powers and functions under the statute. Enforcement involves taking action to ensure compliance with the statute by both the regulatory authority and others whose conduct is regulated by the statute. There are a variety of means of enforcing environmental statutes, including criminal prosecution for offences, civil enforcement proceedings to remedy or restrain statutory breaches, proceedings to impose a civil pecuniary penalty for statutory breaches and administrative orders such as stop work orders and directions for remedial works (Preston 2011: 72).

Implementation and enforcement of environmental statutes are critical to good governance. Good governance is itself a component of achieving ESD (*Hub Action Group v Minister for Planning* (2008) 161 LGERA 136, 141, 157).

Implementation will be enhanced by having dedicated, competent, knowledgeable (including ecologically literate), and well resourced (adequate human, financial and material resources) regulatory authorities exercising powers and functions under the statute. Imposing more duties and obligations, rather than merely discretionary powers, and specifying desired environmental outcomes and standards to be achieved or not to be compromised in the exercise of powers and functions, as recommended earlier, will also enhance implementation.

Good governance will be assisted by measurement, monitoring and reporting on performance in the implementation of the statute. The primary responsibility for measurement, monitoring and reporting should reside with the regulatory authority. Accountability, transparency and responsiveness will be promoted by publication of reports on measurement and monitoring. Integrity will be enhanced if there is an independent audit, from time to time, such as by an Auditor General or by an Environmental Ombudsman. The availability and utilization, from time to time, of merits review and judicial review of the regulatory authority's conduct and decisions will also improve its performance and good governance.

Enforcement of environmental statutes is enhanced by empowering not only the regulatory authority but also citizens to have access to a court or tribunal to enforce the law. Open standing provisions, such as section 123 of the *Environmental Planning and Assessment Act 1979* (NSW), which allow any person to bring civil proceedings to remedy or restrain the statutory breach are a hallmark of most environmental statutes in New South Wales. They empower citizens to enforce environmental statutes against individuals in breach of the statute where the regulatory authority has failed to act and even to bring proceedings against the regulatory authority itself in respect of conduct and decisions in breach of the statute. As I will come to in a moment, an ecocentric approach would extend the right of standing to the environment and components of it, exercisable by a legally recognized representative for the environment.

Access to justice

I turn now to deal with my second general topic of access to justice in environmental matters. Access to justice includes citizens having effective access to judicial and administrative proceedings, including redress and remedy

(*Rio Declaration on Environment and Development*, Principle 10; *Convention on Access to Information, Public Participation in Decision-making and Justice in Environmental Matters*, opened for signature 25 June 1998, 2161 UNTS 447 (entered into force 30 October 2001) article 9(2)–(4) ('*Aarhus Convention*'); *Caroona Coal Action Group Inc v Coal Mines of Australia Pty Ltd (No 3)* (2010) 173 LGERA 280, 287). In order for access to be effective, there needs to be appropriate institutions to whom access for review is available, appropriate procedures for review, financial and other assistance to persons seeking access, and adequate and effective remedies.

Reviewing institutions

As to the first aspect, the reviewing institutions, access for review should be provided to a court of law or another independent and impartial body established by law. Access to justice in environmental matters may be improved by establishment of specialist environmental courts and tribunals. There are many benefits that environmental courts and tribunals can yield (Preston 2008a: 385; Pring and Pring 2009). However, three benefits are of particular significance to the theme of this paper: responsiveness to environmental problems; facilitating access to justice; and development of environmental jurisprudence (Preston 2008a: 406–8).

On responsiveness to environmental problems, I have said elsewhere:

> An environmental court is better able to address the pressing, pervasive and pernicious environmental problems that confront society (such as global warming and loss of biodiversity). New institutions and creative attitudes are required to address these problems. Specialisation enables use of special knowledge and expertise in both the process and substance of resolution of these problems. Rationalisation enlarges the remedies available.
> (Preston 2008a: 406)

An environmental court or tribunal can facilitate access to justice both by its substantive decisions and by its practices and procedures. Substantive decisions can uphold fundamental constitutional, statutory and human rights of access to justice, including statutory rights of public access to information, rights to public participation in legislative and administrative decision-making, and public rights to review and appeal legislative and administrative decisions and conduct (Preston 2008a: 406–7).

An environmental court or tribunal is more likely to adopt practices and procedures to facilitate access to justice, including removing barriers to public interest litigation. An environmental court or tribunal is better able to ensure the just, quick and cheap resolution of proceedings, thereby ensuring that rights of review and appeal are not merely theoretically available but are actually available to all who are entitled to seek review or appeal.

An environmental court or tribunal can better address the inequality of alms between parties. Specialization and the availability of technical experts in an environmental court or tribunal can redress in part inequality of resources and access to expert assistance and evidence (Preston 2008a: 407).

An environmental court or tribunal has more specialized knowledge, has an increased number of cases and hence more opportunity, and is more likely to develop environmental jurisprudence. An environmental court or tribunal by its decisions may develop aspects of substantive, procedural, restorative, therapeutic and distributive justice. The Land and Environment Court of NSW, for example, has displayed leadership in developing jurisprudence in relation to the principles of ESD (principle of integration, precautionary principle, intergenerational equity, conservation of biological diversity and ecological integrity, and internalization of external environmental costs, including the polluter pays principle), environmental impact assessment, public trust, and sentencing for environmental crime (Preston 2008a: 407–8).

Other institutions may also be useful in promoting an environment-centred approach. Some jurisdictions have established an environmental ombudsman or commissioner. New Zealand, for example, has a Parliamentary Commissioner for the Environment, established under the *Environment Act 1986* (NZ). The Commissioner has wide powers to investigate and report on any matter where the environment may be or has been adversely affected, and advise on preventative measures and remedial action to protect the environment. An environmental ombudsman or commissioner has the capacity to represent the environment and components of it and thereby value and provide a voice for the environment.

Procedures

The second aspect under this topic of access to justice in environmental matters is the procedure by which access to justice is to be gained. Where access is to the courts, court practices and procedures can act as barriers to access to justice. Barriers to plaintiffs seeking to preserve the environment include procedural rules governing standing to bring proceedings, requiring an undertaking for damages as a prerequisite for granting interlocutory injunctive relief, requiring the giving of security for costs of proceedings, summary dismissal of proceedings on the ground of laches and ordering an unsuccessful plaintiff in public interest litigation to pay the defendant's costs of the proceedings. These procedural rules particularly act as barriers to access to justice for citizens seeking to enforce environmental law. The consequence is that the public interest in environmental protection risks being unrepresented or, at least, under-represented in the courts (*Caroona Coal Action Group Inc v Coal Mines Australia Ltd (No 3)* (2010) 173 LGERA 280, 289). The procedural rules need to be reformed to remove or reduce these barriers to access to justice (Preston 1993: 165).

The provision of open standing to any person to bring proceedings to remedy or restrain breaches of statutes removes the standing barrier. An ecocentric approach would extend standing to the environment and components of it, such as non-human biota. The fact that the environment and non-human biota are not able to vocalize their claims and concerns is not an insuperable problem. A representative can be appointed to speak on their behalf. Stone, in arguing that natural objects, such as rivers, forests and trees, should have legal rights to make claims to protect against damage or to seek compensation and reparation for damage, has explained how natural objects can vocalize their claims through appointed legal spokespersons (Stone 1972: 450, 1985: 1, 1987).

The other procedural rules I have referred to can be reformed so as to reduce their effect as barriers. For example, the *Land and Environment Court Rules 2007*, pt 4 r 4.2, allows the Court, if it is satisfied that proceedings have been brought in the public interest, not to make an order for payment of costs against an unsuccessful plaintiff in the proceedings, not to make an order requiring the plaintiff to give security for the defendant's costs and to grant an interlocutory injunction or order without requiring the plaintiff to give an undertaking for damages.

Access to justice also requires access to information on governmental decision-making affecting the environment (see *Aarhus Convention* recitals and arts 4, 5). Courts can assist parties' access to justice by adopting procedures that facilitate parties' access to information. Court Rules and practice notes can require regulatory authorities to provide access, at an early stage in proceedings, to all relevant documents and information and to give reasons for decisions. With respect to requirements for access to documents, see, for example, the Land and Environment Court of New South Wales, *Practice Note – Class 1 Residential Development Appeals*, which states that on request, a respondent who is a public authority or public official is to provide the applicant with access to the documents relevant to the residential development application and its decision (if any), within seven days of the request (para 19). With respect to the requirement to give reasons, in proceedings in which a public authority's decision is challenged or called into question, the Land and Environment Court may make an order directing the public authority to furnish to any other party a written statement setting out the public authority's reasons for the decision (*Land and Environment Court Rules 2007* (NSW) Pt 4 r 4.3; Land and Environment Court of New South Wales, *Practice Note – Class 4 Proceedings*, para 14).

Financial assistance

The third aspect under this topic of access to justice is provision of financial assistance. It has been said that there is little point in opening the doors to the court if the litigants cannot afford to come in (Toohey and

D'Arcy 1989: 79). There is a great disparity in the resources (financial, human and material) available to persons seeking to enforce the public interest in environmental protection compared to those promoting economic and social development, being typically government and industry. Consideration needs to be given to the establishment of appropriate assistance mechanisms to remove or reduce these financial and other barriers to access to justice (*Aarhus Convention*, article 9(5)).

Various mechanisms have been suggested, including the establishment and operation of public interest, environmental legal centres, such as the Environmental Defender's Offices, to provide advice and assistance; the provision of legal aid for environmental, public interest litigation; and intervenor funding for persons representing the public interest of environmental protection to participate in and access administrative processes, such as public hearings and inquiries (Preston 1991: 61–5).

Remedies

The fourth and final aspect of this topic of access to justice is remedies and redress. The availability of adequate remedies and redress is fundamental to achieving effective access to justice. Environmental statutes typically empower courts to restrain breaches as well as remedying breaches by injunctive orders, both prohibitory and mandatory. Where the environment has been altered, the order may require reinstatement or remediation to the condition before the breach was committed (see, for example, *Environmental Planning and Assessment Act 1979* (NSW) section 124(2)).

Courts lack, however, power to grant other remedies. Unlike in the United States, courts are unable to make awards for natural resource damages. Natural resource damage assessment involves calculating the monetary cost of restoring injuries to natural resources that result from some statutory breach such as the release of hazardous substances or discharge of oil. Damages to natural resources are evaluated by identifying the functions or services provided by the natural resources, determining the baseline level of the services provided by the injured resources, and quantifying the reduction in service levels caused by the injuries (such as by contamination).

Natural resource damage assessment and restoration of natural resources affected by injuries such as release of hazardous substances or oil are undertaken in the US under the *Comprehensive Environmental Response, Compensation and Liability Act 1980* ('CERCLA') or the *Oil Pollution Act 1990* ('OPA') respectively.

Natural resources include 'land, fish, wildlife, biota, air, water, groundwater, drinking water supplies and other such resources' belonging to, managed by or held in trust by federal, state or local governments or an Indian tribe (*Comprehensive Environmental Response, Compensation and Liability Act* § 101(16), 42 USC § 9601(16) (2008); *Oil Pollution Act* § 1001(20), 33 USC § 2701(20)

(2010)). Natural resource damages are for injury to, destruction of or loss of natural resources including the reasonable cost of a damage assessment (*Comprehensive Environmental Response, Compensation and Liability Act* § 101(6), § 107(a)(4)(C), 42 USC § 9601(6), § 9607(a)(4)(C) (2008); *Oil Pollution Act* § 1001(5), § 1002(b)(2), 33 USC § 2701(5), § 2702(b)(2) (2010)). The measure of damages is the cost of restoring natural resources to their baseline condition, compensation for the interim loss of injured natural resources pending recovery and the reasonable cost of a damage assessment (43 CFR § 11 (2010); 15 CFR § 990 (2011)).

Under both CERCLA and OPA, responsibility for protection of natural resources falls on designated federal, state and tribal trustees. This recognizes that natural resources are held in trust for the public. Trustees are given responsibility for restoring injured natural resources. The two major areas of trustee responsibility are assessment of injury to natural resources and restoration of natural resources injured or services lost due to a release or discharge. One of the mechanisms by which trustees can meet these responsibilities is to sue in court to obtain compensation from potentially responsible parties for natural resource damages and the cost of assessment and restoration planning. If a designated trustee sues a potentially responsible party in court to recover compensation, a natural resource damage assessment done in accordance with the relevant regulations creates a rebuttable resumption. This means that the burden of proof shifts to a potentially responsible party to disprove the trustee's assessment (*Comprehensive Environmental Response, Compensation and Liability Act* § 107(f)(2)(C), 42 USC § 9607(f)(2)(C) (2008); *Oil Pollution Act* § 1006(e)(2), 33 USC § 2706(e)(2) (2010)).

The trustees use the compensation awarded for restoration and replacement of natural resources injured or services lost due to release or discharge or for acquisition of an equivalent natural resource (*Comprehensive Environmental Response, Compensation and Liability Act* § 107(f)(i), 42 USC § 9607(f)(i) (2008); *Oil Pollution Act* § 1006(c), 33 USC 2706(c) (2010)).

Restoration actions are primarily intended to return injured natural resources to baseline conditions but they may also compensate the public for the interim loss of injured natural resources from the commencement of injury until baseline conditions are established (Environment Protection Authority 2011).

Such action for compensation for damage to natural resources could be useful in Australia, giving value and voice to natural resources through natural resource trustees.

Conclusion

I have endeavoured to raise for consideration ways in which environmental law can beneficially embrace ecocentrism. These ways involve extending legal considerateness to all of the Earth's community of life, not just its human members. It also involves taking a holistic view of the community, of its processes and functioning, its integrity and interconnectedness, rather than engaging in Cartesian reductionism. The goal is for law to serve both people and planet.

References

Boulding, K.E. (1970) 'The economics of the coming spaceship Earth', in K.E. Boulding (ed.) *Environmental Equality in a Growing Economy*, reproduced in G. de Bell (ed.) *The Environmental Handbook*, New York: Ballantine Books.

Commoner, B. (1972) *The Closing Circle: Confronting the Environmental Crisis*, London: Jonathon Cape.

Commonwealth of Australia (October 2009) *Australian Environment Act: Report of the Independent Review of the Environment Protection and Biodiversity Conservation Act 1999*.

Council on Environmental Quality (January 1997) 'Considering cumulative effects under the National Environmental Policy Act', online. Available at: <http://energy.gov/sites/prod/files/nepapub/nepa_documents/RedDont/G-CEQ-ConsidCumulEffects.pdf> (accessed 5 October 2013).

Environment Protection Authority (2011) 'Natural resource damages: a primer', online. Available at: <http://www.epa.gov/superfund/programs/nrd/primer.htm> (accessed 19 November 2012).

Krier, J.E. (1970) 'Environmental litigation and the burden of proof', in M.F. Baldwin and J.K. Page (eds) *Law and the Environment*, New York: Walker & Co.

Peel, J. (2011) 'Issues in climate change litigation', *Carbon & Climate Law Review*, 5: 15–24.

Preston, B.J. (1986) 'Third party appeals in environmental law matters in New South Wales', *Australian Law Journal*, 60: 215–23.

Preston, B.J. ((1991) 'Public enforcement of environmental laws in Australia', *Journal of Environmental Law and Litigation*, 6: 39–80.

Preston, B.J. (1993) 'Judicial review in environmental cases', *Australian Bar Review*, 10: 147–75.

Preston, B.J. (2008a) 'Operating an environment court: The experience of the Land and Environment Court of New South Wales', *Environmental and Planning Law Journal*, 25: 385–409.

Preston, B.J. (2008b) 'The environment and its influence on the law', *Australian Law Journal*, 82: 180–95.

Preston, B.J. (2011) 'Enforcement of environmental and planning laws in New South Wales', *Local Government Law Journal*, 16: 72–85.

Pring, G. and Pring, C. (2009) *Greening Justice: Creating and Improving Environmental Courts and Tribunals*, The Access Initiative.

Sax, J.L. (1989) 'The law of a liveable planet', in R. J. Fowler (ed.) *Proceedings of the International Conference on Environmental Law (14–18 June 1989)*, Sydney: National Environmental Law Association of Australia and the Law Association for Asia and the Pacific.

Stone, C. (1972) 'Should trees have standing?: Towards legal rights for natural objects', *Southern Californian Law Review*, 45: 450–501.

Stone, C. (1985) 'Should trees have standing? revisited: how far will law and morals reach? A pluralist perspective', *Southern Californian Law Review*, 59: 1–154.

Stone, C. (1987) *Earth and Other Ethics – the Case for Moral Pluralism*, New York: Harper & Row.

Toohey, J. and D'Arcy, A. (1989) 'Environmental law: its place in the system', in R. J. Fowler (ed.) *Proceedings of the International Conference on Environmental Law (14–18 June 1989)*, Sydney: National Environmental Law Association of Australia and the Law Association for Asia and the Pacific.

Chapter 7

Jurisprudential challenges to the protection of the natural environment

D E Fisher

Human behaviour is governed by the artificial contrivance of law. But humans are also inescapably part of the natural world. Traditional legal doctrine is that humans, not nature, are subjects of the rules of law, while humankind's relationship with or impact on nature may be their object. How might earth jurisprudence equalize nature and humans, both parts of the global environment, in the eyes of the law?

The jurisprudential foundations of environmental law

Ethical approaches

These issues underlie the ongoing discourse about the jurisprudential foundations of environmental law. Are they anthropocentric, ecocentric, both, or neither? If anthropocentric, must nature be excluded from consideration? One view in the context of a human right to an adequate environment has been that:

> [t]he right cannot be conceived as implying or condoning indifference towards the non-human world since in requiring that the non-human environment should be preserved in the condition that is adequate for human health and wellbeing it implies – especially in a world as disrupted by anthropogenic environmental harms as this one now is – rather stringent demands of environmental protection. Moreover, part of its core rationale is to oppose the unbridled pursuit of those rights that do manifest the most 'strongly' anthropocentric tendencies.
>
> (Haywood 2005: 33)

This anthropocentric view of environmental law thus contemplates 'stringent demands of environmental protection'. But it goes somewhat further:

> The more that humans come to understand about the inter-connectedness of their health and wellbeing with that of non-human nature, the more inseparable appear their interests with the 'good' of nature.
>
> (Haywood 2005: 34)

Significantly, while the language betrays an economic perspective of nature, it is in the context of the 'interests' of both humans and nature. And finally, in this context:

> A human right to an adequate environment does not preclude the taking of other, complementary, approaches to environmental and ecological problems. It might also serve in many ways to support them and to enhance their potentiality for success.
>
> (Haywood 2005: 35)

Accordingly a human right to an adequate environment does not exclude recognition that nature has intrinsic value, and possibly even a right to its own intrinsic values.

An ecocentric approach to environmental law is premised upon a need to respect and protect the values of nature for their own sake, but it need not necessarily exclude recognition that the values of nature are important for humans' sake. An ecocentric approach to environmental law has been supported by arguments focused on: interdependence; spiritual harmony; extensionism; and fictionism (Alder and Wilkinson 1999: 66–8). These have been described as:

> Interdependence is the idea that all forms of life are interdependent and must be valued for their interdependence. Spiritual harmony is the feeling that individuals have with nature. In a sense the spirit of individual people is coextensive with the spirit of nature. Extensionism treats the environment and ecosystems as persons in the same way as other entities are afforded legal personality. Fictionism is the device by which a status is afforded to the environment or an ecosystem by deeming it to have rights which it would not otherwise have.
>
> (Fisher 2010: 38)

This suggests that the most important concepts from the law's perspective are personality and status rather than rights. Acknowledging legal personality and status for nature is of little practical value unless the law also creates responsibilities that also 'respond' to this personality and status.

A different but not inconsistent approach to environmental law is biocentrism, which effectively focuses on all living organisms. While humans can identify their own values, the values of non-human living organisms can be identified teleologically:

> Our conceiving of each organism as a teleological centre of life is our recognition of the reality of its existence as a unique individual, pursuing its own good in its own way. By developing the process of heightened awareness of it as the particular individual it is, we achieve a full

understanding of the point of view defined by its good. We then have the capacity needed to make the moral commitment involved in taking the attitude of respect toward it, even though having this capacity does not necessitate our making the moral commitment.
(Taylor 1986: 128–9)

This recognises an intrinsic value, but makes no reference to rights. However, it does require the existence of duties owed to all living organisms, such as a duty not to harm or a duty to compensate wrongs to any living organism (Taylor 1986: 172–92).

A third approach is the doctrine of ecological justice (Bosselmann 2008: 96–9), bringing together the anthropocentric and ecocentric approaches; incorporating in one theory of justice not only social but also ecological justice. Ecological justice is linked to intergenerational justice and intragenerational justice – two elements of social justice. Disguised as intergenerational equity and intragenerational equity, these are already principles supporting sustainability. The introduction of ecological justice moves the discourse somewhat in the direction of an ecocentric approach. Ecological justice as a value within the law can be formalized as 'a duty to pass on the integrity of the planetary system as we have inherited it (ecological integrity)' (Bosselmann 2008: 98).

The need for ecological integrity reflects the concern for the non-human natural world – the concept of inter-species justice. Ecological justice thus comprises intergenerational, intragenerational, and inter-species justice, supported by this duty 'to pass on the integrity of the [inherited] planetary system'. However, rights are not part of this framework.

Rights approaches

The jurisprudential conundrum about the rights of nature began in 1972, with a focus on a procedural right – standing – rather than on substantive rights:

Natural objects would have standing in their own right, through a guardian; damage to and through them would be ascertained and considered as an independent factor; and they would be the beneficiaries of legal awards. But these considerations only give us the skeleton of what a meaningful rights-holding would involve. To flesh out the 'rights' of the environment demands that we provide it with a significant body of rights for it to invoke when it gets to court.
(Stone 1972: 450)

The rules about standing have generally been liberalized over recent years but not to the extent that 'natural objects' have 'standing in their own right'.

Generally, nature receives standing indirectly through human agency. But jurisprudence has evolved to suggest 'what a meaningful rights-holding would involve'. Recognizing nature as a subject within the law is the significant development in legal doctrine. Whether it has rights or not, nature has a personality or a status recognized by the law. This means that its existence is recognized, is capable of protection, and cannot be ignored. In this sense it is not unlike a human right. These rights are not protected immediately as human values, but are capable of protection through an associated set of obligations. They are inchoate rights evolving into protectable rights. But the difficulties inherent in moving from the current philosophy of governance to Earth jurisprudence surface as soon as one mentions 'rights' for animals or the environment – particularly if there are lawyers present (Cullinan 2011: 95).

Arguably it has become a question of relationships rather than one of rights and duties by themselves. The attribution of personality or status to nature as a subject within the law implies that nature is capable of legal relationships with other subjects. The statement which is the locus classicus of this proposition is:

> The universe is a communion of subjects, not a collection of objects. As subjects the component members of the universe are capable of having rights. Every component of the Earth community has three rights: the right to be, the right to habitat and the right to fulfil its role in the ever-renewing processes of the Earth community.
>
> (Berry 2006, quoted by Cullinan 2011: 103)

There is accordingly a relationship between the Earth's human and non-human elements. These are subjects with legal personality and status. It is a specific function of the law to determine precisely what these relationships are. How would a jurisprudential model for this purpose be structured?

Structural approaches

International and national legal instruments have structural features in common: a framework of normative values; competence rules; strategic rules; regulatory rules; liability rules; and market rules (Fisher 2010: 9–11). Because of the nature of international law, international legal instruments tend to comprise statements of normative values, principles and objectives, and only relatively general statements of obligations. National legal instruments are naturally more specific in substance, particularly with regard to obligations. The relationship between their structural elements is important. A statement of normative values simply explains the fundamental ideas and concepts upon which the system is based. Competence rules explain what nation states, and agencies and individuals within them may do. Strategic rules inform the substance of competence rules by explaining the outcomes to be achieved in exercising the powers, while regulatory rules limit how those powers are exercisable. Liability rules provide remedies and sanctions for breach of the rules. Market rules – a more recent phenomenon of environmental law – have effect as economic regulatory instruments.

Equally important is the linguistic, grammatical, and syntactical structure of the statements of the rules. Statements of normative values apply to nobody in particular but everybody in general. Principle, strategy, and outcome statements, while similar, are directed more at particular sets of circumstances. Regulatory statements are more specific again, being directed at identifiable legal persons in defined circumstances. Similarly, liability rules may state a duty owed to a particular person (for example, contractual liability), to a member of an identifiable group (for example, a tortious liability), or to all members of a community (for example, criminal liability). If we ascribe legal personality or status to nature, how can rules be structured to create a legal relationship between nature and humans, as subjects of the law, and rules, that are the objects of the law?

The structure of international instruments

Principled approaches

Consider the structure of international legal instruments. Not surprisingly, the Stockholm Declaration 1972, the World Charter for Nature 1982 and the Rio Declaration 1992 (Sands and Galizzi 2004: 4–23) are cast as statements of principles, most being intrinsically anthropocentric but some being ecocentric. Principle 1 of the Stockholm Declaration is intrinsically anthropocentric, conferring upon 'man' a right and a responsibility. Principle 4 elaborates by identifying 'a special responsibility to safeguard and wisely manage the heritage of wildlife and its habitat' – combining anthropocentric and ecocentric values. In the result 'nature conservation must therefore receive importance in planning for economic development'. Principles 2, 3 and 5 restrict the human use of natural resources – the beneficiary being humankind but incidentally the natural resources themselves. The principal beneficiary of the obligation in principle 6 is an ecosystem, although humankind benefits incidentally. Significantly, in grammatical structure, principles 2, 3, 5 and 6 are in the intransitive or passive voice, meaning the sentence has a subject but not an object. While the subject appears in the nominative case, there is nothing in the accusative case. The objective of the stated obligation is a proposition in what may loosely be described as the dative case. This grammatical analysis may seem unnecessarily arcane, but it is critical in the context of attributing personality and status – and perhaps rights – to non-human subjects. It is an analysis that gives the status of a subject to the 'natural resources of the earth' in principle 2.

The Rio Declaration introduced formally the idea of sustainable development. Its approach is almost entirely anthropocentric. Principle 1 states unequivocally that 'human beings are at the centre of concerns for sustainable development', and are 'entitled to a healthy and productive life in harmony with nature'. While recognized, nature appears a subsidiary element in this approach. Principles 3 and 4 are similarly balanced and again the grammatical structure is passive: principle 3 asserts that the right to development must be fulfilled 'to equitably meet developmental and environmental needs of present and future generations'; under principle 4, environmental protection is an integral part of the development process.

The Rio Declaration imposes upon states something akin to obligations, although they are described as principles: principle 11 requires states to enact effective environmental legislation; principle 13 requires states to develop national laws regarding liability and compensation for victims of pollution and other environmental damage. Clearly, protection of the environment and prevention of environmental damage are elements of achieving sustainable development, but these outcomes are expressed in the accusative case while states are in the nominative case; so the subjects of these arrangements are states while the environment and nature remain the objects.

The World Charter for Nature similarly balances the anthropocentric and ecocentric values, but unlike the Stockholm and Rio Declarations, its focus appears more ecocentric than anthropocentric. Articles 1, 2 and 4 are critical in this regard. Article 1 makes no reference to humankind. It states 'Nature shall be respected and its essential processes shall not be impaired'.

Neither clause in this sentence has an object in the accusative case. Nothing indicates by whom or for what nature is to be respected and its essential processes not impaired. Perhaps, by implication, the obligations are imposed upon humankind. This is consistent with article 24:

> Each person has a duty to act in accordance with the provisions of the present Charter; acting individually, in association with others or through participation in the political process, each person shall strive to ensure that the objectives and requirements of the present Charter are met.

Clearly the duty is imposed upon all persons. Article 24 refers to the Charter's objectives and requirements. Is article 1 an objective or a requirement? It is structured as a requirement, with the beneficiary being nature and its essential processes. Thus, nature and its essential processes are the subjects rather than the objects of these legal arrangements. Article 2 is structured similarly, although with more specific subjects: genetic viability; population levels of all life forms; and necessary habitats. Again, the focus is ecocentric; humankind does not feature. Article 4 has a very clear anthropocentric perspective:

Ecosystems and organisms, as well as the land, marine and atmospheric resources that are utilised by man, shall be managed to achieve and maintain optimum sustainable productivity, but not in such a way as to endanger the integrity of those other ecosystems or species with which they coexist.

The anthropocentric reference to the human use of resources and the objective of optimum sustainable productivity are a counterpoint to the ecocentric reference to the integrity of ecosystems and species. Article 4 thus creates a balance between the two approaches while articles 1 and 2 disclose an ecocentric approach. Significantly, these articles treat nature, its essential processes and its more specific elements as the subjects of their propositions. Grammatically these are in the nominative case; there are no objects in the accusative case, and outcomes are expressed in the dative case.

In the World Charter for Nature, these principles are to be effected through a range of functions and implementation provisions. Article 6 contemplates respect for these fundamental principles and article 14 expects the principles to be reflected in both international and national legal systems. Article 10 goes further, recognizing a set of prescriptive rules: natural resources are to be used 'with a restraint appropriate to the principles' in the Charter and 'in accordance with' four 'rules'. One rule relates to limiting use of living resources. Another is for maintaining productivity of soils. The third deals with the reuse or recycling of water resources. The fourth provides for limited exploitation of non-renewable resources. Once again these elements of the natural environment are given subject status, grammatically; but they are 'rules' in the form of passive (intransitive) requirements. When applied together with article 24 (the duty on each person to strive to ensure that the requirements are met), what emerges from these propositions is nature as a subject of legal arrangements. The legal arrangements are given effect through the obligation (albeit limited) to satisfy the instrument's objectives and requirements. The World Charter for Nature emerges as an interesting model, but it is merely a resolution of the UN General Assembly, not, itself, a binding legal instrument.

Rules-based approaches

In multilateral environmental agreements, obligations designed to achieve the conservation of the relevant natural resources and the protection of the relevant environment are imposed upon nation states. While most multilateral agreements contain competence rules and limitation rules, the emphasis for obvious reasons is upon limitation rules. Equally significantly, the obligations in these limitation rules are imposed for the most part upon nation states. Accordingly, nature and the environment are largely the objects rather than the subjects of these rules. While these arrangements have an anthropocentric focus, ecocentric perspectives are not excluded; that is, nature may also be the beneficiary of these arrangements.

One example is the *Convention Concerning the Protection of the World Cultural and Natural Heritage 1972* (Sands and Galizzi 2004: 646–60). The definition of natural heritage in article 2 states four perspectives for determining the quality of the components of the world natural heritage: aesthetics, science, natural beauty, and conservation. The first three are unambiguously anthropocentric; but conservation includes natural heritage as one beneficiary of these arrangements. This is found in the obligation upon states in article 5(d) to take the appropriate measures necessary for the identification, protection, conservation, presentation and rehabilitation of the natural heritage. Conservation is one outcome but it appears different from the others in that it alone appears directed specifically at non-human perspectives.

Consider also the formulation of the third element of the definition of natural heritage in article 2. It includes the habitat of threatened species of animals and plants of outstanding universal value from the perspective of science or conservation. Science involves the knowledge and understanding of humankind, making humans the beneficiary of these arrangements. However, reference to the point of view of conservation, in this context of the habitat of threatened species, appears designed to allow focus upon the species as such, rather than upon humans' interest in it. This disjunctive reference to science 'or' conservation implies that the habitat of threatened species must also be conserved for the species' benefit. While this may be speculative, these arrangements clearly make some distinction between the human (science) and the non-human (conservation) perspectives of conservation of world natural heritage.

Another example is the *Convention on Biological Diversity 1992* (Sands and Galizzi 2004: 698–724). Article 2 states three objectives, the second and third clearly disclosing a human perspective:

- the conservation of biological diversity;
- the sustainable use of its components;
- the fair and equitable sharing of the benefits arising out of the use of genetic resources.

In common with most multilateral environmental agreements the Convention imposes a series of obligations upon nation states to take a range of measures to achieve its objectives. These obligations are cast in the active rather than a passive form. In-situ and ex-situ conservation measures are separated. The obligations for in-situ conservation in article 8(a) and (b) refer only to means for conserving biological diversity. More specifically, article 8(d) covers only the protection of ecosystems, natural habitats and the maintenance of viable populations of species in natural surroundings. On the other hand, article 8(c) focuses firstly upon the conservation of biological diversity:

> Regulate or manage biological resources important for the conservation of biological diversity whether within or outside protected areas with a view to ensuring their conservation and sustainable use.

Ultimately, then, the objectives of this system are linked to conservation and sustainable use of biological resources.

The Convention's statement of objectives in article 1 distinguishes between conservation and sustainable use. This distinction is carried into the detail of the obligations imposed by article 8. This is not suggesting that the objective of conservation is designed to benefit and to benefit only biological diversity. Focusing on conservation of biological diversity makes that the principal beneficiary of these arrangements, but humans benefit incidentally. In these and other provisions (for example, article 10) the Convention discloses both anthropocentric and ecocentric perspectives. The balance is determined in accordance with precise textual arrangements: in some provisions, the principal focus is conservation of biological diversity for its own sake and sustainable use is an incidental outcome; in others, the focus is reversed. The emerging set of arrangements recognizes the need to use and develop natural resources for human benefit, alongside the need for conservation of nature for its own sake, and incidentally for human benefit. This is moving towards sustainable development.

An integrated approach

The Draft International Covenant on Environment and Development (IUCN Commission on Environmental Law 2000) is one of the best examples of this emerging approach. Although not binding, it is indicative of evolving legal doctrine. Its structure is clear:

- an objective;
- nine fundamental principles;
- general obligations imposed on states and persons;
- more specific obligations relating to natural systems and resources;
- obligations relating to processes and activities;
- obligations relating to global issues;
- provisions for implementation, responsibility, liability and compliance.

These various provisions construct a framework of normative values; competence rules; strategic rules; regulatory rules; liability rules; and market rules. As an international legal instrument it imposes duties or obligations upon the states parties, but there are obligations imposed also upon persons. Particularly important for present purposes is the structure of the objective and the fundamental principles. The objective in article 1 is: 'to achieve environmental conservation and sustainable development by establishing integrated rights and obligations' – a single objective comprising two outcomes linked conjunctively: conservation of the environment; and the sustainable development of its resources. However, the distinctive use of the words 'conservation' and 'development' is important. Protection of the environment is an element of sustainable development, as is environmental conservation. But arguably, for this purpose conservation focuses upon nature conservation as an ecocentric – rather than an anthropocentric – outcome. On the other hand, a sustainable development outcome is clearly anthropocentric.

The fundamental principles guide the states parties in achieving the objective. It is not surprising that the principles are formulated as rules with nature or its elements as their subject rather than their object. For example, article 2 states an unambiguously ecocentric principle:

> Nature as a whole warrants respect. The integrity of the Earth's ecological systems shall be maintained and restored. Every form of life is unique and is to be safeguarded independent of its value to humanity.

Each sentence has a subject and a verb but no object. This is important: in effect, it means the principle is of unrestricted application and, to the extent that there is an obligation, it is imposed upon everyone. Again significantly, the second and third sentences contain obligations also expressed passively – implying these are duties on everyone.

Article 6 is structured differently: 'Protection of the environment is best achieved by preventing environmental harm rather than by attempting to remedy or compensate for such harm'. The outcome here is clearly protection of the environment. The environment is the beneficiary of this limited obligation. The principle instructs how it is to be protected: namely, by preventing, rather than by remedying harm. Again, the instruction is formulated passively, implying an obligation imposed, not upon anyone in particular, but upon everyone in general.

This interpretation is supported by the formulation of article 20, which obliges states parties to take appropriate measures 'to conserve and, where necessary and possible, restore natural systems which support life on Earth in all its diversity'. The obligation thus constitutes the legal mechanism for implementing the objective stated in article 1 and the principles stated in articles 2 and 6. Not surprisingly, this obligation is in active rather than passive form. The Draft Covenant thus indicates how nature and its components can be not only recognized within the legal system but also given the status of a subject. Nature is also the object of active obligations imposed upon the states. A set of relationships is beginning to emerge within the legal system, including relationships between the natural environment and the human environment.

The structure of national instruments

A constitutional approach

National legal systems will naturally adopt a more specific and directed approach to giving legal recognition to nature. It may be recognized directly or indirectly, as a subject or object of the legal system or possibly in other ways. The mechanisms may include constitutional rules, strategic rules, regulatory rules and liability rules (Burdon 2010: 71–7). An example of a unique approach to nature is adopted in the Constitution of Ecuador.[1] The first paragraph of article 71 stipulates:

> Nature, or Pacha Mama, where life is reproduced and occurs, has the right to integral respect for its existence and for the maintenance and regeneration of its life cycles, structure, functions and evolutionary processes.

In grammatical terms nature is the subject. The object is the right to respect for its present and continuing existence into the future. The existence of nature is the subject matter of respect and respect is the subject matter of the right. There is respect 'for' the existence, and again 'for' the maintenance and regeneration of nature. Accordingly, article 71 stipulates not nature's right to its present and future existence but a right to 'respect for' these things. This necessarily raises an important question: respect by, or from what, or whom. The answer lies in subsequent articles.[2] In effect, it is everyone in the community including all natural and legal persons and all agencies of the state.

These constitutional provisions contain a series of competence rules and limitation rules. The competence rules include a power to request public authorities to enforce the rights of nature and the limitation rules include obligations upon the state to protect nature and promote respect for it. Limitation rules include the obligation on the state in article 406 to:

> regulate the conservation, management and sustainable use, recovery, and boundaries for the domain of fragile and threatened ecosystems, including among others high Andean moorlands, wetlands, cloud forests, dry and wet tropical forests and mangroves, marine ecosystems and sea shore ecosystems.

The listed elements of nature are clearly beneficiaries of this obligation. However, nature is not the only beneficiary. Article 83(6) imposes an obligation upon all Ecuadorians: 'To respect the rights of nature, preserve a healthy environment and use natural resources rationally, sustainably and durably'.

Clearly there is a duty to respect the rights of nature but also to use natural resources in a particular manner. It is Ecuadorians who use the resources and therefore they are the beneficiaries of these arrangements. This is supported by article 74: 'Persons, communities, peoples, and nations shall have the right to benefit from the environment and the natural wealth enabling them to enjoy the good way of living'.

The relationship between these provisions suggests two conclusions:

- nature is entitled to respect from humankind;
- humankind is under an obligation to respect nature and at the same time is entitled to benefit from nature.

The Constitution is thus a complex blend of intrinsic values, relatively specific rights and more specific obligations. In structure, form and language, these arrangements contemplate a legal system with capacity to recognize these values, protect the rights and enforce the obligations. The Constitution of Ecuador recognizes the rights of nature in ways not unlike the arrangements of the World Charter for Nature 1992 – there are both human and non-human perspectives. The English translation of the Constitution suggests that, in the context of the Constitution at large, these are rights in relation to nature, as well as rights of nature. Whatever strictly linguistic view is applied to these propositions, nature is given a personality and a status within them.

The contribution of the judiciary

Let us consider some examples of judicial approaches to legal arrangements under which the environment may be a beneficiary. National statutes are implemented by executive action, and executive decisions may be challenged, leading to judicial scrutiny. The way in which national parks are managed was an issue in Australia for the state[3] Supreme Court of Queensland in 2000 in a case concerning a proposal to undertake development works on Lizard Island, a national park (*Cape York Land Council Aboriginal Corporation v Boyland & Anor* [2000] QCA 202). The relevant Act, the National Parks and Wildlife Act 1975 (Qld), contained a 'cardinal principle' for the management of National Parks: 'the permanent preservation, to the greatest possible extent, of their natural condition'.[4] Section 25 of the legislation also required the Director to 'exercise his powers under this Act in such manner as appears to him most appropriate to achieve this objective'.

The justiciable issue for the court was whether the Director had observed the cardinal principle in exercising his powers. The Court's ruling gave clear legal priority to conservation of nature – 'the permanent preservation, to the greatest possible extent, of the natural condition of the park' (*Cape York Land Council Aboriginal Corporation v Boyland & Anor* [2000] QCA 202 at 16) – over its sustainable use. The focus of the management principles for national parks upon the permanent preservation of their natural condition over the sustainable use of nature is consistent with the legislated object, conservation of nature. Significantly, it is a legal priority not an executive priority. Strategic rules, stated as principles and objectives, were accordingly enforced through a careful interpretation of the language of the legislation, to find that in fact, nature was the intended primary beneficiary of the arrangements.

Similar reasoning in 1976 led the United States Court of Appeals for the District of Columbia to interpret legislation as prioritizing the protection of the endangered porpoise over interests of commercial fishing (*Committee for Humane Legislation v Richardson* (1976) 540 F. 2d 1141).[5] The issue was the validity of a fishing permit granted under the Marine Mammal Protection Act of 1972 (16 USCS §§ 1361–1374). The Act had a 'major objective' and a 'primary objective', each directed at protecting the marine mammals in question from over-exploitation by human activity (16 USCS §§ 1361(2), 1361(6)). A critical point was the relevance and significance of the policy stated in the Act and the relationship between that policy, the regulations and the permit.

The Court of Appeals agreed with the District Court 'that the Act was to be administered for the benefit of the protected species rather than for the benefit of commercial exploitation' (*Committee for Humane Legislation v Richardson* (1976) 540 F. 2d 1141 at 1148). The permit applications in question had no 'discussion of the predicted impact of the proposed takings on the optimum sustainable population of the porpoise species involved' nor did they 'display consistency with the purposes of the ... Act' (at 1151). The Act required the permit to be consistent with the regulations and the regulations to be consistent with the purposes and policies of the Act. Granting the permit was inconsistent with the regulations, which in turn were inconsistent with the purposes of the Act. While the Act permitted commercial fishing, its focus was marine mammal protection. By a set of enforceable rules, the prime beneficiary of the legislation was marine mammals. Humankind also benefited but only secondarily.

Evolving liability regimes

The various forms of legal liability may be particularly significant in regard to conservation and protection of nature. If nature has personality and status – and possibly even rights – under law, an infringement of these rights or a breach of associated duties may enliven some form of liability rules. These rules traditionally provide a remedy for loss or damage suffered by a person or entity as a result of another's unlawful conduct. An early attempt at the international level to introduce a civil liability regime, to provide a remedy for damage sustained by nature and natural resources was the *Convention on Civil Liability for Damage Resulting from Activities Dangerous to the*

Environment 1993 (Sands and Galizzi 2004: 1242–62). In 2004 the European Union enacted the Directive on Environmental Liability with the Regard to the Prevention and Remedying of Environmental Damage (Directive 2004/35/EC: 56). Two of the most interesting national responses have been provisions creating liability for destruction or loss of natural resources under the Comprehensive Environmental Response, Compensation and Liability Act 42 USCS §§9601–9607 of the United States, and Germany's Environmental Damage Prevention and Remediation Act 2007 which implements the European Union Directive. These give to natural resources in the United States and to the environment in Germany a degree of personality and status within the legal system to become the beneficiaries of liability regimes.

The United States Act applies to an actual or threatened release of a hazardous substance (42 USCS §9607(a)). The person responsible is liable 'for damages for injury to, destruction of, or loss of natural resources' (42 USCS §9607(a)(4)(C)) consequential upon the activities causing the release. Natural resources are land, fish, wildlife, biota, air, water, ground water, drinking water supplies, and other such resources controlled by the United States, other government agencies or any Indian tribe (42 USCS §9601(16)). While an extensive range of natural resources is covered, liability is restricted to release in a fairly narrow set of circumstances. The Act specifically provides that the President acts on behalf of the public as trustee of the natural resources, for the purpose of recovering compensation for the damage sustained (42 USCS §9607(f)(1)). Thus, the beneficiaries of these provisions are the relevant natural resources through the fiduciary responsibilities of the United States.

The German Act (*Environmental Damage Prevention and Remediation Act 2007*) is structured rather differently. It imposes upon the responsible party three fundamental obligations:

- to inform the competent authority of an imminent threat of environmental damage or the occurrence of environmental damage (section 4);
- to take the necessary preventive measures (section 5);
- where environmental damage has occurred, to take the necessary damage control measures and the necessary remedial measures (section 6).

The responsible party is therefore liable for the costs of preventive measures, damage control measures and remedial measures (section 9(1)), under the supervision of the competent state authority (sections 7–8).

The critical concepts underlying these obligations are the responsible party, an occupational activity and environmental damage. An occupational activity is any activity carried out in the course of an economic activity, business or undertaking, whether private or public, for profit or non-profit (section 2(4)). Environmental damage covers damage to species and natural habitats, water damage, or land damage by impacts on soil functions (section 2(1)). Accordingly, the responsible person is liable for engaging in or controlling an activity which directly causes damage (section 2(3)). Damage more specifically is a measurable, direct or indirect adverse change in or impairment of a natural resource (section 2(2)), being species and natural habitats, water and soil. So liability is restricted to damage directly caused by an occupational activity. The list of occupational activities in Annex 1 is extensive. Most importantly for present purposes, the natural resources – species, natural habitats, water and soil – are recognized for their own sake and in this sense have personality and status. The Act does not go so far as to talk in terms of rights. While the legal mechanisms are structurally traditional, there can be little doubt that the subjects of the legislation – the beneficiaries if its arrangements – are the natural resources in question. The object of the Act is to prevent and remedy environmental damage – that is, environmental damage becomes the object rather than the subject of these rules. The fundamental instruments for preventing and remediating environmental damage are the obligations imposed upon responsible parties. Humans also benefit indirectly from these arrangements. While the focus is ecocentric, it is to this extent anthropocentric.

An emerging jurisprudence of environmental governance

The jurisprudence of environmental governance has traditionally been little different from any other form of governance, having interrelated sets of rights, obligations and liabilities. Rights have been structured as competence rules such as rights of sovereignty under international law and property rights under national laws. Rights are increasingly circumscribed by limitation rules. Humans are traditionally both the subjects and objects of legal arrangements. For the most part, therefore, the law uses an anthropocentric approach. Protection of the environment and conservation of natural resources are recent elements of the paradigm. The right to exploit a natural resource has been constrained by the obligation to protect the environment from which the resource is taken and into which waste is deposited. A complex set of arrangements brings these rights and obligations together, leading ultimately to potential liabilities. It appears that the environment, nature and natural resources are increasingly perceived as having value beyond those of human interest and human benefit. In other words, an ecocentric approach is emerging. It is evolving through the legal system, not only as a responsibility to protect the environment and to conserve natural resources, but also as a human right in relation to these outcomes. Outcomes in the form of strategic rules in the legal system are a significant element of the jurisprudence of environmental law. What has emerged is a set of relationships between statements of value, statements of principle, strategic rules, regulatory rules, and liability rules.

The approach of international law has been to preface international instruments by statements of value, principle, and outcome. But significant instruments such as international declarations and United Nations resolutions have set the context of more specific rights and obligations promulgated in multilateral agreements. The World Charter for Nature has been particularly significant in the context of formulating an ecocentric approach. The Stockholm and Rio Declarations informed a series of multilateral agreements that have implemented these principles and strategies in specific sets of circumstances.

The structure of these instruments has been critical. Grammatically, a passive rather than an active voice has been adopted. The subject of the arrangements has increasingly become the environment, nature or natural resources; the object – the objective of the processes – is their use, development, protection, preservation or conservation. While humans are by no means excluded, the focus has changed to recognize increasingly the intrinsic values of the environment and nature that need to be protected and conserved for their own sake, rather than simply for human benefit.

National legal arrangements have evolved similarly. The incorporation of strategic rules within the system has changed the essence of the relationship between its elements. Common law has largely avoided a consideration of the outcomes of decision-making processes. These have now become an essential element of the system, and, as the objects of the system, outcomes are related increasingly to subjects of the system such as the environment and nature. As the holders of rights in the strict sense and as the subjects of legal relationships, humans have traditionally been subjected to obligations that limit the exercise of these rights. But the nature of these obligations has changed dramatically, with the emergence of a much more detailed and comprehensive set of strategic rules, along with traditional regulatory rules.

The relationship between rights and obligations remains important, even in the context of the environment and nature. It may be premature to suggest that nature and the environment have rights, but recognizing environment and nature under the law arguably affords to them a form of personality and status. Furthermore, a change is discernible in the nature of rights attributed to humans. Certainly humans have personality and status within the law. But, at least in the environmental context, their rights have been eroded substantively, to the point that it is almost meaningless to speak of a human right to exploit the environment except in relation to the obligations that relate to it. In other words competence rules have increasingly been overtaken not only by liability and regulatory rules but also by strategic rules. In this way national legal systems are in many respects following the international legal model.

Two examples are the liability rules for loss of or damage to natural resources under legislation in the United States and Germany. We have also seen an example of liability rules invalidating the authorization of construction activities in a national park, under national parks and wildlife laws in the Australian state of Queensland. Then there is the specific constitutional recognition of nature, coupled with responsibilities towards nature, in the Constitution of Ecuador.

The law has always been about defining the relationship between legal persons. The objects of these relationships have been matters of interest and concern to humans whether they are material, non-material, biological, physical, cultural or spiritual – for example, the human interest in life, physical integrity, reputation, and property. The jurisprudence of environmental law has added to these by including nature and the environment in the traditional form of what may be described as a human right in relation to the environment or to an environment of an acceptable quality. Whether there is such a right depends on the designated subjects and objects of particular legal arrangements. Whether it is appropriately called a right may not matter. It is the substance of the relationship between the subjects and objects of the legal relationship that is important.

The same may well be true of nature and the environment. The recognition of nature for its own values is attributing to it a legal personality or status. Similarly, whether it can be termed a right may not be material. What is important is the relationship between nature as a subject of a legal relationship and the objects associated with this legal relationship. It may well be premature to make this assertion. But law is dynamic, and on the approach argued here, its dynamic processes may be glimpsed moving in this direction.

Notes

1 For English translation of the relevant provisions, see: Ministerio de Relaciones Exteriores de Ecuador, <http://pdba.georgetown.edu/Constitutions/Ecuador/english08.html> (accessed 5 December 2012).
2 Arts 71, 72 and 73, in conjunction with art. 83(6) and (13), and arts 404 and 406.
3 Australia is a federation, with commonwealth, state and local governments, the conservation of nature being generally approached according to sets of rules in the form of strategies and principles, reflecting those acknowledged by international law. Principles in support of environmental management emerged in 1992 through the Intergovernmental Agreement on the Environment together with the National Strategy for Ecologically Sustainable Development. For discussion of these see Fisher 2010: ch. 10.
4 This Act has been repealed, but the cardinal principle as enacted in the current Act is in almost identical terms: 'permanent preservation of the area's natural condition and protection of the area's cultural resources and values': Nature Conservation Act 1992 (Qld), s 17(2).
5 Helpfully referred to in Cullinan 2011: 114.

References

Alder, J. and Wilkinson, D. (1999) *Environmental Law and Ethics*, London: Macmillan Press.

Berry, T. (2006) 'Appendix 2 – ten principles for jurisprudence revision', in T. Berry, *Evening Thoughts: Reflecting on Earth as a Sacred Community*, San Francisco: Sierra Club Books.

Bosselmann, K. (2008) *The Principle of Sustainability: Transforming Law and Governance*, Aldershot: Ashgate Publishing.

Burdon, P. (2010) 'The rights of nature: reconsidered', *Australian Humanities Review*, 49: 69–89.

Cullinan, C. (2011) *Wild Law: A Manifesto for Earth Justice*, 2nd edn, White River Junction, VT: Chelsea Green Publications.

Fisher, D.E. (2010) *Australian Environmental Law: Norms, Principles and Rules*, Rozelle, NSW: Thomson Reuters.

Haywood, T. (2005) *Constitutional Environmental Rights*, Oxford: Oxford University Press.

IUCN Commission on Environmental Law (2000) *Draft International Covenant on Environment and Development*, 2nd edn, Gland: IUCN.

Sands, P. and Galizzi, P. (eds) (2004) *Documents in International Environmental Law*, 2nd edn, New York: Cambridge University Press.

Stone, C. (1972) 'Should trees have standing? – towards legal rights for natural objects', *Southern California Law Review*, 45: 450–501.

Taylor, P. (1986) *Respect for Nature: a Theory of Environmental Ethics*, Princeton, NJ: Princeton University Press.

Chapter 8

Who's afraid of the founding fathers? Retelling constitutional law wildly

Nicole Rogers

In Australian constitutional law, we confront an almost immutable sacred text or rather, as Greta Bird has observed, a hierarchy of sacred texts: the Constitution itself, the case law in which the High Court has interpreted the Constitution, and finally the academic commentary on constitutional law (Bird 1996). The original sacred text, the Australian Constitution, is very much the product of the preoccupations and concerns of its nineteenth century drafters, and is notoriously resistant to change. Constitutional referenda in Australia are rarely successful.[1] As a consequence of this, one constitutional scholar has described Australia as the 'frozen continent' (Sawer 1967: 208).

However, textual restrictions and omissions have not impeded the High Court in its creative interpretation of the Constitution. The High Court's expansive reading of the Commonwealth government's powers,[2] its drawing of implications from the system of representative democracy which our Constitution arguably establishes,[3] and its use of the doctrine of separation of powers and in particular the separation of judicial power in protecting (and also failing to protect) human rights[4] are but some examples of what has been described, often disparagingly, as judicial activism. Such shifts in judicial interpretation demonstrate that the second layer of sacred texts, constitutional case law, may well be sacred in the sense that their authority and status cannot be challenged, but *they* are not immutable. Subsequent High Courts can and do alter their approach to constitutional issues, indirectly or directly overriding earlier decisions. A future High Court could, in fact, interpret the Constitution from a Wild Law perspective. Retelling constitutional law from a wild perspective requires us to interrogate not so much the textual omissions, for these have not prevented innovative interpretations in other contexts, but rather the underlying assumptions about environment, nature, wilderness, and property in the second layer of constitutional sacred texts: High Court constitutional case law.

My intention, in wildly retelling or wildly deconstructing four constitutional cases, is to focus on this second layer of sacred texts, to highlight the ways in which the High Court's interpretation of the Constitution excludes perspectives which a Wild Lawyer might consider important or critical, and to offer suggestions of alternative approaches to constitutional issues. In a wild retelling of constitutional law, we must consider the relevance of the Constitution for the protection of other non-human species, and examine the role which the Constitution can or should play in acknowledging and protecting the rights of other species to exist and flourish. A Wild Law perspective requires us to interrogate existing constitutional provisions which protect trade and property, and to question whether such provisions should be read subject to considerations of environmental impact and the rights of other species. From a Wild Law perspective, abstract questions of public power and constraints upon public power must be anchored in the context of particular places and particular times. If we adopt a Wild Law perspective, we reinsert into constitutional narratives the bodies and places which experience the impact of constitutional decision-making.

The nature of constitutional law

Our so-called Founding Fathers shared far more similarities with John Galsworthy's fictitious Victorian 'man of property', Soames Forsyte (Galsworthy 1906), than with nineteenth century ecologists and advocates of wilderness preservation such as Henry David Thoreau and John Muir. The Forsyte clan's fascination with property might explain why trade, commerce and property were considered worthy of constitutional protection by our Founding Fathers while human rights and environmental values were not. Instead of a Bill of Rights, we have only 'five flimsy freedoms' (Coper 1987: 316) in our constitutional text and, with the exception of section 51(xxxi) which protects property rights, these have not been widely interpreted. Innovative statements about environmental rights, environmental protection and even rights of nature appear in the constitutions of approximately 60 other countries, including South Africa, Kenya, France, India, the Philippines and Ecuador (May and Daly 2011: 329–57); these have sometimes been used successfully in public interest environmental litigation.[5] Such statements are, however, conspicuously absent in the Australian Constitution.

Admittedly the omissions in relation to environmental protection and environmental rights can be explained by lack of scientific knowledge and sheer ignorance. James Crawford, in his discussion of the extent to which our Constitution is or should be responsive to environmental values, has pointed out that the Founding Fathers had little understanding of the vulnerability of the Australian and global environment, and the capacity of human beings to damage these environments irretrievably. He writes:

> The drafters of the Constitution would have emphasised the immensity of the continent, the difficulties in 'overcoming' it, rather than the fragility of many of its ecosystems or the problems in managing it once

it had been 'overcome'. To the extent that they thought of 'the environment' as a distinct issue, they regarded it as essentially a local issue, that is, one to be left to the States, and like most other issues they saw as local, would not have mentioned it.

(Crawford 1992: 2)

There is, he points out, only one cursory reference to environmental issues in the Constitution (Crawford 1992: 2). This is section 100, which prevents the Commonwealth 'by any law or regulation of trade and commerce' from abridging the rights of a State or its residents 'to the reasonable use of the waters of rivers for conservation or irrigation'. This section was not intended to be an absolute guarantee of environmental rights. It confers a qualified right on the States in respect of the use of rivers and also, to a limited extent, protects the rights of residents of States, but not against State interference (Crawford 1992: 3). It has, thus far, been explicitly confined in its application to Commonwealth laws which deal with trade and commerce (*Commonwealth v Tasmania* (1983) 158 CLR 1, Mason J at 153–5, Murphy J at 182, Brennan J at 248–9) and the Court continued to apply a narrow interpretation of this section in a recent case in which a group of farmers argued unsuccessfully that the section applied to restrictions on their bore licences (*Arnold v Minister administering the Water Management Act 2000* (2010) 240 CLR 242).

Helen Irving has suggested that our Constitution would have looked very different if it had been drafted by a group of Founding Mothers (Irving 1994). In the same way that environmental matters were not mentioned and therefore left, by implication, to the States, so 'the domestic and familial' were consigned by constitutional silence to the States (Irving 1994: 196). She argues that the Constitution reflects 'a male perspective in politics and a "gendered notion" of what was and what was not "essentially federal"' (Irving 1994: 190).

Our Constitution would also look markedly different if it had been drafted by a group of Wild Lawyers or deep ecologists. Constitutional storytelling can incorporate the voices and perspectives of those who played no role in constructing the text. However, constitutional narratives, as they are currently shaped by the High Court, tend to exclude rather than include such alternative perspectives.

Wild law storytelling

Margaret Thornton points out that the process of 'constitutionalisation' necessarily involves the identification and resolution of issues at a 'very high level of abstraction' (Thornton 1999: 754). Within this rarefied sphere, the 'body of an individual complainant' disappears or becomes 'a mere spectre behind the text' (Thornton 1999: 754). Thornton is referring to human bodies but even less visible in constitutional case law is the corporeal presence of other species which are affected, altered, destroyed or protected as an incidental byproduct of the constitutional resolution of issues.

Emotion is also erased from the constitutional realm (Thornton 1999: 755). Thornton observes that 'constitutionalisation legitimises the recounting of narratives that are likely to be unrecognisable to the complainants' (Thornton 1999: 756). Such narratives, despite the rhetoric of justice, neutrality and universality, are still 'storytelling'. They are 'fictionalised accounts' which become 'the authoritative texts of constitutional jurisprudence' and they exclude the perspective of the 'other' (Thornton 1999: 756).

Thornton has highlighted the need for a feminist critique of constitutional law, which requires us to look under its supposed neutrality and universality to the particular (Thornton 1999: 771). Rewriting constitutional stories is part of a broader feminist project, in which feminist scholars have retold 'official court stories' (Sarmas 1994: 703) by focusing on the voices which have been excluded. Wild Law storytelling, or retelling legal narratives from a Wild Law perspective, shares many similarities with this feminist project. Its focus is also on the marginalized, the powerless; its goal is to uncover the biases and partiality in official narratives. However, unlike other forms of alternative storytelling, Wild Law storytelling must try to find a voice for the voiceless. Wild Law storytelling requires us to retell constitutional stories from the perspective of other non-human species, and to question the authority of abstract concepts such as property and trade in an interpretative framework in which these concepts are assumed to be more important than the survival of other species.

Attempting to speak in another's voice, particularly when we can never discover what the 'other' is thinking or feeling, is inherently problematic. As Lisa Sarmas puts it, we are 'silenc[ing] the voices of "others" and ... replac[ing] them with our own more privileged voices' (Sarmas 1994: 727). The legitimacy of such feats of ventriloquism is particularly questionable when the 'other' does not and cannot have a human voice. How can we extrapolate from our human needs and desires and speak for crayfish or thousand-year-old trees with any degree of credibility?

Sarmas also points out that challenging official narratives or 'stock stories' may be counter-productive; 'it is sometimes preferable, indeed necessary, to employ strategies which utilise dominant narratives towards the end of winning the case' (Sarmas 1994: 727). For instance, in the *Tasmanian Dams* case (*Commonwealth v Tasmania* (1983) 158 CLR 1), a conventionally framed, constitutional narrative generated a positive outcome for an area of wilderness and the diverse species contained within it without any judicial acknowledgment of the intrinsic value of wilderness and other species. Thus Wild Law storytelling may well generate the same outcome as that in the original constitutional decision. A wild retelling of the *Tasmanian Dams* case would surely end, as did the case itself, with the Court upholding the legislation which protected the World Heritage area from desecration.

A pragmatist may therefore question the value of wild storytelling. It could, in fact, be argued that a strict adherence to traditional legal reasoning and positivism may be more successful in achieving wild outcomes than wild storytelling which challenges such well-entrenched and seemingly politically neutral traditions.

However, the tradition of legal positivism is not and has never been politically neutral. I agree with Lucinda Finley, who points out in her feminist critique of legal language and legal discourse that the use of dominant narratives 'creates a stark dilemma: in light of the power of existing meanings, can we change the meanings of terms while still using those terms?' (Finley 1989: 908). Wild storytelling is both a challenge and a threat to traditional modes of legal reasoning. Importantly, irrespective of outcome, it is a process by which the dominant paradigm can be shifted. It allows us to envisage different possibilities and new realities. As Thornton points out, 'bringing in the narratives, experiences and perspectives of formerly objectified others is deeply corrosive of the bland constitutionalized abstractions that presently parade across legal texts' (Thornton 1999: 772). When we try to tell constitutional law stories with a different voice, we can see more clearly the fictions and cultural stereotypes which support such abstractions, and we can thus contest their continued legitimacy and authority. We can also expose the fallacies in the oft-expressed view that legal positivism is politically neutral.

The constitutional law narratives which I have selected for the purposes of my wild law storytelling exercise are all, in some way, connected with other species and the ongoing survival of other species. The four narratives are both emblematic and remarkable in their failure to acknowledge and address ecological concerns. Instead, the High Court focused on the scope of the external affairs and other heads of Commonwealth power, the relevance of just terms compensation for a mining company with leases in a World Heritage area, the ability of activists to conduct their protest activities in restricted areas, and the permissible restrictions on the trade of live crayfish between the States.

Wilderness (and wild bodies) as taboo

The *Tasmanian Dams* case (*Commonwealth v Tasmania* (1983) 158 CLR 1) is an appropriate starting point for this exercise. The case determined the fate of an extraordinary area of wilderness in southwest Tasmania, an area widely acknowledged to have outstanding natural and cultural value by the World Heritage Committee when it was included on the World Heritage List in 1982. This area, however, had been set aside by the then Tasmanian government for the construction of a dam, a development which would have destroyed many of the unique characteristics of this area of wilderness. In 1983, a newly elected Commonwealth government under the leadership of

Bob Hawke enacted legislation to prevent the construction of the dam. The matter then came before the High Court. The Court's task was to decide on the constitutional validity of the Commonwealth legislation.

Although the High Court could hardly fail to be aware of the political significance of the case, and the contentious nature of the dispute between the Commonwealth and Tasmanian governments over the fate of this area of wilderness, the judges took great pains to ostensibly distance themselves from the political issues. They maintained, with the conviction of committed legal positivists, that they were deciding the case purely on its legal issues. This point was clearly made in their preface to their judgements in which they stated that 'the Court is in no way concerned with the question whether it is desirable or undesirable, either on the whole or from any particular point of view, that the construction of the dam should proceed' (at 58–9).

As if that were not enough, Gibbs CJ and Deane J reiterated in their judgements that the Court was dealing only with legal issues, and that it was not up to the judges to decide whether the construction of the dam should proceed (Gibbs CJ at 60, Deane J at 250.). Even more poignantly, according to Phillip Toyne, the Court refused to view photographs of the Franklin River lest such images 'inflame the minds of the Court with irrelevancies' (Toyne 1994: 44) and corrupt their otherwise purist examination of the scope of the external affairs, corporations and race heads of power.

Outside the courtroom, the High Court judges could not possibly have avoided the extensive media coverage of the Franklin Dam blockade and the widely circulated photographs of the threatened area of wilderness, in particular Peter Dombrovskis' iconic image of Rock Island Bend in the Franklin River. Images of the Franklin River and commentary on the blockade were everywhere in the period prior to the pivotal 1983 federal election which swept the Hawke government into power, with a significant percentage of voters writing 'No Dams' on their ballot papers. Yet in the *Tasmanian Dams* case, wilderness was the unacknowledged subtext to an exhaustive (and constitutionally groundbreaking) exposition of the scope and ambit of Commonwealth constitutional powers. This case was indeed an illustration of wilderness as taboo.

It is easy to understand why the judges sought refuge in positivist reasoning, particularly when their conclusions had such an overtly political impact. This apparent disavowal of politicized and emotive reasoning on the part of the judges did not protect them from a barrage of criticism. Critics denounced the majority judges for their seemingly radical departure from constitutional orthodoxy.

It was not only wilderness which was ignored in the *Tasmanian Dams* case. The 2,613 participants (The Wilderness Society 1983: 9) in the Franklin Dam blockade, described by one commentator as Australia's 'most celebrated' environmental blockade (Bonyhady 1993: 50), had used their bodies to defend wilderness in what was often a carefully choreographed 'theatre on the river' (Cohen 1997: 67). Yet their highly effective embodied performances of protest are neither documented nor acknowledged in the constitutional sacred text which is the *Tasmanian Dams* case. The wild bodies, which had confronted barges in duckie flotillas, deliberately trespassed on Hydro-electric Commission property, climbed crane booms, and languished in Risdon Gaol after refusing to accept bail conditions which prevented their return to the wild, have also been erased from the *Tasmanian Dams* case.

How can we reinsert these missing elements in the constitutional narrative? Where were these wild bodies while the High Court deliberated over its findings? We find a clue in one blockader's narrative. It was July 1983. It was freezing cold, midwinter in southern Tasmania. She and a small committed group of blockaders were maintaining their vigil around a campfire in the Tasmanian wilderness, at the site of the proposed dam. We can locate some of the missing wild bodies in her moving account of the nerve-wracking wait for the outcome of the High Court's decision:

> The 10 a.m. news came and went with no mention of the subject uppermost in our minds... During the interminable wait some of us knitted and crocheted or chewed fingernails, while others whittled. Apprehension was a lump in my throat, my belly. Then, suddenly, the crackly voice of the newsreader: 'The dam cannot be built; I repeat, the dam cannot be built.'
>
> (The Wilderness Society 1983: 119)

What did the protesters think about the High Court's refusal to acknowledge the importance of wilderness in its decision? This narrator adopts a pragmatic perspective, writing that 'although the High Court judgement was made without the question of wilderness, with all its intrinsic worth, being raised, it is a positive affirmation of all that is natural, infinite, whole' (The Wilderness Society 1983: 119). In fact, the High Court decision was not politically radical in the Court's adherence to positivist reasoning and eschewal of ecocentric viewpoints; in fact, it highlights the resistance of constitutional law discourse to the values and tenets of ecocentrism or Wild Law.

Nor did the decision necessarily pave the way for further environmental victories. The expanded definition of the external affairs head of power,[6] which provided much of the constitutional significance of the decision, can easily have adverse environmental consequences. Not all international treaties and conventions impose human rights and environmental responsibilities upon nation states. The so-called 'free trade' agreements strengthen corporate domination of the global economy at the expense of human rights and at the expense of the environment. It is ironic that an expansive interpretation of the Commonwealth's external affairs head of power not only facilitated the domestic implementation of treaties which protect human rights and the environment, but also facilitated the implementation of treaties which intensify the control of multinational corporations over the Australian economy, and weaken our existing standards in the areas of human rights and environmental protection.

One commentator has described the decision as 'at best, a minor setback to the conquest of nature in Australia' (Lines 2006: 217).

Sterilizing the wild

Some six years after the *Tasmanian Dams* case, the Hawke government was embroiled in yet another environmental controversy over the fate of Coronation Hill in the Northern Territory. This area was both ecologically and culturally significant, as a sacred site for the Jawoyn people. After a Resources Assessment Commission inquiry into the feasibility of mining operations in Coronation Hill, the government eventually decided to incorporate the area within Kakadu National Park. The mining industry was incensed by this outcome, which meant that further mining operations were prohibited. According to Hugh Morgan, Managing Director of Western Mining Corporation, the decision was a 'shocking defeat', akin to 'the fall of Singapore in 1942' and an attack on the nation's prosperity (Hamilton 1996: 15). In the *Newcrest* decision (*Newcrest Mining (WA) Ltd v Commonwealth* (1997) 190 CLR 513), the High Court had to determine whether Newcrest, as the holder of existing mining leases over parcels of land in Coronation Hill, had a constitutional entitlement to compensation.

Some of Newcrest's mining leases were gold mining leases and others were mineral leases. The Commonwealth had not acquired these leases, nor Newcrest's property rights in the relevant minerals, by including Coronation Hill within a World Heritage area. However, as two judges observed, the 1991 Commonwealth proclamation 'sterilised the benefits' which otherwise might have flowed to Newcrest as a consequence of these leases (Brennan J at 530-1, Gummow J at 635). The majority judges concluded that depriving Newcrest of the benefits of its mining leases amounted to an acquisition of property and thereby attracted the operation of the just terms compensation provision in section 51(xxxi) of the Constitution. However Justice McHugh, in his dissenting judgement, pointed out that 'both as a matter of substance and form, the Commonwealth obtained nothing which it did not already have' (McHugh J at 573).

From a Wild Law perspective, the omissions and exclusions in the High Court judgements are all the more startling given the use of the terminology of sterilization in relation to property rights. In a wild retelling of the *Newcrest* case, the focus would surely be on other forms of sterilization. Coronation Hill is located in the heart of what the Jawoyn people refer to as 'sickness country'. It is the resting place of Bula, the Jawoyn people's creation god; if disturbed they believe that he will become angry and unleash a wave of destruction (Hamilton 1996: 4). What, in fact, would have been sterilized or rendered impotent according to this system of knowledge if the proclamation had not been made? The Jawoyn people believe that it is mining which would have destructive if not completely apocalyptic consequences for humanity. According to the Jawoyn people, 'to desecrate this site, also known as sickness country, would be akin to opening the gates of Western society's hell and letting a demon loose' (*Koori Mail* 1991: 1).

Despite the mining industry's scepticism about the validity and credibility of the Jawoyn people's claims, the Hawke government agreed that Coronation Hill should be protected. The invocation of the terminology of sterilization in relation to Newcrest's property rights can be viewed as a form of colonizing appropriation and inversion of Jawoyn arguments about 'sickness country' but also, interestingly, as an appropriation and inversion of the arguments of environmentalists about the destructive impact of mining on the 'ecological integrity' of the area.[7]

The High Court paid no heed to the relevance of sterilization in other contexts and other systems of knowledge while considering the constitutional significance of the sterilization of property rights. The looming threat of sterilization posed by mining for an almost pristine area of wilderness, and the destructive sterilization of humanity which could ensue if a creation god (or significant uranium deposits) were disturbed and the consequences of widespread radiation were felt, were absent from the constitutional debate. Instead, the High Court focused upon the sterilization of something with meaning only in law, the sterilization of an abstraction which lies at the heart of our legal system: namely, property rights.

It is quite apparent from the judgements in the *Newcrest* case that property rights are of paramount importance in the abstract worldview of constitutional law. Justice Kirby in particular drew upon a number of international Declarations and other constitutions (at 657–60) in support of his argument that provision for just compensation in the event of governmental interference with property rights is a 'universal and fundamental' human right, an essential requirement in a 'civilised society' (at 660). Yet the environmental ramifications of interpreting a so-called sterilization of property rights as acquisition seemed to be lost on all the judges. Karla Sperling has drawn parallels between this blinkered reasoning and the reasoning of United States judges in the 'taking' cases, which have effectively thwarted a number of governmental interventions to restrict land use in the public interest (Sperling 1997: 432).

Justice Callinan, in a later case, would invoke the sterilization arguments from the *Newcrest* case in commenting on the Court's findings in the *Tasmanian Dams* case. In the following extract, the extent to which the sterilization of property rights can overshadow the more pertinent issues of loss of wilderness, and the potential sterilization or elimination of natural ecosystems by inappropriate development, is clearly apparent. In constitutional terms, it would seem that only the proprietary status of wilderness has any meaning; the legal focus is on the capacity of human stakeholders to exploit and to continue to exploit its 'conventional, commercially exploitable attributes'.

> The very nature of the Commonwealth's powers and the flexibility and ingenuity with which they can be exercised mean that what a dispossessed owner has lost, in the hands of the Commonwealth or some other beneficiary of the Commonwealth's enactment, may assume an entirely different, even elusive shape or character, from what it possessed earlier. After the enactment of the legislation to ensure placement of the region of the Franklin River in Tasmania upon the World Heritage List, that region remained in exactly the same natural state, and title to it continued to reside in the State of Tasmania, as it had before that enactment. But in proprietary terms it had assumed a quite different character. It had become an area of land from which almost all of the conventional, commercially exploitable attributes had been stripped or rendered highly conditional. In short, almost all of the components of the sum of the property rights had been effectively taken away. To use the language of Gaudron and Gummow JJ in the present matter, there was also 'an effective sterilisation [of many] of the rights constituting the property in question'.
>
> (*Smith v ANL* (2000) 204 CLR 493, per Callinan J at 547)

This is an extreme expression of the philosophical approach to private property which dominates constitutional law and is manifested so clearly in the *Newcrest* decision: a sensitivity to the need to protect property owners from governmental interference with their property rights, and an apparent insensitivity to the deleterious ecological consequences of failure on the part of governments to control the exercise of such property rights in vulnerable environments.

The obdurate activist

I have already commented on the erasure of the wild bodies of the Franklin Dam blockade activists from the constitutional narrative of the *Tasmanian Dams* case. In the *Levy* case (*Levy v Victoria* (1997) 189 CLR 579), also known as the duck shooting case, the Court was required to consider whether the wild bodies of activists were engaged in a form of political communication and, if so, whether their activities attracted some form of constitutional protection.

Animal rights activist Laurence Levy had been charged under the *Wildlife (Game) (Hunting Season) Regulations 1994* (Vic) with entering a permitted hunting area during prohibited times without a licence. He argued that the

Regulations were invalid insofar as they prevented him from protesting about duck hunting and protesting about the Victorian legislation which facilitiated and legalized this activity. Levy's presence in designated duck hunting areas was not only designed as a form of protest. Levy and his supporters also entered these areas to retrieve wounded and dead ducks, including members of protected species.

Levy was relying upon a recently discovered implied freedom of political communication (*Australian Capital Television v Commonwealth* (1992) 177 CLR 106; *Nationwide News v Wills* (1992) 177 CLR 1) in arguing that the Regulations, which inhibited him in his attempts to convey a potent political message about duck hunting to the Australian population, were invalid. The judges were prepared to acknowledge that Levy was engaged in a form of political communication (*Levy v Victoria*, Brennan CJ at 594–5, Toohey and Gummow JJ at 613, McHugh J at 622–3 and Kirby J at 637–8). Non-verbal direct action fell within this category; in fact, as McHugh J pointed out, political communication encompasses 'signs, symbols, gestures and images' (McHugh J at 622–3). It is, however, clear that, from a judicial perspective, some forms of political communication are more privileged and credible than others. McHugh J acknowledged that the implied freedom extended to 'false, unreasoned and emotional communications as well as true, reasoned and detached communications' (McHugh J at 623); this juxtaposition of adjectives suggests that the emotive, including imagery designed to trigger an emotive response, is to be distrusted whereas the path to truth lies in reasoned and dispassionate argument. As Lucinda Finley has observed, 'law is a language firmly committed to the "reason" side of the reason/emotion dichotomy' (Finley 1989: 892).

The judicial acceptance of direct action as a persuasive form of political communication constitutes an important milestone for environmental activists. The image events produced by environmentalists who engage in direct action are more than attention-grabbing devices. They are, Kevin De Luca maintains, designed to 'move the meanings of fundamental ideographs' (De Luca 1999: 52) such as progress and nature (De Luca 1999: 46). Protesters, physically enact and demonstrate their interdependence with nature through the strategic placement of their bodies in areas of threatened wilderness, and thus contest not only the meaning of key ideographs but also the anthropocentric assumption that human beings dominate nature (De Luca 1999: 56). This process of displacing key assumptions and contesting meanings can be, in De Luca's view, as profoundly unsettling as Foucault's experience upon reading Borges' description of the fictitious, and to the Western brain, wildly improbable categories in a Chinese encyclopaedia (De Luca 1999: 52). Direct action is a subversive and highly effective form of political communication, in that it can challenge our most fundamental assumptions about humanity and the natural world.

Notwithstanding this important judicial concession, the *Levy* case was hardly a victory for animal rights activists. The court acknowledged that the Regulations had a restrictive impact on political communication and prevented Levy and his colleagues from communicating their message in the most effective way possible. Nevertheless the Regulations were valid as they were reasonably appropriate and adapted to achieving an end which was 'compatible with the maintenance of the constitutionally prescribed system of representative and responsible government and the procedure prescribed by section 128' (Brennan CJ at 599, Dawson J at 608-9, Toohey and Gummow JJ at 614-15, Gaudron J at 619, McHugh J at 626-7 and Kirby J at 648). This end was the protection of public safety. As Justice Dawson put it, the legitimate end was that of 'ensuring the safety of persons with conflicting aims who would be likely to be present in the vicinity of duck shooting at the opening of the 1994 season' (Dawson J at 609).

This statement is revealing. Restrictions on access to duck shooting areas did not affect the general public. The Regulations were designed to protect animal rights activists like Levy from risking their own lives to save the lives of members of other species. Environmental direct action is a performative enactment of various ideologies, including an ecocentric ideology. The vast majority of participants are engaged in performances which express their own values and philosophical position on humans, nature and wilderness. Protesters place their vulnerable bodies between death-dealing weapons and machinery and other living non-human species in defiant challenge. They are prepared to risk their lives for other species and this is a tangible demonstration of their commitment to the discourse of ecocentrism, according to which humans do not dominate nature but co-exist with and within nature (De Luca 1999: 52-4).

In enacting and upholding legislation which prevented such performances, the State and the court were expressing quite different values, anthropocentric values which assume that human beings dominate nature and that human lives are more important than the lives of other species. In a wild retelling of the *Levy* case, the wellbeing and protection of other species would be as important as considerations of public safety in evaluating the validity of legislation which restricts the activities of animal rights activists.

The crayfish as citation

It may seem peculiar to conclude my wild retelling of constitutional law with *Cole v Whitfield* (1988) 165 CLR 360 (*Cole v Whitfield*), the unanimous constitutional law decision which finally settled the interpretation of section 92 of the Constitution after decades of extensive litigation. After all, section 92 is about freedom of trade and commerce and this, one would have thought, is a subject far removed from Wild Law even if the environmental implications of section 92 have attracted some academic commentary (Crawford 1992; Taberner and Lee 1991).

In *Cole v Whitfield*, in the High Court's discussion of section 92 and its drafting and litigious history, there is no judicial expression of concern for the objects, or living entities, being traded. There is certainly no reference to the underlying ethical issues which might arise in relation to such trade. However, the judgement in *Cole v Whitfield* opens with extracts from a statement of agreed facts from the magistrate's court (*Cole v Whitfield* at 380–1) and here we find some of the missing Wild Law subtext.

The respondents operated and managed the Boomer Park Crayfish Farm in Tasmania, a business which bought and marketed live crayfish throughout Tasmania, Australia and overseas. They had purchased crayfish from South Australia; of these, 60 male and 37 female crayfish were under the prescribed size for crayfish in Tasmania. The respondents were charged with possession of undersized crayfish. The following three 'facts', reproduced from this document, gesture towards the sufferings and fate of the controversial crayfish and yet, from the judicial perspective, these facts are completely irrelevant to any interpretation of section 92.

(a) The crayfish in question were brought to Tasmania chilled but still alive in packages. They were put into saltwater ponds to revive them.
(b) Those sufficiently revived were chilled in brine to minus five degrees centigrade and shipped in bags to the United States of America.
(c) Those that did not revive sufficiently were held by the Respondents pending final determination as to their disposal.

(*Cole v Whitfield* at 381)

The Court's concern in *Cole v Whitfield* was to clarify the interpretation of a constitutional section for which 'judicial exegesis ... has yielded neither clarity of meaning nor certainty of operation' (at 384). In so doing, the judges had to revisit 'the approximately 140 decisions of this Court and of the Privy Council which have attempted to illuminate the meaning and operation of the section' (at 385) and look at constitutional history. Ultimately, they adopted an interpretation 'favoured by history and context' (at 407), concluding that section 92 was offended by discriminatory laws of a protectionist kind. This outcome of *Cole v Whitfield* is well understood.

In applying this test to the Tasmanian Regulation which prohibited possession of undersized crayfish, the Court held that there was no discriminatory protectionist purpose (at 409–410). Instead, the Regulation was designed for the 'protection and conservation of an important and valuable natural resource, the stock of Tasmanian crayfish' (at 409). It could not be enforced effectively without also applying to imported crayfish.

The crayfish have no real role to play in this constitutional story. Their individual sufferings as they were chilled, partially revived, and chilled again (or disposed of), are irrelevant. As a species, they constitute 'an important and valuable natural resource' because of their commercial rather than intrinsic value. They are effectively excluded from the 'institutions, codes, interests and the corporeality of power relations' (Threadgold 1997: 214) which comprise constitutional law. In writing about the exclusion of battered women who kill their husbands from the network of power relations which make up the law, Terry Threadgold has pointed out that:

> stereotypes ... rush to fill the semiotic void of your exclusion. There you may well be read as a citation of a story you were never in, heard as performatively enacting realities you never knew, written as other by men whose categories cannot contain you.
> (Threadgold 1997: 214)

This, indeed, is the lasting fate of the 97 long deceased, undersized, crayfish delivered to the Boomer Park Crayfish Farm in 1982; they are nothing more than a citation in a celebrated constitutional narrative about permissible restrictions on trade and commerce.

Conclusion

This wild retelling exercise has highlighted some significant impediments to the incorporation of Wild Law principles into Australian constitutional law. For High Court judges, and indeed most judges, violence against nature and other species remains an abstraction. Patricia Wald states that violence against the environment 'is only a fledgling idea in the law, implemented sporadically in practice' (Wald 1992: 103). In contrast, violence directed towards other species becomes tangible, threatening and very real for environmental activists who interpose their bodies between machinery and weapons, and trees and other creatures.

Furthermore, judges lack the awareness of place which is, according to De Luca, 'the keystone to resistance to industrialism now and then' (De Luca 1999: 159). Environmental activists often physically embed themselves in a region and create a corporeal physical relationship with place (De Luca 1999: 160). Legal performances, on the other hand, are overtly separated from place. Courtrooms are what Victor Turner would describe as liminal or threshold spaces (Turner 1987: 34), physically divorced from the conflicts which are resolved therein. In these spaces, 'a distanced replication' of the conflict is presented (Turner 1987: 34).

I would suggest that wild constitutional law is impossible without some form of experiential rethinking on the part for the High Court judges, a process which must involve being embedded in place and in contact with other species. The legal performances of constitutional law and the parameters of constitutional argument must incorporate both place and the non-human. It is only through creating new and innovative performances of constitutional law, performances which are both located in and celebrate place, that missing bodies and endangered places will find some belated recognition in the sacred texts of constitutional case law.

Rather than focusing on textual limitations, Wild Lawyers must address the existing performative and ideological barriers to the recognition of Wild Law principles in Australian constitutional law.

Notes

1 The procedure in section 128 must be followed, which requires a majority of voters in a majority of States to vote in favour of the proposed change in a constitutional referendum. Only eight of forty four such referenda have been successful.
2 This expansive reading is apparent, for instance, in the *Tasmanian Dams* case (*Commonwealth v Tasmania* (1983) 158 CLR 1) discussed below. In the context of environmental management, as James Crawford has noted, the expansive reading of Commonwealth powers has conferred upon the Commonwealth power to legislate in relation to 'most large-scale mining and environmental matters' (Crawford 1991: 30).
3 Most famously, the Court found an implied freedom of political communication in two cases in 1992: *Australian Capital Television v Commonwealth* (1992) 177 CLR 106 and *Nationwide News v Wills* (1992) 177 CLR 1. The judges elaborated on the scope and application of the implied freedom in a sequence of cases including *Levy v Victoria* (1997) 189 CLR 579 discussed below.
4 See, for instance, *Kable v Director of Public Prosecutions (NSW)* (1996) 189 CLR 51, *South Australia v Totani* (2010) 242 CLR 1 and *Wainohu v New South Wales* (2011) 243 CLR 181 as examples of the application of the separation of judicial power to protect individual rights.
5 May and Daly cite a number of such cases (May and Daly 2011: 333-335) while also arguing that successful constitutional environmental litigation requires the overcoming of substantial hurdles. One of the most well-known of these cases is *Re Minors Oposa v Secretary of the Department of Environment and Natural Resources* (1994) 33 ILM 174, which the Philippino Supreme Court held that logging contracts violated the constitutional right of the people and future generations to 'a balanced and healthful ecology in accord with the rhythm and harmony of nature'.
6 The most expansive reading of the external affairs head of power appears in the judgment of Murphy J, who explained his interpretation in terms of the global imperative for environmental protection: 'Again, suppose that in the next few decades, because of the continuing rapid depletion of the world's forests and its effect on the rest of the biosphere, the survival of all living creatures becomes endangered. This is not a fanciful supposition; see The Global 2000 Report to the President of the United States, (1980). Suppose the United Nations were to request all nations to do whatever they could to preserve the existing forests. Let us assume that no obligation was created (because firewood

was essential for the immediate survival of people of some nations). I would have no doubt that the Australian Parliament could, under the external affairs power, comply with that request by legislating to prevent the destruction of any forest, including any State forest. Again, without any treaty but in order to avert threatened military or economic sanctions by another nation, the Parliament could legislate on a subject which was otherwise outside power' at 170–171.
7   According to Clive Hamilton (Hamilton 1996: 6), 'the idea of the integrity of the Park underlay much of the deliberation' over the issue of mining at Coronation Hill, and the potential impact of mining operations on the ecological integrity of the Park was a major concern for environmentalists.

References

Bird, G. 'Sacred text: reading the father's law', paper presented at Australasian Law and Society Conference, La Trobe University, Melbourne, December 1996.
Bonyhady, T. (1993) *Places Worth Keeping: Conservationists, Politics and Law*, Sydney: Allen and Unwin.
Cohen, I. (1997) *Green Fire*, Sydney: Angus and Robertson.
Coper, M. (1987) *Encounters with the Australian Constitution*, North Ryde: CCH Australia.
Crawford, J. (1991) 'The Constitution and the environment', *Sydney Law Review*, 13: 11–30.
Crawford, J. (1992) 'The Constitution', in T. Bonyhady (ed.) *Environmental Protection and Legal Change*, Sydney: Federation Press.
De Luca, K.M. (1999) *Image Politics. The New Rhetoric of Environmental Activism*, London and New York: Guilford Press.
Finley, L. (1989) 'Breaking women's silence in law: the dilemma of the gendered nature of legal reasoning', *Notre Dame Law Review*, 64: 886–910.
Galsworthy, J. (1906) *The Man of Property*, New York and London: G P Putnam's Sons.
Hamilton, C. (1996) 'Mining in Kakadu. Lessons from Coronation Hill', a lecture presented to the Parliamentary Library 'Vital Issues' Seminar Series, Parliament House, Canberra, 19 June; online. Available at: <www.tai.org.au/file.php?file=discussion_papers/DP9.pdf> (accessed 1 October 2012).
Irving, H. (1994) 'A gendered constitution? Women, federation and heads of power', *Western Australian Law Review*, 24: 186–98.
Koori Mail (1991) 'Court decision will not end coronation dispute', 19 June, 1.
Lines, W.J. (2006) *Defending Australia's Natural Heritage*, St Lucia: University of Queensland Press.
May, J.R. and Daly, E. (2011) 'Constitutional environmental rights worldwide', in J.R. May (ed.) *Principles of Constitutional Environmental Law*, Chicago, IL: American Bar Association.
Sawer, G. (1967) *Australian Federalism in the Courts*, Melbourne: Melbourne University Press.
Sarmas, L. (1994) 'Storytelling and the law: a case study of *Louth v Diprose*', *Melbourne University Law Review*, 19: 701–28.

Sperling, K. (1997) 'Going down the takings path: Private property rights and public interest in land use decision-making', *Environmental and Planning Law Journal*, 14: 427–36.

Taberner, J.G. and Lee, D.J. (1991) 'Section 92 and the environment', *Australian Law Journal*, 65: 266–9.

The Wilderness Society (1983) *Franklin Blockade by the Blockaders*, Hobart: The Wilderness Society.

Thornton, M. (1999) 'Towards embodied justice: Wrestling with legal ethics in the age of the "new corporatism"', *Melbourne University Law Review*, 23: 749–72.

Threadgold, T. (1997) 'Performativity, regulative fictions, huge stabilities: Framing battered women's syndrome', *Law Text Culture*, 3: 210–31.

Toyne, P. (1994) *The Reluctant Nation*, Sydney: ABC Books.

Turner, V. (1987) *The Anthropology of Performance*, New York: PAJ Publications.

Wald, P.M. (1992) 'Violence under the law. A judge's perspective', in A. Sarat and T.R. Kearns (eds) *Law's Violence*, Ann Arbor, MI: University of Michigan Press.

Part III

The rights of nature

Chapter 9

Decolonizing personhood

Erin Fitz-Henry

At a time when the dominant approaches to environmental protection at the UNEP and among the major conservation organizations remain unequivocally marked-based and corporate-sponsored, it is perhaps not surprising that, all across the social sciences and humanities, the narrowly anthropocentric definitions of nature's value that implicitly undergird such approaches are being challenged by scholars working in the post-human tradition (Latour 1998; Plumwood 2009; Bennett 2010; Kirksey and Helmreich 2010; Morton 2010). However, what *is* surprising – at least from the perspective of critical social scientists – is that the principal social movements involved in attempting to expand conceptualizations of how properly to honour the multitude of natures that surround us (beyond the dominant 'natural capital' and 'ecosystem services' frameworks) have received so little attention up until now. So complete, in fact, has been the neglect among critical human geographers and environmental anthropologists that as recently as 2012 Kenneth MacDonald and Catherine Corson (2012) have been able to lament what they see as a 'striking reduction in the opposition to the idea of a natural world defined as capital' (Arsel and Buscher 2012: 57). As Noel Castree (2003) has recently summarized in an important review article, the treatment of nature as a form of 'natural capital' (or, in other terms, the 'neoliberalization of nature') has become ubiquitous in policy circles as natural resources throughout much of the global south are privatized, subjected to eighteenth-century style enclosure, 'conserved' via NGO-corporate partnerships that frequently bypass the state, priced in dogmatically quantitative terms that often feel reductive to the communities that surround them, and traded on new ecosystem markets (Castree 2003, 2008a, 2008b; Bakker 2005; Heynen et al. 2007).

So ubiquitous has this orientation become that, from the perspective of theorists like Bram Buscher and Murat Arsel, there is simply little in the way of formidable resistance to it (Arsel and Buscher 2012; MacDonald and Corson 2012; Peluso 2012). Nature has become yet another trademarked commodity: Nature, Inc. The prolific geographer Erik Swyngedouw (2013) has perhaps best described this 'post-political environmental consensus' about the necessity of market-solutions to market-problems in the most discouraging of terms. As he summarizes:

> [That] consensus is one that is radically reactionary, one that forestalls the articulation of divergent, conflicting, and alternative trajectories of future environmental possibilities and assemblages. There is no contestation over the givens of the situation… there is only debate over the technologies of management, the timing of their implementation, the arrangements of policing, and the interests of those whose stake is already acknowledged, whose voice is recognized as legitimate.
> (Swyngedouw 2013: 4)

While the continued quantification and commodification of ecosystem services is unquestionably the dominant trend among those 'whose voice is recognized as legitimate,' on the streets from Philadelphia, Pennsylvania to Quito, Ecuador, a wide-ranging conversation is unfolding about the degree to which nature can be said to have a very different kind of value – that is, the rights and legal protections of something like human personhood. This is a conversation that, in the United States, has aimed to embolden local communities in their struggles against the natural gas industry by re-asserting local democratic practices long submerged or sidelined by environmental decision-making at the state level. And it is one that, in much of Andean Latin America, seeks to extend conceptions of human personhood to rivers and mines and wetlands in ways that are both radically novel (given the region's deeply rooted legacies of colonial racism) and continuous with indigenous visions and histories (de la Cadena 2010). It is in Ecuador – the first country in the world to include the rights of nature in its constitution – that these processes are currently most visible, and it is from there that this article proceeds.

In what follows, building principally on environmental theorists of and from Latin America, I argue that students of the neoliberalization of nature would do well to attend more closely to the plethora of rights-based movements – particularly in the Global South – that are at the forefront of contesting the ongoing capitalization of nature at the hands of transnational corporations and their government allies. But just as importantly, and this is the crucial second part of my argument, because this neo-liberalism is so deeply entrenched (in the form of rapidly proliferating 'green economy' experts and UN-sponsored workshops on 'sustainable growth'), students of the rights of nature on the other hand would do well to listen more closely to the perspectives of those who either resist such a rights-framework, find it of limited use, or attempt to co-opt it for ends that are insufficiently sustainable.

In recent years, lawyers have provided solid and subtle defences of the philosophical viability, soundness, and necessity of earth justice (Burdon 2011, 2012; Cullinan 2011), and some (notably, Burdon) have pointed to the limitations of fundamentally individualizing rights-discourses in the absence of broader market reforms. However, few – at least in English-language publications – have robustly engaged the tangled specificities of the political terrain on which those rights are actually being implemented and, more specifically, the often conflicting ways in which they are currently being both imagined and defended against by actors across the NGO-government-corporate spectrum. Given the epistemic omnipresence of assertions that the green economy is the only way forward, we need to worry actively, it seems to me, about the ways in which the movement for the rights of nature (or what some have called, this 'dream of a new beginning') is being heard, contested, and transformed on the ground in particular cultural contexts.

I should be clear at the outset, however, that I am not offering a critique of the rights of nature movement in Ecuador. Quito-based activists and lawyers are working long hours to push for the development of secondary legislation which will further concretize these rights and to challenge the forms in which they are currently being instantiated in environmental codes. I do not mean to diminish their work in the least. Indeed, I am keenly aware that the shift in consciousness that Thomas Berry hoped would be initiated by an extension of law to the natural world is a shift that will likely take generations and, along the way, occasion its fair share of ridicule and rejection.

On the contrary, my aim in this chapter is to explore the ways in which ideas about the rights of nature are being understood, ignored, contested, and reshaped on the ground in Ecuador today as the country undergoes what leftist-populist President Rafael Correa calls, 'a citizen's revolution'. More specifically, I explore the limitations of such rights in the context of the government's largest development project to date – the construction of a 300,000 barrel-a-day oil refinery and petrochemical complex in the coastal province of Manabi. By exploring in fine-grained ethnographic detail the ways in which the rights of nature articles from the constitution of 2008 are being understood and implemented by a diversity of actors concerned with the Refinery of the Pacific, I argue that rights-discourses in Ecuador – while productive of important conceptual expansions – are currently being read by many not as a form of necessary intellectual and moral decolonization by which to shake off the shackles of the excessively anthropocentric 'Rights of Man' that restrict the moral community to the human, but as a kind of posturing on the international stage that is either (a) essentially useless, (b) secondary to the demands of a much more pressing anti-neoliberalism, or (c) consistently trumped by sets of competing rights.

The rights of nature in coastal Ecuador

On 24 July 2008, in the dusty inland city of Montecristi in Ecuador's westernmost coastal province, the Constituent Assembly convened by newly-elected leftist president, Rafael Correa, approved the most far-reaching draft constitution the country has ever produced. Approved by 94 of the 130 assembly-people dominated by Correa's political party, Alianza Pais, the constitution became the first in the world to recognize what it called, 'the rights of nature'. Part of a broader shift in overall development framework – from the straightforward economic growth that has long been pushed by Western economic experts to *sumak kawsay*, or ecologically harmonious 'good living' – those rights are spelled out most substantially in articles 71–4. 'Nature, or Pacha Mama', begins Article 71, 'where life is reproduced and occurs, has the right to integral respect for its existence and for the maintenance and regeneration of its life cycles, structure, functions and evolutionary processes' (Ecuadorian constitution 2008). While the vagueness and breadth of this assertion make it difficult to either contest or to implement consistently, article 72 makes matters somewhat more concrete, legalizing the rights of all communities – and not just those directly affected by environmental damage who traditionally have legal 'standing' – to bring cases on behalf of nature into Ecuadorian courts. And article 73 goes on to demand specific actions on the part of the state when the projected violence done to a given ecosystem is likely to be permanent. The text summarizes: 'The State shall apply preventive and restrictive measures on activities that might lead to the extinction of species, the destruction of ecosystems and the permanent alteration of natural cycles.' In a country that has seen billions of gallons of crude oil spilled in the Amazon by Chevron-Texaco and the state-owned PetroEcuador, the intensification of Canadian-led mining throughout the cordillera, the second worst rate of deforestation on the continent, and, since 1990, some of the most sophisticated and systematic indigenous organizing in the Western hemisphere, it was perhaps only a matter of time before nature would be granted such historic rights in Ecuador.

Observers of the Ecuadorian constitutional process have paid important attention to the philosophical and legal complexities involved in this extension of moral personhood to ecosystems – both celebrating and worrying about the radical shift that it entails from visions of nature as 'property' to visions of nature as 'person' (Gudynas 2009a, 2009b). In her introduction to the 2011 edited collection, *La Naturaleza con Derechos*, Esperanza Martinez, for example, persuasively argues for a (somewhat clichéd, but nevertheless crucial) rupture with those foundations of Cartesian thought that have pitted nature against culture, and that have thereby allowed the former to be consistently constructed as mere 'property'. To effect this rupture, Martinez argues, is to continue the work of decolonization that began over four centuries ago with the resistance to the Spanish occupation. The philosophical trajectories of Andean thought so long ago repressed by that occupation – with their focus not on an unproductive and ultimately destructive separation of nature and culture, but on complementarity, relationality, and multi-tiered exchange – provide increasingly important counterweights, she believes, to the excessively mechanistic and externalizing constructions of nature that continue to undergird its status in Western law as property. It is thus in dialogue with contemporary Andean communities that we can recover a long-subjugated 'cosmovision' that recognizes nature not as a thing or a what, as activists in Quito often point out, but a being and a whom. As Martinez summarizes: 'The capacity to understand what other species are saying, to read what Nature is expressing through her changes... this we can learn *only* in intercultural dialogue with those communities who maintain close relationships with nature' (Martinez and Acosta 2011: 16).

But while supporters of the rights of nature in Ecuador have made strong claims for the necessity of something like a thorough-going decolonization of Western legal thought via a return to the suppressed traditions and trajectories of the pre-hispanic Andean world, a range of scholars in Latin America have questioned this focus on rights. Many have done so not because of the standard legal worries about the degree to which nature can be said to have will or intentionality (necessary for the prosecution of rights) or because of the widespread 'judicialization of the state' that has accompanied the retraction of the welfare state in many parts of the world (in which rights become imperfect and distracting replacements for a fundamentally broken social contract), but precisely because of what they take to be a romanticized essentialization of Andean thought (Comaroff and Comaroff 2008; Mansilla 2011a, 2011b; Sanchez-Parga 2011). From their perspective, this return to 'animism' is a form of what Gayatri Spivak would call 'strategic essentialism' that is being used primarily to divert attention from the core dynamics of capitalism that continue to lead inevitably to the commodification of nature. The enemy, in this view, is not Western anthropocentrism per se, but the dynamics of predatory capitalism; the challenge is not to undo too strict a legal dichotomy between property and person, but to challenge the 'fetishism of commodities' by which *all* beings are emptied of their livingness; and the solution is not some semi-mystical return to the 'invented traditions' of Andean cosmologies, but a frontal attack on the violence of neoliberal economics. Much as Charles Hale has explored the ways in which discourses of multiculturalism have been used by neoliberal governments throughout Latin America to simultaneously present the appearance of indigenous inclusiveness while blocking the sorts of actual economic reforms that might result in indigenous sovereignty, critics fear that the rights of nature or the rights of Pachamama (the Incan mother-goddess) are similarly little more than a 'reactionary utopianism' that wraps in the fashionable air of 'postmodern animism' projects that are more environmentally damaging than ever before (Hale 2002; Sanchez-Parga 2011). Indeed, as Eduardo Gudynas (2009a) has pointed out, there is a new and increasingly violent extractivism at work throughout the region that is perhaps only being masked, as Sanchez-Parga (2011) has gone on to argue vehemently, by an 'indigenous hyper-constitutionalism' (Gudynas 2009a; Sanchez-Parga 2011: 36).

These debates about whether rights are productively decolonizing at a time of such massive commodification of 'environmental services' or, on the contrary, mystifying of the fundamental dynamics of capitalism, are exceedingly important. And to understand their implications in empirically grounded ways – that is, to trace how they are inflecting the actual implementation of the rights of nature in Ecuador – I want to suggest that we return now to the scene of the writing of the 2008 constitution. By dwelling on the historico-political particularities that surrounded, structured, and sustained its writing, we can better understand, it seems to me, how these tensions between decolonization and anti-capitalism continue to play out in local responses to what these rights should – or might – mean in actual practice.

Anti-neoliberalism in Ecuador

The tiny inland city of Montecristi, Manabi was chosen strategically by the socialist administration of Rafael Correa for its weighty symbolic power. The birthplace of Ecuador's most famous liberal revolutionary from the late nineteenth century – General Eloy Alfaro, it was selected as the site from which to initiate the 'citizen's revolution' because of the explicit parallels that Correa has consistently drawn between himself and his forefather. Throughout the country, and particularly throughout Manabi, Eloy Alfaro is praised (and now, in countless museums, iconized) for the strength with which he battled the Catholic hierarchy in the highlands in the last decades of the nineteenth century, fought the concentration of oligarchic power among the elites of the capital city of Quito, defended the sovereignty of the nation against the incursions of foreign capitalists (to whom the country had been opened by his conservative predecessors), pushed for secular education and opened schools to women, and, perhaps most importantly, began the construction of a railroad that would have for the first time unified the highlands and the coast. For these radical affronts to the Catholic powers of the time, he was brutally killed in Quito on 28 January 1912 – his body set on fire in the downtown *Parque Ejido* after having been dragged through the streets by conservative mobs. Eloy Alfaro's project – so we are told by the Correa administration as part of the president's weekly radio addresses – was a project of regional unification, modernization, and, perhaps what made it all possible, the defence of national sovereignty. While the historical veracity of at least some of this history is questionable, as scholars on the right and opponents of the regime are quick to point out, it is the story that Correa has emphasized (if not constructed) to provide a nineteenth century charter for his own struggle to institute what he calls, 'socialism for the twenty-first century' against the dictates of 'foreign imperialists' such as the World Bank and the International Monetary Fund. A fierce and decisive leader, his is a project of radical anti-neoliberalism in the service of enhanced equity, regional integration, reduced poverty, and a powerful reassertion of national sovereignty. As new highways financed by the citizen's revolution connect parts of the country which, just four years ago, would have taken days to reach, and the railroads of Eloy Alfaro are begun anew, the vision is clear: this is a nation-building project in the spirit of late nineteenth century modernization that rejects – at least discursively – what Correa has called, the 'long night of neoliberalism'. After years of devastating Washington Consensus-led reform that saw the collapse of the Ecuadorian currency in 1999 and the bleeding of oil profits at the hands of US-based companies like Occidental and Chevron-Texaco, the economic policies of Correa's 'twenty-first century socialism' include dramatically increased taxes on imported goods, enhanced assistance to the poorest of the poor, and the extraction of sizeable percentages of the profits of transnationals working principally in the energy sector.

While rates of poverty have declined throughout Ecuador over the past six years, however, Correa remains a wildly controversial figure, and there is heated – even violent – disagreement in the country about what, precisely, is involved in this citizen's revolution, who, precisely, should be included among its citizens and what, precisely, is the enemy of that revolution. To sketch the disagreement in starkest terms: is the revolution a revolution against neo-liberalism and unrestrained, US-dominated capitalism (as the Correa administration believes) or is it a revolution against Western modernity more generally, with its deeply flawed conceptions of the relationship between human and non-human (as indigenous and growing numbers of environmental organizations suppose)? Is it principally against the World Bank and its flawed economic prescriptions that drove so many millions into abject misery, or is it more thoroughgoing than that – an assault on the very architecture of Western colonial (and colonizing) thought that has treated the human and the non-human as separable? Arturo Escobar has recently described this tension throughout the Andean region as a tension between 'alternative modernization' – which principally involves a contestation of the neoliberal economic development model – and 'de-colonization', which instead involves a more fundamental questioning of the dualist and hierarchical ontologies of Western thought that continue to undergird relationships of subjugation, particularly in regard to the natural world (Escobar 2010). Throughout most of the Andean region, Escobar tells us, the State is pursuing 'alternative modernization', while indigenous and environmental movements are struggling for a more comprehensive 'de-colonization'.

It is this tension that both runs through the Ecuadorian constitution – rendering it, at times, so laden with 'rights' that it is practically incoherent – and that makes ongoing responses to the rights of nature so multi-layered and often conflicted. Drawing on interviews with opponents of the state-owned Refinery of the Pacific, unconvinced community members, and environmental engineers from the oil company responsible for its construction, what follows are two brief snapshots of some of the competing ways in which the rights of nature are currently being drawn upon as part of the country's most ambitious nationalist development project to date. I focus here on the state-owned refinery and petrochemical complex because it provides perhaps the clearest example in Ecuador today of the ways in which these rights – part of an effort to unlearn the colonialism inherent in Western relationships to the natural world – are being challenged, restrained, and muted by an aggressively nationalist anti-neoliberal development model.

The utility of 'rights' in the context of 'strategic priorities'

As early as 2007, the Correa administration announced that it was planning to begin construction of what is slated to be the largest oil refinery and petrochemical complex in South America. After conducting no fewer than seven environmental impact assessments (of which only three are currently available, and none to the general public), as well as 'socializing' the project in all the communities projected to be affected in the coastal province of Manabi, in 2009 the government decided on 3,800 hectares of dry forest (*bosque seco*) near the sparsely-populated village of El Aromo some 20 kilometres from the coast. At the edge of one of the country's most biodiverse national parks, Parque Pacoche, and in a crucial micro-climate responsible for the capture and retaining of condensation in a zone of high and increasing aridity, the state-owned Refinery of the Pacific is currently scheduled to go operational in 2015. According to the general manager of the project, Pedro Merizalde, by 2016 its capacity per day is expected to be approximately 300,000 barrels of heavy Ecuadorian and Venezuelan crude, plus thousands of gallons of diesel, alcohol, benzene, xylene, and polypropylene – all of which will be pumped from the facility via two pipelines to a port just south of the major tuna-exporting city of Manta.

The clearing of the terrain for this refinery, however, has not gone uncontested on environmental grounds – and ones that make active use of the rights of nature of the constitution of 2008. While the vast majority of local inhabitants support the facility because of the 2,000-plus jobs that it promises over the 40 years of its projected operation, enduring questions have been raised about the degree to which it violates the rights of nature in a zone of particularly dense biodiversity. Perhaps most important among the voices of the dissenters has been a group of nine academics based at the local university in the city of Manta (Universidad Laica Eloy Alfaro de Manta) and a support team of five community members who, in 2009, authored a 13-page technical analysis of the basic 'terms of reference' provided by the two state-owned oil companies responsible for the construction of the facility – the Ecuadorian PetroEcuador and the Venezuelan PDVSA. At the time, these 'terms of reference' were the only statistics that the surrounding communities had been offered by the Refinery even as construction went aggressively forward. The resulting academic analysis of the terms draws explicitly upon the rights of nature in arriving at its conclusion (a) that the refinery should not go forward in its present location; and (b) that it should not 'affect the resources that nature offers us and which allow for the harmonious development of the region' (Erazo, Camino et Al. 2009). Using the rights framework to contest the narrowness of the geographical circumference to which the Refinery of the Pacific had restricted its 'area of study', the report explains:

> It is inappropriate and exaggeratedly limited to consider as the population 'directly affected' only those within the area designated 'the study area' where the project will be located... They [the oil companies] need to widen the concept of 'Direct Affect' to include concepts of 'the good life' [sumak kawsay, or 'buen vivir'], the rights of nature, and the development models of the provinces and cities... They have also not considered the necessity of amplifying the conception of 'Indirect Affect' to include understandings of the connectedness of the territory and the environment to larger regional and inter-regional circuits.
> (Erazo, Camino et al. 2009: 2).

Drawing explicitly on the rights of nature, these academics pushed PDVSA and PetroEcuador to think more broadly about their conceptions of who, precisely, might be considered 'directly' and 'indirectly affected' and to widen their understandings of the connections between the water sources necessary for the refining of the oil, the aqueducts that will carry it from the dams to the plant, and the marine life whose migration patterns will be impeded by the daily ships leaving the port with thousands of gallons of gasoline and diesel. Unfortunately, however, and largely because of the tense political climate in university higher education at the time, after presenting their findings to the head of the university in Manta in 2009, they never received a response nor any confirmation that the report had been received by the government. Members of the academic community involved now believe that the report was never forwarded to the Ministry of the Environment, President Correa, or the Refinery of the Pacific out of fear that the university – which was undergoing a review of its accreditation at the time – might lose its status if it presented findings at odds with the official developmentalist narratives of the current administration.

In late December 2012, I met with the head of the technical team based at ULEAM. In a tiny second floor office that housed the six-person Department of Environmental Studies, he explained that the team had done all that it could in an environment that was growing increasingly hostile to such concerns. In their technical report they had made repeated reference to the rights of nature in order to call attention to the number of ecosystems likely to be affected in this zone of impressive biodiversity, and to recommend that the refinery be constructed at a greater remove from both the human populations living in the region and the nature reserve, which is home to – among other beings – howler monkeys, vampire bats, and some of the smallest frogs in the world. From the perspective of the head of this team, the rights of nature enshrined in the constitution are, and will essentially remain, useless in practice so long as the government is able to speak the language of 'strategic priorities'. All talk of environmental rights, he explained, is a sort of beautiful rhetoric used to entice support for Ecuador from the international community, but one that is not only lacking in teeth but fundamentally incapable of teeth. So long as the same constitution that enshrined the rights of nature recognizes that the state has 'strategic priorities' according to which those rights may be violated if it is in the interests of the nation's 'development', there are only shaky constitutional grounds on which to contest the most highly unsustainable industries such as the refinery and petrochemical complex. Indeed, while the State's National Development Plan (2007–2010) recognizes – among its 12 principles – the importance of environmental sustainability, it talks ominously (from the perspective of environmentalists) of 'strategic areas' that deserve the special attention of the state, including industries like mining, hydrocarbons, technology, and telecommunications. In the years since the signing of the constitution, these 'strategic priorities' have been frequently invoked to justify the increase in highly extractive projects in both the highlands and the coast, which currently include not only the refinery, but a massive, Chinese-financed hydroelectric dam in the neighbouring city of Chone and numerous Chinese and Canadian-financed gold and copper mines in the southern highlands. From the perspective of this author, then, the rights of nature – no matter how clearly defined, how accurately measured, or how intricately elaborated in secondary legislation – will thus always be susceptible to being upended and nullified by the state's ever-accelerating 'strategic priorities'. As he concluded most bluntly: 'Once you have strategic areas, there are no rights.'

The rights of nature versus the right to energy sovereignty

While such priorities suggest that it will likely prove difficult to find sustained constitutional grounds on which to lodge cases against the violators of nature's rights, those rights find perhaps even greater obstacles in a range of competing rights that are enormously malleable, open to interpretation, and often deployed discursively by the administration as part of its nationalist reclamation of the state apparatus. As noted earlier, Correa has styled himself as a faithful descendant of the liberal modernizer, reformer, and fighter for social justice against the Catholic oligarchies of the highlands, General Eloy Alfaro. Like his forefather, he is passionately committed first and foremost to the reclamation of all forms of national sovereignty, and arguably most important among these forms of twenty-first-century sovereignty is that of 'energy sovereignty', or *soberania energetica*. Despite the fact that – according to the scientists, architects, and historians based at the ULEAM – the refinery will likely result in the out-migration of at least three species of seasonal birds and the death of the humpback whales who breed in the warm waters of the Pacific in early June (and it is thus a relatively clear violation of the rights of nature), it is and remains fundamentally constitutional from the administration's perspective because it will allow for that most cherished national good: energy sovereignty. While Ecuador has massive, though dwindling, oil reserves in the Amazon region, as well as two existing (if considerably dated) oil refineries, it has never been able to refine the quantity of heavy crude necessary for the satisfaction of growing domestic demand. As a result, the country continues to import refined products (principally diesel and gas), and at significant cost. By refining more than 300,000 barrels of heavy Ecuadorian and Venezuelan crude a day, the Refinery of the Pacific, according to the administration and company executives, promises to rectify this situation – not only allowing the country to satisfy its own domestic demand, but to export vast amounts to the flourishing Asian, and especially Chinese markets.

Refinery personnel recognize and even emphasize the importance of the 'rights of nature' of the 2008 constitution, and as the general manager, Pedro Merizalde, explained to me in late 2012, they are doing all that they can to ensure the most sustainable facility possible. Not only will they abide by the strictest European standards of greenhouse gas emissions and use the most advanced refining technology, but – much to the amusement of many of the *campesinos* of Manabi who know only too well what it is like to live in a province that has historically witnessed droughts lasting six, seven, or even eight years – they are planning to plant what will be, if successful, the largest man-made forest in all of South America directly around the installation. The forest will be made up exclusively of native plants that, according to refinery personnel, will both absorb the carbon dioxide from the facilities and serve as construction material for neighbouring communities, thereby simultaneously meeting the social and environmental needs of the surrounding community. While it remains unclear just how profound the company's commitment to such environmental responsibility runs (some four years in, for example, they have still not identified the water sources that will be used to irrigate the trees), what is clear is that refinery representatives believe that the right to energy sovereignty is a right that trumps the rights of nature.

And they are not alone in this belief. While howler monkeys may have to change the paths that they have historically used to move through the forests of Pacoche and the whales may have to breed somewhat further down the coast, the head environmental engineer from the Refinery told me, it is *people* who need development first and foremost, and it is deeply offensive to assert otherwise. In a province in which thousands of children live beneath the poverty line and many rural homes lack electricity, gas, and running water, it is the state's responsibility to provide lower cost electricity and diesel. And it is the refinery – so the public relations campaign goes – that will ensure that this right to energy sovereignty is honoured. Often couched in deeply nationalist terms that bring us back to both the birthplace of Eloy Alfaro and the site of the writing of the constitution in 2008, the refinery is frequently constructed as the modern-day equivalent of the late nineteenty century railway built by Eloy Alfaro. Just as the general modernized the country in the late 1880s with the construction of the railway – bringing coast and sierra within reach for the first time in the history of the country, so, too, refinery personnel insist, Rafael Correa is modernizing the country in the early 2000s by bringing cheaper and cheaper electricity to households formerly disconnected from infrastructural grids. 'The Refinery of the Pacific', read exuberant colourful signs all throughout the city of Manta, 'Progress for Manabi'.

Scholars like Sanchez-Parga have rightly noted that the rights of nature in articles 71–4 are heavily constrained by rights that seem – at least potentially – to be in conflict with them, including the right of 'persons, communities, and nationalities to benefit from the environment and natural resources that allow for the good life' in ways that may be construed by some as violating the rights of nature (Sanchez-Parga 2011: 41). In the case of the Refinery of the Pacific, the range of potentially conflicting rights is larger still, with the right to energy sovereignty being consistently construed in powerfully nationalist terms as part of the necessary rebuilding of the state after the 'long night of neoliberalism'. At a time when anti-neoliberal discourses of reclaiming national sovereignty from the IMF, the World Bank, and the bankers that work within and alongside those development organizations is persuasive to growing numbers of Ecuadorians, the right to energy sovereignty remains a particularly potent idiom. While supporting the rights of nature (and, indeed, more than 65 per cent of the Ecuadorian population supports those rights), residents of the province of Manabi overwhelmingly also stand behind the rights of communities to make use of their natural resources and, more specifically in the case of the refinery, their rights to energy sovereignty. Thus, given the large number of competing rights claims currently existent in the constitution, coupled with the emergence of extremely potent, even propagandistic, discourses of anti-neoliberal nationalism on the part of the administration, it appears unlikely for the time being that the rights of nature will prove fundamentally capable of arresting or redirecting the state's growing investment in extractive projects.

Conclusion

The preamble to Ecuador's historic constitution is a powerful collective assertion of the importance of a spiritual and conceptual decolonization that simultaneously de-centers the human, embraces the cultural diversity of the country, and proclaims its continuity with the anti-colonial independence struggles of Simón Bolívar and Eloy Alfaro. 'Celebrating nature (Pachamama) of which we are a part and which is vital to our existence', the preamble begins, '...[and] heirs to social liberation struggles against all forms of domination and colonialism...[we] hereby decide to build a new form of public co-existence, in diversity and in harmony with nature, to achieve the good way of living, the *sumak kawsay*' (Constitution of Ecuador 2008). In the years since the approval of this charter for decolonization, Quito-based activist organizations have worked creatively to explore ways in which to best implement this radically biocentric legislation, even winning their first victory on behalf of a river against the provincial government of Loja in 2011 – a subject that I have explored in detail elsewhere (Fitz-Henry 2012). However, as I have suggested throughout this short chapter, the current administration is committed principally not to the sort of decolonization for which indigenous and radical environmentalists are calling, but to a vehemently passionate anti-neoliberalism that has arguably made life better for many millions of Ecuadorians, but at a serious and deepening cost.

While opening up vast and rich new conceptual terrain, and continuing to spark productive debate, the rights of nature are seriously limited by tensions in the constitution itself between what Escobar (2010) has called, 'alternative modernization' and 'decolonization' – tensions that continue to play out on the international stage at Rio+20 and elsewhere between the 'green economists' (who are looking for alternative market mechanisms to ensure the safeguarding of the natural world) and rights-based activists (who are looking to fundamentally transform the ways in which nature is imagined). The stakes in these competing framings are most apparent in Ecuador's current mega-projects, by far the most ambitious of which is the Refinery of the Pacific. While academics at the local university in Manta attempted to use the rights of nature to encourage the administration to build the refinery in a location that would not threaten such high levels of biodiversity, they soon discovered that in the context of a resurgent nationalism that allows the president to designate 'strategic development priorities', those rights held little sway. Furthermore, as refinery personnel themselves pointed out, there are strongly competing rights throughout the constitution – and in particular, the right to energy sovereignty – that are simply more pressing from the perspective of the administration than a few possible species extinctions. In a country where millions survive on just under 300 dollars a month and there remains a pressing need for ever-greater revenue to fund the government's portfolio of social programs, to talk of wounded butterflies or new pathways through the forest for monkeys or panthers is simply offensive to many non-activists.

The rights of nature are a vitally important step toward the thoroughgoing decolonization of human/non-human relations for which radical environmentalists, indigenous communities throughout the Americas, and the post-humanists with which I opened this chapter are all actively pushing. But these rights are being developed in emerging world contexts in which the overriding need to turn away from the neoliberalism that brought so much devastation to the region beginning in the 1980s presents a serious obstacle to their enforceability. They are, as Andreu Viola Racasena has recently suggested, though perhaps in somewhat too black and white a language, 'a rhetorical adornment with no practical effect or, in the worst of cases, a juridico-political error that could generate a [sizeable] increase in conflicts in the future' (Sanchez-Parga 2011: 36). While I do not share Racasena's critique of rights as mere 'rhetorical adornment' – precisely because such rhetoric has historically always taken generations to become anything less than 'adornment' – I share his fear that they may perhaps be insufficient in the heavily conflicted and increasingly litigated context of Ecuador today, in which, after the brutal decades of spiralling hyperinflation and bank betrayal that culminated in full economic collapse in 1999, the need for development remains enormous. As in much of the world, rights discourses of all sorts are currently proliferating in Ecuador as part of calls for a continuation of the struggle against the colonialism of the IMF and the internal colonialism of mestizo administrations. But in practice, the rights of nature are being consistently either over-ridden by the state's strategic development priorities or forced to compete with other sovereign rights that many experience to be far more pressing. While the citizenry is enthusiastically supportive of these rights, they are simply not prepared, as the administration has repeated on many an occasion, to be 'beggars sitting on a pile of gold'.

References

Arsel, M. and Buscher, B. (2012) 'Nature, Inc: Changes and continuities in neoliberal conservation and market-based environmental policy', *Development and Change*, 43(1): 53–78.

Bakker, K. (2005) 'Neoliberalizing nature? Market environmentalism in water supply in England and Wales', *Annals of the Association of American Geographers*, 95: 542–65.

Bennett, J. (2010) *Vibrant Matter: A Political Ecology of Things*, Durham, NC: Duke University Press.
Burdon, P. (2011) 'Earth rights: A theory', *IUCN Academy of Environmental Law*, 1: 1–12.
Burdon, P. (2012) *Environmental Protection and the Limits of Rights Talk*, online. Available at: <http://rightnow.org.au/topics/environment/environmental-protection-and-the-limits-of-rights-talk/> (accessed 10 August 2012).
Castree, N. (2003) 'Commodifying what nature?', *Progress in Human Geography*, 27(3): 273–97.
Castree, N. (2008a) 'Neoliberalising nature: The logics of deregulation and reregulation', *Environment and Planning A*, 40: 131–52.
Castree, N. (2008b) 'Neoliberalising nature: Processes, effects, evaluations.' *Environment and Planning A*, 40: 153–73.
Comaroff, J. and Comaroff, J. (2008) *Law and Disorder in the Postcolony*, Chicago, IL: University of Chicago Press.
Cullinan, C. (2011) *Wild Law: A Manifesto for Earth Justice*, Totnes: Green Books.
De la Cadena, M. (2010) 'Indigenous cosmopolitics in the Andes: Conceptual reflections beyond politics', *Cultural Anthropology*, 25(2): 134–70.
Erazo, Camino et al. (2009) *Analisis Tecnico de 'los Terminos de Referencia' del Proyecto: Complejo Refinador y Petroquimico del Pacifico, Provincia de Manabi, Ecuador*. Manta, Ecuador: Universidad Laica Eloy Alfaro Manabi.
Escobar, A. (2010) 'Latin America at a crossroads', *Cultural Studies*, 24(1): 1–65.
Fitz-Henry, E. (2012) 'The natural contract: From Levi-Strauss to the Ecuadorian Constitutional Court', *Oceania*, 82(3): 264–79.
Gudynas, E. (2009a) 'Diez tesis urgentes sobre el nuevo extractivismo', *Extractivismo, Politics, y Sociedad*. Quito, Ecuador: CAAP and CLAES.
Gudynas, E. (2009b) *El Mandato Ecológico: Derechos de la Naturaleza y Políticas Ambientales en la Nueva Constitución*, Quito: Abya-Yala Press.
Hale, C. (2002) 'Does multiculturalism menace? Governance, cultural rights, and the politics of identity in Guatemala', *Journal of Latin American Studies*, 34(3): 485–524.
Heynen, N., McCarthy, J., Prudham, S and Robbins, P. (2007) *Neoliberal Environments: False Promises and Unnatural Consequences*, London: Routledge.
Kirksey, S. and Helmreich, S. (2010) 'On the emergence of multispecies ethnography', *Current Anthropology*, 25(4): 545–76.
Latour, B. (1998) 'To modernize or to ecologize: That is the question,' in N. Castree and B. Willems-Bram (eds) *Remaking Reality: Nature at the Millennium*, London: Routledge.
MacDonald, K. and Corson, C. (2012) 'TEEB begins now: A virtual moment in the production of natural capital', *Development and Change*, 43(1): 159–84.
Mansilla, H.C.F. (2011a) 'Desigualdad, medio ambiente, y desarrollo sostenible en el Area Andina de America Latina', *Ecuador Debate*, 82: 81–98.
Mansilla, H.C.F. (2011b) 'Ideologias oficiales sobre el medio ambiente en Bolivia y sus aspectos problematicos', *Ecuador Debate* 84: 89–106.
Martinez, E. and Acosta, A. (2011) *La Naturaleza con Derechos: De la filosofia a la politica*, Quito: Abya-Yala Press.
Morton, T. (2010) *The Ecological Thought*, Cambridge, MA: Harvard University Press.

Peluso, N. (2012) 'What's nature got to do with it? A situated perspective on socio-natural commodities', *Development and Change*, 43(1): 79–104.

Plumwood, V. (2009) 'Nature in the active voice', *Australian Humanities Review*, 46, May: 113–29.

Sanchez-Parga, J. (2011) 'Discursos Retrovolucionarios: Sumak kawsay, derechos de la naturaleza, y otros pachamismos', *Ecuador Debate*, 84: 31–50.

Swyngedouw, E. (2013) 'The non-political politics of climate change', *ACME*, 12(1): 1–8.

Chapter 10

Building an international movement for Rights of Nature

Mari Margil

In 2008 Ecuador became the first country in the world to recognize Rights of Nature in its constitution. Article 71 of the constitution states:

> Nature, or Pachamama, where life is reproduced and occurs, has the right to integral respect for its existence and for the maintenance and regeneration of its life cycles, structure, functions and evolutionary processes. All persons, communities, peoples and nations can call upon public authorities to enforce the rights of nature.

In 2011, the first lawsuits were filed in Ecuador to defend and enforce the rights of ecosystems facing threats from construction, mining, and other types of development. In early 2013, indigenous and environmental organizations filed a suit against the Ecuadorian national government and the Chinese mining company Ecuacorrientes SA (ECSA) to stop a proposed copper mine in the Cordillera del Condor, a mountain range in southern Ecuador. The government signed a mining contract with ECSA in March 2012.

Meanwhile, Ecuador's President Correa remains largely unsupportive of the Rights of Nature constitutional provisions. Despite Ecuador's long history of environmental harm from extractive industries, Correa has promoted efforts to expand mining and oil drilling with proposals for new development being due in spring 2013.

In December 2012, Ecuador's Minister of Foreign Affairs, Trade and Integration hosted the last in a series of seminars on the Rights of Nature and its implementation. The seminar, for members of Ecuador's judiciary, was described as a training for judges on how to implement the Rights of Nature constitutional provisions and international trends with the Rights of Nature. As an attendee and presenter, I had numerous discussions with representatives of environmental organizations within Ecuador, before and at the event, as to why the Correa administration would be holding such a seminar. Their answers were remarkable in their consistency – that the seminar was intended to paint a picture of Correa and his government as 'green', despite the administration's efforts to prevent any real implementation of the Rights of Nature as it seeks to expand extractive and other industrial development in Ecuador.

I was asked to speak at the seminar on the *Universal Declaration on the Rights of Mother Earth*. The *Universal Declaration* came out of Bolivia's 2010 *World People's Conference on Climate Change and the Rights of Mother Earth*. The intention of the declaration was to model itself after the UN-adopted *Universal Declaration on Human Rights*. Such declarations are aspirational, as well as non-binding, providing a vision of the kinds of law and policy that we hope will become binding law in countries around the world. By having the opening panel at the seminar focused on the *Universal Declaration on the Rights of Mother Earth*, it became clear that the Correa administration was attempting to promote the declaration as its Rights of Nature work, understanding that if adopted by the UN, it would have no legal enforceability in Ecuador or anywhere else in the world. Promoting the document is a way for the administration to appear supportive of Rights of Nature abroad, while systematically neglecting it at home.

This resistance by Ecuador's national government to enforce the Rights of Nature provisions should not be considered a failure of this emerging movement. Rather, it must be understood within the context of how movements build, how resistance and response to changes in the status quo must be anticipated, and with a recognition that fundamental change takes generations, and comes neither quickly nor easily.

Ecuador's constitutionalizing of nature's rights, and efforts ongoing in the United States, where local municipalities first began passing Rights of Nature laws in 2006, demonstrate the growing interest in moving to a rights-based approach for nature's protection. The following examines why Rights of Nature is needed if we are to achieve sustainability, how this movement is growing in the Americas and around the world, and key lessons that can be learned from past movements for rights.

Why the need for rights of nature?

Under existing structures of environmental law around the world, governments try to protect ecosystems through environmental regulation that attempts to limit the degree of harm that can be inflicted upon the natural environment. Environmental regulations thus *legalize certain harms* to occur, while attempting to regulate the extent of those harms. For instance, mining corporations are issued environmental permits to extract coal, with those permits establishing permissible levels of pollution that can occur through mining.

Under these structures of law, ecosystems and natural communities are treated as *property* – either as private property where use is individually regulated, or as the state's property where use is controlled to guarantee equal use and access by all aspects of society. Thus, traditional environmental laws are designed to regulate how we *use* nature, legalizing environmental harms by regulating how much destruction of nature can occur under law. As this structure of law has spread around the world, by almost every criterion, the condition of the environment has worsened. We see this with species loss, ocean acidification, the destruction of fisheries, deforestation, as well as global warming which is far more advanced than even the leading climate scientists predicted.

Over 30 municipalities in the United States and the country of Ecuador have begun to pioneer a new form of environmental jurisprudence which establishes legally enforceable Rights of Nature. These laws change the status of ecosystems from being regarded as *property* under the law to being *rights-bearing* entities. While recognizing the rights of ecosystems and natural communities to exist and flourish, these laws also grant legal authority to residents and local governments to enforce and defend those rights. Further, these laws provide that any damages that may be awarded for violations of an ecosystem's rights are to be awarded for the purpose of, and in the amount necessary to, restore the ecosystem to its pre-damaged state.

Under a rights-based system of law, a river may be recognized as having the right to flow, fish in a river may be recognized as having the right to exist and evolve, and the flora and fauna that depend on a river may be recognized as having the right to thrive. This legal framework seeks to protect the natural ecological balance of that habitat. Recognizing Rights of Nature does not put an end to fishing or other human activities, rather it places them in the context of a healthy relationship where our actions do not threaten the balance of the system upon which we depend. Further, these laws do not stop all development, rather they halt only those uses of land that interfere with the very existence and vitality of the ecosystems which depend upon them.

The emerging rights of nature movement

As we study successful peoples' movements, we see that they grow from an initial few to become many. Those few, at the beginning, who begin to have a discussion about what they see wrong with the world, often have those conversations privately, secretively, for fear of reprisal if revealed outside a trusted circle. These movements grow from this small group, or pockets of small groups, who then begin to expand their discussions into a more public forum, hoping to reach others who share a similar concern, to bring them into their growing movement.

Reaching out beyond those inner circles can bring consequences. Abolitionists in the United States were called radical and extreme, they saw their businesses burned, their printing presses destroyed, and they were subject to mob violence. Over a century later, seeking to have the rights driven into the US Constitution by the Abolitionists finally and fully implemented and enforced, members of the Civil Rights Movement similarly saw their houses burn, their property destroyed, and they faced violence from those seeking to preserve the status quo which systematically subordinated blacks in America.

As those early discussions begin to grow, we find those who took to the written word, perhaps instead of the spoken, have often been essential to the origins of a movement. Those who write bear witness to the immorality and illegitimacy of the current state of affairs, and often call for change. People like the prolific American Abolitionist William Lloyd Garrison, who in the early days of that movement began writing his newspaper, the *Liberator*, which he published for over 30 years advocating for the urgent end of slavery while blasphemously calling the US Constitution – which codified slavery – a 'covenant with death, an agreement with hell' (Nelson 1966: 234). Incidentally, Garrison, who not only wrote widely but also publicly spoke about the need for abolition, would burn the constitution at rallies, which to those in attendance provided perhaps the clearest indication of how tightly the problem of slavery was woven into the American framework, and thus how deeply the work of the Abolitionists needed to go (Nelson 1966).

Where did the idea of Rights of Nature begin? When were the words 'Rights of Nature' first spoken, or perhaps written? That's difficult to say, but many look to the American law professor Christopher Stone for first taking hold of it, building on an increasing concern for the health of the environment. In his seminal law review article *Should Trees Have Standing?* Stone (1972) explores how the law treats nature as 'right-less', with no legally recognized rights of its own to defend and enforce. Thus, much like slaves once were, nature is today treated by the law as a thing, as *property*, existing for the use of its owner. Stone examined what it might mean for nature to move from *rights-less* to *rights-bearing*. For example, whether a tree may have standing to defend its right to existence, to life, in a court of law.

In 1989, another American academic, Professor Roderick Nash, published *The Rights of Nature* tracing the evolution of environmental law and ethics over centuries. He explained how throughout history, the *right-less* – slaves, women, others – have struggled to expand the body of legal rights to include themselves (Nash 1989). Nash's book helped advance the discussion about nature's rights, providing a context for how and why the body of rights is moving in the direction of expanding to perhaps one day include nature. Following this, in 2001, the author and religious leader Thomas Berry wrote his essay *The Origin, Differentiation, and Role of Rights* in which he described how all members of the Earth community possess inherent rights. Building on Berry's insights, in 2002, South African attorney Cormac Cullinan published *Wild Law: A Manifesto for Earth Justice*. Together, Berry and Cullinan opened up a new front on nature's rights – adding a significant spiritual and moral element to the legal and historic discussion begun by Stone and Nash.

Each of these writers has played an important role in driving a shift in thinking regarding the relationship between humankind and nature. Such shifts in culture – as the Abolitionists, Suffragists, and other rights-based movements have found – are essential for driving an expansion of the body of legal rights. But alone they are not enough. Rather, such cultural change must be paired with legal change.

History shows us how cultural change can drive change in law, and similarly, changes in law can drive change in the culture. And when it comes to the question of rights – that is, expanding the body of legal rights to include those who are currently without rights – such change can take generations, if not centuries.

Moving from the *idea* of Rights of Nature to the *codification* of those rights occurred for the first time in 2006. In the small community of Tamaqua Borough, in Schuylkill County, Pennsylvania, located in the northeastern part of the US, Tamaqua was for generations a coal mining town. Seeking to ban waste corporations from dumping toxic sewage sludge in the community, the elected members of the borough council adopted a local ordinance banning corporate sludging and recognizing the Rights of Nature.

In Tamaqua, for the first time, we see a move from *discussion* to *practical application*. Why does this happen, that a first community or country is willing to make that leap to expand the body of legal rights? Why would Tamaqua be willing to be the first community, the very first place in the US or the world, to establish Rights of Nature?

Chris Morrison, mayor of Tamaqua Borough at the time of the ordinance's adoption, explained it this way: 'If you are taking away my clean soil or my clean drinking water or my clean air to breathe, you're actually just taking my civil right away. By damaging the ecosystem, you're damaging me. You're damaging the community' (Mena 2007: 34).

Tamaqua's actions represented a recognition that harming the environment was harmful not just to a river or a wetland, but to people and their community. It was an understanding that we are part of the natural environment, we depend on it, and that if we are to survive, if we are to achieve any semblance of ecological balance, we must change how we protect it.

So let's trace how, since Tamaqua's passage of its ordinance in 2006, a movement for Rights of Nature has grown:

- Between 2007 and this writing in early 2013, over three dozen communities in seven states in the US – Pennsylvania, Ohio, New Mexico, New York, Maryland, New Hampshire, and Maine – have followed in Tamaqua's footsteps, passing local laws which codify nature's rights. These local laws, drafted with the assistance of the *Community*

Environmental Legal Defense Fund (CELDF) based in Mercersburg, Pennsylvania, emerged out of efforts to stop threats to the local environment from proposed industrial factory farms, sewage sludge application on farmland, corporate water privatization, and shale gas drilling and hydraulic fracturing, or 'fracking'. The largest of these communities is the City of Pittsburgh, with over 300,000 people, located in Western Pennsylvania. The ordinance recognizing Rights of Nature passed unanimously by the Pittsburgh City Council in November 2010, as part of a ban on shale gas drilling and fracking within the city limits.

- In 2008, the country of Ecuador became the first country in the world to recognize the Rights of Nature in its national constitution. Quito-based NGO *Fundación Pachamama* learned of the work of CELDF in the US working with communities to recognize Rights of Nature. CELDF and Fundación Pachamama met with elected delegates to the Ecuador Constituent Assembly to discuss establishing Rights of Nature in the new constitution. Through a national referendum in September 2008, the people of Ecuador approved their new constitution, becoming the first nation to constitutionalize nature's rights.
- In 2010, Bolivia held the *World People's Conference on Climate Change and the Rights of Mother Earth*. A key aspect of the conference was the drafting and release of the *Universal Declaration on the Rights of Mother Earth*. Modeled on the UN adopted *Universal Declaration of Human Rights*, the declaration states that the rights of Mother Earth are 'inalienable' and 'inherent', and that the 'rights of each being are limited by the rights of other beings and any conflict between their rights must be resolved in a way that maintains the integrity, balance and health of Mother Earth'. Following the conference, Bolivia submitted the declaration to the UN General Assembly for its consideration. As of this writing, no action has been taken at the UN.
- In 2010, the *Global Alliance for the Rights of Nature* was formed at a meeting held in Tamate, Ecuador. With founding members from Africa, Australia, as well as North and South America, the alliance was founded to build an international Rights of Nature movement. In announcing its formation, the Global Alliance issued the *Tungurahua Volcano Declaration* stating: 'Recognizing that exploitation, abuse, and contamination have caused great destruction, degradation and disruption of Mother Earth, putting all life at risk through phenomena such as climate change... Convinced that in an interdependent living community it is not possible to recognize the rights of only human beings without causing an imbalance within Mother Earth... Believe that the universal recognition and effective implementation of the Rights of Nature is essential to avert catastrophic harm to humanity and life as we know it... calls upon all organizations and people of the Earth... to bring forth the universal adoption and effective implementation of the Rights of Nature.'

(The Tungurahua is an active volcano in Ecuador, in view of which the alliance founders first met.)
- In 2011, the first Rights of Nature lawsuits were decided in Ecuador under the country's constitutional provisions, upholding the rights of ecosystems. The first case, heard by the Provincial Court of Justice of Loja, featured the Vilcabamba River as the plaintiff. Thus, the river itself was able to defend its own rights to 'exist' and 'maintain itself' – as it sought to stop a government highway construction project that was interfering with the natural flow and health of the river. The court ruled that the project be stopped. However, the ruling has not yet been enforced, which may mean that further legal action is required.
- In 2012, Bolivia adopted its *Law Under the Mother Earth and Integral Development for Living Well.* Passed by Bolivia's Plurinational Legislative Assembly, the law recognizes the Rights of Mother Earth in statutory law. Civil society and indigenous peoples in Bolivia, much like in Ecuador, have great concerns with the new law and whether it will, in fact, uphold the rights of ecosystems to ensure the 'continuity of the regenerative capacity of the components, parts and systems of life of Mother Earth' (for more information, see http://www.pachamama.org/blog/stepping-in-the-right-direction-giving-mother-earth-rights). Bolivian President Evo Morales, much like Ecuador's President Correa, seeks to appear 'green' even as he proposes major development and extraction projects that will bring severe environmental impacts.
- In 2012, the first Rights of Nature organization formed in Italy, called *Diritti della Natura Italia.* The organization is seeking to raise public awareness about the need to move to a rights-based structure of environmental protection, as well as work to advance the first Rights of Nature laws in Italy.
- In 2012, the Kathmandu-based *Center for Economic and Social Development (CESOD)*, in partnership with CELDF, proposed draft Rights of Nature constitutional provisions to the Nepal Constituent Assembly. With the Himalayan glaciers melting due to global warming and developing nations such as Nepal seeing little progress through the UN climate change negotiations, CELDF developed a *Right to Climate* legal framework under which the atmosphere, as well as human and natural communities, have the right to a healthy, functioning climate free from human alteration and pollution. This would create a legal platform whereby at-risk countries could hold major polluters around the world responsible for their global warming impacts. CESOD and CELDF presented the draft provisions to elected delegates to the Constituent Assembly, who have been engaged in a multi-year constitutional drafting process. In May 2012, the Nepal Supreme Court dissolved the assembly as it failed to promulgate a new constitution by an established

spring deadline. As of this writing, elections for new assembly delegates are scheduled for late 2013.
- In 2012, it was announced that the national government of New Zealand had reached agreement with the Whanganui River iwi, a local Maori people, to recognize a legal persona for the Whanganui River. That is, an agreement to recognize a form of legal standing for the river. The agreement recognizes the river as 'Te Awa Tupua' – an integrated, living whole. With Maori rights to the river long in dispute, the agreement puts in place a shared guardianship whereby the government and the iwi will determine protection measures for the river.
- In 2012, a campaign was launched in India by *Ganga Action Parivar*, a civil society organization, to recognize rights of the Ganga River Basin. Recognized as a holy river, and long managed under traditional forms of environmental regulatory laws which regulate use of the river, it is an ecosystem in collapse. Ganga Action is partnering with CELDF to draft a *National Ganga River Rights Act* which would establish the river's right to exist, thrive, regenerate, and evolve; prohibit activities that would interfere with the river's rights; and empower people, communities, civil society, and governments within India to protect and defend the rights of the river.

Building a movement: key lessons

Building any movement to expand and establish rights is fraught with challenges. The primary being that entire cultures and economies are built on structures of law and governance which depend on those treated as *right-less* remaining that way – women, slaves, nature. As the above chronicle of the emerging Rights of Nature movement demonstrates, this work takes time to develop and grow. And yet time, of course, is of the essence as we face ecosystem collapse around the world. Thus as we look forward, it behooves us to look back, to our predecessors who sought to recognize rights for the right-less, and who did so understanding the immense barriers they had to overcome. They learned difficult, but essential lessons, which we can both learn from and apply in our own work.

So, how does the movement for Rights of Nature grow, build, and strengthen? What challenges, changes, setbacks, and opportunities will we need to anticipate? There are some key lessons that my organization has learned from past people's movements in the United States – such as the Abolitionists and Suffragists – movements which sought to establish legal rights for those the legal system treated as 'right-less'. These are lessons we are applying in our organizing in the US and in our work in other countries to establish Rights of Nature.

First, movements start not only small, but local – and they often are initiated with people who are personally impacted by a harm legalized by the existing constitutional structure. They begin with conversations among people with shared belief systems and then broaden to an ever-widening group. These discussions are all part of building a base of support for fundamental change and identifying people with the passion and capacity capable of leveraging those conversations to engage a more geographically and philosophically diverse population. The strategy, then, is to bring together more and more people who support structural change and who are willing to engage in an effort to make that change happen. As more and more people and communities are engaged, the task remains to bring these groups together to form a larger movement working to drive change outward and upward, from the grassroots to national levels.

The second key lesson from these past movements is that they started slowly and took significant time to build. Fundamental structural change comes neither easily nor quickly. In today's culture of immediacy, activists are considered to have failed if their work doesn't generate headlines or thousands of Facebook fans. Thus, advocacy – and organizations that fund advocacy – is tailored to generate the immediate headlines and create the online storm of e-mails, blogs, tweets, and web postings that suggest something is happening. But a listserv does not a movement make. And headlines are only as good as they are able to advance the organizing on the ground. By themselves, they have no value.

A third key lesson is that these movements are characterized by traditional failures. In the early days of the Abolitionist movement in the US, anti-slavery organizations in Ohio, Massachusetts, Vermont, and elsewhere sent thousands of petitions to the US Congress, asking for an end to slavery in the District of Columbia and nationally. For years, the US House of Representatives and Senate – led by their Southern members – deliberately ignored these petitions by voting to table or outright reject them, rather than give them consideration or a hearing. Thus, by traditional measures, the petitioners failed repeatedly to gain traction in the halls of Congress. The Abolitionists, however, were able to wield the overwhelming inaction in the Capitol to slowly build their movement, using the actions and words of slavery's defenders to bring more people into their fold.

For more than a century, Suffragists in the US similarly struggled and suffered in their efforts to gain rights for women, including the right to vote. In the 1870s, following ratification of the Fourteenth Amendment to the US Constitution, which recognized rights for newly freed slaves, Suffragists attempted to use the new amendment to recognize universal suffrage. The courts uniformly rejected their efforts. The Suffragists continued to attempt to cast their ballots in elections and were arrested for their efforts. Why bother, some may ask, to vote if you know you'll just be stopped and arrested? What was defined by some as failure, was recognized by the Suffragists as an opportunity to strengthen and deepen their movement – understanding that with each attempt at the ballot box, they were shining an increasingly bright light on the injustice and illegitimacy of laws denying women's rights – thus adding fuel to a movement that remained a constant between confrontations.

A fourth key lesson is that when people advocate for fundamental change – advocating for rights for those without rights – they are described as treasonous and radical, their ideas are ridiculed, and even those who sympathize with their cause argue that the changes they seek are too big and come too fast. As part of the early Abolitionist movement in the US, Ted Weld and his students at Lane Seminary in Ohio were forcibly ejected from the seminary for their views. Indeed, the Abolitionists and Suffragists faced ridicule and were shunned by their families and society at large for the ideas they expressed. As Professor Christopher Stone explained in *Should Trees Have Standing?*:

> The fact is, that each time there is a movement to confer rights onto some new 'entity' the proposal is bound to sound odd or frightening or laughable. This is partly because until the rightless thing receives its rights, we cannot see it as anything but a thing for the use of 'us' – us being, of course, those of us who hold rights.
>
> (Stone 1972: 8)

The final key lesson is to know what your goal is, and not allow that goal to be diluted by others. There is a growing tendency to throw the emerging Rights of Nature movement into the category of conventional environmental activist work.

Traditional environmental laws seek to regulate our use of the environment, and environmental activists find their advocacy focused on making these existing laws a little bit better. What does it mean for these environmental laws to work *better*? It means more regulation of how much pollution or exploitation of nature can occur from mining, drilling, or other activities. That is, we may be able to emit a little less carbon into the air or frack wastewater into streams. At best, these new regulations may slow down somewhat the rate of destruction of the natural environment that otherwise would occur. These laws and regulations, therefore, are not intended or designed to achieve sustainability.

As existing environmental laws operate under the premise that nature is property, these laws legalize ecosystem harm. Rather than working to protect ecosystems as a whole, and ensuring that they remain healthy, functioning, and resilient, today's environmental laws piecemeal the environment into different flora and fauna, waterways and trees.

To understand this and why it is important that we should not put the Rights of Nature work in the same basket as conventional environmental work, let's consider slavery. In the US, there were the Abolitionists who sought to end slavery and recognize rights of the freed slaves. And there were folks, known as the American Colonization Society (ACS), who also represented themselves as anti-slavery. With founding members who were themselves slave owners, the goal of the ACS was not abolition, but rather to relocate freed slaves to Africa while keeping the existing structure of law in place which constitutionally protected slavery and slave owners.

It became incumbent upon the Abolitionists not only to distinguish themselves from the ACS, but to knock the ACS out of the picture altogether. Why? Because if the ACS was allowed to continue in its work, unchallenged, they would provide that 'easy out' for those concerned with slavery. That is, the ACS did not seek to change the status quo. Yet movements for rights come up against the brick wall that is the status quo, and must break it down.

The Abolitionists – Ted Weld, John Brown, and so many others – came up against an economy, a culture, and a structure of law and governance which not only codified slavery, but protected and promoted it. Challenging that status quo was tantamount to taking on the impossible.

And as we've seen through the ages, people and organizations and governments and those in power, will do everything to protect themselves from change. They will seek the easiest way out of the situation, the path of least resistance. Those options, in today's world, mean creating blue ribbon commissions and study groups to suggest that the problem, that is, whatever the rabble happens to be rabbling about that day, is being dealt with. Or they'll pass non-binding resolutions expressing their outrage about this or that, whatever the rabble is up in arms about, and then do nothing more. That is, they will take the least number of steps possible to preserve the status quo – their power, their way of life – without making any real change, but doing so in a way that makes it appear they did make change. So the ACS offered a wonderful alternative to the Abolitionists – appearing to do something about slavery, when in fact they would do nothing other than making sure that freed slaves could not inflame their brethren in chains because they had been conveniently removed from the continent.

And thus we find ourselves in a similar situation today with the budding work on Rights of Nature. By throwing it into the same bucket with other 'green' laws, it will ensure that we don't move to a system of environmental protection based on rights. But rather, that we will maintain the existing environmental legal structure based on treating nature as right-less, as property, but appear to be doing something different and thus making people feel that things are taken care of and nothing more needs to be done.

If we are to make steps toward real change – that is, fundamental change in how we treat nature in law and practice to create a new relationship between humankind and the natural environment – we must not settle for the idea that anything that happens in the name of the planet is worthwhile. It's not.

When we paint everything with the same brush, that means we're validating the existing structure, and it's the existing structure which ensured slavery would continue in perpetuity, that women would forever be subordinate to men, and that we will never achieve any semblance of ecological balance with nature because our laws, and our culture that supports and protects it, are not intended to achieve sustainability, rather quite the opposite.

Conclusion

More and more communities and countries are now beginning to consider Rights of Nature legal frameworks as they increasingly see that existing environmental laws are not able, and were never intended, to protect nature. They see ecosystem collapse, species extinctions, and degradation of the natural systems upon which we depend, and wonder why – with so many environmental laws and regulations on the books – things don't seem to be getting any better. It is this questioning, this wondering, that is taking people, organizations, communities, and even countries in a new direction.

References

Berry, T. (2001) 'The origin, differentiation, and role of rights', paper presented at the Earth Jurisprudence Conference, Warrenton, Virginia, April 2001.
Cullinan, C. (2002) *Wild Law: A Manifesto for Earth Justice*, South Africa: Siber Ink.
Global Alliance for the Rights of Nature (2010) *Tungurahua Volcano Declaration.* Available at: <http://therightsofnature.org/ga-declaration/> (accessed 10 February 2013).
Mena, C.R. (2007) 'Tamaqua discusses dumping ban again', *The Morning Call*, Allentown, PA, 5 April.
Nash, R.F. (1989) *The Rights of Nature*, Madison, WI: The University of Wisconsin Press.
Nelson, T. (ed.) (1966) *Documents of Upheaval: Selections from William Lloyd Garrison's The Liberator, 1831–1865*, New York: Hill and Wang.
Stone, C.D. (1972) 'Should trees have standing? Toward legal rights for natural objects', *Southern California Law Review*, 45: 450–501.

Chapter 11

'Water as the way'
Achieving wellbeing through 'right relationship' with water

Linda Sheehan

Earth is a water planet – more particularly, a 97.5 per cent salt water planet (UN Water). Salt water flows through our veins as it flows through the sea, connecting us with all life through the eons of evolution. Most of our body is composed of water, which we must consume daily or perish quickly. Our co-habitants on Earth similarly depend on water as a building block of their own bodies and systems. Yet, accessible fresh water is in short supply; for example, lakes and rivers constitute only about 0.3 per cent of all fresh water sources (UN Water). This limited supply, moreover, is decreasing due to over-diversion, pollution and other threats.

Many governing bodies are beginning to recognize a 'human right to water' to address growing water challenges. However, few recognize the needs and rights of the natural systems from which we draw our water. If this does not change, our perceived rights may become as dry as the paper they are printed on.

This chapter examines the need to recognize in law both human and environmental rights to water in order to achieve flourishing lives in harmony with nature. It begins by assessing water threats and outlining efforts to address those challenges. Next, it assesses the limitations of our dualistic approach to water management, which treats water as property separate from humans, rather than as an integral partner. It then offers alternative governance methodologies grounded in the collective, shared rights of people and the natural world to the water that all need for wellbeing. Finally, it calls for the righting of our relationship with the natural world through broad recognition and implementation of the rights of nature to exist, thrive and evolve, as a family member on our wondrous, shared planet.

Water status and threats

> In an age when man has forgotten his origins and is blind even to his most essential needs for survival, water... has become the victim of his indifference.
>
> (Rachel Carson, in Carson 2002: 39)

Despite the fragile state of waters globally, we have developed a deeply dysfunctional relationship with this essential element of life and livelihood. Misuse through over-diversion and pollution drains and contaminates waterways, while climate change exacerbates impacts by disrupting sensitive hydrologic cycles. While some governments are responding with new initiatives to conserve and restore waterways, others are responding by commodifying water for sale to the highest bidder, regardless of the needs of local human and environmental communities.

Water over-diversion, which already has contributed to the destruction of powerful ancient civilizations (Diamond 2005), is accelerating globally despite unequivocal indications that such practices cannot be sustained (Pearce 2012). More than half of extracted water is not returned to original watersheds, drying out whole regions (Bigas 2012: 27). Groundwater is particularly vulnerable; the rate of disappearance of global groundwater stocks more than doubled between 1960 and 2000 (UNEP 2012: 196). Though agriculture is the major user, energy development represents 40 per cent of total water withdrawals in the United States and European Union, with associated pollution impacts (UNEP 2012: 120).

The impacts of the race for ever more water span the globe:

- over 1.4 billion people currently live in river basins where the use of water exceeds minimum recharge levels;
- in 60 per cent of European cities with more than 100,000 people, groundwater is being used faster than it can be replenished;
- by 2025, 1.8 billion people will be living in regions with absolute water scarcity, and two-thirds of the world's population could be under water stress conditions (UN Water).

Ongoing over-diversions also devastate ecosystems and species. Globally, freshwater biodiversity has declined 35 per cent since 1970, greater than in terrestrial or marine ecosystems, and new data often demonstrate more widespread effects than expected (Bigas 2012: 27).

Pollution also is a concern. In the United States, over half of monitored rivers and streams nationwide, and almost 70 per cent of lakes, reservoirs and ponds, still cannot meet one or more established beneficial uses such as swimming, fishing or habitat (US EPA 2010). The assembled nations at the 2012 UN Conference on Sustainable Development ('Rio+20') agreed unanimously on the 'need to adopt measures to significantly reduce water pollution and increase water quality' (UN General Assembly 11 September 2012: 124).

Climate change will exacerbate these impacts. The World Bank found that a potential, 'devastating' 4°C increase by 2100 would prompt 'substantially exacerbated water scarcity in many regions' (The World Bank

November 2012: v, 7). Large-scale biodiversity losses are also expected, 'driving a transition of the Earth's ecosystems into a state unknown in human experience' (The World Bank November 2012: 7).

As clean, reliable fresh water supplies dwindle, incentives increase for 'water grabbing' (National Geographic December 2012) and privatization for profit. At least one top economist expects 'a globally integrated market for fresh water', opining that:

> Once the spot markets for water are integrated, futures markets and other derivative water-based financial instruments… will follow. There will be different grades and types of fresh water, just the way we have light sweet and heavy sour crude oil today. Water as an asset class will… become eventually the single most important physical-commodity based asset class, dwarfing oil, copper, agricultural commodities and precious metals.
>
> (Lubin 2011)

The derivates market for mortgage-backed securities set off the global financial crisis of 2008. Global financial speculation around water could have implications far beyond even these major impacts, reaching to the fundamental ability of people to survive (Kaufmann 2012: 469–71; Keim 25 October 2012).

Ignoring the lessons of the lost empires of the past, the headlong rush to claim 'our' water is accelerating, driven most recently by vastly expanding oil and gas mining through water-intensive hydraulic fracturing, or 'hydro-fracking' (Klare 2012: 118–22). If over-diversion, pollution, privatization and climate change continue as expected, not only will negative impacts to human health, environment and economics expand, but peace and security will also be threatened, with water potentially used 'as a weapon or to further terrorist objectives' (US National Intelligence Council 2 February 2012: iii). As observed by former UN Secretary-General Kofi Annan, 'water issues contain the seeds of violent conflict' (UNESCO: 3). New, effective water governance strategies are needed now to prevent such impacts and create a mutually flourishing relationship with each other and the world's waters.

Water management strategies in a dichotomous world

Limits of dualistic water management

> That which fills the universe I regard as my body and that which directs the universe I consider as my nature.
>
> (Chang Tsai, in Chan, trans. 1963: 497–8)

On the eve of Rio+20, the United Nations Environment Programme (UNEP) released a report assessing progress on long-adopted, international environmental goals. Of 90 goals assessed, significant progress could only be shown for four; none of which addressed waterway health (UNEP 2012: xvii, 101, 127–9).

The global lack of progress is unfortunately not surprising, given that existing governance and economic systems incentivize environmental degradation. We misguidedly assume that we are separate from the natural world; that we can take from and contaminate it with relatively little impact to ourselves. By acting as if we are disconnected from the natural systems on which we depend, we drive degradation of the wellbeing of all.

Examples of core assumptions underlying our governance and economic systems that prevent us from living in harmony with the natural world include:

- The 'free market' maximizes societal wellbeing.
- Environmental regulations hurt balance sheets and therefore hurt our wellbeing.
- Corporations inherently have rights.
- The environment serves humans and does not have rights.

Each of these flawed assumptions ignores the fact that, rather than separated, we and our co-inhabitants on Earth are intimately interconnected, and our governance systems must reflect this to ensure our mutual wellbeing. Current environmental statutes buy time, but they do not substitute for full acceptance of a partnership, rather than master-servant, relationship with nature (Meadows 1999). By changing the foundational assumptions on which our governance systems rest, we will create new systems that motivate actions to achieve thriving waterways.

The practical implications of change are straightforward. If we continue to divert all the water that we feel 'entitled' to, and further pollute water sources, we will leave drained and contaminated landscapes in our wake. From an ethical perspective, our deep bonds with the natural world – arising from our shared past, present and future – call for governance grounded in respect.

Choosing governance that advances 'sustainable communities'

Across industrial societies, and increasingly across the globe, we have so effectively convinced ourselves of the inevitability and effectiveness of our neoliberal economic system that not only have we subjugated nature to it, we have also begun to subjugate ourselves. Even though our economic system is driving ever-greater environmental destruction and expanding the gulfs between rich and poor, we continue to convince ourselves that we and the natural world are best served by economic growth, regardless of its impacts.

'Sustainable development' and the 'green economy', major focus areas of Rio+20, illustrate our addiction to the economy as the goal of society. The spotlight of these terms – 'development' and 'economy' – limited Rio+20 stakeholders to tweaking existing, economy-focused governance. Challenges to underlying assumptions – such as the acceptance of 'infinite growth on a finite planet' – remained relatively ignored.

Rather than focus on 'sustainable development' or the 'green economy', we should ask ourselves how to achieve a larger vision of 'sustainable communities', or thriving, co-evolving human and environmental communities that represent the best of us. Thriving human communities include a well-run economy *as well as* clean drinking water, healthy food, wide circles of family and friends, sanitation, housing, necessary medical care, democratic governance, education, meaningful and appropriately rewarded labour, spirituality – and healthy relationships with a flourishing natural world. Thriving environmental communities similarly require healthy nutrients, clean water, biodiversity, restoration, connected habitats – and healthy relationships with humans, who have the power to destroy and to rejuvenate.

Only by changing the lens by which we view our place in the world can we begin to see the inherent flaws of contorting environmental and societal wellbeing into a system focused on protecting markets and promoting unending economic growth for the few, at the expense of all. An operating system premised on 'development' as the end goal of the exercise in achieving 'sustainability' is not equipped to ask and answer the urgent questions about how we should conduct our lives in an era of growing scarcity. By changing our focus from sustainable development to 'right relationships' within sustainable communities, we will develop the contours of an economy that serves the intrinsic worth and rights of both people and the natural world. Water, the essence of life itself, illustrates how to reach this goal.

Human right to water advances sustainable communities

> The human right to water is indispensable for leading a healthy life in human dignity. It is a pre-requisite to the realization of all other human rights.
> (UN Committee on Economic, Social and Cultural Rights 20 January 2003: 1)

Nations and international bodies have begun to counter the profit-driven focus of our governance systems by recognizing the human right to water for fundamental human needs. Implementation of this right, together with the rights of waterways, will help build 'sustainable communities' of thriving relationships among people, ecosystems and species.

The UN has formally recognized the 'right to safe and clean drinking water and sanitation as a human right that is essential for the full enjoyment of life and all human rights' (UN General Assembly 3 August 2010). The UN reiterated this Resolution at Rio+20, agreeing unanimously to 'reaffirm our commitments regarding the human right to safe drinking water' (UN General Assembly 11 September 2012: 121). A UN Special Rapporteur on the human right to safe drinking water receives allegations of violations of the right to water, and provides advice on measures required to realize the right to water. Her work is informed by the UN General Comment No. 15 (UN Committee on Economic, Social and Cultural Rights 20 January 2003), which defines the 'right to water' as the right to sufficient, safe, acceptable and physically accessible and affordable water for personal and domestic uses.

Constitutional provisions explicitly requiring the protection or provision of clean water are found in at least 18 nations, with the number growing (Bigas 2012: 131). Some courts have also 'found' a constitutional right to water based on the fact that it is a prerequisite to the enjoyment of other human rights, including the right to life (Bigas 2012: 132). Dozens of countries also recognize the right to water in national legislation or policy (Bigas 2012: 133). Together, these efforts are already producing stronger water laws and policies, with accumulating benefits to human wellbeing (Boyd 2012).

The human right to water is increasingly being recognized at a subnational level as well. California Assembly Bill 685 (25 September 2012: 1) declared it 'established policy of the state that every human being has the right to safe, clean, affordable, and accessible water adequate for human consumption, cooking, and sanitary purposes'. The bill's legislative history reports that numerous California families are left entirely without safe water (California Senate Committee on Natural Resources and Water 7 July 2011) due to nitrate pollution from under-regulated agriculture (Harter and Lund 2012: 2). Because '[n]itrate is among the most frequently detected contaminants in groundwater systems around the world' (Harter and Lund 2012: 9), action is needed globally to protect this right.

The UN's Millennium Development Goal (MDG) process took on this effort, committing nations to halve, by 2015, the proportion of people 'unable to reach or to afford safe drinking water' (UN General Assembly 18 September 2000: 19). While the UN asserts this goal has been met five years ahead of schedule, over 600 million people will still lack access in 2015. Moreover, while the MDG target calls for access to 'safe' drinking water, its success has been measured merely by access to an 'improved' source of drinking water. These are not equivalent. As even the UN admits, 'it is likely that the number of people using improved water sources is an overestimate of the actual number of people using safe water supplies' (UN Department of Economic and Social Affairs 2012: 52).

We have much work yet to do to ensure reliably safe drinking water for the world's human populations. The first step must be to question why we maintain governance systems that allow continued over-diversion and pollution. To live in 'right relationship' with the natural world, we must recognize its own inherent worth and express in our laws waterways' right to sufficient, clean water. We will ensure our own wellbeing only by rejecting the idea of waterways as property to be abused for short-term profit, and instead nurturing the natural world that nurtures us.

Waterway rights to water advance sustainable communities

> The river, for example, is the living symbol of all the life it sustains or nourishes...The river as plaintiff speaks for the ecological unit of life that is part of it.
>
> (Justice William O. Douglas, in *Sierra Club v. Morton* 1972: 741–3)

Driven by the furious pace of industrialization over the past 200 years, we have dammed, diverted, pumped and contaminated most of the world's waterways with relatively little thought to consequences – despite the fact that 'the lives, livelihoods and well-being of people and the health of the environment are interrelated and interdependent' (UNEP 2010).

Most water treaties, statutes and policies have been ineffective in protecting the integrity of waterways because they fundamentally legalize ongoing pollution and extraction, rather than focus on ensuring the wellbeing of a rights-bearing Earth partner. Rather than attempting to master waterways, we must learn to live harmoniously with them.

We can begin to course-correct our imbalanced relationship with the environment by examining the nature of rights, and the rights of nature. The Universal Declaration of Human Rights (UDHR) recognizes that '[a]ll human beings are born free and equal in dignity and rights' (UN General Assembly 1948: Art. 1). The UDHR lists numerous rights that protect individuals from the excesses of the state, including the 'right to life, liberty and security of person' (article 3) and the 'right to an effective remedy' for acts violating named rights (article 8).

As articulated by the UDHR Drafting Committee, 'the supreme value of the human person... did not originate in the decision of a worldly power, *but rather in the fact of existing*' (Santa Cruz 1948 (emphasis added)). The basis for the environment's rights is the same as our own: in the fact of its arising and existence on our shared planet. Our failure to recognize the inherent rights of nature has resulted in lifestyles dangerously out of balance with the Earth's systems. By recognizing the rights of the natural world to exist, thrive and evolve, we may begin to rectify this imbalance and ensure the wellbeing of both people and planet. This effort is particularly critical as we face the hard realities of the limits of natural systems.

Nations, regions and municipalities around the world are already beginning to recognize the rights of nature in law. Most notably, in 2008 Ecuador became the first nation to adopt a constitutional provision endowing nature with inalienable, enforceable rights (Constitución de la República del Ecuador 2008). Article 71 states that the natural world has the right to exist, persist, maintain and regenerate its vital cycles, structure, functions and its processes in evolution, and allows for enforcement by individuals and communities. Article 72 further provides the natural world with a right to restoration independent of humans' right to compensation. These provisions were first tested in a successful 2011 case, in which the court found that the Vilcabamba River's constitutional right to flow had been violated by destructive road development practices and ordered its full restoration (*Wheeler y Huddle* 30 March 2011).

The precedent set by the Ecuadorian Constitution led to the adoption, spearheaded by Bolivia, of an international 'Universal Declaration of the Rights of Mother Earth' (UDRME) (22 April 2010). Formally submitted to the United Nations and discussed in a UN General Assembly Dialogue (UN General Assembly April 2011), the UDRME parallels the UDHR by recognizing 'Mother Earth and all beings' as having numerous rights, including the right to life and to exist, the right to water as a source of life, the right to integral health, and the right to full, prompt restoration for violations of these rights. The UDRME also requires humans and their institutions to 'recognize and promote the full implementation and enforcement of' these rights. The Final Declaration of the Rio+20 'People's Summit' specifically called on governments to adopt and implement the UDRME (Cúpula dos Povos June 2012).

Municipalities around the US have also begun adopting ordinances recognizing the rights of the natural world, specifically including waterways. The largest city to recognize these rights, Pittsburgh, Pennsylvania, adopted an ordinance recognizing that '[n]atural communities and ecosystems, including ... water systems, possess inalienable and fundamental rights to exist and flourish' (City of Pittsburgh 1 December 2010).

Water as the way: living in right relationship

> Water is the driving force of all nature.
> (Leonardo da Vinci, in Pfister *et al.* 2009: vi)

Our flawed but deeply-held worldview of 'people over nature' can be overcome by recognizing our integral connections with the natural world, and respecting those connections by recognizing the inherent rights of nature in the laws that guide our behaviour. One obstacle to development of waterway rights, however, has been the perception that they may irreconcilably conflict with human rights to water, to humans' detriment. Article 1, Section 7 of the UDRME recommends a path forward, stating: '[t]he rights of each being are limited by the rights of other beings and any conflict between their rights must be resolved in a way *that maintains the integrity, balance and health of Mother Earth*' (emphasis added). For example, where there are conflicts between water for ecosystem health and for hydrofracking, the damage caused by hydrofracking may weigh against its claim to limited water supplies that ecosystems need for life itself.

Rights to water are not homogenous, but depend upon the needs of the subject entity. As articulated by cultural historian Thomas Berry, '[r]ivers have river rights... Humans have human rights. Difference in rights is qualitative, not quantitative' (Berry 2006: 149-50). Humans have different needs than rivers, but our needs do not automatically exceed the rights of all other species. Waterways have the right to flow with water in an amount and quality necessary for the waterway and their dependent ecosystems and species to exist, thrive and evolve. Human rights to water must be implemented consistent with waterway rights, lest we violate the integrity, balance and health of the waterways that would nourish us.

Since its adoption almost 65 years ago, the UDHR's commitment to basic rights and freedoms has been translated into constitutional, statutory and judge-made law through which human rights have been expressed and increasingly guaranteed. The same can be done on behalf of the rights of nature, creating a 'right relationship' with our waterways that leads toward a shared, thriving future.

Water strategies that serve people and planet

Rights of waterways and humans to sufficient, clean water, consistent with ensuring the 'integrity, balance and health' of the Earth, must be integrated into our governance systems. Numerous opportunities to begin this initiative exist. Efforts such as the UN's post-2015 Millennium Development Goal initiative, the UN's Rio+20 follow-up effort to develop worldwide Sustainable Development Goals, and growing attention at the national level can help advance the concept and implementation of waterway and human rights to water. Language for rights-based advances in law and policy can be gleaned from the UDRME, from constitutional provisions and court decisions such as in Ecuador, and from community ordinances in the United States. A policy model is Ecuador's National Plan for Good Living 2009–2013, which offers administrative and regulatory strategies consistent with the Plan's challenge to 'the notion of material, mechanic and endless accumulation of goods', and its proposal to 'shift from the current prevailing anthropocentrism to what we may call bio-pluralism' (Republic of Ecuador 2010).

Examples of needed language also can be found in 2012 civil society agreements at Rio+20 (Blue Pavilion 21 June 2012) and the 2012 Alternative World Water Forum in Marseille (Alternative World Water Forum 14–17 March 2012). Both declarations, approved by a broad coalition of civil society organizations, strongly agreed that 'water is a commons, not a commodity,' and opposed the 'dominant economic and financial model that is in favour of privatizing and commoditizing water' (Alternative World Water Forum 14–17 March 2012). Both called for recognition of the rights of nature, and for preservation of hydrologic cycle integrity in the context of the rights of ecosystems and species to exist, thrive, and reproduce. The signatories called for local, alternative and sustainable solutions to meet human needs, consistent with economic systems that guarantee wellbeing for communities over 'maximum individual wealth and over-inflated profits for business and finance' (Alternative World Water Forum 14–17 March 2012). Through such agreements, civil society has begun coordinated movements calling for an integrated water governance strategy addressing the needs and rights of both people and environment to water.

Significant insight and lessons can also be drawn from indigenous communities, many of whom implicitly understand humans' inherent integration with the natural world. For example, a 2012 legal agreement between Maori iwi and the New Zealand government recognizes the legal status and standing of the Whanganui River and its watersheds, grounding it in the intrinsic interconnections between the Whanganui River and the wellbeing of people (*Tūtohu Whakatupua: Agreement between the Whanganui Iwi and the Crown* 30 August 2012). The Agreement 'view[s] the Whanganui River as a living being, Te Awa Tupua; an indivisible whole ... including all the physical and metaphysical elements' (Art. 1.2), and supports the role of the Whanganui Iwi to 'care, protect, manage and use the Whanganui River' (Art. 1.3). While the final specifics are still being developed, the Agreement provides model language for other governments to emulate in developing laws protecting the rights of people, ecosystems and species to needed water, including appointment of independent guardians of those rights (Arts 2.18–2.22).

Broader application of the above initiatives will help expand implementation of the rights of people and natural systems globally. To better understand the variables of this path, we consider California, which is trying to develop its own sustainable relationship with its Bay-Delta Estuary, through which drinking water for more than 25 million Californians flows. What is missing from its efforts, however, is a statewide vision that recognizes Californians' integral relationship with the natural world. Instead, the state has adopted two 'co-equal' goals: more reliable water supplies, and protection and enhancement of the Delta ecosystem (*California Public Resource Code § 29702(a)* 2009). However, a 'co-equal goals' presumption allows us to falsely imagine that our own needs are not dependent on the wellbeing of the ecosystems to which we are inextricably linked. It runs counter to the

UDRME, which recognizes that we protect our own wellbeing only by maintaining the 'integrity, balance and health of Mother Earth'. If we do not learn to respect the natural world, it will ensure that that happens in a manner for which we did not plan.

In California and elsewhere, we can begin to address our imbalanced relationship with water by developing and allocating water rights to waterways based on ecosystem needs (e.g., Berry's 'rivers have river rights'). Formalizing and effectuating water rights for ecosystems will ensure that waterway and fish needs are considered up front, planning is effective, implementation and enforcement is clear, and water is shared in a way that ensures that the needs of the state and its ecosystems are met. Implementation could be overseen by independent guardians, appointed in a transparent public process (as under the Whanganui River Agreement). An independent advocate for waterways is essential to success, as agencies tend to balance 'competing' water interests in favour of human uses rights even where the damage is environmentally devastating (Klamath Riverkeeper 2012), particularly if legislation allows them that leverage. For example, the 1987 Oregon Instream Water Rights Act authorized Oregon agencies to apply for instream water rights certificates to support habitat, pollution abatement, and scenic and recreational values. While commendable compared with other states, Oregon's program falls short because diversions for human uses that 'came first' often push aside waterways' established instream flow rights, and because state agencies may 'reserve' unappropriated water for future economic use for up to 20 years, further trumping waterways' rights (Achterman 2006). Independent guardians, paired with rights-based governance and community stewardship, will improve significantly our relationships with the world's waters, to our mutual benefit.

Conclusion: Applying water's lessons to achieve collective wellbeing

> Through water flows the wisdom of the universe.
> (Theodor Schwenk, in Schwenk 1996: 97)

Principle 1 of the 1992 Earth Summit's 'Rio Declaration' states that 'Human beings... are entitled to a healthy and productive life in harmony with nature'. This is only part of the truth. Nature, as well, is entitled to healthy and productive existence. Our existing, dichotomous approach to environmental management (as if the environment, rather than our own behaviour, needed 'managing') contradicts the science and ethics of our deep integration with the natural world. Initial efforts to implement both the human and environmental rights to water provide important lessons for how we can modify our behaviour to live in harmony with each other and nature, consistent with the recognition of nature's rights to exist, thrive and evolve.

Chinese philosopher Lao Tzu observed that water 'comes closest to the way' because it 'excels in benefiting the myriad creatures without contending with them and settles where none would like to be'. He taught that humans are part of the Earth, and that wellbeing flows from living in right relationship with nature. A life lived for the benefit of others, including the natural world, brings deeper connections that in turn generate further peace and wellbeing. By contrast, modern governance, and particularly our economic system, reinforces divisions through its relentless pursuit of power and fortune – the opposite of 'settling where none would like to be'. The result is ecosystems and species driven to extinction and untold numbers of people driven into poverty. Perversely, success under this system brings little pleasure to those who 'win' because the constant attachment to striving by definition fails to cease.

Humans are just one element of the integrated whole of life on Earth. The inherent rights of ecosystems and species, like our own, dictate that all must be allowed to struggle fairly and together. By evolving our laws to acknowledge these rights and enhance the 'integrity, balance and health of Mother Earth', we will begin the process of living in true harmony with nature. This will not only benefit us practically, through physical benefits such as clean water and healthy natural systems. It will also enhance our peace and wellbeing both personally and collectively, which in turn will encourage further actions to benefit others, bringing us all closer to the way.

References

Achterman, G. (2006) 'Sometimes a great notion: Oregon's instream flow experiments', *Lewis & Clark Law School: Environmental Law*, 36(4): 1125–55.

Alternative World Water Forum (14–17 March 2012) *Declaration of the Participants: Marseille*, online. Available at: <http://earthlawcenter.org/static/uploads/documents/FAME_final_declaration.pdf> (accessed 5 January 2013).

Assembly Bill 685 (Eng) (25 September 2012) online. Available at: <http://leginfo.legislature.ca.gov/faces/billNavClient.xhtml?bill_id=201120120AB685&search_keywords=> (accessed 5 January 2013).

Berry, T. (2006) *Evening Thoughts: Reflecting on Earth as Sacred Community*. San Francisco: Sierra Club Books.

Bigas, H. (ed.) (2012) *The Global Water Crisis: Addressing an Urgent Security Issue*, Hamilton, Canada: UNU-INWEH, online. Available at: <http://inweh.unu.edu/wp-content/uploads/2013/05/WaterSecurity_The-Global-Water-Crisis.pdf> (accessed 5 January 2013).

Blue Pavilion, People's Summit (21 June 2012) *Declaration: Rio de Janeiro, Brazil*, online. Available at: <http://earthlawcenter.org/static/uploads/documents/Final_Declaration_Blue_Pavilion_English2.pdf> (accessed 5 January 2013).

Boyd, D.R. (2012) *The Environmental Rights Revolution: Constitutions, Human Rights, and the Environment*, Vancouver: UBC Press.

California Public Resource Code § 29702(a) (2009), online. Available at: <http://leginfo.legislature.ca.gov/faces/codes.xhtml> (accessed 5 January 2013).

California Senate Committee on Natural Resources and Water (7 July 2011) *AB 685 Analysis*, online. Available at: <http://leginfo.legislature.ca.gov/> (accessed 5 January 2013).

Carson, R. (2002) *Silent Spring: 40th Anniversary Edition*, New York: Mariner Books, Houghton Mifflin.

Chan, W. (trans.) (1963) *A Source Book in Chinese Philosophy*, Princeton, NJ: Princeton University Press.

City of Pittsburgh Legislative Information Center (1 December 2010). Online. Available at: <http://pittsburghpa.gov/lic/> (accessed 5 January 2013), and also at: <http://earthlawcenter.org/static/uploads/documents/Marcellus_Shale_Ord_Pittsburgh_1.pdf> (accessed 5 January 2013).

Constitución de la República del Ecuador (2008) Title II, Ch. 7, online. Available at: <http://www.asambleanacional.gov.ec/documentos/constitucion_de_bolsillo.pdf> (accessed 5 January 2013).

Cúpula dos Povos (June 2012) *Final Declaration*, online. Available at: <http://cupuladospovos.org.br/wp-content/uploads/2012/07/FinalDeclaration-ENG.pdf> (accessed 5 January 2013).

Diamond, J. (2005) *Collapse: How Societies Choose or Fail to Succeed*, New York: Penguin Books.

Harter, T., Lund, J. et al. (March 2012) *Addressing Nitrate in California's Drinking Water with a Focus on Tulare Lake Basin and Salinas Valley Groundwater*, Davis, CA, University of California Davis, online. Available at: <http://groundwaternitrate.ucdavis.edu/> (accessed 5 January 2013).

Kaufman, F. (2012) 'Wall Street's thirst for water', *Nature*, 490 (7421): 469–71.

Keim, B. (25 October 2012) 'Public or private: the fight over the future of water', *Wired*, online. Available at: <http://www.wired.com/wiredscience/2012/10/water-derivatives/> (accessed 5 January 2013).

Klamath Riverkeeper (2012) *Tell the Forest Service: Only You Can Prevent Extinction*, online. Available at: <http://org2.democracyinaction.org/o/5834/p/dia/action/public/?action_KEY=11549> (accessed 5 January 2013).

Klare, M. (2012) *The Race for What's Left*, New York: Metropolitan Books, Henry Holt & Co.

Lau, D.C. (trans.) (1963) *Lao Tzu: Tao te Ching*, London: Penguin Books.

Little, J. (ed.) (2000) *Striking Thoughts: Bruce Lee's Wisdom for Daily Living*, Boston: Tuttle Publishing.

Lubin, G. (21 July 2011) 'Citi's Top Economist Says the Water Market Will Soon Eclipse Oil', *Business Insider*, online. Available at: <http://articles.businessinsider.com/2011-07-21/markets/30043464_1_clean-water-water-crisis-water-industry> (accessed 5 January 2013).

Meadows, D. (1999) *Leverage Points: Places to Intervene in a System*, Hartland, VT: The Sustainability Institute, online. Available at: <http://www.sustainabilityinstitute.org/pubs/Leverage_Points.pdf> (accessed 5 January 2013).

National Geographic (December 2012) 'Water Grabbers: A global rush on freshwater', online. Available at: <http://news.nationalgeographic.com/news/2012/12/121214-water-grabbers-global-rush-on-water-threatens-millions/> (accessed 5 January 2013).

Pearce, F. (November 2012) 'Grabbing Water from Future Generations,' *National Geographic*, online. Available at: <http://news.nationalgeographic.com/news/2012/12/121218-grabbing-water-from-future-generations/> (accessed 5 January 2013).

Pfister, L., Hubert, S.H. and Fenicia, F. (2009) *Leonardo Da Vinci's Water Theory*, Wallingford, Oxfordshire: IAHS Press.

Republic of Ecuador (2010) *National Plan for Good Living 2009–2013*, online. Available at: <http://plan2009.senplades.gob.ec/web/en/home>.

Santa Cruz, H. (1948) *Statement on the Universal Declaration of Human Rights*, online. Available at: <www.un.org/en/documents/udhr/history.shtml> (accessed 5 January 2013).

Schwenk, T. (1996) *Sensitive Chaos*, trans. O. Wicher and J. Wrigley, 2nd edn, East Sussex, England: Rudolph Steiner Press.

Sierra Club v. Morton, 405 U.S. 727, 741–43 (1972), online. Available at: <http://supreme.justia.com/cases/federal/us/405/727/case.html> (accessed 5 January 2013).

The World Bank (November 2012) *Turn Down the Heat: Why a 4°C World Must Be Avoided*, Washington DC: The World Bank, online. Available at: <http://climatechange.worldbank.org/sites/default/files/Turn_Down_the_Heat_Executive_Summary_English.pdf> (accessed 5 January 2013).

Tūtohu Whakatupua: Agreement between the Whanganui Iwi and the Crown (30 August 2012) online. Available at: <http://nz01.terabyte.co.nz/ots/DocumentLibrary%5CWhanganuiRiverAgreement.pdf> (accessed 5 January 2013).

UN Committee on Economic, Social and Cultural Rights (20 January 2003) 'E/C.12/2002/11: Substantive Issues Arising in the Implementation of the International Covenant on Economic, Social and Cultural Rights: General Comment No. 15 (2002)', online. Available at: <http://www.unhchr.ch/tbs/doc.nsf/0/a5458d1d1bbd713fc1256cc400389e94/$FILE/G0340229.pdf> (accessed 5 January 2013).

UN Department of Economic and Social Affairs (2012) *The Millennium Development Goals Report*, New York: United Nations, online. Available at: <http://www.un.org/millenniumgoals/pdf/MDG%20Report%202012.pdf> (accessed 5 January 2013).

UN General Assembly (10 December 1948) *The Universal Declaration of Human Rights*, online. Available at: <http://www.un.org/en/documents/udhr/index.shtml> (accessed 5 January 2013).

UN General Assembly (18 September 2000) *Resolution A/RES/55/2: United Nations Millennium Declaration*, online. Available at: <http://daccess-dds-ny.un.org/doc/UNDOC/GEN/N00/559/51/PDF/N0055951.pdf?OpenElement> (accessed 5 January 2013).

UN General Assembly (3 August 2010) 'Resolution A/RES/64/292: The Human Right to Water and Sanitation', online. Available HTTP: <http://www.un.org/ga/search/view_doc.asp?symbol=A/RES/64/292> (accessed 5 January 2013).

UN General Assembly (April 2011) *Interactive Dialogue on Harmony with Nature*, online. Available at: <http://www.un.org/en/ga/president/65/initiatives/HarmonywithNature.html> (accessed 5 January 2013).

UN General Assembly (11 September 2012) 'Resolution A/RES/66/288: The Future We Want', online. Available at: <http://sustainabledevelopment.un.org/futurewewant.html> (accessed 5 January 2013).

UN Water, *Statistics: Graphs & Maps*, online. Available at: <http://www.unwater.org/statistics_res.html> (accessed 5 January 2013).

UNEP (2010) *The Greening of Water Law: Managing Freshwater Resources for People and the Environment*, Nairobi: UNON Publishing Services, online. Available at: <http://www.unep.org/delc/portals/119/UNEP_Greening_water_law.pdf> (accessed 5 January 2013).

UNEP (2012) *Global Environmental Outlook 5*, Malta: Progress Press Ltd, online. Available at: <http://www.unep.org/geo/geo5.asp> (accessed 5 January 2013).

UNESCO, *From Potential Conflict to Co-operation Potential: Water for Peace*, Japan: ICM Company, online. Available at: <http://webworld.unesco.org/water/wwap/pccp/pdf/brochure_2.pdf> (accessed 5 January 2013).

US EPA (2010) *Watershed Assessment, Tracking & Environmental Results*, online. Available at: <http://ofmpub.epa.gov/tmdl_waters10/attains_nation_cy.control> (accessed 5 January 2013).

US National Intelligence Council (2 February 2012) *Intelligence Community Assessment on Global Water Security*, online. Available at: <http://www.dni.gov/files/documents/Special%20Report_ICA%20Global%20Water%20Security.pdf> (accessed 5 January 2013).

Wheeler y Huddle en contra de Director de la Procuraduria General del Estado en Loja (30 March 2011) Juicio No. 11121-2011-10, Casillero No. 826, Corte Provincial de Justica de Loja, online. Available at: <http://earthlawcenter.org/static/uploads/documents/Vilcambamba_River_Decision_3_31_11.pdf> (accessed 5 January 2013); and also online at: <http://therightsofnature.org/first-ron-case-ecuador/> (accessed 5 January 2013).

Universal Declaration of the Rights of Mother Earth (22 April 2010) World People's Conference on Climate Change and the Rights of Mother Earth, online. Available at: <http://pwccc.wordpress.com/programa/> (accessed 5 January 2013).

Chapter 12

Earth laws, rights of nature and legal pluralism

Alessandro Pelizzon

It may appear strange to begin a chapter on the comparative legal implications of Wild Law and Earth Jurisprudence by acknowledging the country upon which the paper is written and in which it is being read. And yet, the act of acknowledging country is a fitting example of a discursive legal action that, at a first glance, does not appear to be necessarily legal. Therefore, I believe it is particularly important to begin this paper by acknowledging both the country where it is written, the country that the Ancestors have entrusted the Bundjalung people with looking after, and the country upon which the reader sits at the moment of reading this chapter, wherever the reader may be.

In so doing, I would like to recognize the legal and political implications contained in such an acknowledgment, which a number of authors have successfully explored elsewhere (Pelizzon and Kennedy 2011). At the very least, I would like to suggest that such an act of acknowledgment raises important questions regarding any hegemonic claim to said country. However, more relevantly to the present chapter, I would like to remind the reader and myself that the concept of country is a varied and multifaceted one. For the Aboriginal peoples of Australia, country is far more than an abstract geopolitical entity (Jackson 2007). Rather, it constitutes a precise statement about a different worldview and it is the expression of an unending and uninterrupted cosmology that speaks strongly to the central argument of this chapter.

In the words of Deborah Bird Rose, country is 'the nexus of shared being' (Rose 1992: 86). Country can be described as the matrix of interconnectedness, identity and relationship. Country is comprised of all beings that surround each one of us at any given time and of all phenomena that shape, connect and bind us all. Country is the totality of the relations among and with such beings and phenomena. Country is all the stories within which such relations are construed and contained. It is with this in mind, then, that I would also like to pay respect to the owners and custodians of such stories, the Elders past, present and future. Furthermore, since country is not only inscribed in place but also in time, I would equally like to pay respect to the readers for the time that they share in engaging with this chapter.

In choosing to begin this chapter by acknowledging a concept of country that is rooted in the worldview of the Aboriginal peoples of Australia, I would like to speak to the central concern of this chapter. That is, that the cultural and normative engagement with the welfare of the environment – however defined – is not the province of a single legal tradition but rather ought to be the collective effort of all distinct legal cultures. Consequently, colonial and post-colonial political issues regarding the status and legal position of Indigenous peoples in contemporary nation states (Howard 2003; Hall and Fenelon 2009) cannot be separated from an engagement with their distinct environmental philosophies and their articulation of such philosophies in normative terms. As Vandana Shiva notes, issues of social justice and environmental sustainability form part of an inseparable continuum (Shiva 2011). Therefore, if we are truly to embrace an *Earth* Jurisprudence and the legal changes that to do so entails, we must be prepared to embrace the totality of the distinct worldviews that form the normative web of all Earth legal communities, we must be prepared to engage appropriately and dialogically with all of the many Earth *laws*.

This chapter will focus on Indigenous worldviews and legal perspectives, given the specific place that they are awarded within the emerging discourse of Wild Law and Earth Jurisprudence. Such are the legal traditions that Glenn defines as the 'chthonic' traditions of peoples living 'in or in close harmony with the earth' (Glenn 2000: 61). This definition, although wide ranging, appears to coincide with the traditions of the peoples involved for over two decades in the drafting of the *United Nations Declaration of the Rights of Indigenous Peoples* (Anaya 1996).

Finally, the theoretical perspectives within which this paper is framed are those advanced by the emerging discourse of Wild Law and Earth Jurisprudence. Furthermore, building upon Boulot and Sungaila's recent suggestion of a 'jurisprudence based on ecological sovereignty' (Boulot and Sungaila 2012) and mirroring other authors' suggestions (Bosselmann 1995), I would like to enlarge the planetary boundaries implicit in the term *Earth* Jurisprudence by referring to an *Ecological* Jurisprudence, thus adopting interchangeably the terms Wild Law, Earth Jurisprudence and Ecological Jurisprudence in the course of this chapter.

Indigenous peoples and the rights of nature

Indigenous peoples and their worldviews have occupied a special position within the emerging discourse of Earth Jurisprudence from the very beginning. Thomas Berry himself powerfully voiced such position in *The Sacred Universe*, where he suggested that

> [o]ne of the most striking things about Indigenous peoples is that traditionally they live in conscious awareness of the stars in the heavens, the

> topography of the region, the dawn and sunset, the phases of the moon, and the seasonal sequence. They live in a world of subjects... not a world of objects.
>
> (Berry 2009: 88)

Berry's words are not isolated. Abram, among others, states that many authors

> have come to recognize that long-established indigenous cultures often display a remarkable solidarity with the lands that they inhabit, as well as a basic respect, or even reverence, for the other species that inhabit those lands. Such cultures, much smaller in scale (and far less centralized) than modern Western civilization, seem to have maintained a relatively homeostatic or equilibrial relation with their local ecologies for vast periods of time, deriving their necessary sustenance from the land without seriously disrupting the ability of the earth to replenish itself.
>
> (Abram 1996: 93–4)

Implicit in the recognition of the long-term sustainability of these ecologically adapted Indigenous worldviews is the assumption that the normative organization of Indigenous societies originates from and is consistent with said worldviews. Cullinan writes:

> [I]t appears that certain cultures did manage to evolve laws and other means of regulating human conduct that enabled them to live successfully over long periods of time as part of a wider community of living and non-living beings... [thus succeeding] in avoiding degrading their environments as we have. To me this suggests that they probably know things that we don't and which would be helpful for us to know. Secondly... the fundamental issue that we are dealing with here, our relationship with the Earth, is as old as humanity itself. We would be foolish indeed not to consult the fantastic library of different techniques of human governance that have succeeded over thousands of years.
>
> (Cullinan 2002: 88–9)

Furthermore, the current 'rights of nature' discourse has also been strongly informed by Indigenous voices. Local Indigenous perspectives have been instrumental to the drafting of the new Ecuadorian Constitution of 2008, through the direct influence of the indigenist-based movement and political party Pachakutik Plurinational Unity Movement (Mijeski and Beck 2011). The vision of nature contained in Andean cosmology, already prominent in the Ecuadorian example, became even more central to the *Universal Declaration of the Rights of Mother Earth*. When Bolivian President Evo Morales, an Aymara man himself, convened the *World People's Conference on Climate*

Change and the Rights of Mother Earth in Tiquipaya, just outside Cochabamba, in April 2010, the presence of Indigenous representatives was overwhelming (Morales et al. 2011). Moreover, local Andean Indigenous perspectives were enshrined in the Declaration itself in the linguistic shift from the concept of 'nature' to the concept of 'Mother Earth', direct translation of the Quechua word 'Pacha Mama' (more aptly translated as 'divine or universal feminine' but linguistically simplified as 'Mother Earth').

The relevance of Indigenous worldviews to the project of an Ecological Jurisprudence, both in a practical as well as a theoretical sense, is certainly seen as uncontroversial. Advocates of Earth Jurisprudence suggest and promote an important dialogue with and among all cultures in regard to the way in which we, as a collective species, engage with the environment, with particular emphasis on a dialogue involving Indigenous voices. It is important to remember, however, that this proposed dialogue is not, at present, based on equal power relationships and thus is open to the risk of incorporating and adopting those cultural traits that appear to be particularly inviting to the dominant culture, while arbitrarily excluding cultural traits that are refused and/or negatively judged. Ramsay Taum cautions 'wild lawyers' – that is, legal practitioners engaged in Wild Law – 'not to think that they have invented anything new' but rather to listen to the politically suppressed voices of those who have engaged with similar principles since the 'time of creation' (Taum 2010).

Ontological landscapes and normative lawscapes

Taum's suggestion reminds us that it is not possible to situate Indigenous voices within the legal discourse of Earth Jurisprudence without at the same time considering the ontological and cosmological terrains within which such voices operate. To highlight this point, Graham notes that

> [i]n English, the definition of the word 'environment' is 'the aggregate of surrounding things' and this reflects, to an extent, a worldview in which people are positioned at its centre and everything else around them. In this view, culture is separate from nature so it is unsurprising that law, being cultural, does not regard itself as derivative of nature. The separation between the physical and metaphysical, between place and people, is almost antithetical to Indigenous jurisprudence.
>
> (Graham 2011b: 263)

Although it might appear distant from the operative world of lawyers dealing with courts and with very precise procedural matters on a daily basis, the constant awareness of the interrelatedness between ontological and epistemological concerns and positive legal issues – between worldviews and law – cannot be forsworn when dealing with legal traditions as distinct and varied as the 'chthonian' ones (Glenn 2000). In engaging with Indigenous worldviews and their normative operativization, it is not possible to limit the discussion to the boundaries of the 'legal' as construed and perceived – however successfully – in Western legal philosophies (Kelly 1992; Freeman 2008).

Swimme and Tucker suggest that since the birth of our species, cultural adaptive strategies have been intrinsically connected to environmental milieus:

> Every place we went, we became that place. That is the brilliant power provided by symbolic consciousness. With their cultural inventions, humans could adapt to new environments much more quickly than would be the case if they had to rely solely upon genetic changes. That's why the humans who decided to follow the reindeer rapidly became reindeer people. They walked the same pathways as the reindeer. They ate some of the same foods. At night, in their feasts and their dancing, they celebrated the thrill of being the reindeer people. Other humans aligned themselves with the whales and became the whale people. Some identified with the birds and began wearing feathers and greeting each dawn with song – their highest fulfillment became the act of joining with the birds' celebration. The early humans did not just journey through Earth's worlds. The spirits of each world captivated their imaginations as they revisioned their lives in terms of that place. They absorbed every color and sound into their life and soul.
> (Swimme and Tucker 2011)

Davis defines these cultural strategies, these many worldviews, as *ethnospheres* and points to the symbiosis between these culturally imagined *ethnospheres* and the biospheres that they inhabit (Davis 2009: 3).

However, humans did not – and do not – only journey through the many possible imagined worlds that Earth offered them, they also adapted their social and normative systems to the environments that they perceived and symbiotically interpreted. Not only did they travel through many biospheres and construe many connected *ethnospheres* that determined their social identity in relation to their environment. They also shaped a variety of *nomospheres*. The term *nomosphere* has been introduced in critical legal geography by David Delaney to describe the cultural-material environments that are constituted by the reciprocal materialization of 'the legal' and the legal signification of the 'socio-spatial' (Delaney 2010). Nicole Graham further adopts the convincing term *lawscape* to describe the intrinsic interdependence between law, property regimes and environmental ontologies (Graham 2011a). Every landscape we see, inhabit and shape, the author argues, is the direct result of a combination of ontological possibilities and legal structures. This web of regulatory mechanisms connected both to cultural worldviews and to the environmental milieus in which cultures exist, this interconnected matrix of *biospheres*, *ethnospheres* and *nomospheres* constitutes, I believe, what Berry poetically defined as the many 'Dreams of the Earth' (Berry 1988).

It is to the richness and variety of these 'Dreams of the Earth' that Davis speaks, when he reminds us that

> [o]ne of the intense pleasures of travel is the opportunity to live amongst peoples who have not forgotten the old ways, who still feel their past in the wind, touch it in stones polished by rain, taste it in the bitter leaves of plants. Just to know that, in the Amazon, Jaguar shaman still journey beyond the Milky Way, that myths of the Inuit elders still resonate with meaning, that the Buddhists in Tibet still pursue the breath of the Dharma is to remember the central revelation of anthropology: the idea that the social world in which we live does not exist in some absolute sense, but rather is simply one model of reality, the consequence of one set of intellectual and spiritual choices that our particular cultural lineage made, however successfully, many generations ago. ... All these people teach us that there are other options, other possibilities, other ways of thinking and interacting with the earth. This is an idea that can only fill us with hope.
>
> (Davis 2009: 1–2)

Earth laws

Any attempt to engage dialogically with Indigenous *nomospheres* requires a distinct epistemological approach capable of considering and embracing the distinct ontological and cosmological parameters within which such *nomospheres* operate. Although the establishment of such an approach is beyond the scope of this chapter, I would like to follow the suggestion of a number of Indigenous colleagues and friends and adopt a narrative approach to briefly introduce a number of examples from which the reader may hopefully gaze into the many Dreams of the Earth that Indigenous cultures offer to the project of an Ecological Jurisprudence. Through these examples I do not wish to present any coherent or cohesive framework of inquiry, but rather indirectly introduce other ontological possibilities than the ones entertained by the Western legal discourse within which the philosophy of Earth Jurisprudence originated.

> 'I want you to remember only this one thing', said the Badger. 'The stories people tell have a way of taking care of them. If stories come to you, care for them. And learn to give them anywhere they are needed. Sometimes a person needs a story more than food to stay alive.'
>
> (Borrows 2007: 13)

Stories are, indeed, the most common epistemological device adopted in Indigenous discourse (Meyer 2004). Swimme and Berry further argue that all cultural knowledge of the cosmos is better understood as a 'story' (Swimme and Berry 1994), including the purportedly universal and 'objective' scientific understanding of the universe, without any of such stories claiming exclusionary and hegemonic prominence. When viewed in this light, creation stories assume a much more complex ecological meaning, they become relevant not only ontologically but also normatively. Black writes that 'by telling a cosmological story from my ancestors' country, I am demonstrating how I am patterned into the web of Law stories that have weaved my ancestors into reality' (Black 2011: 4).

Indigenous creation stories often relate to the time of the Ancestors, a mythical time not to be construed as a time *before* time, but rather as a time *beyond* time, a cosmological referent that constantly positions any epistemological and normative pursuit. Suzuki and Knudtson write that for the Koyukon Indians of subarctic Alaska, 'Distant Time represents nature's timeless substratum. This primal, creative epoch of life on Earth is the fertile, boundless, mythic soil in which *everything – all things human and natural –* in this world is ultimately rooted. Distant Time is a dim but potent memory, illuminated largely by traditional stories and spiritual practices' (Suzuki and Knudtson 1992: 35). The Koyukon Distant Time mirrors, among others, Tjukurpa, the Dreamtime of the Pitjantjatjara people of central Australia, the ancestral mythical time constantly relived in and through Dreaming stories (Berndt and Berndt 1988).

If stories are the universal cognitive matrix within which cultures articulate and orient themselves in relation to 'nature', however, Indigenous narratives add more complex dimensions to this understanding. When asked what it means to be 'Indigenous', Uncle Dootch, a Yuin man from the Illawarra area of southeastern Australia, said 'it's my nature' and, he added

> when I say 'that's my nature' I'm talking about the natural environment out there, because that's my nature. The ocean, the bush... People don't look at it in the context, they look at it as my personality. But I say 'yes, that's my personality' but understand that my nature also is that natural environment right beside you... When I'm in the bush and I say to people 'this is my nature' they understand exactly what I'm saying, because they're in that environment with me and they see how I relate to it. When I'm on Country I walk slow, I want to see everything that surrounds me, the colors of the flowers, the wind in trees, the smell of the plants, the sound of the water running, just a goanna I can spot from a hundred yards off, observing his movements while he's observing mine... Indigenous people who are connected to Country, we look at all of that because they're the spirits of our people, the very trees, the very

rocks, the mountains that we walk on, we're walking on our spirits... That's my nature.

(Pelizzon, 2012: 253)

Indeed, the very Western term 'nature' seems incapable of 'enfolding Native notions of a vast, spiritually charged cosmic continuum, in which [identity,] human society, biosphere, [law,] and the entire universe are seamlessly rolled into one' (Suzuki and Knudtson 1992: 19). For the Bunun people of central Taiwan, for example, no single word is capable of translating the Western concept of 'nature' (Soqluman and Hung, 2010). Instead, two words are used synergistically: *taki*, to describe the totality of the known universe and *asan*, to describe human interactions with it. The word *asan*, literally, can be translated in two ways. Firstly, as 'home', as nature is the place that humans inhabit. Secondly, as 'excrement', since nature is, Soqluman and Hung explain, the place that humans also pollute. The combination of these two literal meanings thus indicates that together with the privilege of inhabiting a place comes the responsibility of maintaining it.

This sense of interconnectedness with 'nature', of identification with and respect for a place of belonging – that is, 'country' for Aboriginal peoples of Australia – is encoded in the words with which traditional Hawaiians declare their identity: 'I he Hawaii', 'I am Hawaii' (Taum 2010). This sense of identity with the Earth, with nature, with country, whereby individual identity and 'country' of belonging are one and the same, is fully realized in what Wade Davis defines as 'sacred geography' (Davis 2009: 116). For the people of the Anaconda of the north-eastern Amazonian basin, for example, rivers are not simply a way of transport and communication, but rather they are the very veins of the earth, the paths along which the ancestors travelled at the beginning of time. At the same time the numerous sacred sites articulated along these pulsating corridors of both life and myth are not only memorials or symbols of distant mythic events, but rather they are living places that eternally inform the present (Davis 2009: 95). Equally, for Australian Aboriginal peoples the entire natural world is saturated with meaning and cosmological significance. Every rock and waterfall embodies a story and everything is more than it appears, for the visible world is only one level of perception. Every plant, every animal, every rock is a distinct physical representation of the same spiritual essence that connects, uninterrupted, all beings, thus making the distinction between humans and the rest of nature utterly devoid of meaning.

The variety, richness and importance of all these 'Dreams of the Earth' is, I believe, self-evident. However, by positioning these stories in relation to the many questions raised by the philosophy of Earth Jurisprudence, it is possible to see that many answers to such questions have already been operativized within Indigenous *nomospheres*. Without any attempt to universalization or abstraction from the contextual and vibrant milieu within which these examples exist, one example among many of this direct continuity between an ethical ontology based on identity with one's 'nature' and a political-articulation of the legal responsibilities that follow is contained in the totemic responsibility common to all Aboriginal people of Australia and could provide a possible answer to the question of 'who' is to represent nature, a question that is crucial to the articulation of rights of nature since Stone's (1972) topical essay.

Aboriginal kinship systems divide human societies into moieties and 'skin names', each represented by a totemic ancestral connection to the Dreaming expressed by a precise element of nature (Berndt and Berndt 1988). Each individual thus shares a series of connections with one's individual and collective totems, or Dreamings, and thus a sense of individual and collective identity not only with nature as a whole, but particularly with some elements of nature. Equally, these elements of nature define the identity of the person and continuously connect him or her to the Dreaming, the creative time of the Ancestors. As a result of this sense of identity, the individual derives a direct responsibility toward one's totems and an absolute taboo toward their harm and, or, consumption. Each individual sharing a totemic connection with a potentially injured element of nature would not only be entitled but also actually required to confront the alleged offender – another individual inscribed within the complex web of interpersonal obligations defined by the kinship system – about the offending behaviour. Consequently, from the point of view of Western environmental economics, this normative strategy charges each individual with responsibilities toward the only 'resource' he or she has no access to. Furthermore, and more importantly for the present argument, from the point of view of the unanswered questions raised by rights of nature legislation, this strategy creates a diffused, specialized and interdependent representation of nature's rights within the human political community.

Where laws collide

The importance of Indigenous voices to the project of an Ecological Jurisprudence has been only further revealed, I hope, by the examples briefly presented above. However, it is not the case that many of the ontological, cosmological and epistemological premises of Indigenous *nomospheres* are readily accepted by non-Indigenous audiences. White Jr asks, "'Do people have ethical obligations toward rocks?" ...To almost all Americans, still saturated with ideas historically dominant in Christianity ... the question makes no sense at all' (White Jr 1967: 1205). However, the question not only makes perfect sense but also has unequivocally positive answers in many Indigenous cultures.

Furthermore, the lack of acceptance – and often of basic understanding – of Indigenous worldviews does not operate on a dialogical terrain where all participants possess the same power. Thus, insofar as a power differential exists and 'regimes of truth' (Foucault 1996) are determined, both directly and indirectly, by processes of power, ecological 'truths' are defined by the dominant paradigm and imposed upon those who are in position of power subordination. 'Many environmentalists', David Suzuki writes, 'are reluctant to allow indigenous people, whose cultures are built around the use of animals and plants, to exploit the land that has always belonged to them' (Suzuki and Knudtson 1992: xxxv). This is immediately apparent, for example, in the resistance against contemporary hunting of dugongs in Northern Queensland, or in the mistrust displayed toward Native American entrepreneurial activities such as the establishment of casinos on tribal lands.

More subtly, however, power differentials exert more indirect colonial impositions. This is what Cepek defines as *environmentality*; that is, the risk that environmentalist programs and movements operate as forms of governmentality in a Foucauldian sense (Cepek 2011). Cepek argues that environmental paradigms are subtly forced upon Indigenous actors in a manner similar to that of governments with their 'subjects' (Cepek 2011). Hence, the result of environmental programs ostensibly directed toward the care and protection of the environment can indirectly cause processes of cultural imposition upon Indigenous worldviews. This is exemplified by a case study of the Cofan people of Zabalo in the far northeastern Amazonian region of Ecuador and their interaction with the Field Museum of Natural History's Office of Environmental and Conservation Programs (ECP). 'Perhaps', the author writes, 'the most important form of alienation involved in Cofan performance of scientific conservation is that of the [Indigenous] workers from the forms of knowledge they produce. Paradoxically, what most interests the ECP in Zabalo is what most complicates its efforts, namely Cofan people's pre-existing practices of community conservation' (Cepek 2011: 507–10).

At present, most Indigenous cultures live in a condition of an asymmetry of power, whereby governments ultimately exert hegemonic power over traditional cultures, as a whole and in relation to specific cultural traits. Dzil Nchaa Si An, 'Big Seated Mountain' in Western Apache, or 'Mount Graham' as also known in colonial times, is considered one of the four holy mountains by Apache people; that notwithstanding, multiple organizations have been allowed to set up a series of large telescopes in a few separate observatories authorized by a Congressional waiver of US environmental laws for – purportedly universal – scientific reasons. The same sense of impotence toward the desecration of one's sacred geography has been experienced, among countless examples, by the Lakota people in relation to the Paha Sapa, or 'Black Hills', or by the Anangu people of Northern Territory in relation to Uluru, or 'Ayers Rock'.

Insofar as Indigenous cultures exist and operate from a position of subordination toward the colonial governments established on their ancestral lands, it is not possible to truly and fully embrace the cultural diversity contained in worldviews coexisting in the same geographical space. Westra writes that

> the interdependence between the basic/survival rights of indigenous peoples, their biological integrity and the ecological integrity of their lands ... is constantly under attack through the economic activities of developed countries that view the use of aboriginal lands and peoples as their right, with little or no consideration for the gravity of the consequences that ensue.
>
> (Westra 2008:17)

As long as this is the case, Indigenous voices are somehow dimmed, if not entirely silenced and consequently, I believe, the project of an 'Earth' Jurisprudence is greatly diminished. This suggests that 'Wild Lawyers' and legal practitioners engaging with Earth Jurisprudence and rights of nature should be cautious so as not to exert forms of environmental colonialism upon all those cultural traits that they reject as not consistent with (unilaterally established) environmental projects. The central message of this chapter is that a paradigmatic shift such as the one advocated by Wild Law and Earth Jurisprudence should be cautious so as not to impose another worldview, however seemingly more enlightened, upon the totality of human communities on the planet.

Some exponents of Earth Jurisprudence have privately suggested to me that 'Indigenous people do not possess a concept of "rights"' and thus the entire articulation of rights of nature ought to be advanced in the Western legal terms in which such concept of 'rights' has evolved. The suggestion is not only, I believe, exclusionary at the detriment of all Indigenous groups actively involved at present in the discourse, but also it is extremely fallacious from the point of view of comparative law. Although it is certainly true that a concept of 'rights' as historically defined in Western cultures is unique to such cultures, this does not mean that there are no 'functional equivalents' in other cultures. Even within the Western legal traditions, after all, how can we be sure that 'right' is an appropriate translation of the German concept '*Recht*', of the French '*droit*', of Italian's '*diritto*'?

Although a comprehensive discussion on legal pluralism is beyond the scope of this chapter (but see Giliessen 1972; Griffiths 1986; Griffiths 2002) legal anthropologists and comparative lawyers have devised a highly refined methodology to engage the question of 'chtonian' law (Llewellyn and Hoebel 1941; Pospisil 1971; Rouland 1988; Sacco 1980). Consequently, I believe it is safe to assume that, whether or not we consider law to be a universal phenomenon and whether or not we consider all cultures as possessing 'legal' protocols, we can certainly consider all cultures to possess 'functional legal equivalents' (Zweigert and Kötz 1977) and thus we can consider all cultures to be legally co-involved in the project of Earth Jurisprudence and in the rights of nature discourse.

The 'function' to be considered equivalent can here be found in the central concern of Wild Law and Earth Jurisprudence; that is, the concept of 'environment'. In this sense, the many concepts of 'environment' (the many *ethnospheres*), and the multiple ways in which human conduct is regulated in relation to them (the many *nomospheres*) constitute the comparative interface between diverse legal traditions. The relation that all human cultures have with the non-human 'other' and the way in which all cultures regulate their social interaction with it become the comparative lens through which regulatory – that is, 'legal' in a comparative sense – mechanisms can be contextualized and interpreted.

This means, firstly, to embrace ontological and cosmological differences as part of the legal terrain to be explored by Wild Law and Earth Jurisprudence. Secondly, it is crucial to acknowledge that political and environmental issues are inextricably inseparable and thus issues of renegotiated sovereignty, political independence and self-determination of Indigenous peoples are fundamental to the project of a truly universal Earth Jurisprudence as issues of environmental protection. Thirdly, it means to draw on disciplines and theoretical perspectives that are effective vehicles for establishing the cognitive bridges required to facilitate an understanding of the cultural and legal milieu of Indigenous worldviews. Finally, this chapter contends, it means to adopt a truly dialogical approach in order to establish meaningful conversations among distinct cultural traditions. This does not mean to accept unquestioningly all cultural traits, arguments and strategies, naturally, since political specificity of contemporary Indigenous issues does not need to equate to a novel form of cultural exceptionalism. Instead, it means to suspend personal judgement and enter into a dialogue as political equals. To become participants, as legal actors, of this dialogue may lead us to feel part of the creative effort of a truly extended family, one comprised not only of seven billion human beings with all their social structures and political institutions but also of all beings and phenomena, both visible and invisible, with whom we are sharing this space and time.

References

Abram, D. (1996) *The Spell of the Sensuous*, New York: Vintage.
Anaya, S.J. (1996; 3rd edn 2004) *Indigenous Peoples in International Law*, Oxford: Oxford University Press.
Berndt, R.M. and Berndt, C.H. (1988) *The World of the First Australians*, Canberra: Aboriginal Studies Press.
Berry, T. (1988) *The Dream of the Earth*, San Francisco: Sierra Club Books.
Berry, T. (2009) *The Sacred Universe*, New York: Columbia University Press.
Black, C.F. (2011) *The Land is the Source of the Law*, New York: Routledge.

Borrows, J. (2007) *Recovering Canada: The Resurgence of Indigenous Law*, Toronto: University of Toronto Press.
Bosselmann, K. (1995) *When Two Worlds Collide: Society and Ecology*, Auckland: RSVP.
Boulot, P. and Sungaila, H. (2012) 'A new legal paradigm: Towards a jurisprudence based on ecological sovereignty', *Macquarie Journal of International and Comparative Environmental Law*, 8(1): 1.
Cepek, M.L. (2011) 'Foucault in the forest: Questioning environmentality in Amazonia', *American Ethnologist*, 38(3): 501.
Cullinan, C. (2002; 2nd edn 2011) *Wild Law*, White River Junction, VT: Chelsea Green Publishing.
Cullinan, C. (2011) 'A History of Wild Law', in Burdon, Peter (ed.) (2011) *Exploring Wild Law*, Kent Town, Adelaide: Wakefield Press.
Davis, W. (2009) *The Wayfinders*, Toronto: House of Anansi Press.
Delaney, D. (2010) *The Spatial, the Legal and the Pragmatics of World-Making: Nomospheric Investigations*, Oxford: Taylor and Francis.
Foucault, M. (1996) 'Truth and juridical forms', *Social Identities: Journal for the Study of Race, Nation and Culture*, 2(3): 327.
Freeman, M.D.A. (2008) *Lloyd's Introduction to Jurisprudence*, 8th edn, London: Sweet & Maxwell.
Giliessen, J. (ed.) (1972) *Le Pluralisme Juridique*, Bruxelles: Editions de l'Université de Bruxelles.
Glenn, H.P. (2000; 4th edn 2010) *Legal Traditions of the World*, Oxford: Oxford University Press.
Graham, N. (2011a) *Lawscape*, New York: Routledge.
Graham. N. (2011b) 'Owning the Earth', in P. Burdon (ed.) *Exploring Wild Law*, Kent Town, Adelaide: Wakefield Press.
Griffiths, A. (2002) 'Legal pluralism', in R. Banakar and M. Travers (eds) *An Introduction to Law and Social Theory*, Oxford: Hart.
Griffiths, J. (1986) 'What is legal pluralism?', *Journal of Legal Pluralism and Unofficial Law*, 24: 1.
Hall, T.D. and Fenelon, J.V. (2009) *Indigenous Peoples and Globalization*, Boulder, CO: Paradigm Press.
Howard, B.R. (2003) *Indigenous Peoples and the State*, DeKalb, IL: Northern Illinois University Press.
Jackson, R. (2007) *Sovereignty*, Cambridge: Polity Press.
Kelly, J.M. (1992) *A Short History of Western Legal Theory*, Oxford: Oxford University Press.
Latour, B. (2004) *Politiques de la nature*, trans. C. Porter (2004) *Politics of Nature*, Cambridge: Harvard University Press.
Llewellyn, K. and Hoebel, E.A. (1941) *The Cheyenne Way*, Norman, OK: University of Oklahoma Press.
Meyer, M.A. (2004) *Ho'oulu. Our Time of Becoming*, Honolulu: 'Ai Pohaku Press.
Mijeski, K.J. and Beck, S.H. (2011) *Pachakutik and the Rise and Decline of the Ecuadorian Indigenous Movement*, Athens, OH: University of Ohio Press.
Morales, A.E., Barlow, M., Shiva, V. and Biggs, S. (2011) *The Rights of Nature: The Case for a Universal Declaration of the Rights of Mother Earth*, San Francisco, CA: Council of Canadians, Fundación Pachamama and Global Exchange.

Pelizzon, A. and Kennedy, J. (2011) 'Welcome to Country: Legal meanings and cultural implications', paper presented at the Ceremonies of Law Conference, Law and Society Association of Australia and New Zealand at the University of Wollongong, Wollongong, December 2011.

Pelizzon, A. (2012) *Laws of the Land. Traditional Land Protocols, Native Title and Legal Pluralism in the Illawarra*, Lambert Academic Publishing.

Pospisil, L.J. (1971) *Anthropology of Law: A Comparative Theory of Law*, New York: Harper & Row.

Rose, D.B. (1992; 2000 edn) *Dingo Makes Us Human*, Cambridge: Cambridge University Press.

Rouland, N. (1988) *Anthropologie juridique*, trans. P.G. Planel (1994) *Legal Anthropology*, London: Continuum International Publishing.

Sacco, R. (1980) *Introduzione al Diritto Comparato*, Torino: Giappichelli.

Shiva, V. (2011) *Vandana Shiva on Biopiracy and the Rights of Nature*, online. Available at: <https://foodfreedom.wordpress.com/2011/06/05/vandana-shiva-biopiracy-rights-of-nature/> (accessed 6 January 2013).

Soqluman, N. and Hung, H. (2010) 'A Bunun perspective', paper presented at the Keeping the Fire Conference, Second Australian Conference on Wild Law and Earth Jurisprudence, Wollongong, July 2010.

Stone, C. (1972, 3rd ed 2010) *Should Trees Have Standing?*, New York: Oxford University Press.

Suzuki, D. and Knudtson, P. (1992) *Wisdom of the Elders*, New York: Bantam.

Swimme, B.T. and Berry, T. (1994) *The Universe Story*, New York: HarperCollins.

Swimme, B.T. and Tucker, M.E. (2011) *Journey of the Universe*, New Haven, CT: Yale University Press.

Taum, R. (2010) 'A Hawaiian Indigenous voice', paper presented at the Keeping the Fire Conference, Second Australian Conference on Wild Law and Earth Jurisprudence, Wollongong, July 2010.

Westra, L. (2008) *Environmental Justice and the Rights of Indigenous Peoples*, London: Earthscan.

White, L.T. Jr (1967) 'The historical roots of our ecologic crisis', *Science*, 155: 1203.

Zweigert, K. and Kötz, H. (1977; 3rd edn 1998) *Einführung in die Rechsvergleichung*, trans. T. Wier (2011) *An Introduction to Comparative Law*, Oxford: Oxford University Press.

Part IV

A Wild Law perspective on environmental stewardship

Chapter 13

Ecological limits, planetary boundaries and Earth Jurisprudence

M Maloney

The idea of ecological limits has been contentious since it was first brought to international attention by the release of the Club of Rome's *Limits to Growth* in 1972 (Meadows et al. 1972). The study examined several possible scenarios for humanity's progress and impact on the environment, based on five variables: world population, industrialization, pollution, food production and resource depletion. Two of the scenarios saw 'overshoot and collapse' of the global system by the mid to latter part of the twenty-first century, while a third scenario resulted in a stabilized world. The study stimulated criticism and debate when it was released, and the scrutiny from some quarters escalated to the extent that by the late 1980s the report had been 'demonized' by a coalition of conservative economists and other groups (Badi 2008). Nonetheless with over 30 million copies of the report sold worldwide, it brought the idea of limits to international attention and triggered a significant body of multi-disciplinary work focusing on the biophysical limits of our planet. The report has received 20 and 30 year 'revisits' (Meadows et al. 1992, 2004) and it continues to withstand rigorous analysis (Turner 2008).

Forty years after its release, its most bleak scenarios have been played out. Humanity's insatiable consumption and destruction of the natural world has brought us to the situation where more than 80 per cent of the world's people now live in countries that are 'biocapacity debtors'. This means they use more than they have and must import resources, deplete their own stocks and/or utilize the global commons of atmosphere and ocean (Global Footprint Network 2011). Ever widening disparities exist between the resource consumption of industrialized and poorer countries, but in aggregate, human societies are now estimated to be using the equivalent of 1.5 Earths to meet their demands (Global Footprint Network 2011).

The ecological crisis brought about by humanity's overshoot is now well documented – deforestation, biodiversity loss, air and water pollution, land degradation and the escalating disruption of entire components of the Earth System, such as anthrogenic climate change (Millennium Ecosystem Assessment 2005). Human influence on the environment has become so significant that some scientists are claiming we have moved into a new geological epoch – the 'Anthropocene' (Crutzen and Stoermer 2000). Given how well documented and studied human impact on the environment is, and the direct threat this poses to our own existence, the logical response is for us to live within our ecological limits; to consume less and to 'limit human consumption so it doesn't exceed the sustainable level of production from natural systems' (Lowe 2006: 62). However, as noted above, human societies continue to escalate into overshoot.

The aim of this chapter is to use Earth Jurisprudence (EJ) and Wild Law to examine the debate about, and offer a practical framework for progressing, the idea of living within our ecological limits. By doing so, I hope to engage directly with the task of this book – to explore how Wild Law may be of practical use in moving us towards restoring a healthy relationship with the Earth Community.

In Part 1 I provide an overview of key elements of EJ and Wild Law and argue that in terms of ecological limits, EJ works as both a critical theory and a practical, constructive tool. As a critical theory it helps us deconstruct and understand the barriers in our modern governance and legal systems to living within our limits, and it offers the necessary 'mind shift' to challenge the dominant pro-growth, destructive world view that is causing the ecological crisis. As a practical tool it helps us ask the key questions that we must answer in order to live within our limits: how do we know our ecological limits? How do we know our place in the world? What governance structures and tools can help us respect valued relationships and live within our limits? And how do we deconstruct our dysfunctional governance systems, and challenge existing power structures, in order to transform our societies to live within our limits and respect the Earth Community?

In Part 2, I apply these questions to aspects of the limits discourse and begin creating an EJ framework for exploring how to live within our limits. I demonstrate that EJ can help us: (i) question and engage with current scientific understandings, including Earth System Science and Planetary Boundaries, to better understand our ecological limits; (ii) engage with a broader, Earth-centred worldview, informed by science, philosophy and traditional knowledge, to create a new vision of our place in the world; (iii) draw on Earth-centred legal and governance constructs such as Rights of Nature, to design new governance approaches; and (iv) link existing, fragmented methods and tools and guide our efforts to challenge existing power structures and transform our societies so that we embrace governance systems that support the Earth Community.

Finally, I also suggest that one of the greatest strengths of EJ is its ability to combine a rational critique of some of our oldest Western legal and governance structures, with a very new worldview that, while built on modern scientific knowledge, also links to a less rational, more emotive call to return to a sacred appreciation of the Earth and the Earth Community.

Part 1: Earth Jurisprudence and ecological limits
Overview

Earth Jurisprudence is an emerging theory of Earth-centred law and governance. Its starting point is that our ecological crisis is caused by anthropocentrism – a belief by people in the modern industrialized world that we are somehow separate from, and more important than, the rest of the natural world. Thomas Berry argued that this anthropocentric worldview underpins all the governance structures of modern industrial society – economics, education, religion, law – and has fostered the belief that the natural world is merely a collection of objects for human use (Berry 1999).

In contrast, Earth Jurisprudence suggests a radical rethinking of humanity's place in the world, to acknowledge the history and origins of the Universe as a guide and inspiration to humanity and to see human beings as one of many interconnected members of the Earth Community (Swimme and Berry 1992). By 'Earth Community' Berry referred to all human and 'other than human' life forms and components of the planet (Berry 1999: 105). He suggested that 'our great work' is to transform human governance systems to create a harmonious and nurturing presence on the Earth (Berry 1999).

Responding to Berry's work, Cormac Cullinan's *Wild Law: A Manifesto for Earth Justice* (2003) was a direct call for our legal profession to engage with Earth Jurisprudence, and to shift our legal system to support the Earth Community. Eco-centrism in the law has been explored by writers such as Christopher Stone in 1972 (Stone 2010), Roderick Nash (Nash 1989), Klaus Bosselmann (Bosselmann 1994) and others. The work of Berry and Cullinan builds on this body of work, but I would argue it also offers something new. In addition to building a growing body of literature (Cullinan 2003; Burdon 2011a), EJ and Wild Law are increasingly becoming practical and constructive tools to guide practice. This is reflected in the growing international movement of people and organizations advocating for Earth-centred law and governance, and who are explicitly building their movements on the work of Berry and Cullinan.[1] It has also been demonstrated by inspiring, real-world examples of social change and Earth-centred law and governance, such as Ecuador's 2008 Constitution, Bolivia's 2010 Act for the Rights of Mother Earth and the several dozen local Rights of Nature ordinances that now exist in the United States (Margil 2014).

Key elements of EJ relevant to limits

There are four elements of Earth Jurisprudence that are particularly relevant to a discussion about ecological limits. First, EJ acknowledges that the Universe is the primary lawgiver (Berry 1999). In contrast to positivist legal systems, that see human laws as the highest authority for human society (and implicitly, for all other life forms and ecological systems), EJ sees the laws of the Universe, the 'Great Jurisprudence' or 'Great Law', as providing the fundamental parameters of the Earth Community, including human societies. Thus, EJ explicitly advocates that human societies live within the 'rules' or limits of the natural world.

Second, EJ sees the Earth as interconnected and argues for a relationship-based existence between humanity and the rest of the Earth Community. This contrasts with the contemporary legal view that creates relationships between people and between people and corporations through constructs like property law, while commodifying and exploiting other aspects of the natural world (Cullinan 2003; Graham 2011; Burdon 2013). This concept of an Earth Community places greater duties and responsibilities on human beings. Rather than permitting unlimited 'use' of the natural world by humans, the concept of an Earth Community requires humans to nurture and support the biosphere. To do this, humans will have to limit their actions so that the rest of the Earth Community can survive, thrive and evolve. Indeed, Berry claimed that 'the primary concern of the human community must be the preservation of the comprehensive community' and he argued for a human world that works to ensure that all members of the Earth Community can thrive and continue their evolutionary journey (Berry 1999: 58).

Third, many advocates of EJ have argued that the Earth Community and all the beings that constitute it have 'rights', including the right to exist, to habitat or a place to be and to participate in the evolution of the Earth Community (Berry 2002). Berry argued that 'nature's rights should be the central issue in any… discussion of the legal context of our society' (Berry 1999: 80). Granting rights to nature is a radical rethinking of the role of our legal system, as it currently grants rights only to humans and selected human constructs such as corporations. Granting rights to nature challenges the supremacy of human interests and forces a rethink of the underpinning objectives and operation of the law. And yet the idea appears to be taking hold in many jurisdictions. The legislation mentioned above, in Ecuador, Bolivia and the United States move Earth-centred ideas from merely a theory, to a practical framework for Earth stewardship.

Fourth and finally, it can be argued that EJ calls for greater creativity, pluralism and 'soul' in our legal system. Cullinan argues that 'if we and the next few generations are to meet the challenge of our age by successfully catalysing huge societal changes, we will have to bring our whole selves to the party' (Cullinan 2003: 19). Through Cullinan's book *Wild Law* and the work of Thomas Berry, we see a call for the legal system to expand its current narrow frame of reference from legal positivism to incorporate different ways of knowing and governing ourselves and the Earth. One of the appealing aspects of the Earth Jurisprudence movement[2] is that it invites a greater engagement by law and legal practitioners, with philosophy, the natural sciences, indigenous knowledge and pluralism; and it emphasizes rather than suppresses human emotional connections to the Earth.

In summary, EJ offers a critique of existing law and governance, a substantive new foundation for Earth-centred legal approaches and calls for doing law and governance differently. It also directly engages with humanity's need to live within its ecological limits. By advocating that all life is bound by the laws of the universe and that all members of the Earth Community have rights, EJ gives us a range of 'boundaries' for human activities. EJ expressly engages with the idea that humanity must rein in its activities and create a harmonious relationship with the Earth Community and it stresses that the way to do this is not by regulating nature, but ourselves.

Before moving to an analysis of how Earth Jurisprudence can be used as a framework for living within our limits, it is important to first reflect on why human societies have so far been unable to transition to living within the biophysical capacity of the Earth.

Barriers to living within our limits

From an Earth Jurisprudence perspective, the reasons for humanity's failure to transition to societal rules that help us live within our ecological limits are complex, but can be grouped under three main headings or barriers.

The first barrier is the powerful combination of two belief systems in modern industrial society: anthropocentrism, which was discussed earlier in this chapter, and the belief in unlimited economic growth. The idea that unlimited growth is critical for the health of national economies developed during the Industrial Revolution and continues to dominate modern political, economic and cultural life (Alexander 2011). The combination of these two worldviews has been a significant barrier to the mind shift necessary to accept and act on the reality of our ecological limits (Berry 1999).

The second barrier to human societies living within their limits is the unequal power structures created and perpetuated by the vested interests who control much of the Earth Community, or the planet's 'natural resources', and currently prevent those concerned with the health of the Earth from transforming our societies. There are now many claims that modern industrial societies are plutocracies rather than democracies (Alexander 2014; Burdon 2013; Preston 2013) and are governed by the interests of wealthy individuals and corporations, in partnership with state-sanctioned policies. The lengths to which private interests have gone to protect their financial interests in industries as diverse as tobacco and fossil fuels have now been carefully documented (Oreskes and Conway 2011). There are also an increasing number of exposés showing the interaction between powerful private interests and their control over the public policy agenda (Sachs 2011). Such power structures mean that the vast majority of the world's population, including civil society and other groups who want to live sustainably and within their ecological limits, are excluded from key decision making roles. This 'pathology' of a society dominated by vested interests and disconnected from its physical realities is a powerful and all-pervading reason why we do not yet live within our limits.

Finally, the fact that industrialized nations have functioned for hundreds of years without any concept of environmental limits means that living *within* limits is new and challenging for our governance and legal systems. Our existing governance systems – our institutions, regulatory systems and 'environmental management tools' – are all built to support human-centred growth and are not yet sufficiently sophisticated or in tune with the Earth Community to help us live within our limits (Salzman 1997; Allenby 2002; Guth 2008).

Earth Jurisprudence can assist in addressing these barriers, by encouraging us to ask some important questions: how do we understand our Earth and our ecological limits? How do we know our place in the world? How do we reconstruct our governance systems to live within our limits and how do we guide ourselves to make the right choices and live within the Earth Community? Finally, by inviting us to transform and transition from where we are now, to building a harmonious relationship with the Earth Community, EJ encourages us to ask: how do we create the earth centred change we need?

Part 2: An EJ framework for living within our limits

In this section I apply these questions to aspects of the limits discourse and begin creating an Earth Jurisprudence framework for exploring how to live within our limits.

How do we know our ecological limits? The great law, planetary boundaries and multi-scalar governance responses

The first step in guiding humanity to live within its limits is to know what our limits are. An ecocentric worldview, on its own, will not help us rein in humanity's devastating impact on the Earth. To do this, all elements of modern society must be transformed to better understand, respond to and set rules and supportive frameworks for living within the physical capacity of the Earth system. This calls for human law and governance to explicitly engage with science and knowledge of the non-human world.

Knowing our earth

Berry argues that modern societies are disconnected from the natural world, and this supports our destruction of it. In industrial society's pursuit of a 'wonderworld' we have created a 'waste world' and 'so completely are we at odds with the planet that brought us into being that we have become strange beings indeed' (Berry 1999: 15). Earth Jurisprudence challenges us to develop a deeper understanding of our universe and home, and all of the life within it. Berry argued that we need to develop this relationship with Earth on various scales; that we need an 'intimate acquaintance with the organic functioning of our local region ... (and) ... we also need a larger sense of the Earth' (Berry 1999: 93). He called on all human institutions, and especially universities and educational institutions, to focus on a deeper understanding of the natural world. He argued that the task of such institutions is to ensure humanity focuses on nurturing, not exploiting, the Earth which supports us (Berry 1999). I would argue that developing this intimate knowledge of the non-human world plays a vital part in enabling modern societies to live within their limits.

Knowing our limits

Within Earth Jurisprudence, the idea of the Great Law is critical to how we know our Earth, and our own limits. Berry argues that human society should recognize the supremacy of the already existing Earth governance of the planet, as a single, yet differentiated community. What are these supreme Earth governance systems and what is 'the Great Law'?

Burdon provides a useful overview of the Great Law, noting that:

> Earth Jurisprudence advocates the existence of two types of law, which exist in a hierarchical relationship. On top is the Great Law which represents the rules or principles of nature, which are discoverable by human beings and relevant to human-earth interaction. Underneath the great Law is Human Law which represents rules articulated by human authorities, which are consistent with the Great Law and enacted for the common good of the comprehensive Earth community.
>
> (Burdon 2011b: 60)

In his exploration of the Great Law, Burdon takes Cullinan's explanation: 'laws or principles that govern how the universe functions', and develops it further. Consistent with other Earth jurists, Burdon contends that the Great

Law should be defined with reference to 'first principles' in the scientific discipline of ecology (Burdon 2011b: 66) and clarifies further the concept of 'ecological integrity' and its role as an objective of Earth jurisprudence (Burdon 2012, 2013). The concept of ecological integrity, which evolved as an ethical concept and has appeared in domestic and international law, connotes a valuable whole, the state of being whole or undiminished, unimpaired. Laura Westra notes that the key elements of ecological integrity are: the autopoietic (self creative) capacities of life to organize, regenerate, reproduce, sustain, adapt, develop and evolve over time at a specific location – thus integrity defines the evolutionary and biogeographical processes of a system as well as its parts of elements at specific location (Westra 2011: 324). She states that 'as it is vital for the right to life, to health and other basic rights, ecological integrity should be foundational for all domestic and international law regimes' (Westra 2011: 325). As pointed out by Klaus Bosselmann, however, the inherent design flaw in all environmental legislation at present, is 'the absence of a fundamental rule to not harm the integrity of ecosystems' (Bosselmann 2011: 204).

While ecological integrity is a useful objective for maintaining and restoring the health of the Earth Community, I would argue that to assist humanity to live within its limits, we need specific parameters to live within. How do we know if our efforts to maintain and restore ecological integrity in a region or ecosystem are enabling us to live within our ecological limits?

Developments in the new area of science called 'Earth System Science' over the past decade have, for the first time, suggested upper limits to guide humanity in its endeavour to understand and live within our natural limits. In particular, the concept of Planetary Boundaries is an important conceptual breakthrough. I would argue that combining EJ's call for Earth-centred law and governance with our growing knowledge about Earth System Science and Planetary Boundaries, gives us, for the first time, 'upper limits' to work within and greater guidance about EJ's 'Great Law'.

Earth System Science (ESS) emerged in the late 1990s and seeks to integrate various fields of academic study to understand the Earth as a system. The science of the whole Earth system is a developing, highly interdisciplinary field that treats the Earth as a single, complex, dynamic system. The primary aim of ESS is 'to discover the Earth's biophysical limits and how to live within them' (Gifford et al. 2010: 1).

In 2009, a group of scientists researching ESS proposed 'a new approach to defining biophysical preconditions for human development', called Planetary Boundaries (Rockström et al. 2009: 472). Noting that our planet's ability to provide an accommodating environment for humanity is being challenged by our own activities, they argued that one way to address the challenge is to determine 'safe boundaries' for humanity, based on fundamental characteristics of the planet and to operate within them. They defined a boundary as a specific point related to a global-scale environmental process beyond which humanity should not go. The nine boundaries are: stratospheric ozone, biodiversity, chemicals dispersion, climate change, ocean acidification, freshwater consumption and the global hydrological cycle, land system change, nitrogen and phosphorus inputs to the biosphere and oceans and atmospheric aerosol loading. It is claimed that three of these boundaries have already been crossed: climate, the nitrogen cycle and freshwater.

Steffen et al. (2011) noted the complexity and difficulty of identifying the planet's 'intrinsic, nonnegotiable limits' and stressed that while local and regional environmental issues continue to be important, the Planetary Boundaries are specifically designed for the global scale. They also stressed that Planetary Boundaries doesn't say anything about resource use, affluence or human population; these are part of the trade-offs that humanity has to negotiate (Steffen et al. 2011).

Planetary Boundaries is an extremely important development for the ecological limits debate. The scientists who developed the concept suggest that while building on earlier efforts, Planetary Boundaries 'takes a rather different approach' as it 'does not focus so directly on the human enterprise… but rather emphasises the Earth as a complex system' and 'for the first time, we are trying to quantify safe limits outside of which the Earth system cannot continue to function in a stable, Holocene-like state' (Rockström et al. 2009: 475).

It is widely agreed that more work is required to refine the concept of Planetary Boundaries and make it operational (Steffen et al. 2011). Nonetheless, it has been argued that the concept has 'profound implications for future governance systems' as it offers 'some of the wiring needed to link governance of national and global economies with governance of the environment and natural resources' (Bass 2009). As one report in the corporate sustainability context noted: 'research suggests many corporate reports describe sustainability as a "journey" with no explicit destination or quantifiable boundaries', and this means 'corporations defer the radical journey necessary and continue business as usual' (Whiteman et al. 2013: 311). In comparison, Planetary Boundaries means for the first time that we have planetary-wide 'targets' for reining in human activities, not just a continual process of improvement.

While the Planetary Boundaries concept is articulated in a human-centred framework, by arguing that these boundaries map out 'the safe operating space for humanity', it would appear obvious that the boundaries also offer the opportunity to create a safe operating space for the Earth Community. By understanding and preserving our Planetary Boundaries, we set the larger parameters, the planetary scale, for then working to preserve and restore the ecological integrity and health of all life and life-supporting systems on Earth. In other words, Planetary Boundaries provides a new, quantifiable benchmark for the Great Law, and in turn, the ecological limits that humans need to operate within.

Operationalizing planetary boundaries and the great law

If Planetary Boundaries can help inform our understanding of the upper limits of the Great Law, and the goal is to ensure ecological integrity of our environment within these upper limits, the next practical question is: how do we create governance structures to support this approach? Today, humanity is organized into a myriad of governance systems, across local, regional, national, supranational and international scales. To transition human societies to live within the supportive limits of the Great Law will require an iterative relationship between integrating knowledge of the natural environment with our existing governance systems, and transforming our governance systems to better understand, respond to and protect, the health of the Earth Community. This will require effort at the local, national and international levels of human interaction, and is no easy task.

The implications of operationalizing the Planetary Boundaries concept are being explored in a wide range of fields. Steffen and other authors of the original research have suggested new global governance institutions for monitoring and implementing Planetary Boundaries (Steffen et al. 2011) and the Stockholm Resilience Institute is exploring how Planetary Boundaries can inform governance structures (Galaz et al. 2012a; Galaz et al. 2012b). A research paper prepared by Peter Roderick is particularly relevant to this discussion, as he examines the potential of legislating for environmental limits in the United Kingdom (Roderick 2011). One of the options he proposes is to use Planetary Boundaries as a foundation for creating national budgets for resource use and management. He suggests creating a national 'Planetary Boundaries Commission' which could explore what national Earth System boundaries should look like in the UK, and extend the existing mechanism of a carbon budget (institutionalized in the UK under the Climate Change Act 2008), to other Earth System processes, to create, for example, a national nitrogen budget and phosphorous budget and so on (Roderick 2011). Roderick's paper offers a good starting point for Earth Jurists to explore how to create Earth-centred national and local governance systems that link to the upper limits of Planetary Boundaries.

Earth Jurists need to explore and articulate the role of the Great Law in order to progress the development of legal and governance systems that can help us live within our limits. Planetary Boundaries, though in its early stages of conceptual refinement and operationalization, offers an important scientific foundation for this work and should be integrated into Earth Jurisprudence research. Rockström has suggested that living within our Planetary Boundaries should be seen as a positive opportunity for humanity, and all we need is the 'mind shift' to get us there (Rockström 2010). I would argue that in addition to exploring the practical aspects of Earth-centred governance structures for living within our limits, by offering a critique of existing governance systems, and new, positive ways to build different systems in the future, Earth Jurisprudence can assist in supporting the necessary mindshift that sees ecological limits and boundaries as a necessary and beneficial aspect of human life.

How do we know our place in the world?

Understanding ecological limits is crucial to our journey to transitioning to a society that lives more harmoniously with the Earth Community. However, this knowledge on its own is not enough. We could (and I would argue many people do) appreciate our ecological limits but still remain focused on the human project – i.e., in a world of diminishing resources, what can we do to ensure the survival of humanity? Earth Jurisprudence stimulates us to question the anthropocentric culture that has evolved with Western industrial civilization, and to explore our role in ensuring the survival of the entire Earth Community, not only humanity.

By working with mathematical cosmologist Brian Swimme and telling 'The Universe Story' (Swimme and Berry 1992), Thomas Berry offers a functional cosmology that can guide our cultural narrative into a new relationship with the Earth Community. Berry suggests, '[w]e might begin to think about our present life-situation by reflecting for a moment on the wonder of Earth, how it came to be the garden planet of the universe and what might be our human role in this context' (Berry 1999: 19).

The existential journey EJ invites us to contemplate is one of the strengths of the movement. It takes us beyond a rational critique of humanity's destruction of the Earth and invites us to contemplate the mystery and wonder of the universe we were born into, and to question our role within the Earth Community. I would argue that it also helps us accept our moral responsibilities to nurture, not destroy, the Earth Community.

How do we create governance structures that help us respect valued relationships and live within our limits?

Once we acknowledge our place in the wider Earth Community and commit ourselves to respect the Great Law, we have to make choices about how to organize ourselves *within these limits and parameters.*

Examining governance structures for an Earth-centred human society is a significant area of work, but given the constraints of this chapter I will only emphasize two points:

(i) Humanity has the power to create its relationship with the Earth Community so we need to be aware of the different outcomes that arise from different governance choices (scenario planning), and the need for Earth-centred ethical tools to help us work through our choices.
(ii) We have an abundance of governance concepts, methods and 'tools' that we currently use to help us 'manage' the environment, including some that aim to quantify our resource use. These approaches are plentiful, fragmented and many are expressions of the flawed thinking that brought us to the ecological crisis we are now experiencing. Earth Jurisprudence can help us redesign our governance structures to ensure all our tools and approaches work within the Great Law and support the Earth Community.

I will briefly outline the first point and discuss the second in more depth.

The power to choose our future

As noted by Steffen et al. (2011), scientific concepts like Planetary Boundaries do not say anything about resource use, affluence or human population; these are part of the trade-offs that humanity has to negotiate. Science and understanding the world is just the starting point for our relationship with the universe. To state the obvious, we need to be aware that humanity has control over how it treats and lives within the natural world. Once we accept that we need to live within our limits, we need to understand that different decisions or scenarios will have different impacts on the Earth Community and if we want governance systems that respect and support valued relationships, we need to create them. This was made obvious by the scenarios presented in *Limits to Growth* (Meadows et al. 1972) and is evident in vast amounts of work carried out by the academic community. As an example, projects like the Great Transition Initiative expressly recognize the fact that humans and the Earth are a global community, and acknowledge the existence of various scenarios for moving into a healthier future (Global Scenario Group 2002).

Once we accept our capacity to change the future, and the importance of scenario planning, we need guidance on how to make our choices. Existing ethical frameworks like the Earth Charter have been demonstrated to be compatible with Earth Jurisprudence and able to provide 'a source of paralegal principles for jurisprudence' (Engel and Mackey 2011: 321).

A cohesive framework for an abundance of tools

EJ can offer guidance on what governance systems and 'tools' are beneficial, in order to organize ourselves to live within our limits and support the wellbeing of the Earth Community.

The 'tools' available to us include all social constructs and governance infrastructure used to organize our societies: law, economics, accounting, institutional structures, rules for political participation and so on. Law plays a special role in these broader governance structures, as we use our legal systems to create the meta-structures for all our other governance systems, including the rules for our financial, taxation, investment, accounting and other systems. As already noted in this chapter, the essence of the Earth Jurisprudence critique is that our governance and legal systems are 'geared' to support anthropocentric and pro-growth objectives. This means that despite the fact that most jurisdictions have created a growing body of environmental law, these laws largely just mitigate the impacts of human activity, they do not aim to circumvent or transform our existing model of material growth and development (Guth 2008). Indeed, our legal system has very few existing frameworks for reducing the overall volume of consumption of natural resources (Maloney 2010). It is argued that we need a significant realignment of key aspects of our legal system to support a culture that can live within its limits, such as linking our planning laws to the physical realities of our local and regional ecosystems (Graham 2011); reversing the onus of proof for new developments and activities (Guth 2008); and the creation of frameworks for managing demand (Salzman 1997).

There are also a range of governance mechanisms relevant to living within our limits that are outside the realm of formal law. A brief perusal of any introductory text book for environmental or resource accounting will reveal the plethora of 'management and accounting tools' that now exist to calculate and track use of natural resources (Hecht 2005). Interestingly, the origins of many of these tools can be directly traced to the publication of *Limits to Growth*. Hecht points out that one of the many responses to the Club of Rome report was that nation states became concerned about running out of finite resources and the first environmental accounts were constructed, independently, by several European countries (Hecht 2007). After the birth of environmental accounts in the 1970s came 'environmental indicators' and 'sustainability indicators' in the 1980s, all aimed at countering or expanding the narrow range of what was 'counted' in the primary indicator for our societies – Gross Domestic Product (GDP). In the 1990s, innovative approaches to resource management began emerging in the private sector, as businesses also began to focus on sustainability and resource use. During the late 1980s and 1990s, concepts like cleaner production (Jackson 2002) and industrial metabolism and industrial ecology emerged (Erkman 2002) and have continued to be developed by corporations and businesses to the present day.

A recent report to the EU identified and outlined 18 'alternative indicators', including those in most common use today – Ecological Footprint, Gross National Happiness, Human Development Index, Genuine Progress Indicator (Hak et al. 2012). All of these represent humanity's search for mechanisms to 'count' what's important, beyond the realm of economic growth. The Ecological Footprint, created in the mid-1990s, was found to be the most widely-used method for environmental accounting in the world (Hak et al. 2012) and deserves special mention. Described by the Global Footprint Network (GFN) as a 'resource management and communications tool that measures how much nature we have, how much we use and who uses what' (Global Footprint Network 2011), it represents the area of biologically productive land and sea (biocapacity) that an individual, population or activity requires to provide the resources it consumes and to absorb its CO_2 (Wackernagel and Rees 1996). One of the strengths of the method is that it can be used at any scale – national, regional, local, organizational, household and individual. The Footprinting method is one of the more successful 'tools' we have created that aim to document and monitor our consumption of the natural world, and it helps us conceptualize 'overshoot' and abuse of the natural world. However, while more than 50 nations have engaged with the GFN about the Footprinting method, only nine countries have formally adopted it as a mechanism for quantifying and measuring their 'use' of the natural world (Global Footprint Network 2011). This demonstrates that we have a long way to go before all human societies are focused on living within their limits.

It is argued that today's tools for understanding and tracking 'resource consumption' are 'primitive' and they do not yet fully capture the complexity of cumulative impacts and feedback systems (Allenby 1999). From an Earth Jurisprudence perspective, most of the tools currently used by us to 'value' and 'track' our use of the natural world, all stem from the same flawed thinking that helped us create the current ecological crisis. In other words, although such tools aim to document and track resource consumption, and increase the efficiency of 'resource use', they still stem from the anthropocentric notion that the natural world is a resource that exists for human use and can be managed and controlled by us. Sagoff covers this perfectly:

> (Today, environmentalists)... construct integrated multiscale ecological-economic models and assessments online, utilising the results of adaptive, biocomplex, computational, cross-cutting, holistic, integrated, interactive, interdisciplinary, multifactorial, multifunctional, multiscale, networked, nonlinear, simulational, synthetic, externally funded research, addressing uncertainties, vulnerabilities, complexities, criticalities, and surprise scenario forecasts. Thus they adopt in a contemporary form the very economic and utilitarian approach their predecessors deplored.
>
> (Sagoff 1994: 155)

Environmental management tools can indeed draw us back into the very mindset that created the current ecological crisis in the first place – a faith in our ability to control the natural world and reliance on technically oriented solutions. But I would suggest that if we're committed to transitioning to a harmonious relationship with the Earth Community, with seven billion humans and 200 major national jurisdictions, humanity will need sophisticated governance tools.

I would argue that Earth Jurisprudence should expand its critique of governance systems into the area of environmental management tools, so that we can deconstruct the pro-growth 'resource consumption' framework that exists today and build an Earth-centred suite of tools that will help human societies regulate themselves to live within our ecological limits. Work is already being done in this space by ethicists, philosophers and others (Sagoff 1994), but further work needs to be done. One area where Earth Jurisprudence is already exploring these ideas, is in the 'stream' of EJ work focused on Rights of Nature. While rights-based discourse comes under, and deserves, continued critique, EJ mechanisms such as Rights of Nature legislation can play an important part in demonstrating practical ways that the rights of the Earth Community can be weighed against the rights of human societies. Any Earth-centred analysis of human development and resource consumption will of course raise issues that people find uncomfortable – complex issues about western lifestyles, consumption and population growth. A world view that aims to support the rights of the Earth Community to exist and thrive will challenge many of our current assumptions about what we can 'have'. Cullinan (2008) touches on this in his paper 'If Nature Had Rights, What Would We Need to Give Up?'. So a further role for Earth Jurisprudence is to play a part in shifting society to accept a new definition of progress and success; and to argue that we wouldn't be giving up anything important if we were to focus on nurturing and saving the Earth Community; that our lives will be richer if our Earth Systems are healthy and our evolutionary companions can join us on our journey into the future.

How do we get there? How do we transition to a society that lives within its limits?

This final question is of course critical to living within our limits. Understanding the science of our ecological limits is of little help if we cannot change our governance structures to respect them. While there is limited space in this chapter to discuss these issues, there are a number of summary points that can be made. As already noted, the task of transitioning to a society that lives within its limits will require change at all levels of governance, and in all spheres of human endeavour. Changing our legal and governance systems will be just one part of a multitude of changes necessary to shift human societies to live within their ecological limits.

If an EJ framework can help us live within our limits, how do we transform existing governance and legal systems to adopt EJ and Wild Law approaches? The most obvious starting point is to use conventional law reform to integrate Earth-centred concepts and frameworks into existing and new legislation and national constitutions. The Ecuadorian Constitution was revised in 2008 to include Rights of Nature provisions (s.71) and new legislation called *The Act for Mother Earth* was introduced in Bolivia in 2011. However, as noted earlier in this chapter, in modern industrialized nations some of the greatest barriers to change are the power structures and vested interests that maintain the dominant, growth-centred worldview in our political, legal and cultural domains. Consequently, conventional law reform may not be the most conducive starting place for transforming our legal systems to an Earth-centred approach.

Two chapters in this book address this issue. Samuel Alexander (2014) suggests a radical rethink of how we create the transition to an Earth-centred governance system. He asks what Earth Jurists should do given the apparent lack of interest by modern industrial state systems in moving towards an Earth-centred, or even a 'weak sustainability' model of governance. He suggests instead 'that perhaps we should be directing more of our energies toward building the new society at a grassroots level; building it beneath the legal structures of the existing society with the aim that one day new societal structures will emerge' (Alexander 2014: 14).

In a similar vein, Burdon argues that the power structures that presently prevent our transformation to a healthy Earth Community can be countered by projects such as 'Earth Democracy'. He argues that attempts to fuse ecocentric ethics with deeper forms of democracy and public participation can help 'shift the power structure that dominates contemporary decision making from private interests, to the collective' (Burdon 2014: 32).

EJ can certainly accommodate the proposals made by Alexander and Burdon, and facilitate 'bottom up' approaches to creating Earth-centred governance. An example of this can be seen in the processes that created Rights of Nature ordinances at the local level in the USA. Margil explains that Rights of Nature provisions have been included in several dozen local ordinances in the US, as part of community-based strategies to empower local groups to protect their local ecosystems from unwanted industrial development (Margil 2014). Grassroots activism also played a part in agitating for the introduction of Rights of Nature provisions into the Ecuadorian Constitution in 2008 (Linzey 2010). As a final point, it's worth noting that Earth Jurisprudence is supportive of non-violent civil disobedience as a 'bottom up' strategy for creating 'top down' change (Burdon 2011b:71).

In conclusion then, Earth Jurisprudence is able to support a range of approaches to changing our legal and governance systems, and transitioning to systems that help us live within our limits.

Conclusion

In this chapter I have argued that Earth Jurisprudence offers a growing body of theory and activism to support the creation of governance structures to help us live within the biophysical capacity or limits of our Earth Community. The simple Earth-centred framework I have outlined offers practical questions that can be used at any scale, as a starting point for exploring how to create governance systems for living within our limits.

To conclude, I would suggest that Earth Jurisprudence and Wild Law offers something unique to an analysis of the governance structures that can help us live within our limits. It engages with our rational capacity for critical thinking, by helping us to critique and analyse our current institutional, regulatory and decision making structures and reshape them to 'fit' within the biophysical realities of the Earth system. But by inviting us to engage personally with the Universe Story, to reconnect with the Earth Community and to find our place in the world, EJ also connects humanity's rational concern for the state of the Earth with something deeper and more powerful – our innate connection with, and love of, our home planet and our 'evolutionary companions'. I would argue that tapping into this powerful connection that human earthlings have with their home is the catalyst we need to implement the societal changes necessary for us to live within our ecological limits.

Notes

1 For example, see the Global Alliance for the Rights of Nature website, which lists organisations from around the world advocating for Rights of Nature and Earth centred governance http://therightsofnature.org/founding-organizations/
2 This is evidenced by anecdotal evidence gathered by the Australian Earth Laws Alliance during its professional and community engagement activities.

References

Alexander, S. (2011) 'Property beyond growth: toward a politics of voluntary simplicity', unpublished thesis, University of Melbourne.
Alexander, S. (2014) 'Wild law from below', in M. Maloney and P. Burdon (eds) *Wild Law in Practice*, London: Routledge Press.
Allenby, B.R. (1999) *Industrial Ecology: Policy Framework and Implementation*, Englewood Cliffs, NJ: Prentice Hall.

Allenby, B.R. (2002) 'Industrial ecology: governance, laws and regulations', in R.U. Ayres and L.W. Ayres (eds) *A Handbook of Industrial Ecology*, Cheltenham, UK: Edward Elgar.

Badi, U. (2008) *Cassandra's Curse: How 'The Limits to Growth' was demonized*, online. Available at: <http://www.clubofrome.org/?p=1893> (accessed 20 March 2013).

Bass, S. (2009) Planetary Boundaries: Keep Off the Grass. *Nature Reports Climate Change*, online. Available at: <http://www.nature.com/climate/2009/0910/full/climate.2009.94.html> (accessed 21 March 2013).

Berry, T. (1999) *The Great Work: Our Way Into the Future*, New York: Bell Tower.

Berry, T. (2002) 'Rights of the Earth: We need a new legal framework which recognises the rights of all living beings', *Resurgence*, online. Available at: <http://www.resurgence.org/> (accessed 19 March 2013).

Bosselmann, K. (1994) 'Governing the global commons: the ecocentric approach to international environmental law', in *Droit de l'environnement et développement durable*, Limoges: Presses Universitaires de Limoges.

Bosselmann, K. (2011) 'From reductionist environmental law to sustainability law', in P. Burdon (ed.) *Exploring Wild Law: The Philosophy of Earth Jurisprudence*, Kent Town, SA: Wakefield Press.

Burdon, P. (ed.) (2011a) *Exploring Wild Law: The Philosophy of Earth Jurisprudence*, Kent Town, SA: Wakefield Press.

Burdon, P. (2011b) 'The Great jurisprudence', in P. Burdon, (ed.) *Exploring Wild Law: The Philosophy of Earth Jurisprudence*, Kent Town, SA: Wakefield Press.

Burdon, P. (2012) 'The future of a river: earth jurisprudence and the Murray Darling', *Alternative Law Journal*, 37(2).

Burdon, P. (forthcoming) *Earth Jurisprudence: Private Property and the Environment*, Routledge.

Burdon, P. (2014) 'Wild law and the project of Earth democracy', in M. Maloney and P. Burdon (eds) *Wild Law in Practice*, London: Routledge Press.

Crutzen, P. and Stoermer, E. (2000) 'The "Anthropocene"', *Global Change Newsletter*, 41: 17–18.

Cullinan, C. (2003) *Wild Law: A Manifesto for Earth Justice*, Totnes, Devon, UK: Green Books.

Cullinan, C. (2008) 'If Nature Had Rights, What Would We Have to Give Up?' *Orion Magazine*, online. Available at: <http://www.orionmagazine.org/index.php/articles/article/500/> (accessed 20 March 2013).

Cullinan. C. (2011) 'A history of wild law', in P. Burdon (ed.) *Exploring Wild Law: The Philosophy of Earth Jurisprudence*, Kent Town, SA: Wakefield Press.

Engel, J.R. and Mackey, B. (2011) 'The Earth Charter, covenants and Earth jurisprudence', in P. Burdon (ed.) *Exploring Wild Law: The Philosophy of Earth Jurisprudence*, Kent Town, SA: Wakefield Press.

Erkman, S. (2002) 'The recent history of industrial ecology', in R.U. Ayres, and L.W. Ayres (eds) *A Handbook of Industrial Ecology*, Cheltenham, UK: Edward Elgar.

Galaz, V., Biermann, F., Crona, B., Loorbach, D., Folke, C., Olsson, P., Nilsson, M., Allouche, J., Persson, A. and Reischi, G. (2012a) 'Planetary boundaries – exploring the challenges for global environmental governance', *Current Opinion in Environmental Sustainability*, 4: 80–7.

Galaz, V. (2012b) 'Global environmental governance and planetary boundaries: An introduction', *Ecological Economics*, 81: 1–3.

Gifford, R.M., Steffen, W. and Finnigan, J.J. (2010) *To Live Within Earth's Limits: An Australian Plan to Develop a Science of the Whole Earth System*, Canberra: Australian Academy of Science.

Global Footprint Network (2011) *Annual Report*, online. Available at: <http://www.footprintnetwork.org/en/index.php/GFN/page/annual_report_2011/> (accessed 19 March 2013).

Global Scenario Group (2002) *Great Transition: The Promise and Lure of the Times Ahead*. Boston, MA: Global Scenario Group.

Graham, N. (2011) 'Lawscape: property, environment and law', *Journal of Environmental Law*, 23(1): 160–4.

Guth, J.H. (2008) 'Law for the ecological age', *Vermont Journal of Environmental Law*, 9: 431–512.

Hak, T., Janouskova, S., Abdallah, S., Seaford, C. and Mahony, S. (2012) *Review Report on Beyond GDP Indicators: Categorisation, Intensions and Impact*. Prague: CUEC.

Hecht, J.E. (2005) *National Environmental Accounting: Bridging the Gap Between Economy and Ecology*, Washington: Resources for the Future.

Hecht, J.E. (2007) 'National environmental accounting: A practical introduction', *International Review of Environmental and Resource Economics*, 1(1): 3–66.

Jackson, T. (2002) 'Industrial ecology and cleaner production', in R.U. Ayres and L.W. Ayres, *Handbook of Industrial Ecology*, Cheltenham, UK: Edward Elgar.

Linzey, T. (2010) *Be The Change: How to Get What You Want In Your Community*, Layton, UT: Gibbs Smith.

Lowe, I. (2006) 'Changing public attitudes to long term issues', *Griffith Review*, 12: 56–63.

Maloney, M. (2010) 'Earth jurisprudence and sustainable consumption', *Southern Cross University Law Review*, 14: 119–48.

Margil, M. (2014) 'Building an international movement for rights of nature', in M. Maloney and P. Burdon (eds) *Wild Law in Practice*, London: Routledge Press.

Meadows, D., Meadows, D.I. and Randers, J. (1992) *Beyond the Limits*, White River Junction, VT: Chelsea Green Publishing.

Meadows, D., Meadows, D.I. and Randers, J. (2004) *Limits to Growth: The 30 Year Update*, White River Junction, VT: Chelsea Green Publishing.

Meadows, D.H., Meadows, D.L., Randers, J. and Behrens III, W.W. (1972) *The Limits to Growth: A Report for the Club of Rome's Project on the Predicament of Mankind*. New York: Universe Books.

Millennium Ecosystem Assessment (2005) *Ecosystems and Well-being: Synthesis*, Washington DC: Island Press.

Nash, R.F. (1989) *The Rights of Nature: A History of Environmental Ethics*, Madison, WI: University of Wisconsin Press.

Oreskes, N. and Conway, E.M. (2011) *Merchants of Doubt: How a Handful of Scientists Obscured the Truth on Issues from Tobacco Smoke to Global Warming*, London: Bloomsbury Press.

Pelizzon, A. (2013) 'Earth laws, rights of nature and legal pluralism', in M. Maloney and P. Burdon (eds) *Wild Law in Practice*, London: Routledge Press.

Preston, B. (2013) 'Internalising ecocentrism in environmental law', in M. Maloney and P. Burdon (eds) *Wild Law in Practice*, London: Routledge Press.

Rivers, L. (2006) 'How to become a wild lawyer', *Environmental Law and Management*, 18: 28–31.

Rockström, J. (2010) 'Planetary Boundaries', TED Conferences, Oxford, July 2010, online. Available at: <http://rs.resalliance.org/2010/08/31/johan-rockstrom-at-ted-on-planetary-boundaries/> (accessed 20 April 2013).

Rockström, J., Steffen, W., Noone, K., Persson, A., Chapin F.S., Lambin, E.F. and Lenton, T.M.L. (2009) 'A safe operating space for humanity', *Nature*, 461: 472–75.

Roderick, P. (2011) *The Feasibility of Environmental Limits Legislation*, London: World Wild Fund for Nature UK.

Sachs, J.D. (2011) *The Price of Civilisation: Reawakening American Virtue and Prosperity*, London: Random House.

Sagoff, M. (1994) *Price, Principle and the Environment*, Cambridge, MA: Cambridge University Press.

Salzman, J. (1997) 'Sustainable consumption and the law', *Environmental Law*, 27: 1243–93.

Steffen, W., Rockström, J. and Costanza, R. (2011) 'How defining planetary boundaries can transform our approach to growth', *Solutions* 2(3), online. Available at: <http://www.thesolutionsjournal.com/node/935> (accessed 12 February 2013).

Stone, C. (2010) *Should Trees Have Standing? Law, Morality and the Environment*, 3rd edn, New York: Oxford University Press.

Swimme, B. and Berry, T. (1992) *The Universe Story: From the Primordial Flaring Forth to the Ecozoic Era – A Celebration of the Unfolding of the Cosmos*, New York: Harper Collins.

Sydes, B. (2014) 'The challenges of putting wild law into practice – reflections on the Australian Environmental Defenders Office movement', in M. Maloney and P. Burdon (eds) *Wild Law in Practice*, London: Routledge Press.

Turner, G. (2008) 'A comparison of the limits to growth with 30 years of reality', *Global Environmental Change*, 18: 397–411.

Wackernagel, M. and Rees, W.E. (1996) *Our Ecological Footprint: Reducing Human Impact on the Earth*, Gabriola Island, BC: New Society Publishers.

Westra, L. (2011) 'Governance for integrity? A distant but necessary goal', in P. Burdon (ed.) *Exploring Wild Law: The Philosophy of Earth Jurisprudence*, Kent Town, SA, Wakefield Press.

Whiteman, G., Walker, B. and Perego, P. (2013) 'Planetary boundaries: Ecological foundations for corporate sustainability', *Journal of Management Studies*, 50(2): 307–36.

Chapter 14

Biodiversity offsets
A dangerous trade in wildlife?

Brendan Grigg

> *Certainly, biodiversity is the greatest wonder and mystery on Earth.*
> (Burdon 2011: 89)

The term biodiversity refers to the myriad forms of life on earth and can be observed at three levels (Gunningham and Young 1997: 247). Genetic diversity denotes genetic variation that allows organisms to evolve and adapt while the concept of species diversity explains 'the numbers, types, and distribution of species within an ecosystem' (Gunningham and Young 1997: 247). Finally, ecosystem diversity 'refers to the variety of habitats and communities of different species that interact in a complex web of interdependent relationships' (Gunningham and Young 1997: 247).

Biodiversity is a fundamental requirement for human life on Earth and its preservation is 'vital for an ecologically sustainable society' (Gunningham and Young 1997: 247). The global decline in biological diversity is now a well-recognized environmental challenge confronting our planet. Land clearing has been regarded as the single most important cause of environmental degradation and the loss and depletion of species and ecological communities both in Australia and abroad (Agius 2001: 483). This chapter considers the use of biodiversity offsets as a means of addressing this problem. It draws on Earth Jurisprudence to analyse two particular examples of biodiversity offsets: the New South Wales biobanking scheme contained in the *Threatened Species Conservation Act* 1995 (NSW) and the concept of the 'significant environmental benefit' set out in the South Australian *Native Vegetation Act 1991* (Saul et al. 2012).

South Australia has one of the highest rates of extinction in Australia: at least 23 mammals, 2 birds and 26 plants are extinct. In South Australia 63 per cent of mammals and 22 per cent of vascular plants are formally listed as threatened (Department for Environment and Heritage 2007). In New South Wales 80 species are considered extinct and there are 1000 species, populations and communities that are either endangered or vulnerable (Burgin 2008: 808). Nationally, up to 70 per cent of Australia's landmass is under private control and as a result the public reserve system cannot be relied on alone to halt and reverse the decline (Nelson and Sharman 2007: 19). Set against the extent of biodiversity loss in these two Australian jurisdictions, the New South Wales and South Australian schemes are important attempts at addressing the problem. Wild Law offers an insightful critique of how they are established and operate.

These observations are clearly relevant globally given that biodiversity offsets have become an increasingly widely-used tool internationally, indeed they have been described as a 'global phenomenon' (Burgin 2008: 808). The use of offsets to mitigate the loss of biodiversity emerged in the United States in the 1970s in an effort to mitigate wetland losses in particular. Biodiversity offset schemes have various names such as setasides, compensatory habitats and mitigation banks. Biodiversity offset schemes offer the promise of enabling development at a particular site while, at the same time, purporting to secure the protection of biodiversity values at another location. They thus, ostensibly, offer a means of balancing the competing demands of conserving and developing the Earth's natural resources (Burgin 2008: 808).

These schemes rely heavily on the legal system's familiarity with, and protection of, property and property rights. Offset schemes are often employed, for example, on land title registration systems to ensure security of interests (Maguire and Phillips 2011: 232). Contract law (Maguire and Phillips 2011: 221), and indeed criminal and civil law mechanisms are also used to create and enforce these rights. Maguire and Phillips (2011: 229) have argued also, for example, that the rights that biodiversity offsets create and enforce conform with the following four kinds of 'common pool resources rights', as analysed by Connors and Dovers. First, is the right of withdrawal: 'the right to obtain the units or products of an environmental resource' (Maguire and Phillips 2011: 229). Second, the right of management referring to 'the right to regulate internal use patterns and transform the environmental resource by making improvements' (Maguire and Phillips 2011: 229). The right of exclusion refers to the right 'to determine who will have access rights and how these rights may be transferred' (Maguire and Phillips 2011: 229). Finally, the right of alienation describes the ability to transfer either or both rights of management and exclusion (Maguire and Phillips 2011: 229).

This chapter investigates biodiversity offset schemes and the property rights they create and enforce in light of the insights that Earth Jurisprudence offers. Section Two introduces market-based biodiversity offset schemes and examines some of the features of the New South Wales biobanking scheme, including the key concept of the biodiversity credit. It argues that this constitutes a commodification of nature. Section Three considers another type of market-based offset scheme, the Australian carbon trading scheme operating under the *Clean Energy Act 2011 (Cth)*. It analyses how that scheme creates personal property in the carbon unit that is traded and draws out a stark contrast between it and the New South Wales scheme. It argues that a carbon trading scheme cannot be equated to a trade in biodiversity and the successes of the former cannot necessarily be transferred to the latter. The carbon unit is analysed as a single, fungible value. That is a characteristic that is not applicable to biodiversity. An understanding of this difference, aided by Earth Jurisprudence is vital to a proper understanding of biodiversity offset schemes. Section Four moves on to consider the South Australian scheme which uses a regulatory rather than a market-based model. This section argues that this model also commodifies nature in the way in which it defines 'native vegetation'. In doing so it has the potential to harm rather than protect nature. Section Five of this chapter concludes by evaluating the property rights that both schemes create in biodiversity in light of some of the understandings offered by earth jurisprudence, particularly those identified by Swimme and Berry who, among others, advocate for a paradigm shift towards an Ecozoic era.

No net loss? Biodiversity offset schemes

Market-based schemes have been widely promoted as a successful form of environmental regulation compared to direct command-and-control regulation (Maguire and Phillips 2011: 216–17). This is due to a number of factors, including their asserted efficiency, effectiveness, financial incentives, flexibility and political legitimacy and what has been considered to be the failure of traditional command-and-control type regulation to achieve successful environmental outcomes (Maguire and Phillips 2011: 216–18). The creation of tradable rights in the environment aims to reverse the market failure associated with the fact that the environmental and social costs of natural resource use are not accounted for or internalized by those who use them (Agius 2001: 490).

Given the popularity of market-based schemes, it is not surprising that market-based schemes have been also used and promoted for biodiversity protection (Agius 2001: 481). Biodiversity offset schemes are designed 'to offset residual, unavoidable damage to biodiversity caused by development activities' (Burgin 2008: 808). They are premised on the idea of allowing development in a way that will ensure 'no net loss of habitat over time' (Maron et al. 2010: 348). They are not, crucially, designed 'to compensate for poor environmental management [and] are additional to other measures that are in place to avoid or minimise environmental damage' (Burgin 2008: 808).

Broadly speaking, the creation of a market-based biodiversity offset scheme involves the following three steps. First is the creation and supply of a credit by a landowner who agrees to undertake works to protect and enhance existing vegetation or to plant new native vegetation in areas where it has been cleared. Second, these credits, once created, are then sold to a central registry. In return for being able to sell the credit to the registry, the landowner is required to sign up to an agreement that requires the ongoing performance of the activity that generated the credit. This agreement can be registered on the title to the land in order to bind all future owners to undertake those actions. Finally, the demand for the credit arises as a result of the need for a developer to clear land as part of a development. Often a condition of the consent or approval to undertake that clearance requires the developer to purchase the biodiversity credits from the central registry.

The New South Wales biobanking scheme

The New South Wales biobanking scheme, contained in the *Threatened Species Conservation Act 1995* (NSW) ('the TSCA') has been operating since July 2008. The biodiversity credit is the central component of this scheme. It is created by carrying out actions that are designed to improve or maintain biodiversity values on a site known as the biobank site. Under the scheme, developers have the option, as an alternative to other statutory requirements (See *Environmental Planning and Assessment Act 1979* (NSW), section 5A) to purchase the number of biodiversity credits that is commensurate with the proposed impact on biodiversity of the development's activities elsewhere. The scheme illustrates all the common pool resources rights noted above.

The biobank site and the management activities are established through a biobanking agreement between the Minister and the landowner pursuant to section 127D of the TSCA. A document called the Biobanking Assessment Methodology, required by the TSCA, is used to determine how many and what type of biodiversity credits are created at the biobank site. Importantly, the Biobanking Agreement must be registered on the title to the land under section 127I of the TSCA. It is binding on all future owners of land (section 127J). The owner of a biobank site may then apply under section 127W of the TSCA to the Director-General of the Department of Environment, Climate Change and Water for the creation of biodiversity credits based on the Biobank Agreement requirements and the Biobanking Assessment Methodology.

A developer who chooses to use the offset scheme applies under section 127ZK of the TSCA for a Biobanking Statement from the Director General that includes an assessment of how many biodiversity credits will need to be retired to ensure that the proposed development improves or maintains the biodiversity values. Once a Biobanking Statement has been issued, the developer may apply to purchase the requisite credits. Pursuant to section 127ZA the developer deposits the requisite monetary amount into a trust fund established by the TSCA and the transfer is registered under section 127ZB.

There are geographical limits to the application of the scheme. The statutory Assessment Methodology provides for so-called red flag areas where biobanking statements may not be issued. Red flag areas are, for example:

- where there is less than 30 per cent vegetation remaining compared to an estimate of what existed in the relevant catchment area as at the year 1750; or
- home to a critically endangered or endangered ecological community listed under New South Wales or Commonwealth law (Department of Environment and Climate Change NSW 2008).

The existence of these red flag areas mean that not all biodiversity values are able to be subjected to trade. Nevertheless, it is clear that the scheme creates a tradable commodity out of nature. The extent to which the biobanking scheme commodifies nature is evident in the expansive definition of biodiversity values, which is central to its operation. Section 4A of the TSCA defines biodiversity values as including:

> the composition, structure and function of ecosystems, and includes (but is not limited to) threatened species, populations and ecological communities, and their habitats.

This is an example of the anthropocentrism of our legal framework which reduces the physical world into 'something that can be owned' (Freyfogle 1993: 49) and an extreme example of what Cullinan (2003: 163) referred to as the transformation of the earth into a 'fictitious commodity' by our legal system.

The extent to which nature is commodified is highlighted starkly by a comparison of the biobanking scheme with another market-based environmental scheme, the Australian carbon trading scheme contained in the *Clean Energy Act 2011 (Cth)* (CEA) which also trades in a 'fictitious commodity', namely units of carbon dioxide. The section below, considers the CEA carbon trading scheme and the specific nature of the tradable carbon unit that it creates.

Market-based environmental schemes: Property in nature

The development of a carbon trading market in Australia illustrates a clear preference for a market-based mechanism, rather than other forms of command-and-control regulation, to achieve a reduction in Australian greenhouse gas emissions. Indeed as Zahar et al. (2012: 167–8) state, the prevalence of market-based mechanisms in a host of different climate change regulatory schemes, ranging from the Kyoto Protocol to regional and domestic regimes, indicate that the market-based approach has been the dominant regulatory approach in the area of climate change.

The economics of market failure, and the need to correct it, are central to these climate change market-based strategies. As the report of the 2008 Garnaut Climate Change Review stated:

> The failure to place a price on greenhouse gas emission had led to over-utilisation of a scarce resource: the atmosphere's capacity to absorb emissions without risk of dangerous climate change.
>
> The correction of this market failure is the central task of climate change policy, in Australia, and the world.
>
> (Garnaut 2008: 299)

While the politics of the response to the Garnaut Report, and the negotiations associated with the development of the CEA have been analysed by others (Zahar et al. 2012; Saul et al. 2012), this chapter's analysis focuses on the way in which property law features in the CEA carbon trading scheme and how this contrasts with the NSW biobanking scheme.

The objects of the CEA, which commenced in Australia in July 2012, are set out in section 3. Primarily they are:

- to give effect to Australia's international obligations under the United Nations Framework Convention on Climate Change and the Kyoto Protocol;
- to support the development of an effective global response to climate change consistent with Australia's national interest in ensuring that average global temperatures do not increase by more than 2 degrees Celsius above pre-industrial levels;
- to take direct action towards meeting Australia's long-term target of reducing Australia's net greenhouse gas emissions to 80 per cent below 2000 levels by 2050;
- to put a price on greenhouse emissions that aims, among other things, to encourage investment in clean energy.

The way in which it achieves particularly this last objective is, broadly speaking, to require that, each year, certain liable emitters surrender to the Clean Energy Regulator the number of what are termed eligible emissions units that corresponds to that entity's emissions for that year (Wilcox and Rennie 2012: 61). The CEA does not compel surrender of eligible emissions units, but any shortfall results in the liable emitter incurring a charge payable to the Commonwealth. When the eligible emissions units are surrendered they are cancelled (Wilcox and Rennie 2012: 61).

Under the CEA there are three types of eligible emissions units: eligible international emissions units, eligible Australian carbon credit and the carbon unit. The ability to surrender eligible international emissions units links the CEA's emissions trading scheme to international carbon trading markets although there are quantitative and qualitative controls on the surrender of eligible international emissions units, designed to maintain the integrity of the scheme (Zahar et al. 2012: 194). The ability to surrender eligible Australian carbon credits provides a link to the scheme whereby carbon offsets are created by activities that store or reduce carbon in the land sector under the *Carbon Credits (Carbon Farming Initiative) Act 2011 (Cth)* 2011.

It is the creation of the carbon unit that illustrates the role of property in this particular market-based regulatory scheme and, in contrast as set out later in this chapter, into the concept of biodiversity offsets. The carbon unit created by the CEA itself is likely to be the primary type of eligible emissions unit that is surrendered (Wilcox and Rennie 2012: 61).

Each carbon unit represents one tonne of CO_2 equivalent (Zahar et al. 2012: 185). Each individual carbon unit is able to be identified by an identification number that, among other things, indicates the year it was created. Section 103 of the CEA provides expressly that a carbon unit is personal property and is transmissible by assignment or by will and can devolve by operation of law. Pursuant to section 103A, the registered holder of a carbon unit is its legal owner and may deal with it as such.

The CEA contemplates two periods of operation. During the first period (from 1 July 2012 to 30 June 2014, the 'fixed price period') the Clean Energy Regulator is required to issue carbon units for a fixed price. Carbon units bought during the fixed price period may not be transferred; however, where an emitter has excess credits due, for example, to greater reductions in emissions than were expected (Zahar et al. 2012: 194) they may be sold back to the Clean Energy Regulator at a discounted price (s116).

Commencing on 1 July 2015 the scheme transitions to a full emissions trading scheme (Zahar et al. 2012: 194) where the price of carbon units issued by the Clean Energy Regulator will be determined at auction. This period is comprised of what the CEA terms flexible charge years. Carbon units acquired in a flexible charge year may be transferred.

The critical component of the scheme, once the flexible charge years commence, is the CEA's carbon pollution cap established under Part 2 of the CEA. It constitutes the maximum permissible level of greenhouse gas emissions for a particular year. Without the carbon pollution cap there would be no carbon market (Wilcox and Rennie 2012: 54). As Wilcox and Rennie (2012: 55) note, its determination is of crucial importance to the success of the carbon trading scheme: if the cap is set too high and, as a result, too many eligible emissions units become available, then their value will be too low and there will be little incentive to reduce greenhouse gas emissions. Where, contrastingly, the cap is set too low, demand for carbon units is likely to outweigh supply, causing problems even for those making genuine efforts to reduce emissions.

Carbon units under the CEA are all functionally interchangeable units of CO_2 equivalent: one carbon unit is the same as another and can be swapped without affecting their value (Mann 2010: 266). Indeed, trading in the carbon credits is the very purpose of their design and operation. In this sense, the emission unit is a fungible piece of property.

As illustrated by the CEA, market-based environmental schemes place vital importance on the concept of property. Indeed the CEA expressly confers the status of property on the carbon unit. This is due to the fact that 'property law defines use, access, and other necessary rights related to the environment [and thus] the legal concept of property is used as an instrument to recognise and allow for control' (Maguire and Phillips 2011: 221).

Unlike the CEA, some market-based environmental schemes, notwithstanding the importance of property and the reliance on the legal system's protections of it, are not as specific about the property status of the commodity that is traded, preferring to refer to the interest as a right (Maguire and Phillips 2011: 227). For example, the rights conferred by the New South Wales biobanking scheme are not expressly stated to be property. This is also the case with the South Australian native vegetation offset scheme which is explored in the next section.

The question is whether a legislative scheme can create property in nature in the absence of express legislative intent. The Australian High Court decision of *ICM Agriculture Pty Ltd v Commonwealth* ('ICM') (2009) 240 CLR 140 assists in answering this question.

In ICM the plaintiffs alleged that the State of New South Wales had breached the Australian Constitution when it carried out a series of legislative water reforms, pursuant to an intergovernmental agreement between it, the Commonwealth of Australia and other Australian states. Pursuant to the agreement, New South Wales converted all water licences which had been granted under the *Water Act 1912* (NSW) in the Lower Lachlan Groundwater System into licences under the *Water Management Act 2000* (NSW) in order to achieve a reduction of 56 per cent in water entitlements in that resource by 1 July 2016. Critically, the 1912 legislation did not expressly state that the bore licences were the property of the licensees. New South Wales provided a package of ex gratia payments to assist licensees to adjust to the impact of these reduced water entitlements. The appellant contended that, nevertheless, the replacement of the licences amounted to an acquisition of property contrary to section 51(xxxi) of the Australian Constitution.

In addressing the question, the High Court referred to criteria set out by the House of Lords in the 1965 case *National Provincial Bank v Ainsworth* [1965] AC 1175. In that case Wilberforce LJ stated that determining whether a right or an interest is property or a property right depends on whether the right or interest is 'definable, identifiable by third parties, capable in its nature of assumption by third parties, and [whether it has] some degree of permanence or stability' (at 1965, 1247–8 per Wilberforce J).

In ICM, the majority of the Court were reluctant to conceptualize flowing water as property. Hayne, Kiefel and Bell JJ, for example, referred to Getzler's attribution to such water of a 'quality of instability' (Getzler 2004: 43) noting that flowing water could not be subjected to physical possession or a right to possession (at 190). In contrast, a majority of the High Court were prepared to characterize the bore licences as property, although ultimately, the majority rejected the appellant's appeal on other grounds. French CJ, Gummow and Crennan JJ noted the commercial value that a bore licence added to land but focused principally on the inherent susceptibility to alteration of statutory rights like the bore licences created under the *Water Act 1912* (NSW). Ultimately French CJ, Gummow and Crennan JJ declined to decide conclusively whether or not the bore licences were property because in their opinion their cancellation did not constitute an acquisition for the purposes of the constitutional just terms guarantee (at 179–81). On the other hand, Hayne, Kiefel and Bell JJ concluded that the bore licences were a 'species of property' (at 201). The rights attaching to the bore licences could be traded, could be used as security for a loan (at 201) and carried with them an entitlement, albeit a fragile one, to a certain quantity of water (at 201). Notwithstanding this position, Hayne, Kiefel and Bell JJ joined with French CJ, Gummow and Crennan JJ in the opinion that there had been no acquisition of property in the sense protected by the just terms guarantee.

On the question of the status of the bore licences, Heydon J (at 218) also considered that the bore licences were 'a form of property' as they were definable, identifiable, by third parties, had a considerable degree of permanence, could be terminated only in certain circumstances and could be transferred either with or without the land to which it related.

This description of property clearly matches the characteristics that the CEA confers upon a carbon unit; however, these characteristics are not applicable to biodiversity. The descriptions of the term biodiversity that were set out at the outset of this chapter belie its inherent complexities. Indeed biologists suggest that the term may well be beyond definition. Edward O. Wilson has noted:

> I recently estimated that the number of known species of organisms, including all plants, animals and microorganisms, to be 1.4 million. This figure could easily be off by a hundred thousand... evolutionary biologists are generally agreed that this estimate is less than a tenth of the number that actually live on Earth.
>
> (Wilson 1992: 132–3)

Biodiversity, understood in this light and comprising all its genetic, species and ecosystem diversity, is complex and varied. Science is yet fully to fathom its depths, wonders and extent. The concept of biodiversity is aligned with flowing water, which the common law has long regarded as beyond property. It is therefore impossible to squeeze the concept into the frame of the legal concept of property. It is equally as difficult to understand how a scheme purports to transform biodiversity into functionally interchangeable units for the purposes of trade. Biodiversity is not a commodity that is fungible in the way a carbon unit is.

Regulatory offsetting: *Native Vegetation Act 1991* (SA)

The *Native Vegetation Act 1991 (SA)* ('the NVA') contains a biodiversity offset scheme that is purely regulatory in nature. It is not a market-based environmental scheme. Rather, the Native Vegetation Council, the regulator established under the NVA, procures the offset either via conditions of an approval to clear native vegetation or its use of funds that have accumulated in the statutory Native Vegetation Fund, through among other things, the payment of money in lieu of a significant environmental benefit, which is described below. Despite the differences between this model and the New South Wales market-based model the South Australian model also offers insights into the creation of property rights in nature.

The predecessor to the NVA was enacted in 1985 in response to what Bates (2010: 457) describes as 'wholesale clearance' of native vegetation in South Australia. Until then, South Australia had no laws specifically directed at the protection and conservation of native vegetation. It was indirectly protected by laws that were principally directed at preventing soil erosion. As Fowler notes, other land management schemes operating in South Australia, such as under the *Crown Lands Act 1929* (SA), encouraged and in some cases actually *required* clearance (Fowler 1986: 49).

From the early 1970s the extent and rate of clearance of native vegetation in South Australia prompted serious calls for action and for reform of the laws governing vegetation clearance (Fowler 1986: 48). Studies had noted, for example, that over half of the native vegetation existing on private land in the South East region of South Australia in 1974 had been cleared by 1981 and that in other areas of the state, such as on the Adelaide Plains and on the Yorke Peninsula less than 10 per cent of the original native vegetation cover remained (Fowler 1986: 49).

The South Australian scheme was the first example in Australia of a comprehensive attempt at controlling native vegetation clearance (Bates 2010: 457). The objects of the NVA are set out in section 6. They include the following:

a. The conservation, protection and enhancement of the native vegetation of the State and, in particular, remnant vegetation, in order to prevent further –

   i. reduction of biological diversity and degradation of the land and its soil and
   ii. loss of quantity and quality of native vegetation in the State; and
   iii. loss of critical habitat

b. The provision of incentives and assistance to landowners to encourage landowners to preserve, enhance and properly manage the native vegetation on their land;
c. The limitation of native vegetation clearance to circumstances where the clearance will facilitate the management of other native vegetation or will facilitate sustainable use of land for primary production.
   ...
e. The encouragement of the re-establishment of native vegetation in those parts of the State that have been cleared or where native vegetation is degraded.

The NVA defines native vegetation as:

a plant or plants of a species indigenous to South Australia including a plant or plants growing in or under waters of the sea.

The key to the NVA is the prohibition, contained in section 26, enforced by criminal and civil penalties, against clearing native vegetation otherwise than in accordance with the Act. It is not surprising, given the objects of the NVA that the scheme contemplates that native vegetation may be cleared with approvals granted under the NVA. Applications to clear are made to the Native Vegetation Council. The matters which the Native Vegetation Council is required to take into account when considering an application to clear are set out in detail in section 29 of the NVA. Its primary duty is to have regard to a number of principles, called principles of clearance of native vegetation, which are set out in Schedule 1 to the NVA. The principles of clearance of native vegetation include, for example, the principle that native vegetation should not be cleared if, in the opinion of the Council:

- it comprises a high level of diversity of plant species, has significance as a habitat for wildlife; or includes plants of a rare, vulnerable or endangered species;
- the vegetation:
- comprises the whole, or a part, of a plant community that is rare, vulnerable or endangered; or

- is significant as a remnant of vegetation in an area which has been extensively cleared; or
- is growing in, or in association with, a wetland environment; or
- contributes significantly to the amenity of the area in which it is growing or is situated; or
- the clearance of the vegetation is likely to contribute to or exacerbate soil erosion or salinity in an area in which appreciable erosion or salinisation has already occurred.

These are, from the perspective of biodiversity conservation, laudable principles. Section 29 mandates the Native Vegetation Council to have regard to these principles and prohibits a decision that is seriously at variance with them. However, their integrity is compromised by provisions such as section 29(3) which require the Native Vegetation Council, in having regard to the principles of clearance of native vegetation, to 'have regard to the applicant's desire to operate the business as efficiently as possible'.

Moreover, and critically for the purposes of this chapter's focus, section 29(4a) of the NVA introduces two offset options that enable the Native Vegetation Council to consent to the clearance of native vegetation where the clearance would actually be seriously at variance with the principles of clearance of native vegetation. The first offset option is based on the applicant for consent proposing to undertake replanting and maintenance operations on the land that is cleared or on adjacent land. If the Native Vegetation Council is satisfied that these actions will, after allowing for the loss of the vegetation that is cleared, result in a significant environmental benefit it may grant consent to clear. The replanting and maintenance is enforced via a condition imposed on the consent to clear.

This trade-off in biodiversity is expanded by the second offset option which enables an applicant for clearance consent to propose a monetary payment into a fund established pursuant to the NVA instead of a significant environmental benefit where it was not possible to undertake actions that generate the significant environmental benefit (section 28(4) and section 28(3)(b)(B)). The Native Vegetation Council has the power to require this payment by means of a condition imposed upon the consent to clear.

The Native Vegetation Fund is established by section 21 of the NVA and includes funds appropriated by Parliament, fees paid for applications to clear, fines and penalties recovered for offences against the Act. Section 21(3)(c) importantly provides that payments in lieu of a significant environmental benefit are also invested in the Native Vegetation Fund. Section 21(6) is explicit about how money paid into the Fund pursuant to section 21(3)(c) is to be used. It must, as far as practicable, be used to establish or regenerate and to preserve and maintain once established or reinstated, native vegetation on land that is within the same region of South Australia as the land that was cleared and on land that has been selected by the Native Vegetation

Council having had regard to an applicable approved Regional Biodiversity Plan for the region.

An understanding of the diversity, complexity and variety of nature which is set out below in section 5 highlights the significant difference between the two offset options contained in the NVA. The first option maintains something of a close physical connection between the land where the clearance occurs and the land where the offset activities occur: the offset activities must take place either on the land that is cleared or on land that is adjacent to that land. The connection between the cleared land and the offset provided where the clearance is accompanied by a payment into the Native Vegetation Fund is far more tenuous. The significant environmental benefit concept assumes, mistakenly, that the diversity, complexity and variety of nature destroyed in one area can be reproduced exactly on selected land within the same region of South Australia as the land that was cleared.

Like the 'red flag' areas in the biobanking scheme, there is one significant limitation under the South Australian scheme that means that not all native vegetation can be cleared and offset. Under section 27(2) the Native Vegetation Council cannot consent to the clearance of native vegetation that is substantially intact. Section 3A provides that substantially intact vegetation means vegetation that has not been degraded by human activity in the preceeding 20 years or the only form of degradation has been by fire.

The South Australian scheme reflects many of the characteristics of a biodiversity offset scheme that have been noted above. It does not explicitly invoke the language of property, but relies on a range of conventional legal mechanisms to create and enforce a range of rights in nature. The ability to determine the significant environmental benefit, for example, falls within Connor and Dover's right of withdrawal. The right of management can be discerned in the conditions imposed by the SA Native Vegetation Council in a consent to clear. The procurement, by the Native Vegetation Council of the offset, funded through the Native Vegetation Fund is an example of the exercise of the right of exclusion.

These rights, just like the rights created and enforced under the New South Wales biobanking scheme illustrate the worldview, described by Cullinan, in which it is:

> right and proper for human subjects unilaterally to dominate all other aspects of the Earth Community as objects. By defining land as a commodity, the dominant legal philosophies legitimise and facilitate our exploitative relations with Earth.
>
> (Cullinan 2003: 177)

Biodiversity offset schemes, whether market-based or not, however, go beyond the commodification of land. They commodify nature itself.

Biodiversity offsets: A dangerous trade in wild life?

Advocates of biodiversity offset schemes argue that giving a financial value to biodiversity turns it into a source of revenue and thereby ensures that it is protected. Doing so turns biodiversity from being a liability into an asset (Nelson and Sharman 2007: 19). This kind of valuation, characteristic of the relationship between a 'master and chattel' (Cullinan 2003: 166), is far from the reciprocal relationship between human and non-human nature that earth jurisprudence advocates (Cullinan 2003: 165–6).

Laws designed, ostensibly to protect nature, are from a Wild Law perspective doing it damage, continuing humankind's exploitative relationship with nature and perpetuating a threat to biological diversity. It continues humankind's 'virtual excommunication' from the Earth Community and the alienation of humankind's 'deeper self' (Cullinan 2003: 170). These problems constitute one aspect of the current global environmental crisis. Berry asserts that the only viable option for the Earth at a time of environmental crisis is to move, paradigmatically, from the current harmful Cenozoic period to the Ecozoic period which is one of 'an integral community that will include all the human and non-human components that constitute planet Earth [and its] first principle ... is the recognition that the Universe is primarily a communion of subjects, not a collection of objects' (Berry 1991: 1).

Swimme and Berry (1992) have highlighted three principles that lie at the heart of the Ecozoic period: communion or interconnectedness, differentiation, autopoiesis. These characteristics provide insight into the operation of a biodiversity offset scheme and a means by which any scheme can be assessed.

As Burdon (2011: 86) elaborates, the principle of communion asserts that the universe is 'an integrated whole, rather than a hierarchical collection of dissociated parts'. The principle of differentiation recognizes that the universe is characterised by its 'diversity, complexity, variation and multiform nature' (Burdon 2011: 86). Autopoiesis refers to 'life's continuous production of itself' (Burdon 2011: 90), and 'the power each thing has to participate directly in the cosmos-creating endeavour' (Burdon 2011: 90).

Biodiversity offset schemes, like those considered above, do little to contribute to the paradigm shift that Berry argues is required. These schemes permit and facilitate the destruction of part of the natural world on the dangerous premise that it can be reproduced identically elsewhere. They perpetuate the hierarchy of dissociated parts of nature: human life is able to trade in non-human life. Like the Biobanking Assessment Methodology, a key aspect of the Biobanking Scheme noted above, and which purports to create 'a currency so that offsets could be determined by objective means rather than... the negotiation leverage of the parties' (Solomon 2011: 94), they are anathema to the notion that nature is diverse, complex, varied and multiform and that has the power to participate in its own creation and recreation. Instead nature is subjected to various property rights and turned into tradable commodity that is treated, like a carbon unit, as though it is functionally interchangeable.

Burdon (2011: 92) asserts that an understanding of the Earth as characterized by communion, differentiation and autopoiesis has 'the potential to move society beyond the outdated and harmful anthropocentric paradigm' and that 'the assimilation and application of these ideas is the *great work* before the present generation'.

An understanding of the principles that lie at the heart of the Ecozoic age offers an insight into both the New South Wales and South Australian biodiversity offset schemes. The earth jurisprudence principles considered in this chapter illustrate the difficulties associated with the commodification of nature. Ultimately, however, they reveal that the attempts to do so are anthropocentric and harmful.

Earth jurisprudence reveals the fiction of property in nature and the potential for property rights in nature to be destructive. The carbon unit which the CEA creates as a piece of personal property is an extreme example of the fiction. It may, as an important component of the market, be crucial in securing the objects of the CEA's carbon trading scheme. It is, however, a piece of property that is fungible. It is functionally identical to other carbon units. In light of the nature of biodiversity, illustrated by Swimme and Berry, a biobanking scheme biodiversity credit, cannot, despite all attempts at an objective quantification, be functionally identical to another biodiversity credit so that it can be destroyed in one place and rebuilt in another. This highlights the danger of transplanting, uncritically, the mechanisms of one market-based scheme into an entirely different context.

Earth Jurisprudence also illuminates the danger in attempting to reproduce the diversity, complexity and variety of nature in the ways permitted by both the New South Wales and South Australian schemes.

In the face of a clear trend towards the development of market-based biodiversity offset schemes Earth Jurisprudence could call upon the neo-liberal language of the market-based world, as Robinson (2009: 221) has done, and argue that as biodiversity is a capital asset, its maintenance ought to be 'financed from societal income not by selling off the capital base'. Doing so ought to question the place of such schemes in our society. At the very least, understanding nature and the complexity of biodiversity in an ecocentric way would ensure that such schemes are severely limited in scope and operation. Offset schemes, where they must be developed, could draw on the red flag areas concept from the New South Wales biobanking scheme or expand on the idea of the substantially intact vegetation concept from the South Australian scheme. Similarly, reflecting some of the insights of earth jurisprudence, harmful elements, such as the potential for the offset site to be located at a great distance from the development site could be avoided.

Doing so may help biodiversity offset schemes move beyond their current dangerous and anthropocentric paradigm.

References

Agius, J. (2001) 'Biodiversity credits: Creating missing markets for biodiversity', *Environmental and Planning Law Journal*, 18(5): 481–4.

Bates, G. (2010) *Environmental Law in Australia*, 7th edn, Sydney: LexisNexis Butterworths.

Berry, T. (1991) *The Ecozoic Era*, online. Available at: <http://www.earth-community.org/images/The%20Ecozoic%20Era.pdf> (accessed 21 February 2011).

Burdon, P. (2011) 'Eco-centric paradigm', in P. Burdon (ed.) *Exploring Wild Law: The Philosophy of Earth Jurisprudence*, Kent Town, SA: Wakefield Press.

Burgin, S. (2008) 'BioBanking: An environmental scientist's view of the role of biodiversity banking offsets in conservation', *Biodiversity Conservation*, 17: 10.

Cullinan, C. (2003) *Wild Law: A Manifesto for Earth Justice*, Dartington: Green Books.

Department of Environment and Climate Change NSW (2008) *Biobanking Assessment Methodology*, online. Available at: <http://www.environment.nsw.gov.au/resources/biobanking/08385bbassessmethod.pdf> (accessed 3 January 2013).

Department for Environment and Heritage (2007) *No Species Loss: A Nature Conservation Strategy for South Australia 2007–2017*, Department for Environment and Heritage, South Australia.

Fowler, R.J. (1986) 'Native vegetation clearance controls in South Australia – a change of course', *Environmental and Planning Law Journal*, 3: 48–66.

Freyfogle, E.T. (1993) *Justice and The Earth: Images for our Planetary Survival*, New York: Free Press.

Garnaut, R. (2008) *The Garnaut Climate Change Review: Final* Report, Cambridge: Cambridge University Press.

Getzler, J. (2004) *A History of Water Rights at Common Law*, Oxford: Oxford University Press.

Gunningham, N. and Young, M. (1997) 'Toward optimal environmental policy: The case of biodiversity conservation', *Ecology Law Quarterly*, 24(2): 243–96.

Maguire, R. and Phillips, A. (2011) 'The role of property law in environmental management: An examination of environmental markets', *Environmental and Planning Law Journal*, 28(4): 215–42.

Mann, T. (ed) (2010) *Oxford Australian Law Dictionary*, Oxford: Oxford University Press.

Maron, M., Dunn, P.K., McAlpine, C.A. and Apan, A. (2010) 'Can offsets really compensate for habitat removal? The case of the endangered red-tailed black cockatoo', *Journal of Applied Ecology*, 47: 348–55.

Nelson, R. and Sharman, B. (2007) 'More than tilting at windmills: A bird's eye view of a bio-offsets scheme under the EPBC Act', *Environmental and Planning Law Journal*, 24(17): 17–34.

Robinson, D. (2009) 'Strategic planning for biodiversity in New South Wales', *Environmental and Planning Law Journal*, 26: 213–35.

Saul, B., Sherwood, S., McAdam, J., Stephens, T. and Slezak, J. (2012) *Climate Change and Australia: Warming to the Global Challenge*, Sydney: The Federation Press.

Solomon, E. (2011) 'Security for biodiversity offsets in New South Wales', *Environmental and Planning Law Journal*, 28(2): 92–110.
Swimme, B. and Berry, T. (1992) *The Universe Story*, SanFrancisco, CA: Harper and Row.
Wilcox, M. and Rennie, M. (2012) *Australian Emissions Trading Law*, Sydney: Thomson Reuters.
Wilson, E.O. (1992) *The Diversity of Life*, New York: W W Norton and Co.
Zahar, A., Peel, J. and Godden, L. (2012) *Australian Climate Law in Global Context*, Cambridge: Cambridge University Press.

Chapter 15

Emissions trading and Earth Jurisprudence
Will liabilities protect the atmospheric commons?

Felicity Deane

Early economists such as Adam Smith regarded long term economic and population growth as unlikely; limits would eventually slow or stop growth, and the process would end with most people living at a subsistence level. These early economists understood that capitalism should balance growth with social objectives (Karr 2008: 103). As stated by Smith:

> Every species of animals naturally multiplies in proportion to their means of subsistence, and no species can ever multiply beyond it... the liberal reward of labour, by enabling them to provide better for their children, and consequently bring up a greater number, naturally tends to widen and extend those limits.
>
> (Smith 1776: 182)

Industrialisation has led to a capacity for population that far exceeds what these early economists would have thought possible. However, the impact of industrialization has been significant. One of these impacts is climate change. As Berry notes:

> ...this devastation of the natural world [is] due to an industrial economy that is willing to wreck the entire planet for financial gain or some so-called improvement in the human condition.
>
> (Berry 1999: 74)

In the face of the catastrophic predictions associated with climate change the implementation of emissions trading schemes may appear a drastic *under-reaction* on the behalf of policymakers and legislators. However, one must pause before making this criticism to understand precisely what it is these schemes achieve. Thus, this chapter seeks to evaluate the environmental effectiveness of emissions trading frameworks generally – and the specific legal frameworks in particular – using the principles of Earth Jurisprudence as the theoretical framework.

In order to do this, this chapter undertakes three tasks. First the principles of Earth Jurisprudence and Wild Law are considered to develop criteria that will be used to analyse emissions trading schemes. Second, the effects of emissions trading schemes will be examined so as to understand the legal impacts of this economic and environmental measure. Finally, the emissions trading schemes of the European Union, New Zealand and Australia will be considered against the criteria enunciated in the first part of the chapter. Before undertaking each of these tasks, this chapter begins with a brief description of the principles of Earth Jurisprudence and Wild Law.

This chapter argues that the existing emissions trading schemes implemented in the EU, Australia and New Zealand do little to promote the rights of nature and therefore cannot be described as wild laws. There are many positive aspects of these schemes, and certainly the introduction of a price on GHG emissions represents environmental progress. However, these frameworks are preoccupied with maintaining a status quo in society that is unsustainable. It is the argument of this chapter that in order to promote the rights of nature, and take measurable steps for mitigating climate change these schemes must enable a forward movement, that may potentially lead to a new societal norm.

Earth Jurisprudence and Wild Law

> Environmental problems raise fundamental questions of ethics and philosophy about the ends we should pursue.
>
> (Desjardins 2006: 7)

If environmental problems raise questions about the ends policies should pursue, Earth Jurisprudence provides one set of answers to these questions. Earth Jurisprudence is the critical legal theory fundamental to the formation of Wild Law (Cullinan 2011a: 10). It provides the 'philosophical and theoretical basis for governance systems that foster wild law' (Cullinan 2002: 118). Earth Jurisprudence is similar to other critical legal theories in that it identifies problems with the current legal system and society as a whole. This philosophy promotes the belief that many problems within human society stem from the anthropocentric view that human beings are the centre and purpose of existence and that they exist independently of nature (Burdon 2009: 41–2). The theory of Earth Jurisprudence is based on the idea that humans are only one part of a wider Earth community, rather than being the centre of it (Burdon 2009: 41).

Earth Jurisprudence is promoted in Wild Laws. Wild Laws are laws that capture the importance of preserving the natural environment for the benefit of all Earth's ecosystems and natural entities (Cullinan 2011b: 10). Wild Laws challenge the tradition of the anthropocentric legal system and shift the focus within this system from humans to the Earth community as a whole.

Wild Law recognizes the rights of all beings to coexist and fulfil their respective roles within the natural world. These laws may take many forms, as there is no prescription for their structure (Cullinan 2011b: 10, 76).

In order to complete the analysis of this chapter the specific requirements of the critical legal theory of Earth Jurisprudence must be examined. For the purposes of evaluating economic instruments using Earth Jurisprudence as a theoretical framework, specific criteria must be developed here. To do this provides some guidance on whether it may be said, with any degree of certainty, that a legal framework promotes the principles of Earth Jurisprudence and can therefore be described as a Wild Law. Although to label an economic instrument as a Wild Law may appear irregular, it is important to remember that diversity of law and governance is one of the key principles of Wild Law (Cullinan 2011b: 10, 76).

The Earth Jurisprudence criteria for climate change mitigation frameworks

To develop criteria for Earth Jurisprudence enables the evaluation of whether a particular legal framework effectively promotes Earth Jurisprudence. Cullinan suggests that systems of governance that promote the ethics underpinning Earth Jurisprudence will have four common elements. The following criteria are quoted from 'Wild Law':

i. Recognition that the source of the fundamental 'Earth rights' of all members of the Earth Community is the universe, rather than human governance systems;
ii. A means of recognising the roles of non-human members of the Earth community and of restraining humans from unjustifiably preventing them fulfilling those roles;
iii. A concern for reciprocity and the maintenance of a dynamic equilibrium between all the members of the Earth Community determined by what is best for the system as a whole (Earth justice); and
iv. An approach to condoning or disapproving human conduct on the basis of whether or not the conduct strengthens or weakens the bones that constitute the Earth Community.

(Cullinan 2011b: 117)

Having recognized these concepts it is possible to extrapolate criteria that may be applied to environmental legal frameworks.

Earth Jurisprudence criteria for emissions trading schemes

The first criterion requires recognition of the Earth rights. This recognition must serve a more meaningful purpose than only recognizing that the Earth, specifically the ecosystem of the planet, has the right to be free from the pollution inflicted upon it by the human species. Any effective recognition must have implications beyond paying lip service to this inherent right.

This is a principle that must be evident throughout a legal framework, and cannot be evidenced by one element in isolation. Therefore, this criterion can only be demonstrated by examining a legal framework as a whole. This may be evidenced by: the object and purpose of the law; by the language used within the law itself; but most importantly, by the overall impact of the framework. This criterion is therefore informed in part by the strength and enforceability of the framework.

The second criterion also has an element of recognition, but at the same time requires that human behaviour is restrained in pursuit of this recognition. Therefore the important element of this criterion for the purposes of this chapter is that there is a restraint on the human behaviour that potentially leads to damage of the environment and other life forms. Thus, this element suggests a need for the prohibition of behaviour that causes excessive emissions of greenhouse gases (GHGs).

The third element necessitates a degree of reciprocity. Reciprocation requires a response where one is required (Soanes et al. 2010: 626). Indeed reciprocity indicates that where one entity assists another, consideration and assistance is returned. Therefore for a governance system to support this element it must require that where damaging behaviour takes place, steps must be taken to correct the damage or indeed, reverse it.

Finally, the fourth element introduces a need to either condone or disapprove of human conduct, depending on the impact of that conduct. This may mean that incentives need to be offered to behave in an environmentally responsible manner and likewise disincentives applied for behaviour that has a damaging impact. In this regard, the more undesirable the behaviour the more sizeable the disincentive should be.

Considering this, we may expand on Cullinan's criteria for the purposes of this chapter. These criteria may be rephrased for the subject matter of this chapter accordingly:

i. A legal framework must ensure legal recognition of the rights of the ecosystem of the planet and the life forms that rely on the proper functioning of the Earth's ecosystem. For a climate change mitigation framework this requires legal recognition of the need to maintain the Earth's ability to regulate the climate through the natural processes. Furthermore we must recognize that human behaviour should not have a dramatic impact on the climate of the planet.
ii. A legal framework should restrain human behaviour that damages the proper functioning of the planetary ecosystem. This criterion requires prohibition on the excessive emissions of GHGs, such as those released through industrial processes.

iii. A legal framework should ensure reciprocation that corrects or reverses any damaging behaviour. For a climate change framework this requires that any damage caused should be corrected by the party causing the damage. This could be achieved in part through recycling revenue acquired through a liability imposed for the emission of GHGs.

iv. A legal framework must include disincentives for environmentally undesirable behaviour. A classic economic disincentive is the imposition of a liability for damaging behaviour. The alternative side of this is an economic incentive, or a subsidy for behaviour that reduces environmental damage.

Each of these criteria may be applied to the legal frameworks of existing emissions trading schemes. This is done to evaluate whether these schemes can promote the principles of Earth Jurisprudence, and in doing so, protect the atmospheric commons. Before undertaking this task it is necessary to consider what it is that emissions trading schemes achieve, and why they have been implemented to mitigate climate change.

The theory of using emissions trading schemes for climate change

> More than half of the population of the developed world lives in countries with emissions trading schemes.
> (Garnaut 2011: 58)

When responding to the question of whether an emissions trading scheme can promote Earth Jurisprudence it is important that the justification for using economic instruments for climate change must feature in the response. However, whether an economic instrument is the quintessential framework for mitigating climate change is not the concern of this paper. One must acknowledge that no singular legal framework will rectify the global problem of climate change. However, it is relevant to examine whether an economic instrument *should* be used, alongside other methods, for mitigating climate change. For this reason, it is important to review the theory of applying a price to GHG emissions through emissions trading schemes.

Climate change and externalities

The cause of climate change is the greenhouse effect (IPCC 2007a, 2007b). The natural greenhouse effect of the Earth's climate system is amplified through anthropogenic GHG emissions. When GHGs are emitted to a degree that the Earth's ecosystem cannot adequately regulate them through natural processes, the consequence is a warming of the climate (Durrant 2008: 55).

Therefore, GHG emissions are an externality (Stern 2006: 308). These emissions are a cost imposed on third parties by the entities causing them (Freebairn 2010: 220). Karr notes that the onset of capitalism in the industrial world has hidden one of the secrets of wealth accumulation:

> the… 'dirty little secret' of capitalism, is that during the accumulation of capital by capitalists, the capitalists do not pay their bills. Indeed, social and environmental consequences, called externalities by economists, are borne by society at large, while the profits accrue to a few capitalists.
> (Karr 2008: 103)

Economists suggest that the most appropriate method for regulating externalities is to charge those who cause them (Ippolito 2005: 230). The concept of taxing to internalize externalities was first suggested by Pigou in 1920 (Kaplow 2008: 20). Known as a Pigouvian tax, the purpose of such a charge is to wholly internalize the costs of the environmental damage caused by a given activity. Pigouvian taxes can be considered corrective taxes, as they correct the bias of using an apparently *free* resource and bring the price of a product closer to the social cost of production (Ippolito 2005: 240). In essence, a Pigouvian tax internalizes the costs of externalities. A true Pigouvian tax wholly internalizes the marginal costs of behaviour – caused by an entity – upon that same entity (Daly and Farley 2011: 430).

Therefore, the question arises, what impact does internalizing the marginal costs of behaviour have on the rights of both the entities polluting and those suffering the damage caused by the pollution? To determine whether economic instruments, specifically emissions trading schemes, can promote principles of Earth Jurisprudence requires that we answer this question. First, it is essential to understand what the existing rights and duties are in relation to the preservation of the atmosphere.

Pricing externalities and the impact on rights and duties to pollute

The principles of Earth Jurisprudence require that rights are extended to the Earth and all its subjects. As such, the relationship between a nation state and its environmental resources could not be considered proprietary, but fiduciary (Sand 2004: 48). Indeed, international law imposes a duty on states to respect and preserve areas of *res communis* (Aust 2010: 40). These areas include those beyond national jurisdiction 'such as the high seas, the ocean floor [and] outer space' (Schrijver 1997: 246), and, as this chapter suggests, is likely to include the atmospheric commons. However, even if this terminology does not extend to the atmosphere, the scientific literature presents a plethora of evidence suggesting GHG emission pollution will cause substantial damage to other areas of *res communis* (IPCC 2007a). Thus, one may present a logical argument that there is a state-based duty to preserve the atmosphere and limit GHG emissions. Certainly based on the international principle of *res communis* states can no longer claim to have a right to release unlimited quantities of GHG emissions (Soroos 2005).

The international climate change regime reinforces the idea that states no longer have a right to use the atmosphere as an unlimited waste disposal for GHG pollutants. Although the text of the United Nations Framework Convention on Climate Change (UNFCCC) requires signatories show 'voluntary restraint' for releasing emissions, the Kyoto Protocol goes further and imposes mandatory targets on Annex I parties (Soroos 2005: 46). Importantly, recognition of this duty does not cause individual entities to be legally prohibited from releasing GHG emissions into the atmosphere.

Daly and Farley (2011) note that when an entity is not restricted from polluting that entity is the holder of a privilege. This means that those who endure the effects of the pollution have no rights. To impose a price on pollution alone does not prevent this behaviour, nor does it change the rights of injured parties, but it does create an obligation on the polluters to pay compensation (Daly and Farley 2011: 424–30). Having said this, an emissions trading scheme is legally different from a tax. Some suggest that emissions trading schemes create property rights to pollute. In contrast to this, Daly suggests that the imposition of a Pigouvian tax and an emissions trading scheme have the same effects. In order to determine which of these claims is correct we must consider emissions trading schemes in more detail.

Units, credits and permits

Emissions trading schemes generally do two things within standard legal frameworks. First, these schemes impose liability on emitters. Second, these schemes create units of trade that can be surrendered for payment of this liability. Therefore, the purchase of emissions trading schemes implies the purchase of value. However, some commentators may suggest that this purchase may also be akin to a right to pollute. In order to consider what it is these units represent and therefore determine the rights associated with them we must explore the different types of tradeable instruments in more detail.

At the centre of any emissions trading market is the object of trade. It is for the trade of this object that a market exists. Indeed the object can exist without the market but the market cannot exist without the object. The object, for which an emissions trading market exists, is a *tradeable instrument* that represents a set quantity of GHG emissions. There are a number of labels assigned to different types of GHG tradeable instruments. As such it is important to resolve the labels that this chapter will use to describe these categories.

First is a 'GHG unit'. GHG units are the central feature of any trading system designed to reduce GHG emissions and mitigate climate change. These units as created by the regulator, represent a particular quantity of GHG emissions and are either issued or auctioned to entities liable to surrender payment for GHG emissions. Commentators have described these units as accounting units. This is because it is through these units that a regulator may track and record where emissions have occurred (Wemaere et al. 2009: 37).

Throughout the world, GHG units have different labels depending on which system they exist within. For example, the Australian carbon pricing mechanism (CPM) legislation labels these units as 'carbon units', where the European Union Emissions Trading Scheme Directive (EU ETS) refers to them as 'allowances'.

Another unit of trade for GHG emissions trading schemes is the 'GHG credit'. A regulator only issues credits when an activity deemed eligible results in the removal or avoidance of GHG emissions (Wemaere et al. 2009: 44). The generation of credits under a program or framework is contingent on whether that framework has approved methodology for a project (Deatherage 2011: 175).

In order to gain a thorough understanding of these instruments we must compare GHG units and GHG credits to GHG permits. The dictionary definition of 'permit' describes this type of instrument as 'an official document giving permission to do something' (Soanes et al. 2010: 555). Therefore, a permit is only required where one must acquire permission to overcome a duty not to behave in a particular manner, or where a right does not already exist to act accordingly. Legal frameworks for emissions trading schemes may include a prohibition on damaging behaviour, in which case a permit or a licence will be required.

The criteria of Earth Jurisprudence and Emissions Trading Schemes

Having considered the legal impacts of emissions trading generally we must evaluate whether the existing frameworks exhibit features that promote the criteria of Earth Jurisprudence. To do this one must consider each criteria in turn against the legal frameworks of three emissions trading schemes currently implemented. These are the EU ETS, the New Zealand Emissions Trading Scheme (NZ ETS) and the Australian CPM.

Legal recognition of the rights of nature

As noted earlier, legal recognition is more than paying lip service. Therefore in order to find evidence of this first criterion it is essential to read figuratively between the lines. Although, it is recognized that frameworks will not generally impart rights themselves to nature, it is suggested that the mere imposition of economic instruments demonstrates that the sustainability of the planet outweighs the importance of economic growth.

Although attempts will be made to draw appropriate conclusions here, it is important to keep in mind that it is impossible to review all aspects of the schemes within the confines of this chapter. Certainly, for the purposes of considering whether the rights of nature have been recognized a conclusion that they have not formally been recognized may be quickly arrived at. Indeed, the objects of the legislation indicate that this is the case. However, this issue cannot be resolved by considering only one part of a framework in isolation. The following paragraphs examine: (i) the objects of the Acts establishing the emissions trading schemes of the EU, New Zealand and Australia; (ii) the enforceability of the frameworks; and, (iii) the breadth and strength of these Acts.

Objectives of the frameworks

The EU ETS, established by the 2003 Council Directive, notes that the subject matter of the Directive is to 'promote reductions of greenhouse gas emissions in a cost-effective and economically efficient manner'. Although this distinctly lacks recognition of the importance of these reductions, the Directive does note the objective of the UNFCCC in paragraph 3 of the preamble of the Council Directive (2003/87/EC: Preamble [3]):

> The ultimate objective of the United Nations Framework Convention on Climate Change, which was approved by Council Decision 94/69/EC of 15 December 1993 concerning the conclusion of the United Nations Framework Convention on Climate Change (6), is to achieve stabilisation of greenhouse gas concentrations in the atmosphere at a level which prevents dangerous anthropogenic interference with the climate system.

This statement does present an indication that the stabilization of the atmosphere and preventing anthropocentric interference with the Earth's systems is indeed the purpose of the introduction of the framework. In this regard, specific reference to the 'climate system' and the importance of preventing human interference with this system aligns with Wild Law principles. The same cannot be said of the other emissions trading schemes considered by this chapter.

The objective of the EU ETS Directive can be compared to the objects of the Australian *Clean Energy Act 2011*: s3. The objects of the Clean Energy Act suggest this framework is implemented:

(a) to give effect to Australia's obligations under:

  (i) the Climate Change Convention; and
  (ii) the Kyoto Protocol;

(b) to support the development of an effective global response to climate change, consistent with Australia's national interest in ensuring that average global temperatures increase by not more than 2 degrees Celsius above pre-industrial levels.

Once again, the objects of the Act recognize the obligations of the Kyoto Protocol and the UNFCCC. However, one may argue that there is almost a degree of acceptance of interference within the objects of the Australian act through recognition of the inevitable increase of two degrees. Further, these objectives could be described as introspective, considering the global problem of climate change only through the lens of the Australian community, rather than the Earth community as a whole. It is suggested here that this does little to promote recognition of the importance of maintaining the Earth's ecosystems.

Similar to the Australian framework the objects of the New Zealand legislation do not present promising evidence of a robust framework designed to prevent anthropogenic interference with the climate system. The purpose of the *New Zealand Climate Change Response Act* 2002 (section 3) is to:

(a) enable New Zealand to meet its international obligations under the Convention and the Protocol, including –

  (i) its obligation under Article 3.1 of the Protocol to retire Kyoto units ...

Similar to the objects of the Australian legal framework, the New Zealand Act in no way considers the underlying objective of the UNFCCC and the Kyoto Protocol. Indeed, there is no recognition of the rights of fellow human beings, and certainly no recognition of the global Earth community. For this reason, the Australian and New Zealand Act's objects could be described as clinical rather than holistic. The objects of the Acts are not indicative of frameworks designed to shift the focus from the anthropogenic society to acknowledge the rights of other natural entities other than human beings. Having said this, these are but one indication of the legal recognition of the rights of nature.

Enforcement, breadth and strength of liability

Each of the EU ETS, the NZ ETS and the Australian CPM include provisions for penalties within the relevant legislative instruments. Therefore, the obligations contained within the schemes are enforceable. This inclusion does not necessarily give the schemes the strength required to label these frameworks Wild Law. In this respect, the relative strength of the schemes may be more accurately ascertained by the breadth of the liability provisions and the desired targets of the schemes.

The EU ETS covers approximately 45 per cent of European carbon dioxide emissions. This translates to 30 per cent of total EU GHG emissions (European Commission, 2005: 7). Initially only carbon dioxide was included in the ETS; however, the second phase of the scheme included nitrous oxide emissions. The liable parties are stationary installations including combustion plants, oil refineries, coke ovens, iron and steel factories and factories making cement, glass, lime, brick, ceramics, pulp and paper (Haywood 2009: 312). The EU has committed to reduce emissions by 21 per cent from 2005 levels by 2020 (IETA, 2012: 1). Although the EU ETS only covers 30 per cent of total emissions, the target reductions apply to the entire EU emissions inventory.

The somewhat narrow coverage of the EU ETS is not indicative of a legal framework designed to support the rights of nature. Rather, it demonstrates the importance of taking some action, but qualified by the importance of maintaining the status quo within the European community. The recognition of the rights of nature is not a part of this status quo. For this reason the coverage of the EU ETS does little to promote these valuable rights.

The Australian CPM is designed to price four of the six Kyoto named GHGs. The CPM covers approximately 60 per cent of Australia's emissions (Australian Government 2011a: 32). Under the CPM, approximately 500 polluters will pay for each tonne of pollution they release (Australian Government 2011b) The targets for emissions reductions under the Australian scheme are somewhat modest, and currently Australia has only committed to a five per cent reduction from 2000 levels by the year 2020 (Australian Government 2011b).

Similar to the EU ETS, the Australian CPM is concerned with taking some action towards mitigating climate change. However, the five per cent reduction target is little more than a token gesture on behalf of the Australian legislators and therefore – as was noted above – clearly the status quo of society is valued more than the continued existence of life on Earth.

The New Zealand Climate Change Response (Moderated Emissions Trading) Amendment Act (2009) uniquely incorporates all sectors, including agriculture, and all GHGs into the NZ ETS by 2015. The inclusion of the agricultural sector in the NZ ETS, although unique, is essential for the effectiveness of the NZ ETS; electricity in New Zealand is currently 67 per cent renewable (Johnson 2008: 195), and the majority of New Zealand GHG emissions are from the agricultural sector (Price et al. 2009: 96).

Ministry for the Environment, Parliament of New Zealand (2011) has committed to reduce emissions by 50 per cent from 1990 levels by 2050. The New Zealand short-term targets are more specific than those of the EU and Australia. For example, there is a commitment to reduce agricultural emissions by 300,000 tonnes of carbon dioxide equivalent by 2013 (NZ ETS Review Panel 2011: 97–8). There are also short-term commitments on forestry area, vehicle efficiency and renewable energy. Arguably, these specific targets will be more easily monitored for compliance than general reduction targets.

Despite some weaknesses in the coverage of the New Zealand scheme, the inclusion of agricultural emissions in the schemes is a positive indication of the purpose of the scheme. This inclusion promotes change in what could be described as New Zealand's most valuable economic sector. Further, the inclusion of short-term as well as long-term targets by the legislators is vital for accountability and future scheme success.

Despite recognizing these positive elements there is little doubt that none of the schemes described here take the requisite steps needed to adequately promote the rights of nature. The above discussion leaves little assurance that the legal frameworks implementing the emissions trading schemes in the EU, New Zealand and Australia give any recognition to the rights of nature generally. Certainly, this is not done in a literal manner. Similarly, the breadth and strength of liability are considered, the measures do not appear robust enough to achieve outcomes needed to maintain the stability of the Earth's climate system.

Prohibition of damaging behaviour

The second criterion of Earth Jurisprudence is the requirement to prohibit damaging behaviour. An example of an ETS that exists concurrently with a prohibition on emissions is the EU ETS. Within the EU, there is indeed a duty for particular entities not to release emissions, unless the entity is the holder of a permit (2003/87/EC: Article 4). However, the EU permits are not the same as EU allowances. Permits allocated in the EU ETS are not transferable as the purpose of these instruments is to impose particular conditions on distinct installations (2003/87/EC: Articles 5–6). The EU ETS permit sets out reporting and monitoring conditions and is to be reviewed by the authority every 5 years (2009/29/EC: Article 1). In addition to holding a permit the installation is required to surrender a relevant number of allowances at the end of each year (2003/87/EC: Article 6). The EU prohibition – in part at least – satisfies the requirement to prohibit any damaging behaviour (Schrijver 1997: 244).

Within the Australian CPM framework there is no prohibition imposed on liable entities from releasing GHG emissions into the atmosphere. Accordingly, within this framework there is no instrument that can be labelled a permit, as there is no requirement for liable entities to seek permission to release emissions. Similarly, there is no prohibition on emissions included within the NZ ETS. However, in the recent NZ ETS review one recommendation of the Review Panel was to prohibit 'knowingly releasing synthetic greenhouse gas emissions' (NZ ETS Review Panel 2011: 88).

Reciprocation through revenue recycling

The third criterion conceptualized within this chapter is the requirement of reciprocation. This means that where damaging behaviour occurs, the entity causing the damage should be required to rectify any injury caused. In the context of climate change, it would be near impossible for the entities that have caused the damage rectify the injury. However, this criterion could be achieved in part if any revenue collected for emissions released was recycled for climate change mitigation purposes.

There is no direct specification within any of the existing emissions trading schemes that the revenue collected from the sale of units or allowances is recycled for climate change mitigation purposes. However, there is some assurance that a portion of revenue from countries with these schemes will find its way to climate change mitigation programs.

In the EU, proposals have been submitted to allocate revenues from certain revenue collected to be used for the purposes of climate action in developing countries (Euractiv 2012). However, these suggestions have been accompanied by rhetoric that any action of this sort would be to aid diplomacy rather than mitigate climate change and restore the Earth's ecological integrity. As noted, '[d]edicating revenues to climate action in developing countries would help restore their trust and garner support for a resolution to the debate around including aviation in the ETS' (Euractiv 2012).

Likewise the implementation of the Australian CPM has not been accompanied by suggestions of recycling revenue for climate change mitigation. The Revised Explanatory Memorandum of the Clean Energy Bill notes: 'Because the carbon price raises revenue, it provides an opportunity to cut other taxes' (Australian Government 2011a: 14).

This is a practice that is not uncommon in relation to carbon pricing schemes. Many carbon taxes implemented throughout the world have the same objective, that is to increase taxes on undesirable behaviour but reduce taxes on the good (Speck and Jilkova 2009: 39). However, some carbon tax frameworks do specify that revenue should be used for environmental purposes. For example, India's *Finance Act* 2010 requires that funds from the Clean Energy Cess (2010) are used to promote clean energy initiatives (*Finance Act 2010*, section 3). Likewise the funds for the Italian carbon tax are used to finance bilateral and multilateral activities in developing countries (Ministry for the Environment, Land and Sea November 2009: 7–1). Despite recognizing these environmental steps forward, we cannot suggest that any of these actions indicates that reciprocation or rectification occurs in any legal framework sufficiently to have any genuine impact.

Implementation of economic disincentives

As noted by Cullinan in *Wild Law*, 'by holding polluters liable for environmental damage we are demonstrating what we value' (Cullinan 2011a: 225). The implementation of an economic disincentive for carbon pollution is precisely what an emission trading scheme is designed to do. In simple terms, emissions trading schemes impose a liability in the same way as classical taxation regimes. The most notable difference between emissions trading schemes and taxation is the ability to satisfy liability through surrendering units rather than currency.

Although it is acknowledged here that the schemes of the EU, New Zealand and Australia all impose a liability on the damaging behaviour of releasing GHG emissions, this liability is partially offset in each of these schemes. The EU ETS has generally issued permits free, generally using grandfathering rather than auctioning to distribute allowances (Clò 2009). In addition to this the EU ETS has provision within the 2009 Council Directive for free allowance allocation where there is intensity and risk of carbon leakage (2009/29/EC: Articles 15–18).

The Australian scheme has significant programs of assistance resulting in free permits for liable entities (Lyster 2011: 459–64). Similar to the Australian CPM, the NZ ETS includes measures of assistance for emissions intensive to moderately intensive eligible industries under the *Climate Change Response (Moderated Emissions Trading) Amendment Act 2009*: sections 81–5. These assistance measures all have the impact of reducing the liability and thus effectively lessening the disincentive required for this damaging behaviour. Certainly, these assistance measures are in opposition to the principles of Earth Jurisprudence.

The principles of Earth Jurisprudence and Wild Law lead one to suggest that if firms cannot financially survive when their own costs are imposed upon them then the costs of the entity are greater than the benefits produced (Daly and Farley 2011: 430–1). These theories eliminate the need to provide assistance when liabilities are imposed for an externality.

Recommendations

The analysis in this chapter has described why the existing emissions trading schemes implemented in the EU, Australia and New Zealand do not take the requisite steps to promote the rights of nature and thus be described as 'Wild Laws'. Therefore, it is now important to briefly consider what exactly could be done in order to achieve this environmental objective.

First, the objectives of the legal frameworks must recognize the importance of maintaining the Earth's climate system, *for the purpose of continuing life* – of continuing all life – for an indefinite period. The legal obligations of the UNFCCC and Kyoto Protocol are of course important, but secondary to the obligations to other species and generations.

Second, the schemes must be robust. Any preoccupation with society's status quo must be set aside in order to ensure steps are taken to manage what is a global environmental problem.

Third, the damaging behaviour must be prohibited. Where the damaging behaviour cannot be avoided, there must be requirements to correct the effects of it.

Fourth, it will be vital for the restoration of the climate system to have sufficient financial resources. For this reason, the revenue recycling must not be used to alleviate the economic impact of the price assigned to GHG emission pollution. Indeed, it is this impact that must be one of the drivers of major societal change if the climate system is to be restored effectively.

Conclusion

For a law to be wild that law must serve the public good. This means it must preserve the Earth's ecosystem and foster life. Laws that serve the 'false idol of industrial capitalism that benefits the few at the expense of the many' contradict this principle (Karr 2008: 103).

Not one of the existing emissions trading schemes examined fall within the category of a Wild Law. This is apparent through the brief analysis of these schemes provided above. Having said this, each of these schemes represents a step in a positive environmental direction, but it is a minor step at best. Certainly, if a legal framework establishing an emissions trading scheme presented features conforming to the criteria of Earth Jurisprudence as enunciated within this chapter it is possible that such a framework could be described as a Wild Law. Indeed, to accept that these criteria promote the principles of Earth Jurisprudence suggests that an emissions trading scheme, and any economic instrument, can recognize the rights of nature, and therefore be 'wild'.

References

Australian Government (2011a) *Revised Explanatory Memorandum, Clean Energy Bill 2011*, Canberra: Commonwealth of Australia.
Australian Government (2011b) *Securing a Clean Energy Future: The Australian Government's Climate Change Plan*, Canberra: Commonwealth of Australia.
Aust, A. (2010) *Handbook of International Law*, 2nd edn, Cambridge: Cambridge University Press.
Berry, T. (1999) *The Great Work*, New York: Bell Tower.
Burdon, P. (2009) 'Earth jurisprudence', *Chain Reaction*, 106: 41–2.
Clò, S. (2009) 'The effectiveness of the EU Emissions Trading Scheme', *Climate Policy*, 9(3): 227–41.

Council Directive 2003/87/EC of the European Parliament and of the Council of 13 October 2003 establishing a scheme for greenhouse gas emission allowance trading within the Community and amending Council Directive 96/61/EC [2003] *Offical Journal of the European Communities* L275/46, 32.

Council Directive 2009/29/EC of the European Parliament and of the Council of 23 April 2009 amending Directive 2003/87/EC so as to improve and extend the greenhouse gas emission allowance trading scheme of the Community [2009] *Offical Journal of the European Communities* L140/52, 63.

Cullinan, C. (2002) *Wild Law*, Claremont, South Africa: Siber Ink.

Cullinan, C. (2011a) *Wild Law*, 2nd edn, Claremont, South Africa: Siber Ink.

Cullinan, C. (2011b) *Wild Law: A Manifesto for Earth Justice*, 2nd edn, White River Junction, VT: Chelsea Green Publishing.

Daly, H.E. and Farley, J. (2011) *Ecological Economics: Principles and Applications*, 2nd edn, Washington, DC: Island Press.

Deatherage, S. (2011) *Carbon Trading Law and Practice*, Oxford: Oxford University Press.

Desjardins, J.R. (2006) *Environmental Ethics: An Introduction to Environmental Philosophy*, 4th edn, Belmont, CA: Thomson Wadsworth.

Durrant, N. (2008) 'The role of law in responding to climate change: emerging regulatory, liability and market approaches', unpublished thesis, Queensland University of Technology.

Euractiv (2012) 'EU's Aviation Carbon Funds Could Aid Developing World', online. Available at: <http://www.euractiv.com/climate-environment/eu-aviation-carbon-funds-aid-dev-news-512568> (accessed 9 May 2012).

European Commision (2005) *EU Action Against Climate Change: EU Emissions Trading – An Open Scheme Promoting Global Innovation*, online. Available at: <http://www.pedz.uni-mannheim.de/daten/edz-bn/gdu/05/emission_trading2_en.pdf> (accessed 24 October 2013).

Intergovernmental Panel on Climate Change (2007a), *Climate Change 2007: Impacts, Adaptation and Vulnerability*, Contribution of Working Group II to the Fourth Assessment Report of the Intergovernmental Panel on Climate Change, Cambridge: Cambridge University Press.

Intergovernmental Panel on Climate Change (2007b), *Fourth Assessment Report: Climate Change, Mitigation of Climate Change*, Cambridge: Cambridge University Press.

International Emissions Trading Association (2012) Briefing on the EU's emissions trading scheme' (Briefing Paper, International Emissions Trading Association, 13 April 2012).

Freebairn, J. (2010) 'Carbon taxes vs tradable permits: Efficiency and equity effects for a small open economy', in I. Claus, N. Gemmell, M. Harding and D. White (eds) *Tax Reform in Open Economies: International and Country Perspectives*, Cheltenham: Edward Elgar, 219.

Garnaut, R. (2011) *The Garnaut Review 2011*, Cambridge: Cambridge University Press.

Haywood, C. (2009) 'The European Union's emissions trading scheme: International emissions trading lessons for the Copenhagen Protocol and implications for Australia?', *Environmental and Planning Law Journal*, 26: 310–29.

Ippolito, R.A. (2005) *Economics for Lawyers*, Princeton, NJ: Princeton University Press.

Johnson, D.L. (2008) 'Electricity and the environment: Current trends and future directions', *New Zealand Journal of Environmental Law*, 12: 195–232.

Kaplow, L. (2008) *The Theory of Taxation and Public Economics*, Princeton, NJ: Princeton University Press.

Karr, J.R. (2008) 'Protecting society from itself: reconnecting ecology and economy', in C.L. Soskolne (ed.) *Sustaining Life on Earth*. Lanham, MD: Lexington Books, 95.

Lyster, R. (2011) 'Australia's clean energy future package: Are we there yet?', *Environmental and Planning Law Journal*, 28(6): 446–77.

Ministry for the Environment, Land and Sea (November 2009), *Fifth National Communication under the UN Framework Convention on Climate Change*, Italy.

Ministry for the Environment, Parliament of New Zealand (2011) *Gazetting New Zealand's 2050 Emissions Target: Minister's Position Paper*, online. Available at: <http://www.mfe.govt.nz/publications/climate/nz-2050-emissions-target/index.html> (accessed 23 February 2012).

New Zealand Emissions Trading Scheme Review Panel (2011) *Doing New Zealand's Fair Share: Emissions Trading Scheme Review 2011, Final Report*, Ministry for the Environment, Parliament of New Zealand.

Price, K., Daniell, L. and Cooper, L. (2009) 'New Zealand climate change laws', in W. Gumley and T. Daya-Winterbottom (eds) *Climate Change Law: Comparative, Contractual and Regulatory Considerations*, Pyrmont, NSW: Lawbook Co, 89.

Sand, P.H. (2004) 'Sovereignty bounded: Public trusteeship for common pool resources?', *Global Environmental Politics*, 4(1): 47–71.

Schrijver, N. (1997) *Sovereignty Over Natural Resources: Balancing Rights and Duties*, Cambridge: Cambridge University Press.

Smith, A. (1776) *An Inquiry into the Nature and the Wealth of Nations*, London: W. Strahan and T. Cadell.

Soanes, C., Hawker, S. and Elliot, J. (eds) (2010) *Oxford English Dictionary*, Oxford: Oxford Press.

Soroos, M.S. (2005) 'Garrett Hardin and tragedies of global commons', in P. Dauvergne (ed.) *Handbook of Global Environmental Politics*, Cheltenham: Edward Elgar Publishing Limited, 35.

Speck, S. and Jilkova, J. (2009) 'Design of environmental tax reforms in Europe', in M. Skou Andersen, and P. Ekins (eds) *Carbon Energy Taxation: Lessons from Europe*. Oxford: Oxford University Press, 24–54.

Stern, N. (2006) *The Economics of Climate Change: The Stern Review*, Cambridge: Cambridge University Press.

Wemaere, M., Streck, C. and Chagas, T. (2009) 'Legal ownership and nature of Kyoto units and EU allowances', in D. Freestone and C. Streck (eds) *Legal Aspects of Carbon Trading: Kyoto, Copenhagen and Beyond*, Oxford: Oxford University Press, 35.

Chapter 16

Wild Law and animal law
Some commonalities and differences

Steven White

This chapter explores points of overlap and difference between two nascent legal disciplines, animal law and Wild Law. Animal law only emerged as a distinct discipline in the United States in the early 1990s, with much of the impetus coming from developments in other disciplines, especially the philosophical challenges to prevailing law posed by the animal rights arguments of Tom Regan, and by the utilitarian arguments of Peter Singer. Wild Law has emerged even more recently, with the publication in 2002 of the first edition of Cormac Cullinan's *Wild Law: A Manifesto for Earth Justice* a defining moment, in turn building on the pioneering work in Earth Jurisprudence by Thomas Berry.[1]

The extent of the similarities between the challenge to the status quo posed by Wild Law, and that posed by a progressive animal law, is striking. First, there is a shared concern with the role played by law in facilitating exploitation. A constant refrain in the Wild Law literature is the extent to which the law legitimizes the exploitation of the environment; a similarly pervasive refrain can be found in the animal law literature, with the law criticized for institutionalizing the exploitation of animals.

Second, the use of a rights-based discourse has been one of the dominant responses in seeking to undermine the foundations of prevailing law and to provide a vision for ending exploitation. One of the prominent bases for rethinking our relationship with animals is located in the natural rights tradition, philosophically most notably developed by Tom Regan, and legally, most significantly developed in the work of Gary Francione. On this approach, the status of animals needs to be transformed – from objects to subjects, with the intrinsic value of animals recognized through personhood rights. Wild Law is underpinned by an Earth Jurisprudence which seeks to have nature, its living and non-living components, valued for their inherent worth, not according to human advantage or exploitation, and to have this worth recognized through the vehicle of rights.[2]

Hand-in-hand with the invocation of rights is a commitment to reforming property doctrine. This is consistent with a shared concern not just to rethink the theoretical basis of our relationship with animals and nature respectively, but also of thinking about how best to advocate and achieve change in the law, to translate theory into practice.[3] However, I argue that it is at this point that some important differences between the two disciplines emerge. One key difference relates to the extent of the challenge to property doctrine. The challenge posed by much theorizing in animal law is in fact much less radical than that posed by Wild Law.

Another key difference, or at least potential tension, concerns what should be understood as 'nature' or the 'environment'. Should animals be understood as just one aspect of the wider category of 'nature' or do they need to be considered in their own right? Are animals in a domesticated setting part of nature or the environment, or does nature include only free-living or wild animals? These are difficult questions which will test the boundaries and compatibility of animal law and Wild Law. I argue that in exploring the boundaries of these disciplines, animal law may be shown to be too narrow in the way in which a revised understanding of the significance of animals is commonly conceptualized, while the implications of Wild Law for all animals – not just wild animals – are yet to be fully explored.

The animal welfare model: anthropocentrism writ large

The basic legal approach to the treatment of domesticated animals was established in the mid-nineteenth century, following the passage of anti-cruelty legislation in the United Kingdom, beginning in 1822 (Radford 2001; White 2007). It has been refined over time, but not radically changed in substance. In Australia, for example, each State and Territory jurisdiction prohibits cruelty to animals.[4] Cruelty is variously defined to include the imposition of pain or harm on animals. While cruelty provisions govern what may *not* be done to an animal, positive obligations are also imposed on those in charge of animals. In two jurisdictions (*Animal Care and Protection Act 2001* (Qld) section 17; *Animal Welfare Act 1993* (Tas) section 6), these positive obligations are explicitly identified as a statutory 'duty of care'. In Queensland, section 17 of the *Animal Care and Protection Act 2001* (Qld) provides some substance for what constitutes the duty of care. The duty of care is modelled very closely on the Five Freedoms, requiring a person in charge of an animal to take reasonable steps to provide or allow for appropriate food and water; appropriate accommodation; the display of normal patterns of behaviour; treatment of disease; and appropriate handling.

The scope of these protective provisions – the cruelty prohibitions and duty of care obligations – is potentially broad. If applied in an expansive way the conditions could be created not just for protection against harm, but also for a form of animal flourishing. In practice this potential is not realized.

Companion animals are perhaps best protected, but even here the recognition is limited. Cullinan sums this up very well when he states:

> [T]oday, legally speaking, it is not possible to murder an animal ... no matter what the magnitude of the slaughter is or what degree of brutality, depravity or cruelty is involved. At worst one might fall foul of animal cruelty laws (which are probably mainly intended to protect human sensibilities) ...
> (Cullinan 2011c: 70–1)

Outside a companion animal context, there are significant barriers to the application of anti-cruelty or duty of provisions in a way which would meaningfully protect animals from harm. The key barrier is that most regulation of the suffering of animals is not directly governed by statutes at all. For most categories of animal, including farm animals, animals used in research and animals used in entertainment, exemptions or defences from cruelty and duty of care offences are provided. It is on this basis, for example, that a range of cruel farming practices are legally entrenched in Australia.[5] Although the regulatory form may differ in other Western jurisdictions, including in the United States, the United Kingdom and New Zealand, the outcomes are broadly the same.[6]

On this basis, animal welfare legislation is characterized as being utilitarian in nature, but in a way which values the interests of humans much more highly than the interests of animals. There is no explicit, enforceable legal recognition of the moral standing of individual animals, on the basis that they are inherently worthy of protection. In some jurisdictions there is at least formal recognition of the sentience of animals; however, the significance of this recognition is limited to emphasizing the need to pay due regard to the welfare of animals. For example, the European Union now explicitly recognizes the sentience of animals in one of its foundation treaties, the *Treaty on the Functioning of the European Union* (opened for signature 7 February 1992, [2009] OJ C 115/199 (entered into force 1 November 1993). Article 13 of this Treaty provides:

> In formulating and implementing the Union's agriculture, fisheries, transport, internal market, research and technological development and space policies, the Union and the Member States shall, since animals are sentient beings, pay full regard to the welfare requirements of animals, while respecting the legislative or administrative provisions and customs of the Member States relating in particular to religious rites, cultural traditions and regional heritage.

The essential premise of all regulation of the welfare of animals is that we should treat animals 'humanely', protecting their interests but only so far as these do not conflict with human interests. This a balancing exercise, but one in which the interests of humans, even where trivial, will most often outweigh concerns about the wellbeing of animals. For Francione this regulatory model reflects what he calls legal welfarism, and it is based on the objectification of animals as personal property:

> First, legal welfarism characterizes animals as the property of human beings ... Second, legal welfarism interprets the property status of animals to justify the treatment of animals exclusively as means to human ends. Third, legal welfarism provides that animal use is 'necessary' whenever that use is part of a generally accepted social institution. Fourth, legal welfarism does not proscribe 'cruelty' as that term is understood in ordinary discourse. Rather, legal welfarism interprets 'cruelty' to refer to animal use that, for the most part, fails to facilitate, and may even frustrate, that animal exploitation.
> (Francione 1995: 26)

Francione's contention is that virtually any use of animals that leads to some economic or social benefit will be justified, necessary or reasonable. This is because animal welfare law merely reflects and reinforces a property regime, and does not significantly alter it. Francione is principally concerned with domesticated animals. Animal welfare statutes generally have little to say about the protection of wild animals, with nature conservation or wildlife legislation much more significant. Francione does address wild animals, though, and suggests the same arguments apply. Although wild animals in their natural state may, in strict legal terms, be ownerless, the State routinely stakes a claim to them. Regardless of the validity of that claim, the State has unfettered power to reduce wild animals to ownership, and the result is that wild animals are routinely exploited.

Arguably, though, a more nuanced approach is required with respect to wild animals than Francione allows. On this approach a hierarchy of legal protection exists, with rare or endangered native animals at the top of the list, enjoying extensive formal protection (including through the domestic implementation of international agreements such as the *Convention on International Trade in Endangered Species of Wild Fauna and Flora*), through to introduced wild animals at the bottom of the list, enjoying very little protection from harm at all (Thiriet forthcoming).[7] Even at the top of the list, though, as Cullinan points out, 'this type of [protection] does not confer rights on non-humans, it merely restricts some aspects of human behaviour, usually to ensure that other humans can continue to enjoy wild areas and creatures' (Cullinan 2011c: 64).

The instrumentalist, property-based nature of the orthodox animal welfare model is clearly analogous to prevailing environmental regulation. Just as in animal welfare law, where human interests (principally economic, but also social and cultural) and animal interests are 'balanced', so in nature conservation law we see a balancing exercise between human interests (again, economic, social and cultural) and the environment, principally through the rubric of 'sustainability'. The concept of ecologically sustainable development, emerging from a report of the World Commission on Environment and Development, defines sustainable development as that which meets the needs of present generations while not compromising the ability of future generations to also meet their needs. Governments around the world have picked up this definition. As with animal welfare law, though, the balancing exercise inherent in an idea such as sustainability undermines meaningful protection of the environment. In its most common form in Western jurisdictions it 'fails to recognize the finite capacity of ecological systems and the fact that these systems are being eroded by the cumulative impact of individual actions' (Taylor and Grinlinton 2011: 12; see also Bosselmann 2011: 206–9). In words which could equally apply to the protection of animals under animal welfare law, Taylor and Grinlinton suggest that:

> if we pay serious attention to the continuing and accelerating decline of Earth's ecological systems (across multiple scales), even in the light of half a century of environmental law and policy, we would have to conclude that environmental law is failing to meet society's objectives, particularly when viewed from the perspective of intra and intergenerational equity.
> (Taylor and Grinlinton 2011: 11)[8]

The problem, as for animals, is the human-centred idea of property. While the focus in an animal context is the personal property status of animals, in the context of nature the focus is real property (and especially private ownership). As Burdon suggests, '[i]n western society, property law provides some of the most foundational ideas about the land and about our place in the environment', and '[w]hile much more can be said, it should be plain that this image of ownership stands in the way of environmental protection. The implications of this view are exacerbated further by the fact that our law stacks rights in favour of human beings and corporate persons' (Burdon 2010a: 63). Cullinan is even more stringent in grounding the failings of protection of the environmental in a property paradigm:

> In the eyes of [Western] law today, most of the community of life on Earth remains mere property, natural 'resources' to be exploited, bought, and sold just as slaves were. This means that environmentalists are seldom seen as activists fighting to uphold fundamental rights, but rather as criminals who infringe upon the property rights of others. It also means that actions that damage the ecosystems and the natural processes on which life depends, such as Earth's climate, are poorly regulated.[9]
> (Cullinan 2011b: 232)

On the proviso that prevailing ideas of property are undermining the meaningful protection of animals and the environment respectively, how are we to respond to the limits of property?

Challenging the animal welfare model through an appeal to rights and reform of property

To begin with animals, one response to the legal categorization of animals as property is to acknowledge that such categorization may be problematic, but to argue that even if it persists, significant gains can still be made in the protection of animals. Radford, for example, accepts that animals' status as property has a range of detrimental consequences (Radford 2001: 103). These include that in the absence of animal welfare or other legislation, it leaves the owner of an animal with complete autonomy as to how the animal should be treated. Further, the idea of property exerts a powerful rhetorical constraint on interference. The classical and still persuasive idea that the State should interfere with property rights as little as possible makes it difficult for those advocating increased protection for animals. The fact is that if animals are to be better protected, this necessarily requires further State intervention to place additional constraints on those property rights. Finally, again in rhetorical terms, the language of property shapes attitudes towards animals. Especially for farm animals and animals used in other commercial endeavours, such as research and entertainment, categorization as property turns the animals into mere commodities. As commodities in a market system, there is inevitably the risk of compromising welfare in the pursuit of profit.

However, notwithstanding these potential detrimental consequences associated with the classification of animals as property, the argument is made that it is still possible to improve the lot of animals without a change in legal status. Radford takes the pragmatic position that the legal status of animals is unlikely to change in the foreseeable future and that more effective legal regulation and enforcement is a more viable way to proceed. In a related vein, Sunstein argues that existing animal welfare legislation amounts to a de facto bill of rights, if we understand rights to mean legal protection against harm (Sunstein 2004).[10] What is needed is a more vigorous commitment to enforcing existing rights to protection. A state or government, he argues, could do a great deal to prevent animal suffering, without going as far as stipulating that animals cannot be owned. For example, apart from better enforcement of existing law, it remains possible to make other legal reforms, such as reforming standing rules to allow actions to be brought on behalf of animals by a wider range of plaintiffs, without making them persons or changing their property status.

A similarly pragmatic approach is advanced by Favre, who argues for a *modification* of property status, rather than abolition. Certain animals could be recognized as 'living property', capable of self-ownership (with human guardians holding legal title, and animals beneficial title). Animals could have actions brought in their own names, or as part of a group, to protect their interests. Those interests would be underpinned by a range of legal rights, including the right not to be harmed, to be cared for, to have living space, to be properly owned, to own property, to enter into contracts and to file tort claims (Favre 2010: 1061–70).

Despite the creativity of an approach such as that advocated by Favre, if the property critique of Francione is accepted, the answer to the problem of objectification is to reject the property status of animals, even in a modified form, and recognize their moral claim to be persons. Although acknowledging his debt to the rights theory of Regan, who appeals to the cognitive abilities of animals to ground his rights arguments, Francione argues sentience is enough to ground this moral claim. In legal terms, this shift to animals as persons would require the abolition of ownership of animals in any form, and a prohibition on using animals for food, in biomedical research, in entertainment and so on.

An analogous approach is embraced by Wild Law. Burdon argues that '[t]he challenge before Wild Law is to develop both theory and law that reflects [a non-instrumentalist] modern understanding of the earth and our relationship to the natural world' (Burdon 2010a: 64). One of the key strands within the Wild Law movement is the rejection of property in nature and the legal recognition of the rights of nature (Burdon 2010a: 63–4). These rights, for sentient and non-sentient beings, include the right to be, the right to habitat or a place to be, and the right to fulfil their role in the ever-renewing processes of the Earth community (Cullinan 2011c: 103).

Animal jurisprudence: anthropocentrism redux?

While arguments challenging property are a key aspect of both Wild Law and animal law, the Wild Law approach seems much more thorough-going than that in much animal jurisprudence. This reflects a key difference in approach, within each discipline, underpinning the critique of property and prevailing law. The difference lies in the foundations on which the rights of animals, or of nature, should be recognized. In Wild Law and Earth Jurisprudence:

> [T]he rights of all beings are derived from the most fundamental source of all, the universe. Since the universe is, in [Berry's] words 'a communion of subjects and not a collection of objects', it follows that all the component members of the universe are subjects capable of holding rights and have as much right to hold rights as humans. One of the beauties of this approach is that it avoids the difficulties that have bedevilled those

who have tried to argue that only certain 'sentient' or 'higher' forms of life should have rights.

(Cullinan 2011c: 96)

The last part of this quote goes directly to the limited nature of the rights approach in much animal jurisprudence. Francione explicitly limits his critique of property to its effect on the interests of animals, and makes no wider claims about the shortcomings of property doctrine. He simply wants animals extricated from private property doctrine. And there is no doubt that whether it's Regan and Francione relying on a natural rights discourse, or Singer relying on preference utilitarianism, these proponents for the moral significance of animals have in common a reliance on either the sentience of animals or the cognitive abilities of animals to ground their arguments. Bryant labels this the 'similarity argument'. The recognition of animals as subjects depends on the extent to which they can demonstrate capacities relevantly similar to humans (Bryant 2007). This reflects an anthropocentric prejudice (Steiner 2005). The measuring stick for animals is human understanding of suffering or human understanding of cognitive abilities. And, if the benchmark levels are met, the ethical remedy is to extend the model of universal, individual rights to animals.

By contrast, Wild Law and Earth Jurisprudence would see the recognition of animals as subjects as just a first step in broader reform of governance arrangements, as part of the recognition of the reciprocal relationship between humans and the rest of nature (Filgueira and Mason 2011: 194–5). It is particularly notable that '[a]n anthropocentric perspective of the earth boasts few contemporary advocates and has lost all credibility in philosophy and science. Its current place in law reflects more the slow moving nature of the institution, than the views of the profession' (Burdon 2010a: 63). The same cannot be said with respect to perspectives on animals. Whereas much theorizing about rights in an animal law domain is focused on an extension of individual rights to some animals,[11] Wild Law emphasizes a more inclusive approach. While such an approach is not without problems (Burdon 2010b: 77–83), by encompassing all of nature and its components, and emphasizing community and interconnectedness,[12] the Wild Law project is liable to pose a much sterner challenge to private property doctrine than the so far dominant approaches in animal law.

Animals and nature/environment

The focus of Wild Law on 'nature' points to another difference, or least a potential tension, between theorizing in animal law and in Wild Law. Writing in the context of the recent *Declaration of the Fundamental Rights of Mother Earth*, and the broader claims of Wild Law about the rights of living and non-living beings, Burdon recognizes this 'introduces an important point of engagement between earth rights, animal rights and human rights ... the central tension is what is meant by the term 'nature'' (Burdon 2011: 5). This tension reflects different conceptions of what should be the proper focus of concern in ethical debate. It is reflected in the opposition which still bubbles along between advocates of, on the one hand, an animal ethic, including an animal rights or utilitarian ethic, primarily concerned with the wellbeing of individual animals, and, on the other hand, advocates of an environmental ethic, concerned with the environment as a whole. While it is beyond the scope of this chapter to provide a detailed account of this debate, some key positions are worth highlighting, since they point to similar potential tensions between animal law and Wild Law.

Sagoff declared animal liberation and environmental ethics to be a 'bad marriage requiring a quick divorce' (Sagoff 1984). In particular, Sagoff zeroed in on the human-centred nature of much animal ethics, suggesting that a 'humanitarian ethic – an appreciation not of nature, but of the welfare of animals – will not help us to understand or to justify an environmental ethic. It will not provide the necessary or valid foundations for environmental law' (Sagoff 1984: 306–7). Baird Callicott similarly sought to clearly separate the individualism of animal liberation from a holistic environmental ethic, and was scathing about moral concern for domestic animals:

> There are intractable practical differences between environmental ethics and the animal liberation movement. Very different moral obligations follow in respect, most importantly, to domestic animals, the principal beneficiaries of the humane ethic. Environmental ethics sets a very low priority on domestic animals as they very frequently contribute to the erosion of the integrity, stability, and beauty of the biotic communities into which they have been insinuated.
> (Baird Callicott 1980: 337)

On the other hand, Regan, in his treatise developing the case for animal rights, was equally scathing about the implications of a holistic environmental ethic. In contemplating the overriding of human and/or animal rights in favour of ecosystem protection, Regan argued that such an ethic reflected a form of 'environmental fascism' (Regan 2004: 361–2). Regan insists that:

> A rights-based environmental ethic remains a live option, one that, though far from being established, merits continued exploration. It ought not to be dismissed out of hand by environmentalists as being in principle antagonistic to the goals for which they work. It isn't. Were we to show proper respect for the rights of the individuals who make up the

biotic community, would not the *community* be preserved? And is not that what the more holistic, systems-minded environmentalists want?

(Regan 2004: 363)[13]

It is noteworthy that over time Baird Callicott has moderated his response to an animal ethic grounded in concern for individual, sentient animals, acknowledging the moral significance of such animals, even if not the claim that this should be the foundation for recognition of rights (Khoo 2009: 62). This shift foreshadows the work of philosophers such as Jamieson (2002), Varner (2002) and Taylor (1986) who in different ways seek to reconcile animal ethics and environmental ethics. Jamieson, for example, has argued that while there may be some theoretical differences between animal liberationists and environmental ethicists the two can hold many of the same normative views. It requires recognition that 'many of our most important issues involve serious threats to both humans and animals as well as to the non-sentient environment; because animal liberationists can value nature as a home for sentient beings; and because animal liberationists can embrace environmental values as intensely as environmental ethicists ...' (Jamieson 2002: 209).[14]

A similar evolution in sensibility can be found in Wild Law.[15] In the first edition of *Wild Law* Cullinan acknowledges that he 'had previously regarded an animal rights approach to environmental law as well-intentioned but ultimately unhelpful and potentially counter-productive to scientific conservation methods' (Cullinan 2002: 149). By the end of *Wild Law* those qualms have disappeared, to the point where constitutional recognition of animals as sentient beings in Germany and Switzerland reflects 'wildness breaking out in the world's governance systems' (Cullinan 2002: 206, 2011c: 160). The evidence to date suggests that such recognition is largely of symbolic significance only, with an orthodox animal welfare ethic still the dominant ethic (Wagman and Liebman 2011: 266–9). It is notable too that such provisions address all animals, including domesticated animals. Baird Callicott's observation that environmental ethics sets a low priority on domesticated animals, cited earlier, is one which is yet to be fully addressed in Wild Law.[16] Consideration of animals as part of nature or the environment usually denotes 'wild animals' in their natural state, not domesticated animals.[17]

And yet the *Declaration of the Fundamental Rights of Mother Earth* is ambiguous about the rights which might be extended to domesticated animals. Article 1 provides that '[j]ust as human beings have human rights, all other beings also have rights which are specific to their species or kind and appropriate for their role and function within the communities within which they exist'. Article 2 includes a commitment, for all beings, to a right to life, the right to be respected, and the right to wellbeing and to live free from torture or cruel treatment by human beings (Cullinan 2011c: 192–5).

At face value, the *Declaration*, especially through Article 2, could entail the extension of the relevant prescribed rights to domesticated animals. The application of these rights in unqualified form would necessitate a substantial reduction in the current exploitation of animals, especially in farm and research contexts. It would compromise significant cultural, traditional and religious practices. The issue, of course, is to what extent and in what form specific rights are to be granted to different species of animals. This takes us back to the tension, highlighted earlier, between human rights, animal rights and earth rights, and how we are to understand nature.

One manifestation of this tension – the question of whether domesticated animals are part of the 'environment' or not – is vividly illustrated by a court case in Australia which arose out of protest action targeting the live export of sheep. The Federal Court of Australia was faced with the issue of the extent to which environmental protection encompasses farm animal welfare. In *Rural Export & Trading (WA) Pty Ltd v Hahnheuser* (2007) 243 ALR 356, Ralph Hahnheuser and Animal Liberation SA defended a claim that they were in breach of section 45DB of the *Trade Practices Act 1974* (Cth) (TPA), by substantially hindering a live export company from engaging in trade or commerce. Hahnheuser placed processed pig meat into a food trough for sheep set to be exported to the Middle East. It was not contested that the act did hinder the export of the sheep. However, the respondents argued that they were entitled to rely on the defence of environmental protection under section 45DD(3) of the TPA.

The trial judge accepted this argument, stating (at 376):

> It is clear that the environment comprehends living things, including animals, and the conditions under which they live... Farm animals are as much a part of the environment as are wild animals, feral animals and domestic animals. There is no reason why the protection of the conditions in which farm animals are kept should be excluded from the concept of environmental protection.

The Full Federal Court overturned this decision.[18] The Full Court did acknowledge that '[d]omestic animals bred for the production of food, just as crops bred for that purpose, form part of the environment' (at 456). However, 'the context of the artificial introduction of human activity, such as the breeding of plants or animals for food, shows that that particular part of the environment has been created for a particular purpose from which it does not need protection' (at 456).

Is the Full Court decision one that Wild Law can or should endorse? Animal agriculture is one of the leading contributors to the major environmental challenges of today, including climate change, habitat and biodiversity loss through land clearing, pollution and so on (see e.g. Henning 2011). For this reason alone Wild Law will have a great deal to contribute to the critique of modern industrial farming methods, as well as of open pasture animal farming.[19] But to approach the use of animals from this perspective only would be to take a purely instrumentalist approach to the interests of the domesticated animals implicated in such practices. Given the central idea of interconnectedness which emerges from Wild Law, should domesticated animals such as farm animals be considered a part of 'nature' or the 'environment' broadly conceived?[20] Is such a broad conception of 'nature' defensible or would it undermine the theoretical coherency of Wild Law? Certainly, if 'nature' or the 'environment' does include all animals, then Wild Law, as part of its larger ecocentric project, necessarily requires drastic rethinking of our prevailing relationship with animals, wild or domesticated, native or introduced.

Notes

1. For a detailed account see Cullinan (2011a).
2. Burdon situates the development of Earth Rights as progressing out of the utilitarian discourse of Jeremy Bentham, and Bentham's argument for the recognition of the significance of animal suffering (Burdon 2011: 4).
3. At least in the animal law literature, this commitment to concrete reform reflects the dominant influence of Anglo-American analytical philosophy. Continental philosophy has been much less influential in critiquing, and especially prescribing reform of, prevailing legal norms, although this may change given that in the last few years 'the status of animals has been given renewed attention and interpretation within continental theory and philosophy' (Mussawir 2011: 58; see also Calarco 2008).
4. See, for example, *Prevention of Cruelty to Animals Act 1979* (NSW) ss 5(1), 6(1) (aggravated cruelty); *Animal Care and Protection Act 2001* (Qld) s 18(1); *Prevention of Cruelty to Animals Act* 1986 (Vic) ss 9, 10 (aggravated cruelty).
5. For an account of these practices see Sharman forthcoming.
6. Wagman and Liebman, in their survey of comparative animal law, state that '[n]ot surprisingly, most countries' domestic laws protect only the animals who their societies regard as worthy of protection. Because some classes of animals are more highly regarded than others, those animals are protected while other animals whose exploitation is more institutionalized are left legally unprotected. In practice, this means that companion animals receive more protections than farmed animals or animals used in research' (Wagman and Liebman 2011: 16-17).
7. This hierarchy of protection is open to contestation. For example, it might be questioned whether such a generalized schema achieves succinctness at the cost of a more nuanced account of the relationship between humans and animals in their wild state. White has suggested that '[t]he ways in which animals are valued are perhaps more complicated than this [hierarchy of protection] suggests' (White 2011: 68).
8. Citing global statistics from the World Watch Institute, Burdon argues that '[e]ven regulations and environmental laws have not fundamentally altered the power structure of law or its effective facilitation of economic development. Perhaps the clearest way to make this point is to reflect on the fact that despite 50 years of awareness of environmental issues and 35 years of environmental law, all of the important indicators are worsening' (Burdon 2012: 82).

9 Cullinan points out that '[a]nimals, plants and almost every other aspect of the planet are, legally-speaking, objects that are either the property of a human or artificial "juristic person" such as a company, or could at any moment become owned, for example by being captured or killed' (Cullinan 2011c: 63).

10 Cullinan would strongly resist this characterization. He points out that 'a person may beat his or her dog with impunity unless there is a provision in the law that prohibits them from doing so ... Of course many countries have laws that prohibit cruelty to animals ... However, it is important to appreciate that in this scenario the dog has no legal right not to be beaten. The law does not describe the relationship between a person and a dog, since the dog is not a legal subject. The legal analysis deals only with the extent of the powers, rights and obligations of humans and state institutions' (Cullinan 2011c: 99).

11 This is not to overlook the range of alternative conceptions that have been advanced, but to reflect the foundation accounts represented by utilitarian and rights approaches (for a succinct summary of other perspectives see Garner 2005).

12 Cullinan states that '[r]adical as completely rethinking property law may seem, on a wider evaluation of the costs and benefits, it seems fully justified. The challenge that now faces us is how to begin the process of undoing the property systems that impede a proper relationship with land and to build a workable alternative in its place' (Cullinan 2011c: 145).

13 In a creative example of 'continued exploration' in this area, Hadley develops the idea of conferring property rights on nonhuman animals, including the right to securely access the natural resources required to meet their needs and those of their offspring. Hadley argues that '[a]ttributing property rights to nonhuman animals would secure for natural areas, and the animals which inhabit them, a level of legal and political protection, not to mention normative significance, which surpasses that currently afforded to them' (Hadley 2005: 306).

14 Jamieson is optimistic about the potential for shared approaches, pointing out that '[w]e are in the midst of a transition from a culture which sees nature as material for exploitation, to one which asserts the importance of living in harmony with nature. It will take a long time to understand exactly what are the terms of the debate. What is important to recognize now is that animal liberationists and environmental ethicists are on the same side in this transition' (Jamieson 2002: 212).

15 That is, a shift to recognition of the value of the different ethics. This is distinct from the form that recognition might take. Varner and Taylor, for example, pursue an argument based on biocentric individualism, clearly at odds with the communitarian basis of Wild Law.

16 The available empirical evidence suggests that environmental organizations continue to focus on non-domesticated animals. For example, in a study of 15 US environmental organizations, Freeman found that they 'only tended to protect the rights of individual animals if they were human, endangered, or charismatic mega-fauna' (Freeman 2010: 271).

17 So, for example, environmental law textbooks generally have very little, if anything, to say about domesticated animals (other, perhaps, than the threat that so-called 'pest' or 'feral' animals pose to endangered animals).

18 On the basis that the respondents were not seeking to protect the environment in which the sheep were held, the feedlot, or the environment to which they were to be moved, the ship. They were trying to prevent the sheep from *moving* to the environment of the ship: *Rural Export & Trading (WA) Pty Ltd v Hahnheuser* (2008) 249 ALR 445.

19 There is empirical evidence that environmental groups are sensitive to the need to address animal agriculture as a response to challenges such as climate change, including through dietary changes. Bristow and Fitzgerald analysed written documents (such as advocacy group materials, government and industry publications and news media) to assess discursive activity about industrial animal agriculture's effects on global climate change. They found that 'the animal welfare/rights groups by and large constructed industrial animal agriculture as a risk to the global climate and integrated it into their campaigns to promote vegetarian and/or vegan diets. Most of the environmental organizations also defined industrial animal agriculture as constituting a risk and encouraged dietary changes, albeit ones often not as drastic as those recommended by the animal rights/welfare groups' (Bristow and Fitzgerald 2011: 222). Freeman reaches a broadly similar conclusion, but argues that more drastic dietary changes are required, since 'to practice ideological consistency in food discourse for those [environmental organizations] who identify with deep ecology principles and/or seek deconstruction of dualisms privileging culture's domination over nature, they would need to do more than just suggest Americans cut back a burger a week or switch to non-GM, vegetarian-fed fish' (Freeman 2010: 271).
20 In a recently revived proposal for an International Treaty for Animal Welfare, Favre sets out model provisions for an umbrella convention. One of the fundamental principles identified by Favre, set out in Article 1, is that '[h]umans and animals co-exist within an interdependent ecosystem' (Favre 2012: 265).

References

Baird Callicott, J. (1980) 'Animal liberation: a triangular affair', *Environmental Ethics*, 2: 311–38.

Bosselmann, K. (2011) 'From reductionist environmental law to sustainability law', in P. Burdon (ed.) *Exploring Wild Law: The Philosophy of Earth Jurisprudence*, Kent Town, SA: Wakefield Press.

Bristow, B. and Fitzgerald, A.F. (2011) 'Global climate change and the industrial animal agriculture link: the construction of risk', *Society & Animals*, 19: 205–24.

Bryant, T.L. (2007) 'Similarity or difference as a basis for justice: Must animals be like humans to be legally protected from humans?', *Law and Contemporary Problems*, 70: 207–54.

Burdon, P. (2010a) 'Wild law: The philosophy of earth jurisprudence', *Alternative Law Journal*, 35: 62–5.

Burdon, P. (2010b) 'The rights of nature: Reconsidered', *Australian Humanities Review*, 49: 69–89.

Burdon, P. (2011) 'Earth rights: The theory', *ICUN Academy of Environmental Law e-Journal*, Issue 2011 (1): 1–12, online. Available at: <http://www.iucnael.org/en/e-journal/previous-issues/157-issue-20111.html> (accessed 8 November 2012).

Burdon, P. (2012) 'Earth jurisprudence and the Murray-Darling: The future of a river', *Alternative Law Journal*, 37: 82–5.

Calarco, M. (2008) *Zoographies: The Question of the Animal from Heidegger to Derrida*, New York: Columbia University Press.

Cullinan, C. (2002) *Wild Law: A Manifesto for Earth Justice*, 1st edn, Westlake: Siber Ink.

Cullinan, C. (2011a) 'A history of wild law', in P. Burdon (ed.) *Exploring Wild Law: The Philosophy of Earth Jurisprudence*, Kent Town, SA: Wakefield Press.

Cullinan, C. (2011b) 'If nature had rights what would we need to give up?', in P. Burdon (ed.) *Exploring Wild Law: The Philosophy of Earth Jurisprudence*, Kent Town, SA: Wakefield Press.

Cullinan, C. (2011c) *Wild Law: A Manifesto for Earth Justice*, 2nd edn, White River Junction, VT: Chelsea Green Publishing.

Favre, D. (2010) 'Living property: A new status for animals within the legal system', *Marquette Law Review*, 93: 1021–71.

Favre, D. (2012) 'An international treaty for animal welfare', *Animal Law*, 18: 237–80.

Francione, G.L. (1995) *Animals, Property and the Law*, Philadelphia, PA: Temple University Press.

Filgueira, B. and Mason, I. (2011) 'Wild law: Is there any evidence of earth jurisprudence in existing law?', in P. Burdon (ed.) *Exploring Wild Law: The Philosophy of Earth Jurisprudence*, Kent Town, SA: Wakefield Press.

Freeman, C.F. (2010) 'Meat's place on the campaign menu: How US environmental discourse negotiates vegetarianism', *Environmental Communication: A Journal of Nature and Culture*, 4: 255–76.

Garner, R. (2005) *Animal Ethics*, Cambridge: Polity Press.

Hadley, J. (2005) 'Nonhuman animal property: Reconciling environmentalism and animal rights', *Journal of Social Philosophy*, 36(3): 305–15.

Henning, B.G. (2011) 'Standing in livestock's 'long shadow': The ethics of eating meat on a small planet', *Ethics and the Environment* 16(2): 63–93.

Jamieson, D. (2002) 'Animal liberation is an environmental ethic', in *Morality's Progress: Essays on Humans, Other Animals and the Rest of Nature*, Oxford: Clarendon Press.

Khoo, O. (2009) 'A new call to arms or a new coat of arms? The animal rights and environmentalism debate in Australia', *Journal of Animal Law*, 5: 49–70.

Mussawir, E. (2011) *Jurisdiction in Deleuze: The Expression and Representation of Law*, Abingdon: Routledge.

Radford, M. (2001) *Animal Welfare Law in Britain: Regulation and Responsibility*, Oxford: Oxford University Press.

Regan, T. (2004) *The Case for Animal Rights*, Berkeley, CA: University of California Press.

Sagoff, M. (1984) 'Animal liberation and environmental ethics: Bad marriage, quick divorce', *Osgoode Hall Law Journal*, 22: 297–307.

Sharman, K. (forthcoming) 'Farm animals and welfare law: an unhappy union', in P. Sankoff, S. White and C. Black (eds) *Animal Law in Australasia: Continuing the Dialogue*, 2nd edn, Sydney: Federation Press.

Steiner, G. (2005) *Anthropocentrism and Its Discontents: The Moral Status of Animals in the History of Western Philosophy*, Pittsburgh, PA: University of Pittsburgh Press.

Sunstein, C.R. (2004) 'Can animals sue?', in C.R. Sunstein and M.C. Nussbaum (eds) *Animal Rights: Current Debates and New Directions*, New York: Oxford University Press.

Taylor, P.W. (1986) *Respect for Nature: A Theory of Environmental Ethics*, Princeton, NJ: Princeton University Press.

Taylor, P. and Grinlinton, D. (2011) 'Property rights and sustainability: Toward a new vision of property' in D. Grinlinton and P. Taylor (eds) *Property Rights and Sustainability: The Evolution of Property Rights to Meet Ecological Challenges*, Leiden: Martinus Nijhoff.

Thiriet, D. (forthcoming) 'Out of eden – wild animals and the law', in P. Sankoff, S. White and C. Black (eds) *Animal Law in Australasia: Continuing the Dialogue*, 2nd edn, Sydney: Federation Press.

Varner, G. (2002) 'Biocentric individualism', in D. Schmidtz, and E. Willott (eds) *Environmental Ethics: What Really Works*, New York: Oxford University Press.

Wagman, B.A. and Liebman, M. (2011) *A Worldview of Animal Law*, Durham, NC: Carolina Academic Press.

White, R. (2011) *Transnational Environmental Crime: Toward an Eco-global Criminology*, Abingdon: Routledge.

White, S. (2007) 'Regulation of animal welfare and the emergent commonwealth: Entrenching the traditional approach of the states and territories or laying the ground for reform?', *Federal Law Review*, 35: 347–74.

Index

Aarhus Convention 88, 90
Abolitionists 151–2, 157, 158–9
Abram, D. 178
access to justice 87–92; funding 90–1; institutions 88–9; procedures 89–90; remedies 91–2
administrative rationalism 59, 63–4
Agenda 21 50
agriculture 257–8; GHG emissions in New Zealand 240, 241; nitrate water pollution 166; use of water 162
Agricultural Revolution 33
Albert, Michael 26
Alexander, Samuel 208
Alfaro, General Eloy 138–9, 143, 144, 145
alienation, common pool resource rights 214
Alternative World Water Forum 170
American Colonization Society (ACS) 159
American Legislative Exchange Council 23
Animal Care and Protection Act 2001 (Qld) 248
animal law, compared to wild law 247–58
animal liberation 255–6
animal rights 122–4, 247, 250, 255, 256; modification of property status 252–3
Animal Welfare Act 1993 (Tas) 248
animal welfare model 248–53
animals, objectification of 250
Anangu people 185
Annan, Kofi 163
Anthropocene 194
anthropocentric worldview 19, 195

anthropocentrism 195, 197, 231–2, 248–51; biodiversity offsets 217; definition 20–1
anti-neoliberalism 138–40
Apache people 185
Arab revolt 21
Arsel, Murat 133
atmospheric commons 230–46
Atomism 13
Australia: Bill of Rights 64; carbon pricing mechanism 237, 240, 241, 242, 243; *Clean Energy Act 2011* 217, 238–9; constitution 64, 113–29; hostility to human rights 64; international environmental agreements and 63, 64; legal system 63–6; state governments and environmental law 63; water licences 220–1
Australian National Strategy of Ecologically Sustainable Development 86

Basque region 26–7
Bates, G. 222
Bengalla coalmine 76
Berry, Thomas 24, 27, 46, 135, 152, 169, 177–8, 181, 182, 195, 196, 197, 199, 203, 215, 226, 227, 230, 247, 253
Bill of Rights, Australia 64, 114
biobanking, New South Wales scheme 213, 216–17, 220, 225, 227
biobanking agreements 84–5
Biobanking Assessment Methodology 216, 226
Biobanking Statement 216
biocapacity debtors 193
biocentrism 96–7

biodiversity: observed at three levels 213; water over-diversion and 162, 163
biodiversity offsets: global phenomenon 214; market-based schemes 215–16, 217–22, 227–8; *Native Vegetation Act 1991* (SA) 213, 222–5; New South Wales biobanking scheme 213, 216–17, 220, 225, 227; regulatory offsetting 222–5
Bird, Greta 113
Black, C. 182
Bolívar, Simón 145
Bolivia 47, 51, 150, 154, 155, 168, 178–9, 195, 196, 208
Bookchin, Murray 20, 40
Boomer Park Crayfish Farm 124–6
bore licences 220–1
Bosselmann, Klaus 10, 12, 13, 26, 27, 69–70, 195, 200
Boulot, P. 177
Brown, John 159
Bryant, T.L. 254
Bunun people 183
burden of proof 4, 81–3, 92; transfer of 7
Burdon, Peter 12, 19–30, 68, 134–5, 199–200, 208, 226, 227, 251, 253, 255
Buscher, Bram 133

California; Bay-Delta Estuary 170–1; co-equal goals 170–1; right to water 166
Callicott, Baird 255, 256
capitalism 21, 22, 23–4, 27, 137, 138, 139, 235, 244
carbon budget (UK) 202
carbon capture 8
Carbon Credits (Carbon Farming Initiative) Act 2011 (Cth) 85, 219
carbon offsets projects 84–5
carbon pollution cap 219–20
carbon pricing mechanism 237, 240, 241, 242, 243
carbon trading 214–15, 217–22, 227; property law and 218
carbon units 214, 215, 217–22, 237; as property 220, 227
Carson, Rachel 161
case law 113
Castree, Noel 133
Cenozoic period 226
Center for Economic and Social Development (CESOD) 155
Cepek, M.L. 185

Charter of Universal Responsibilities 53
Chevron-Texaco 136, 139
chlorofluorocarbons (CFCs) 7
citizen participation, administrative decision making 59–60
citizens: access to justice 87–92; enforcement of environmental statutes by 87
citizen's revolution 135, 138–9
civil disobedience 25, 208
Civil Rights Movement 151–2
civil society 48–52; global networks 50
Clean Energy Act 2011 (Australia) 214, 217, 221; carbon unit as property 220, 227; economic disincentives 243; modest targets of CPM 240; objects of 218, 238–9; reciprocation 242
Clean Energy Regulator 218, 219
Clean Water Act (US) 25
Cleary, P. 8, 9
ClientEarth 60
climate change 5, 8, 217–22, 230; earth jurisprudence criteria for emissions trading schemes 232–4; earth jurisprudence criteria for mitigation frameworks 232; and externalities 234–5; water scarcity and 162–3
Climate Change Act 2008 (UK) 202
Club of Rome 46, 193, 205
coal 5, 7, 8, 9, 76, 79, 80
Cofan people 185
Cole v Whitfield case 124–6
'command-and-control': environmentalism 36–7; regulatory control 65
commercial fishing 107
commodification 196; animals 252; of nature 133–4, 215, 217, 225; of water 162, 163, 170
common law system 63
common pool resources rights 214, 216
communal councils, Venezuela 26
community-based organizations, EDOs 67
Community Environmental Legal Defense Fund (CELDF) 68–9, 153–4; *National Ganga River Rights Act* 156; *Right to Climate* legal framework 155
companion animals 249
compensation, constitutional entitlement to 120–2
compensatory habitats *see* biodiversity offsets

Comprehensive Environmental Response, Compensation and Liability Act 1980 (CERCLA) (US) 91–2, 108, 111
conflict, between objects clauses 76–7
conservation, *Convention on Biological Diversity* (1992) 102–3
conservation agreements 84
constitution, Australian 64, 113–29; compensation entitlement 120–2; environmental statements in 114; male perspective 115
constitutional law: feminist critique of 116; nature of 114–15; Wild Law principles in 126–7
constitutional provisions for water 166
constitutionalisation 115–16
consuming users, burden of proof 82
consumption of resources 193–4
Convention Concerning the Protection of the World Cultural and Natural Heritage (1972) 102
Convention on Biological Diversity (1992) 65, 102–3
Convention on Civil Liability for Damage Resulting from Activities Dangerous to the Environment 1993 107–8
Convention on International Trade in Endangered Species of Wild Fauna and Flora 250
Cordillera del Condor 149
Coronation Hill 120–2
corporate power 39
corporations, interests of 9
Correa, Rafael 135, 136, 138–9, 140, 141, 143, 144, 149, 150, 155
Corson, Catherine 133
costs, procedural rules and 89, 90
country, concept of 176, 177
Crawford, James 114–15
crayfish 124–6
creation stories, Indigenous 182
Crown Lands Act 1929 (SA) 222
cruelty to animals 248–9, 250
Cullinan, Cormac 9, 47, 66, 152, 178, 195, 196–7, 199, 207, 217, 225, 232, 233, 243, 247, 249, 250, 251, 256
cumulative impacts 5, 7–8, 80–1
customary law 41–2

Daly, H.E. 236
DAMAGE 10, 12
damages: for injuries to natural resources 91–2, 108; undertaking for 90; violation of ecosystems rights 151
Das Kapital 22
Davis, W. 180, 181, 183
de-colonization 136, 137, 138, 139, 145, 146
Declaration of the Fundamental Rights of Mother Earth 254, 256–7
defendant, consuming users as 82
Delaney, David 180
De Luca, Kevin 123, 126
democracy 25–7; environmental anarchists and 40
Democracy Schools 68–9
democratic change 38–9
deregulation 37, 65
derivatives market, water 163
development, biobanking schemes 216–17 *see also* sustainable development
Directive on Environmental Liability with Regard to the Prevention and Remedying of Environmental Damage (EU) 108
Diritti della Natura Italia 155
discretionary powers, regulatory authorities 83–4
Distant Time, Koyukon Indians 182
Dombrovski, Peter 118
domesticated animals 248–50, 256–7, 258
Draft International Covenant on Environment and Development 103–5
'Dreams of the Earth' 181
duck shooting case *see Levy* case
duty of care, animals 248–9

Earth Charter 13, 26, 51, 204
Earth Community 24–7, 46, 51, 52, 98, 152, 194–209, 231–2, 239; humankind's 'virtual excommunication' from 226
Earth Democracy 25–6, 208
Earth Jurisprudence 12, 13, 14, 19, 24–7, 247; anarchist challenge to 31–44; animals and 253–4; biodiversity offsets 213, 214–15, 227; ecological integrity starting point 25; ecological limits 195–8, 199, 203, 204, 206–7, 209; emissions trading schemes and

criteria of 232–4, 237–43; principles contravened by legal system 59; rights of nature 176–89
earth laws 176–87
Earth rights 232–3
Earth System, holistic and biosphere-based 46
Earth System Science 194, 200
eco-centrism, environmental law and 75–94, 195
ecocide 12
Ecological Citizens 27
Ecological Footprint 205–6
ecological integrity 25, 53, 65, 97, 200
ecological jurisprudence 177
ecological justice 97
ecological limits 193–212; barriers to living within 197–8; EJ framework for living within 198–202
ecological sovereignty 177
ecologically sustainable development 6, 62, 64–5, 69–70, 76, 77, 78, 86, 251
economic growth 33–4, 165; growth fetish 31
Economically Sustainable Development (ESD) 6, 69–70, 76–7, 79, 80, 86, 87; environmental courts and principles of 89
ecosystems, as property 150–1
Ecozoic era 215, 226, 227
Ecuacorrientes SA (ECSA) 149
Ecuador: citizens revolution 135, 138–9; constitution and rights of nature 11, 47, 64, 86, 105–6, 111, 114, 134, 136, 139–40, 145, 149–50, 154, 155, 168, 178, 195, 208; law suits 149, 155; National Plan for Good Living 169; oil refinery 140–5
eligible emissions units 218–19
emissions trading schemes 232–4; enforcement, breadth and strength of liability 239–41; objectives of frameworks 238–9; prohibition of damaging behaviour 233, 234, 241–2; reciprocation 233, 234, 242; implementation of economic disincentives 233, 234, 243; theory of using schemes 234–7
endangered native animals 250
energy development, use of water 162
energy sovereignty 142–5
enforcement 5–6, 8–9; of statutes 87
Environment Act 1986 (NZ) 89

Environment Protection and Biodiversity Act 1999 (Australia) 65, 69; objects clauses 77; relevant matters 80
environmental accounts 205
environmental anarchists 40
environmental colonialism 186
environmental courts and tribunals 88–9
Environmental Damage Prevention and Remediation Act 2007 (Germany) 108–9, 111
Environmental Defender's Office movement 58–71; categories of work 60–1; collaborative nature 67; historical development 60–1; objectives 62
Environmental Education for Sustainable Societies and Global Responsibility Treaty 53
environmental ethics 255–6
environmental impact assessments, Ecuador 140
environmental law: ethical approaches 95–7; jurisprudential foundations of 95–112; rights approaches 97–8; structural approaches 98–9; three broad approaches 35–8; *see also* international instruments; national instruments
Environmental Planning and Assessment Act 1979 (NSW) 79, 85, 87, 91, 216
Environmental Protection Act 1994 (Qld) 78
environmental regulation: legalise harms 150–1; market-based versus command-and-control 215
Escobar, A. 139, 145
ethnospheres 180, 181, 187
European Union, animal welfare 249
European Union Directive on Environmental Liability with Regard to the Prevention and Remedying of: Environmental Damage (EU) 108
European Union Emissions Trading Scheme 237; economic disincentives 243; narrow coverage 240; objectives 238; prohibition on damaging behaviour 241; reciprocation 242
exclusion, right of 214, 225
expert evidence 7; independent assessment 8; past evidence evaluated 7
exploitation, legitimized by law 247
extensionism 96

externalities: climate change and 234–5; pricing 235–6
extinction rates 213–14

Farley, J. 236
farm animals 249, 252, 257–8
farming practices 249, 257–8
Favre, D. 252–3
fictionism 96
financial assistance, public interest environmental litigation 90–1
Finley, Lucinda 117, 123
Fisheries Management Act 1994 (NSW) 77
flexible charge years 219
Founding Fathers 114
Fowler, R. 11, 222
fracking 154, 163, 169
Francione, Gary 247, 250, 253, 254
Franklin Dam blockade 118–19, 122
Franklin River 118, 122
'free market' environmentalism 35–6
'free trade' agreements 119–20
freedom of trade 124–6
future, capacity to change 204
future generations, legal standing 6, 8

Gaia theory 46
Galsworthy, John 114
Ganga River Basin 156
Garnaut Climate Change Review 218
Garrison, William Lloyd 152
Germany: animals as sentient beings 256; Environmental Damage Prevention and Remediation Act 2007 108–9, 111
Glenn, H.P. 177
Global Alliance for the Rights of Nature 154
Global Citizen's Movement 52, 55
global financial crisis 163
Global Footprint Network 193, 206
global norms 64–5
global warming 151, 155
Godden, L. 63–4
good governance, regulatory authorities 87
governance structures/systems 193–209; flawed assumptions 164, 165; Planetary Boundaries and 201, 202
Graham, Nicole 12, 179, 180
grassroots 32–3, 40–3; EDO 67–8
Great Law 196, 198–204
Great Transition Initiative 204

Great Transition Report 51–2
green economists 145
green economy 134, 135, 165
greenhouse gases 84, 143, 217–18, 219–20, 233, 238; credits 237; permits 237; units 237
greenwash 34
Grinlinton, D. 251
Gross Domestic Product (GDP) 13, 34, 205
groundwater *see* water
growth: industrial capitalism and 21–4; model of progress 33–5; unlimited 197–212
growth fetishism 31, 33, 35
Gudynas, Eduardo 137–8

Hale, Charles 137
Hall, K.L. 9
hard/soft law 48–50
Hawke, Bob 117–18, 120, 121
HEALTHIER 11
Heritage Act 1977 (NSW) 84
heritage agreements 84
Heritage Regulations 2005 (NSW) 84
Higgins, P. 12
Holmes, Oliver Wendell 9
Horowitz, Morton 22–3
Howard, John 64
howler monkeys 142, 144
human right to water 165–7, 169
human rights: adequate environment 95–6; hostility in Australia 64, 66; property rights as 121
Hung, H. 183

ICM case 220–1
incentives/disincentives, emissions trading schemes 233, 234, 243
independent assessment, environmental impacts 8
independent guardians, advocate for waterways 170, 171
Index of Biological Integrity 25
India: carbon tax 242; *Ganga Action Parivar* 156; judiciary 7
indigenous cosmologies 47, 54
indigenous peoples 49, 170, 179–87; customary laws 41–2; and rights of nature 177–9
individualism 10
Industrial Revolution 21, 22–3, 197

industrialisation 33, 230
information, access to 90
interconnectedness 24, 93, 183, 196, 226, 254, 258
interdependence 96
intergenerational justice 97
International Court of Justice 12
international environmental agreements, Commonwealth and 63, 64–5
international instruments, structure of 99–105, 110; integrated approach 103–5; principled approaches 99–101; rules-based approaches 101–3
international law, duty on states 235
International Monetary Fund (IMF) 139, 144
International Mother Earth Day 47
inter-species justice 97
intragenerational justice 97
Irving, Helen 115
Italy: carbon tax 242; *Diritti della Natura Italia* 155

Jamieson, D. 256
Jawoyn people 120–1
judicial activism 113
Judicial Review 79
judicial scrutiny 106–7; Marine Mammal Protection Act 1972 (US) 107; National Parks and Wildlife Act 1975 (Queensland) 106–7, 111
judiciary, training in environmental science 7

Kakadu National Park 120
Karr, J.R. 235
Knudtson, P. 182
Koyukon Indians 182
Krugman, Paul 23
Kyoto Protocol 217, 218, 236, 239, 240, 244

Lakota people 185
Land and Environment Court of NSW 5, 9, 896; practice notes 90
Land and Environment Court Rules 2007 90
land clearing 213, 222
'land ethic' 25
land title registation systems 214
Landauer, Gustav 28
landowners, statutory obligations 84–5, 86

language, used in objects clauses 76
Lao Tzu 172
law, re-conceptualising concept of 24–5
law reform, work of EDO's 61, 62, 70
Law Under the Mother Earth and Integral Development for Living Well (Bolivia) 155
laws of the universe 197
lawscape 180–1
lawyers, practice Wild Law in EDOs 66–7, 68
legal education workshops 67
legal positivism 24, 117, 197
legal systems, shaped by growth paradigm 34
legal welfarism 250
legislation: development under administrative rationalism 59; objects clauses in statutes 75–8
Leopold, Aldo 25, 47
Levy case 122–4
Levy, Laurence 122–4
liability regimes 107–9
Limits to Growth 193, 204, 205
linguistic structure: Constitution of Ecuador 105–6; international instruments 99–105
Livingston, John 20
Lizard Island 106–7
Lovelock, J. 46

MacDonald, Kenneth 133
Maguire, R. 214, 215
management, right of 214, 225
management and accounting tools 205
Manifesto of the Peoples' Sustainability Treaties 52
Manila Bay case 84
Maori 156, 170
Margil, Mari 68, 208
Marine Mammal Protection Act 1972 (US) 107
market-based environmental schemes 217–22
'market-based' regulatory control 65–6
Martinez, Esperanza 136–7
Marx, Karl 21, 22, 31
Marxists 39; differences between environmental anarchists and 40
materialism 12 *see also* consumption of resources
mental determinism 21
mining leases 120–1

mitigation banks *see* biodiversity offsets
Mondragon Corporation 26
Morales, Evo 155, 178–9
Morrison, Chris 153
Muir, John 114
multinational corporations 120

Nash, Roderick 152, 195
National Environmental Policy Act 1969 (US) 80–1
national instruments, structure of 105–9, 110; constitutional approach 105–6; contribution of judiciary 106–7; evolving liability regimes 107–9
national parks 106–7, 111
National Parks and Wildlife Act 1974 (NSW) 78, 84
National Parks and Wildlife Act 1975 (Queensland) 106–7, 111
Native Vegetation Act 1991 (SA) 84, 213, 222–5; objects 222–3; *two offset options* 224
Native Vegetation Act 2003 (NSW) 84
Native Vegetation Council 222, 223–5
Native Vegetation Fund 222, 224–5
natural capital, nature as 133
natural law 24
Natural Resources and Environmental Protection Act 1994 (Michigan) 82–3
Natural Resources Management Act 2004 (SA) 84
natural use, private property 22
nature, as property 136–7
neoliberal growth economics 19, 21–2
neoliberalism 133–48
neoliberalization of nature 133–4
Nepal 155–6
New South Wales Land and Environment Court 5, 9, 89, 90
New Zealand: legal standing for Whanganui River 6, 156, 170; Parliamentary Commissioner for the Environment 89
New Zealand ETS 231; all sectors included 240; economic disincentives under 243; objectives of *Climate Change Response Act 2002* 239; prohibition under 241–2; targets 240–1
Newcrest case 120–2
nitrogen budget 202
nomospheres 180, 181, 183, 184, 187

non-governmental organisations 45, 52
non-human biota, standing in proceedings 90
Noxious Weeds Act 1993 (NSW) 84

objects clauses, statutes 75–8
Occidental 139
Occupy movement 21, 27, 39
Oil Pollution Act 1990 (US) 91–2
ombudsman, environmental 87, 89
Oregon Instream Water Rights Act 171

Pachakutik Plurinational Unity Movement 178
participatory budgeting 26
participatory economics 26
PDVSA 141
Peel, J. 63–4
Peoples' Sustainability Treaties (PSTs) 45–57; antecedents of 48–52; shared drivers with Wild Law 46–8; Wild Law credentials of 52–5
PetroEcuador 136, 141
Philippines 6, 84, 114
Phillips, A. 214, 215
phosphorous budget 202
Pigouvian tax 235, 236
Pittsburgh 154, 168
place, judicial lack of awareness of 126–7
plaintiff, non-consuming users as 82
Planetary Boundaries 46, 177, 194, 200–3, 204; United Kingdom and 202
pluralism 196–7
plutocracies 197–8
plutocracy, environmental protection in 22–4
political class 9
political communication, direct action as 122–4
pollution: nitrates from agriculture 166; rights and duties 235–6; water quality and 162
population growth 230
Porto Alegre 26
precautionary principle 5, 62, 65, 69, 70, 81–2
procedural rules, access to justice and 89–90
prohibition of behaviour, emissions trading schemes 233, 234, 241–2

property and property rights: animals as living property 253; carbon units 219, 220; ecosystems/nature as 150–1; human-centred idea of 251; in nature 221–2, 227; interference by state 252; sterilization of 121–2
property doctrine 247–8
Protection of the Environment Administration Act 1991 (NSW) 81–2
public funding, EDOs 67
public interest, independent assessment 8
public interest environmental lawyers, role of 58–60
public policy agenda, private interests and 198
public trust doctrine 69

quality of life 10, 12, 78, 86

Racasena, Andreu Viola 146
Radford, M. 252
Radical Ecological Democracy Treaty 53
Raskin, P. 10, 12
reason/emotion dichotomy 123
reciprocation, emissions trading schemes 233, 234, 242
red flag areas 216–17, 225, 227
Refinery of the Pacific 135–42
Regan, Tom 247, 253, 254, 255–6
regulation: burden of proof 81–3; implementation and enforcement of statutes 86–7; (statement of) relevant matters 78–81; statutory objects 75–8; substantive rights, duties and obligations 83–6
regulatory authorities: discretionary powers 83–4; implementation of statutes 86–7; statutory duties 83–4
regulatory offsetting 222–5
Rennie, M. 219
res communis 235–6
resource consumption 204–7
rights, relationship to obligations 110
rights and duties, pollution 235–6
Rights for Sustainability Treaty 53
Rights of Mother Earth Treaty 53
Rights of Nature 196, 207, 208, 253; building movement for 149–60; emergence of movement for 151–6; energy sovereignty and 142–5; indigenous peoples and 177–9; key lessons in establishing 156–60; legal recognition of 237–8; need for 150–1

rights of nature laws, United States 150, 151, 153, 168, 195, 196, 208
Rio+20 45, 47, 145, 162, 165, 168, 169, 170; outcome document 54–5
Rio Declaration (1992) 88, 99, 100, 110, 171
Rivers, Elizabeth 67, 70
Robinson, D. 227
Rockström, J. 202–3
Roderick, Peter 202
Rome Statute 12
root causes of environmental crisis, search for 20–2
Rose, Deborah Bird 176
Rudd, Kevin 38

sacred geography 183, 185
Sagoff, M. 206, 255
Sanchez-Parga, J. 138, 144
Sandon Point 76
Sarmas, Lisa 116
Sax, J.L. 85–6
science and knowledge, engaging with 198–9
scientific evidence 4–5
scientific panels 7
setasides *see* biodiversity offsets
shale gas drilling 154
sheep 257
Shiva, Vandana 177
Should Trees Have Standing 152, 158
Singer, Peter 247, 254
slavery 151–2, 157, 158–9
Smith, Adam 230
social change, three strategies for 38–41
Soqluman, N. 183
Spain 26–7
specialized knowledge, environmental courts 89
Sperling, Karla 121
spiritual harmony 96
Spivak, Gayatri 137
Stand Your Ground Laws 23
standard of proof 4–5; overhaul 7
standing, nature's right 97–8
standing barrier, access to justice 90
state, environmental anarchists and the 40
state-capitalism 23
statutes: burden of proof 81–3; implementation of 86–7; objects clause 75–8; (statement of) relevant matters 78–81; rights, duties and obligations 83–6

statutory duties, regulatory authorities 83–4
statutory obligations, landowners 84–6
statutory rights 86
Steffen, W. 201, 202, 204
sterilization, *Newcrest* case 120–2
Stockholm Declaration (1972) 99, 110
Stockholm Resiliance Institute 202
Stone, Christopher 47, 90, 152, 158, 184, 195
stories 181–2
strategic priorities, Ecuador 140–2, 145
Sungaila, H. 177
Sunstein, C.R. 252
Supreme Court of Queensland 106–7
sustainable communities 164–5; human right to water advances 165–7; waterway rights advance 167–8
sustainable development 5, 6, 34, 36, 45, 54, 62, 64–5, 69–70, 76, 77, 78, 86, 100, 104, 165, 251; *see also* Rio+20
Suzuki, David 182, 185
Swimme, B.T. 180, 182, 203, 215, 226, 227
Switzerland, animals as sentient beings 256
Swyngedouw, Erik 133–4
systems of power 23

Tamaqua 153
Tasmanian Dams case 116, 117–20, 122
Taum, Ramsay 179
Taylor, P. 251
Taylor, P.W. 256
test cases, EDOs and 69
'The Future We Want' 54–5
The Origin, Differentiation, and Role of Rights 152
The Rights of Nature 152
The Sacred Universe 177–8
'The Universe Story' 203
Thiong'o, Ng'ang'a 42
Thoreau, Henry David 114
Thornton, Margaret 115–16, 117
Threadgold, Terry 126
Threatened Species Conservation Act 1995 (NSW) 84, 85, 213, 216
Thurow, Lester 14
'top down' change 31–3, 38, 39, 41, 42–3
Toyne, Phillip 118

tradeable instruments, GHG emissions 236–7
Trainer, Ted 40
Treaty on the Functioning of the European Union 249
trees: legal standing 6; offset projects 85; Refinery of the Pacific 143
trustees, assessment of injuries to natural resources 92
Tucker, M.E. 180
Tungurahua Volcano Declaration 154
Turner, Victor 126

Union of Concerned Scientists 19
United Kingdom, Planetary Boundaries and 202
United Nations: civil society and policy-making processes 48; climate change negotiations 155; Conference on Environment and Development (Rio 1992) 50, 88, 99, 100, 110, 171; Conference on Sustainable Development (Rio+20) 45, 47, 54–5, 145, 162, 165, 168, 169, 170; Environment Programme (UNEP) 133, 164; Framework Convention on Climate Change (UNFCCC) 236, 238, 239, 244; Millennium Development Goal (MDG) 166–7, 169; Millennium Ecosystem Assessment (MEA) 19; right to water and 166
United Nations Declaration on the Rights of Indigenous Peoples (DRIP) 48–50, 177; active engagement of civil society 49–50; soft law status 49
United States: Community Environmental Legal Defense Fund 68–9, 153–4; Comprehensive Environmental Response, Compensation and Liability Act 91–2, 108, 111; constitution and slavery 152; Marine Mammal Protection Act 1972 107; natural resource damage assessment 91; Rights of Nature laws 150, 151, 153, 168, 195, 196, 208; 'taking' cases 121
Universal Declaration of Human Rights 154, 167, 169
Universal Declaration of the Rights of Mother Earth (UDRME) 51, 154, 168, 169, 171, 178

Universal Declaration of the Rights of Nature, proposal for 47

Varner, G. 256
Venezuela 26
vested interests 197–8, 208
Victoria (state) 60, 61, 69
Vilcabamba River 155, 168

Wald, Patricia 126
water: access to 115; beyond property 222; commodification of 162, 163, 170; constitutional provisions for 166; groundwater 162 ; human right to 165–7, 169; limited supply 161; management strategies 163–8; millennium Development Goal (MDG) 166–7; over-diversion 162; status and threats 161–3
Water Act 1912 (NSW) 220–1
water grabbing 163
Water Management Act 2000 (NSW) 77, 220–1
Weld, Ted 158, 159

wellbeing, water and collective 171–2
Westra, Laura 25, 186, 200
Whanganui River 156, 170, 171
White, L.T. Jr. 184
Wilcox, M. 219
wild animals 248, 250, 256, 257
Wild Law: A Manifesto for Earth Justice 66, 152, 195, 197, 247, 256
wilderness, ignored in *Tasmanian Dams* case 117–20
Williams, Rowan 14
Wilson, Edward O. 221
withdrawal, right of 214, 225
World Bank 139, 144, 162–3
World Charter for Nature (1982) 99, 100–1, 106, 110
World Heritage List 117, 122
World People's Conference on Climate Change and the Rights of Mother Earth 51, 150, 154, 178–9
World Women's Congress for a Healthy Planet 50

Zahar, A. 217